CHRISTIAN WORSHIP

CHRISTIAN WORSHIP

And when I bear my humble part
In heaven's eternal song,
Wonder and joy shall tune my heart,
And love command my tongue.

Isaac Watts

EXETER:
THE PATERNOSTER PRESS

International Standard Book Numbers
Words only, Standard Edition: 0 85364 191 9
Words only, Presentation Edition: 0 85364 193 5
Music and words, Standard Edition: 0 85364 192 7
Music and words, Presentation Edition: 0 85364 194 3

AUSTRALIA
*Emu Book Agencies Pty., Ltd.,
63, Berry Street, Granville,
N.S.W. 2142*

SOUTH AFRICA
*Oxford University Press
P.O. Box 1411, Buitencingle Street,
Cape Town*

*Made and Printed in Great Britain for
The Paternoster Press Ltd Paternoster House
3 Mount Radford Crescent Exeter Devon
by Redwood Burn Limited Trowbridge and Esher*

CONTENTS

PREFACE AND INTRODUCTION

THE NEW LIFE ALWAYS DECLARES ITSELF IN THE NEW SONG. FROM THE SINGING of the redeemed slaves of Israel on the far side of the Red Sea, described in the book of Exodus, to the praises of the ransomed hosts in heaven, described in the book of Revelation, the Bible is full of song – thanksgiving, praise, adoration, worship – as a spontaneous response to a personal experience of the grace of God, or as the writer of the Letter to the Hebrews put it, "a sacrifice of praise to God, that is, the fruit of lips that acknowledge His name".

This quite novel feature of the early Christian church impressed that perceptive historian Pliny. The religions of Greece and Rome gave their devotees little cause for singing, but, wrote Pliny of second-century Christians, "They meet at daybreak to sing an hymn to one Christ as God". Greece and Rome, like others of earth's proud empires, have gone, but the stream of praise, so far from dying, remains and grows for ever and shall not pass away.

But it was the publication and free availability of the King James' version of the Bible in 1611, followed by the birth of Isaac Watts in 1674 and of Charles Wesley in 1707, that resulted during the 17th and 18th centuries in a vast outpouring of hymns in English without parallel in other languages. Indeed, the missionary movement from the British Isles during the 19th and 20th centuries has resulted in the translation of many English hymns into other languages, so that, apart from these translations, it would be virtually impossible to find an original collection as varied as the present volume in any other tongue.

Yet, although its main flowering was in these two centuries, the full heritage of English hymnody covers all Christian time so far. The present collection includes hymns written as early as the 3rd century and as late as the 3rd quarter of the 20th century. While therefore any truly representative collection of hymns in English will always lead with Wesley and Watts, closely followed by James Montgomery and Horatius Bonar, with outstanding contributions by Cooper, Dix, Doddridge and Newton, and the translations of Caswall, Neale, and others, there are enough worthy contributions from so many other sources to bring the total number of authors and translators in the present collection to well over 400 names, with almost as many composers, arrangers and sources of music, providing nearly 600 different tunes.

From this rich variety of material, the present selection contains 716 hymns, chosen on the basis of three major principles. First, the selection should be as catholic as possible, in the true sense of that word. Nowhere does the true unity of those who are in fact "children of God, members of Christ, and inheritors of the Kingdom of Heaven," exhibit itself more clearly or more enthusiastically than in hymns. The head of a mediaeval monastery ("Jesus, the very thought of Thee!") joins hands across the centuries with a modern Archdeacon ("Tell out, my soul, the greatness of the Lord!"); J. N. Darby ("Rest of the saints above, Jerusalem of God!") is at one with the 12th century Bernard of Cluny, ("Jerusalem, my happy home!"); Quaker and Catholic, Dissenter and Conformist, Presbyterian and Episcopalian, all have made individual contributions to the sung praise of the continuing church of God which are as valid today as when they were first written because they were based, not on the man-made differences of the moment, but on the eternal verities of God's revelation in Christ.

Second, the opportunity has been taken to draw upon the choice heritage of spiritual hymnody that arose out of what came to be called, soon after its commencement over 150 years ago, the Brethren movement. These hymns have hitherto been confined to specialist hymnbooks, and are in danger of being lost to the whole church of God through a number of these books going out of print. Many of these hymns would grace any collection. For instance, Mary Bowly Peters' magnificent hymn beginning, "O blessèd Lord, what hast Thou done, how vast a ransom paid?" is fully worthy to stand side by side with Charles Wesley's "O love divine, what hast Thou done?"; Robert Cleaver Chapman's "Show me Thy wounds, exalted Lord!" parallels Wesley's "Ah, show me that happiest place"; John Nelson Darby's "Hark, ten thousand voices crying 'Lamb of God' with one accord!" is no mean companion to Isaac Watts' "Behold the glories of the Lamb"; while Alexander Stewart's "Lord Jesus Christ, we seek thy face," is as good a hymn of spiritual devotion and worship as can be found anywhere. And the same quality can be found in hymns by Edward Denny, J. G. Deck, J. Denham Smith, S. Trevor Francis, Thomas Kelly, Douglas Russell, and others. The hymnody of this movement is particularly rich in hymns for the Lord's supper, as this selection shows.

The third principle has been to draw upon both these sources in order to provide an adequate coverage of hymns for all requirements of a local Christian church in worship and service, except for the special needs of small children. The classified list of contents will show how this plan has been worked out, and to get full value from this book this plan should be studied and used. Especially valuable is the last section of the book, entitled "Mainly for Private Devotion". Here are hymns of particularly high spiritual and poetic quality, which can occasionally be used for public services, but which are most suitable for personal use.

In a broadcast review, Dr. Cyril Taylor, at that time Principal of the Royal School of Church Music, said, "Anyone who has had a hand in compiling a hymnbook knows quite well with what brave ideals you set out. Good poetry, good theology, good music; let's have them all! But by No. 4 or 5, you are having to pull your horns in, because compiling a hymnbook is the art of the possible". If so great an authority feels like that, who are we to be surprised if we feel the same?

But the possible, particularly in words, can still be worthy. Since this is not an eclectic selection for experts, but a book for regular use by ordinary people, we have one main principle of choice – we will not include a hymn which we would not use ourselves. That said, let the choice be as wide and as high as possible. Omit, rather than alter unduly; and do not chase "original texts" at *all* costs. It is not necessary, for instance, to revert to Isaac Watts' original "*Our* God, our help in ages past," (five "ours" in four lines!) when even in Watts' lifetime it was beginning to be sung with the vocative "O", which is not only consonant with the Psalm on which the hymn is based, but transforms the first verse from a theological statement in the third person into a reverent approach to God.

Good words are worthy of good tunes. But what makes a good tune? First, last, and all the time, *singability*. A hymn tune must be capable of being sung by ordinary people, or it is useless. Therefore a hymn tune must have a strong melodic line, a definite and pleasing rhythm, with a marked and recognisable beat. Beat without rhythm is monotonous, rhythm without beat is formless, while either or both without melody cannot be a tune. It must be reasonably easy for an ordinary congregation not merely to follow in the first verse, but to remember most of it for the second verse, and to have it reasonably well by the third.

In selecting the tunes, therefore, the aim has been to combine worthy music with practical usefulness in the regular services of a local church. So, just as Wesley and Watts still lead in words, Dykes, Sullivan, Gauntlett, S. S. Wesley and Barnby are still important figures in music. But we include valuable compositions from more modern composers, such as Vaughan Williams, Walford Davies, E. H. Thiman, Arthur Somervell, Malcolm Williamson, John Ireland, George Thalben-Ball, Malcolm Brierley, Gordon Hartless, and others. A notable feature of this book is the inclusion of a number of most "singable" Welsh tunes of high musical quality, with memorable melodies, yet still largely unknown outside Wales. These both enlarge and enrich this collection.

In considering tunes the following four points must be borne in mind:

1. There are some tunes that choose themselves. For instance, any editor who sets "The day Thou gavest, Lord, is ended" to any tune other than St. Clement, is wasting his time. It has been tried, but has always failed.

2. The temptation to use tunes of undoubted excellence and popularity too often must be resisted. We have made it a rule to use as few tunes as possible more than once, and none more than twice. This has greatly increased the variety of tunes available for selection by users of this book. In addition to this, there are more than 300 suggestions for alternative tunes, further increasing the practical usefulness of the work.

3. There is no such thing as a "right" tune to any particular hymn. True, some hymns are wedded to some tunes, and it would be foolish to attempt arbitrarily to make a change. But how readily congregations will prefer and accept a better tune in place of an established one is seen by the way in which Vaughan Williams' *Sine Nomine* replaced almost entirely Barnby's *Pro Omnibus Sanctis*. Yet the latter is by no means a bad tune and can be used with discretion in any hymnbook.

4. Not only is there no "right" tune to any particular hymn, but sometimes a tune will be "right" for half a hymn, and "wrong" for the other half! Writers of great spiritual poetry cannot be bound by metric feet. Especially is this true of Watts, who achieves some of his most striking effects by starting occasional verses in an iambic poem, where the stress comes on the second syllable, with a trochee, in which the stress is on the first syllable. Consequently any tune which is "right" for some verses of "When I survey the wondrous cross" or "Nature with open volume stands" is automatically "wrong" for other verses of the same hymn! But this does not unduly concern ordinary folk, otherwise who could explain the world-wide popularity of a hymn whose "right" tune makes everyone sing the first four syllables as "*Er-r-r*-bide with me"?

It should not be necessary to say, but it is, that the best way to get value out of this book is to use it. It can be, as John Wesley said of the first Methodist Hymn Book, "a little body of experimental and practical divinity." This is one reason why, in the music edition, the words are still printed as poetry, and not spread out between the music staves. Do not leave it on your shelves, to be taken once a week for an hour or two to a service where you will be told what to sing! Keep at least a copy of the words edition on your bedside table, and read a hymn or two at night or in the morning. If you play an instrument, work right through the music edition till you have mastered it all. Learn three or four new hymns and tunes each week, and you will not only have employment for more than a year, but will have increased in wisdom and spiritual stature.

The type face and size, and the style of setting of both words and music have been carefully planned to make the book easy to read as well as to handle.

There are many whose kindness during the years of preparation of this hymnbook I must gladly acknowledge. First, there is my wife Eleanor and my son and colleague, Jeremy, without whose patience and encouragement over many years the task might well not have been completed. Dr. Charles Sims, of Exeter, who first expressed in a letter published more than 25 years ago the need for a hymnbook such as this, has helped continually with advice and many readings of proofs. To Mr. A. E. F. Tipler who read the final proofs of the words and Mrs. B. G. Alford who played every note of the music, my thanks are due. I am most grateful to my personal staff at The Paternoster Press, who laboured long and diligently with checking and counter-checking and seemingly endless indexing. And last but by no means least, to my friend and colleague Mr. F. A. J. Tonkin, organist at Belmont Chapel, Exeter, I acknowledge a very deep debt of gratitude for his willingness to undertake any amount of hard work, such as compiling card-index digests of nearly every known hymn tune, and also for giving of his time and musical skill in arranging, suggesting, revising, and gently correcting some of my grosser errors!

I want to express my appreciation of the co-operation of fellow-Christian publishers who, in these difficult days for us all, have made available copyright material in their possession which has enabled us to cut corners and so decrease frustrating delays in production. The Rev. Ronald W. Thomson, Secretary and Manager of the Psalms and Hymns Trust, has helped in this way over several years, and a special word of thanks is due to him. Similarly, we acknowledge the kindness and co-operation of the Baptist Union of Wales, the Methodist Conference, the Scripture Union, Tyndale Press, the Union of Welsh Independents and the United Reformed Church. The permission of individual copyright owners for the use of words and/or tunes of hymns will be found in the list of Acknowledgements at the end of the book. I would also like to pay belated tribute to my two Professors at the Guildhall School of Music and Drama, Walter Hyde and Allan Brown. Not even their hard work and skill could make a musician of me, but they opened a window on a wide new world and inculcated standards which I have tried not to debase.

This book is a better book because of the varied help of these and other friends, but the ultimate responsibility is mine alone.

Most of all, gratitude must be expressed to the Lord Himself, who has given health and time and has maintained enthusiasm for what would have been, had we known in advance, a daunting task. It is now gladly made available to His people, and if by it His praise and worship can be increased, no greater reward could be asked. "O magnify the Lord with me, and let us exalt His name together."

Exeter, Devon, U.K.   B. HOWARD MUDDITT
All Saints Day, 1975

MILTON ABBAS   664.6664.

ERIC H. THIMAN, 1900-1975

COME, Thou Almighty King,
Help us Thy name to sing,
Help us to praise:
Father all-glorious,
O'er all victorious,
Come and reign over us,
Ancient of days.

2 Come, Thou Incarnate Word,
Gird on Thy mighty sword,
Our prayer attend:
Come, and Thy people bless,
And give Thy word success;
Spirit of holiness,
On us descend.

3 Come, Holy Comforter,
Thy sacred witness bear,
In this glad hour:
Thou who almighty art,
Now rule in every heart,
And ne'er from us depart,
Spirit of power.

4 To the great One in Three
Eternal praises be,
Hence evermore:
His sovereign majesty
May we in glory see,
And to eternity
Love and adore.

Author unknown, c. 1758

This hymn may also be sung to **Moscow,** No. 2, or **Malvern,** No. 220

MOSCOW 664.6664

Adapted from F. GIARDINI, 1716-96

DESCANT (*lines 4 to end*)

JOHN HUGHES, 1896-

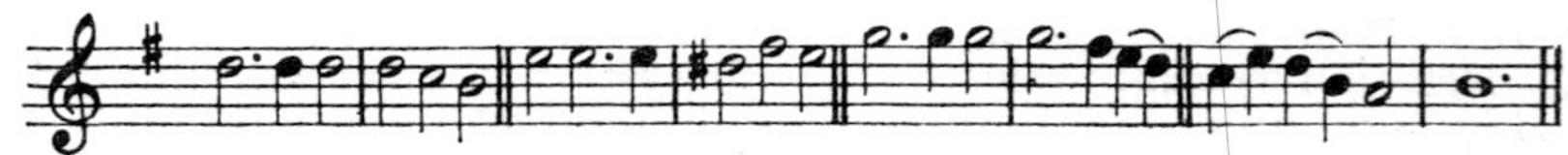

THOU, whose almighty word,
   Chaos and darkness heard,
   And took their flight;
Hear us, we humbly pray,
And where the gospel day
Sheds not its glorious ray,
   Let there be light!

2 Thou, who didst come to bring,
   On Thy redeeming wing,
   Healing and sight—
Health to the sick in mind,
Sight to the inly blind—
Oh now to all mankind,
   Let there be light!

3 Spirit of truth and love,
   Life-giving, holy Dove,
   Speed forth Thy flight!
Move on the waters' face,
By Thine almighty grace,
And in earth's darkest place
   Let there be light!

4 Blessed and holy Three,
   Most glorious Trinity,
   Wisdom, Love, Might:
Boundless as ocean's tide
Rolling in fullest pride,
O'er the world far and wide
   Let there be light!

John Marriott, 1780–1825

DIADEMATA D.S.M.

G. J. Elvey, 1816-93

FATHER, in whom we live,
  In whom we are, and move,
The glory, power, and praise receive
  Of Thy creating love.
  Let all the angel throng
  Give thanks to God on high;
While earth repeats the joyful song,
  And echoes to the sky.

2 Incarnate Deity,
  Let all the ransomed race
Render in thanks their lives to Thee,
  For Thy redeeming grace.
  The grace to sinners showed
  Ye heavenly choirs proclaim,
And cry: Salvation to our God,
  Salvation to the Lamb!

3 Spirit of Holiness,
  Let all Thy saints adore
Thy sacred energy, and bless
  Thine heart-renewing power.
  Not angel tongues can tell
  Thy love's ecstatic height,
The glorious joy unspeakable,
  The beatific sight.

4 Eternal, Triune Lord!
  Let all the hosts above,
Let all the sons of men, record
  And dwell upon Thy love.
  When heaven and earth are fled
  Before Thy glorious face,
Sing all the saints Thy love hath made
  Thine everlasting praise.

Charles Wesley, 1707–88

This hymn may also be sung to **Eden,** No. 193

CHRISTE SANCTORUM   11.11.11.5

French Church Melody
from the *Cluny Antiphoner*, 1686

FATHER most holy, merciful and loving,
Jesus, Redeemer, ever to be worshipped,
Life-giving Spirit, Comforter most gracious,
    God everlasting;

2 Three in a wondrous unity unbroken,
One perfect Godhead, love that never faileth,
Light of the angels, succour of the needy,
    Hope of all living;

3 All Thy creation serveth its Creator;
Thee every creature praiseth without ceasing;
We too would sing Thee psalms of true devotion;
    Hear, we beseech Thee.

4 Lord God Almighty, unto Thee be glory,
One in Three Persons, over all exalted;
Thine, as is meet, be honour, praise, and blessing,
    Now and for ever.

Latin, c. 10th century
tr. Alfred Edward Alston, 1862–1927

REGENT SQUARE   87.87.87   HENRY SMART, 1813-79

GLORY be to God the Father,
Glory be to God the Son,
Glory be to God the Spirit—
  Great Jehovah, Three in One!
    Glory, glory
  While eternal ages run!

2 Glory be to Him who loved us,
    Washed us from each spot and stain!
  Glory be to Him who bought us,
    Made us kings with Him to reign!
      Glory, glory
    To the Lamb that once was slain!

3 Glory to the King of angels,
    Glory to the Church's King,
  Glory to the King of nations!
    Heaven and earth, your praises
        bring;
      Glory, glory
    To the King of Glory bring!

4 "Glory, blessing, praise eternal!"
    Thus the choir of angels sings;
  "Honour, riches, power, dominion!"
    Thus its praise creation brings;
      Glory, glory,
    Glory to the King of kings!

                Horatius Bonar, 1808–89

This hymn may also be sung to **Triumph,** No. 625

6

NICÆA 11.12.12.10

J. B. DYKES, 1823-76

HOLY, holy, holy! Lord God Almighty!
Early in the morning our song shall rise to Thee;
Holy, holy, holy! merciful and mighty,
God in three Persons, blessèd Trinity!

2 Holy, holy, holy! all the saints adore Thee,
Casting down their golden crowns around the glassy sea,
Cherubim and seraphim falling down before Thee,
Which wert, and art, and evermore shalt be.

3 Holy, holy, holy! though the darkness hide Thee,
Though the eye of sinful man Thy glory may not see,
Only Thou art holy; there is none beside Thee,
Perfect in power, in love, and purity.

4 Holy, holy, holy! Lord God Almighty!
All Thy works shall praise Thy name in earth and sky and sea;
Holy, holy, holy! merciful and mighty,
God in three Persons, blessèd Trinity!

Reginald Heber, 1783–1826

THE HOLY TRINITY

SECOND TUNE

TERSANCTUS 1112.1210

GORDON HARTLESS, b. 1913

CROFT'S 136TH   66.66.88   W. CROFT, 1678-1727

WE give immortal praise
   To God the Father's love,
For all our comforts here,
   And better hopes above;
He sent His own eternal Son,
To die for sins that man had done.

2   To God the Son belongs
     Immortal glory too,
  Who bought us with His blood
     From everlasting woe;
  And now He lives and now He reigns,
  And sees the fruit of all His pains.

3   To God the Spirit's name
     Immortal worship give,
  Whose new-creating power
     Makes the dead sinner live.
  His work completes the great design,
  And fills the soul with joy divine.

4   Almighty God, to Thee
     Be endless honours done,
  The undivided Three,
     And the mysterious One!
  Where reason fails with all her powers,
  There faith prevails, and love adores.

Isaac Watts, 1674–1748

See also
313   Father of heaven, whose love profound
510   Father, to seek Thy face
534   Our Father, we would worship
607   God hath spoken
653   Father, in high heaven dwelling
654   Hail, gladdening light
687   Father, Son and Holy Ghost

BETHANY 87.87.D   H. SMART, 1813-79.

"ABBA, Father," Lord, we call Thee,
  Hallowed name—from day to day:
'Tis Thy children's right to know Thee,
  None but children "Abba" say.
This high glory we inherit,
  Thy free gift, through Jesu's blood;
God the Spirit, with our spirit,
  Witnesseth we're sons of God.

2 Abba's purpose gave us being,
  When, in Christ, in that vast plan,
Abba chose the Church in Jesus,
  Long before the world began.
Oh what love the Father bore us!
  Oh how precious in His sight!
When He gave His Church to Jesus,
  Jesus—His whole soul's delight.

3 Though our nature's fall in Adam
  Seemed to shut us out from God,
Thus it was His counsel brought us
  Nearer still, through Jesu's blood.
For in Him we found redemption,
  Grace and glory in the Son.
Oh the height and depth of mercy!
  Christ and we, through grace, are one.

4 Hence, through all the changing seasons,
  Trouble, sorrow, sickness, woe—
Nothing changeth God's affection,
  Abba's love shall bring us through.
Soon shall all the blood-bought children,
  Round the throne their anthems raise;
And, in songs of rich salvation,
  Shout to Abba endless praise.

Robert Hawker, 1753–1827

This hymn may also be sung to **Love Divine**, No. 9

LOVE DIVINE　87.87.D　　　　　　　　　　　J. ZUNDEL, 1815-82

"ABBA, Father!" we approach Thee
　In our Saviour's precious name:
We, Thy children, here assembling,
　Now the promised blessing claim.
From our sins His blood hath washed us;
　'Tis through Him our souls draw nigh;
And Thy Spirit, too, has taught us,
　"Abba, Father," thus to cry.

2 Once as prodigals we wandered,
　In our folly, far from Thee;
But Thy grace, o'er sin abounding,
　Rescued us from misery.
Thou Thy prodigals hast pardoned,
　Loved us with a Father's love;
Welcomed us with joy o'erflowing,
　E'en to dwell with Thee above.

3 Clothed in garments of salvation,
　At Thy table is our place;
We rejoice, and Thou rejoicest,
　In the riches of Thy grace.
"It is meet", we hear Thee saying,
　"We should merry be and glad,
I have found my once lost children,
　Now they live, who once were dead."

4 "Abba, Father!" all adore Thee,
　All rejoice in heaven above;
While in us they learn the wonders
　Of Thy wisdom, grace, and love.
Soon before Thy throne assembled,
　All Thy children shall proclaim,
"Glory, everlasting glory,
　Be to God and to the Lamb!"

James George Deck, 1802–84

This hymn may also be sung to **Bethany**, No. 8

TE LAUDANT OMNIA 77.77.77 J. F. SWIFT, 1847-1931

ALL things praise Thee, Lord most high;
Heaven and earth and sea and sky,
All were for Thy glory made,
That Thy greatness thus displayed
Should all worship bring to Thee;
All things praise Thee: Lord, may we.

2 All things praise Thee; night to night
Sings in silent hymns of light;
All things praise Thee; day to day
Chants Thy power, in burning ray;
Time and space are praising Thee,
All things praise Thee: Lord, may we.

3 All things praise Thee; round her zones
Earth, with her ten thousand tones,
Rolls a ceaseless choral strain;
Roaring wind and deep-voiced main,
Rustling leaf and humming bee,
All things praise Thee: Lord, may we.

4 All things praise Thee; high and low,
Rain and dew and seven-hued bow,
Crimson sunset, fleecy cloud,
Rippling stream and tempest loud;
Summer, winter, all to Thee
Glory render: Lord, may we.

5 All things praise Thee; gracious Lord,
Great Creator, powerful Word,
Omnipresent Spirit, now
At Thy feet we humbly bow,
Lift our hearts in praise to Thee;
All things praise Thee: Lord, may we.

George William Conder, 1821–74

ALL people that on earth do dwell,
Sing to the Lord with cheerful
voice;
Him serve with mirth, His praise forth
tell;
Come ye before Him and rejoice.

2 Know that the Lord is God indeed;
Without our aid He did us make;
We are His flock, He doth us feed,
And for His sheep He doth us take.

3 Oh enter, then, His gates with praise,
Approach with joy His courts unto;
Praise, laud, and bless His name
always,
For it is seemly so to do.

4 For why? The Lord our God is good
His mercy is for ever sure;
His truth at all times firmly stood,
And shall from age to age endure.

William Kethe, 16th cent.

ANGEL voices, ever singing
  Round Thy throne of light,
Angel harps, for ever ringing,
  Rest not day nor night;
Thousands only live to bless Thee,
  And confess Thee
    Lord of might.

2 Thou who art beyond the farthest
    Mortal eye can scan,
  Can it be that Thou regardest
    Songs of sinful man?
  Can we know that Thou are near us
    And wilt hear us?
      Yea, we can.

3 Yea, we know that Thou rejoicest
    O'er each work of Thine;
  Thou didst ears and hands and voices
    For Thy praise design;
  Craftsman's art and music's measure
    For Thy pleasure
      All combine.

4 In Thy house, great God, we offer
    Of Thine own to Thee,
  And for Thine acceptance proffer,
    All unworthily,
  Hearts and minds and hands and voices,
    In our choicest
      Psalmody.

5 Honour, glory, might, and merit
    Thine shall ever be,
  Father, Son, and Holy Spirit,
    Blessed Trinity.
  Of the best that Thou hast given,
    Earth and heaven
      Render Thee.

Francis Pott, 1832–1909

SANCTUS 87.87.D   JOHN RICHARDS (ISALAW), 1843-1908

BRIGHT the vision that delighted
  Once the sight of Judah's seer;
Sweet the countless tongues united
  To entrance the prophet's ear.
"Lord Thy glory fills the heaven;
  Earth is with its fulness stored;
Unto Thee be glory given,
  Holy, holy, holy Lord."

2 Round the Lord in glory seated,
  Cherubim and seraphim
Filled His temple, and repeated
  Each to each the alternate hymn.
Heaven is still with glory ringing,
  Earth takes up the angels' cry,
"Holy, holy, holy," singing,
  "Lord of hosts, the Lord most
    high."

3 With His seraph train before Him,
  With His holy Church below,
Thus unite we to adore Him,
  Bid we thus our anthem flow:
"Lord, Thy glory fills the heaven;
  Earth is with its fulness stored;
Unto Thee be glory given,
  Holy, holy, holy Lord."

Richard Mant, 1776–1848

This hymn may also be sung to **Laus Deo, No. 22**

LASST UNS ERFREUEN (EASTER ALLELUIA)   L.M. with Alleluias
Geistliche Kirchengesang, Cologne, 1623
Arr. by R. VAUGHAN WILLIAMS, 1872–1958

BY every nation, race and tongue
Be heartfelt praises ever sung,
Praise the Father, Alleluia!
For pardoned sin, and death o'ercome,
And hopes that live beyond the tomb,
Alleluia! Alleluia! Alleluia!
Alleluia! Alleluia!

2 Saints, who on earth have suffered long
For Jesus' sake enduring wrong,
Ever faithful, Alleluia!
Where faith is lost in sight, rejoice
To sing with never-wearied voice
Alleluia! Alleluia! Alleluia!
Alleluia! Alleluia!

3 Let earth and air and sea unite
To celebrate His glorious might,
Their Creator, Alleluia!
And all the orbs of endless space
Echo the song of human race,
Alleluia! Alleluia! Alleluia!
Alleluia! Alleluia!

Hereford Brooke George, 1838–1910

COME, ye that love the Lord,
And let your joys be known;
Join in a song with sweet accord,
And thus surround the throne.
Let those refuse to sing
Who never knew our God;
But children of the heavenly King
May speak their joys abroad.

2   The God that rules on high,
That all the earth surveys,
That rides upon the stormy sky,
And calms the roaring seas:
This aweful God is ours,
Our Father and our love;
He will send down His heavenly
powers,
To carry us above.

3 The hill of Zion yields
A thousand sacred sweets,
Before we reach the heavenly fields,
Or walk the golden streets.
There shall we see His face,
And never, never sin;
There from the rivers of His grace
Drink endless pleasures in.

4   The men of grace have found
Glory begun below;
Celestial fruits on earthly ground
From faith and hope may grow.
Then let our songs abound,
And every tear be dry:
We're marching through Immanuel's
ground
To fairer worlds on high.

Isaac Watts, 1674-1748

WINCHESTER NEW L.M.

From a chorale in the
Musikalisches Handbuch, Hamburg, 1690
Arr. by W. H. HAVERGAL, 1793-1870

B LESS thou the Lord, my soul, and
raise
To Him thy grateful song of praise;
Bless Him for all His love to thee,
For mercies countless, rich, and free.

2 While from destruction's power
secure,
Through His redemption, strong and
sure,
His loving-kindness crowns thy head,
And tender mercies round are shed.

3 Thy mouth with good things He doth
fill,
So that thy youth is vigorous still,
E'en as the eagle's strength renewed,
And with fresh grace from heaven
endued.

4 Bless Him for all the hourly love,
Gently distilling from above,
Which fills thy soul and makes thee
blest
Amidst this dreary world's unrest.

5 Bless Him for hopes of coming peace,
When all thy griefs and pains shall
cease;
Bless Him that thou His face shalt see,
And like Him evermore shalt be.

6 Bless thou the Lord, my soul, and raise
To Him thy grateful song of praise;
Oh, deeply in thy heart record
The unnumbered mercies of thy Lord!

Author unknown

17

FESTUS L.M.

Adapted from a melody in
FREYLINGHAUSEN'S *Gesangbuch*, 1704

ETERNAL Power! whose high abode
  Becomes the grandeur of a God:
Infinite lengths beyond the bounds
Where stars revolve their finite rounds.

2 Thee while the first archangel sings,
He hides his face beneath his wings,
And throngs of shining thrones around
Fall worshipping, and spread the
    ground.

3 Lord, what shall earth and ashes do?
We would adore our Maker too;
From sin and dust to Thee we cry,
The Great, the Holy, and the High!

4 Earth from afar has heard Thy fame,
And babes have learnt to lisp Thy
    name;
But oh the glories of Thy mind
Leave all our soaring thoughts behind!

5 God is in heaven, and men below;
Be short our tunes, our words be few;
A sacred reverence checks our songs,
And praise sits silent on our tongues.

Isaac Watts, 1674–1748

18

Words at foot of next page

RICHMOND C.M.

Adapted from T. HAWEIS, 1734-1820,
by S. WEBBE (the Younger), 1770-1843

GERONTIUS C.M.

J. B. DYKES, 1823-76

18 *Tune at foot of previous page*

FILL Thou my life, O Lord my God,
  In every part with praise,
That my whole being may proclaim
  Thy being and Thy ways.

2 Not for the lip of praise alone,
    Nor e'en the praising heart,
  I ask, but for a life made up
    Of praise in every part:

3 Praise in the common things of life,
    Its goings out and in;
  Praise in each duty and each deed,
    However small and mean.

4 Fill every part of me with praise;
    Let all my being speak
  Of Thee and of Thy love, O Lord,
    Poor though I be and weak.

5 So shalt Thou, Lord, from me, e'en me
    Receive the glory due;
  And so shall I begin on earth
    The song for ever new.

6 So shall no part of day or night
    From sacredness be free;
  But all my life, in every step,
    Be fellowship with Thee.

              Horatius Bonar, 1808–89

This hymn may also be sung to
Beatitudo, No. 198

19

FATHER, how wide Thy glory shines!
  How high Thy wonders rise!
Known through the earth by thousand
    signs,
  By thousands through the skies.

2 Those mighty orbs proclaim Thy
      power,
    Their motions speak Thy skill;
  And, on the wings of every hour,
    We read Thy goodness still.

3 Part of Thy name divinely stands
    On all Thy creatures writ;
  They bear the fashion of Thy hands
    Or impress of Thy feet.

4 But, Father, in Thy great design
    To save rebellious man,
  We see both truth and mercy shine
    In free salvation's plan.

5 Here Thy full character is known,
    Nor can a creature trace
  Which of the glories brighter shone,
    The justice or the grace.

6 Now the full glories of the Lamb
    Adorn the heavenly plains;
  Bright angels learn Emmanuel's name,
    And sing their choicest strains.

7 And when I bear my humble part
    In heaven's eternal song,
  Wonder and joy shall tune my heart,
    And love command my tongue.

              Isaac Watts, 1674–1748

20

ST. PHILIP (PRO OMNIBUS SANCTIS)   10.10.10.4   J. BARNBY, 1838-96

For all the love that from our earliest days
Has gladdened life and guarded all our ways,
We bring Thee, Lord, our song of grateful praise,
Alleluia! Alleluia!

2 For all the truth from wisdom's lighted page,
Undimmed and pure, that shines from age to age,
God's holy Word, our priceless heritage,

3 For all the hope that sheds its glorious ray
Along the dark and unknown future way,
And lights the path to God's eternal day,

4 For all the strength that has been gained through prayer,
To face life's tasks, its eager quests to share.
Till ampler powers fulfil its promise fair,

5 For Christ the Lord, our Saviour and our friend,
Upon whose love and truth our souls depend,
Our hope, our strength, our joy that knows no end,
Alleluia! Alleluia!

L. J. Egerton Smith, 1879–1958

This hymn may also be sung to **Sine Nomine**, No. 211

BODMIN L.M.

A. SCOTT-GATTY, 1847-1918

GIVE to our God immortal praise,
Mercy and truth are all His ways;
Wonders of grace to God belong,
Repeat His mercies in your song.

2 Give to the Lord of lords renown;
The King of kings with glory crown:
His mercies ever shall endure,
When lords and kings are known no
more.

3 He built the earth, He spread the sky,
And fixed the starry lights on high:
Wonders of grace to God belong,
Repeat His mercies in your song.

4 He fills the sun with morning light,
He bids the moon direct the night:
His mercies ever shall endure,
When suns and moons shall shine no
more.

5 He sent His Son with power to save
From guilt and darkness and the grave:
Wonders of grace to God belong,
Repeat His mercies in your song.

6 Through this vain world He guides
our feet,
And leads us to His heavenly seat:
His mercies ever shall endure,
When this vain world shall be no more.

Isaac Watts, 1674–1748

22

LAUS DEO 87.87

R. REDHEAD, 1820-1901

G OD and Father, we adore Thee,
Now revealed in Christ the Son,
Joying in Thy holy presence
Through the work that He has done.

2 Filled with praise we bow before Thee,
Thou art evermore the same,
With adoring hearts we bless Thee,
Magnify Thy holy name.

3 Worship, honour, praise and glory,
Would we render unto Thee;
Heights unsearched and depths un-
fathomed
In Thy wondrous love we see.

4 All Thy glory shines transcendent
In the person of the Son,
Jesus Christ, Thy well-belovèd,
Who redemption's glory won.

5 In Thy presence we behold Him
Object of Thy heart's deep love;
Boundless theme of adoration
In that scene of joy above.

6 In Thy grace Thou now hast called us
Sharers of Thy joy to be,
And to know the blessèd secret
Of His preciousness to Thee.

E. H. Chater, 1845-1915

WORSHIP 777.6 FIRST TUNE S. T. FRANCIS, 1834-1925

SECOND TUNE

REMEMBRANCE 777.6 Composer unknown

GRACIOUS God, we worship Thee,
Reverently we bow the knee;
Jesus Christ our only plea:
Father, we adore Thee.

2 Vast Thy love, how deep, how wide,
In the gift of Him who died;
Righteous claims all satisfied:
Father, we adore Thee.

3 Low we bow before Thy face,
Sons of God, oh wondrous place;
Great the riches of Thy grace:
Father, we adore Thee.

4 By Thy Spirit grant that we
Worshippers in truth may be;
Praise, as incense sweet to Thee:
Father, we adore Thee.

5 Yet again our song we raise,
Note of deep adoring praise;
Now, and soon through endless days:
Father, we adore Thee.

Samuel Trevor Francis, 1834–1925

ASCALON 668.D

Silesian Melody

How pleased and blest was I
To hear the people cry,
Come, let us seek our God to-day!
Yes, with a cheerful zeal
We haste to Zion's hill,
And there our vows and homage pay.

2 Zion, thrice happy place,
Adorned with wondrous grace,
And walls of strength embrace thee
round;
In thee our tribes appear,
To pray and praise, and hear
The sacred gospel's joyful sound.

3 There David's greater Son
Hath fixed His royal throne;
He sits for grace and judgment there.
He bids the saints be glad,
He makes the sinner sad,
And humble souls rejoice with fear.

4 May peace attend thy gate,
And joy within thee wait,
To bless the soul of every guest:
The man that seeks thy peace,
And wishes thine increase,
A thousand blessings on him rest.

5 My tongue repeats her vows,
Peace to this sacred house!
For there my friends and kindred dwell.
And, since my glorious God
Makes thee His blest abode,
My soul shall ever love thee well.

Isaac Watts, 1674–1748

I'LL praise my Maker while I've breath;
And when my voice is lost in death,
  Praise shall employ my nobler powers:
My days of praise shall ne'er be past,
While life, and thought, and being last,
  Or immortality endures.

2 Happy the man whose hopes rely
  On Israel's God! He made the sky,
    And earth, and sea, with all their train:
  His truth for ever stands secure;
  He saves the oppressed, He feeds the poor,
    And none shall find His promise vain.

3 The Lord pours eyesight on the blind;
The Lord supports the fainting mind;
  He sends the labouring conscience peace;
He helps the stranger in distress,
The widow, and the fatherless,
  And grants the prisoner sweet release.

4 I'll praise Him while He lends me breath;
And when my voice is lost in death,
  Praise shall employ my nobler powers;
My days of praise shall ne'er be past,
While life, and thought, and being last,
  Or immortality endures.

Isaac Watts, 1674–1748

26

ST. DENIO 11.11.11.11

Welsh Hymn Melody

IMMORTAL, invisible, God only wise,
In light inaccessible hid from our eyes,
Most blessèd, most glorious, the Ancient of Days,
Almighty, victorious, Thy great name we praise.

2 Unresting, unhasting, and silent as light,
Nor wanting, nor wasting, Thou rulest in might;
Thy justice like mountains high soaring above
Thy clouds, which are fountains of goodness and love.

3 To all, life Thou givest, to both great and small;
In all life Thou livest, the true life of all;
We blossom and flourish as leaves on the tree,
And wither and perish: but nought changeth Thee.

4 Great Father of glory, pure Father of light,
Thine angels adore Thee, all veiling their sight;
But of all Thy rich graces this grace, Lord, impart—
Take the veil from our faces, the veil from our heart.

5 All laud we would render; oh help us to see,
'Tis only the splendour of light hideth Thee;
And so let Thy glory, Almighty, impart
Through Christ in the story, Thy Christ to the heart.

Walter Chalmers Smith, 1824–1908

GWALCHMAI 74.74.D

J. D. Jones, 1827-70

King of glory, King of peace,
    I will love Thee;
And that love may never cease,
    I will move Thee.
Thou hast granted my request,
    Thou hast heard me;
Thou didst note my working breast,
    Thou hast spared me.

2 Wherefore with my utmost art
    I will sing Thee,
And the cream of all my heart
    I will bring Thee.
Though my sins against me cried,
    Thou didst clear me;
And alone, when they replied,
    Thou didst hear me.

3 Seven whole days, not one in seven,
    I will praise Thee;
In my heart, though not in heaven,
    I can raise Thee.
Small it is, in this poor sort
    To enrol Thee:
E'en eternity's too short
    To extol Thee.

George Herbert, 1593–1632

LUCKINGTON   10.4.66.66.10.4   BASIL HARWOOD, 1859-1949

LET all the world in every corner sing:
    My God and King!
The heavens are not too high,
His praise may thither fly;
The earth is not too low,
His praises there may grow.
Let all the world in every corner sing:
    My God and King!

2 Let all the world in every corner sing:
    My God and King!
The Church with psalms must shout,
No door can keep them out:
But, above all, the heart
Must bear the longest part.
Let all the world in every corner sing:
    My God and King!

George Herbert, 1593-1632

MONKLAND 77.77   Arr. by J. B. WILKES, 1785-1869

L ET us with a gladsome mind
Praise the Lord, for He is kind:
For His mercies aye endure,
Ever faithful, ever sure.

2 He, with all-commanding might
Filled the new-made world with light:
For His mercies aye endure,
Ever faithful, ever sure.

3 He His chosen race did bless
In the wasteful wilderness:
For His mercies aye endure,
Ever faithful, ever sure.

4 All things living He doth feed;
His full hand supplies their need:
For His mercies aye endure,
Ever faithful, ever sure.

5 Let us then with gladsome mind
Praise the Lord for He is kind:
For His mercies aye endure,
Ever faithful, ever sure.

John Milton, 1608–74

30

STUDLAND S.M.D.

E. A. Burroughs, 1882-1935

Lord God, from whom all life,
  And all true gladness springs,
Whose love and care shine everywhere
  Among earth's common things;
  Be present while we lift
  Our song to Thee, and pay
Heart-gratitude for all things good
  About our path to-day.

2 We thank Thee for the grace
  In friend and brother found;
For human love that points above
  To where all love is crowned;
  Oh, may such friendship here
  To us Thy sons be given,
As shall endure, deep, fair, and pure,
  Till all be one in heaven!

3 But most we bless Thee, Lord,
  That here Thy Spirit's breath
Blows clear and strong to baffle wrong
  And win our lives from death;
  Oh, may each heart accept
  The entrance of Thy power,
And take Thee hence for sure defence
  And help in evil hour!

4 So, when the lives, to-day
  Within one circle brought,
Are sundered wide along the tide
  Of human work and thought,
  One song shall yet be ours,
  One life, one family,
One pathway still, by vale or hill,
  Shall lead us home to Thee.

Edward Arthur Burroughs, 1882–1934

MARYTON L.M.   H. P. SMITH, 1825-98

LORD of all being, throned afar,
Thy glory flames from sun and star;
Centre and soul of every sphere,
Yet to each loving heart how near.

2 Sun of our life, Thy quickening ray
Sheds on our path the glow of day;
Star of our hope, Thy softened light
Cheers the long watches of the night.

3 Our midnight is Thy smile withdrawn,
Our noontide is Thy gracious dawn,
Our rainbow arch, Thy mercy's sign;
All, save the clouds of sin, are Thine.

4 Lord of all life, below, above,
Whose light is truth, whose warmth is
    love,
Before Thy ever-blazing throne
We ask no lustre of our own.

5 Grant us Thy truth to make us free,
And kindling hearts that burn for
    Thee,
Till all Thy living altars claim
One holy light, one heavenly flame.

Oliver Wendell Holmes, 1809–94

This hymn may also be sung to **Birling**, No. 608

CROFT'S 136TH   66.66.88   W. CROFT, 1678-1727

L ORD of the worlds above,
How pleasant and how fair
The dwellings of Thy love,
The heavenly mansions are;
To thine abode
Our hearts aspire
With warm desire
To see our God.

2 Oh happy souls that pray
Where God appoints to hear!
Oh happy men that pay
Their constant service there!
They praise Thee still;
And happy they
That love the way
To Zion's hill.

3 There is Thy throne of grace,
And there the sprinkled blood;
There lives, before Thy face,
Our great High Priest, O God;
His name our plea,
We now draw near,
In holy fear
To worship Thee.

4 We go from strength to strength,
Through this dark vale of tears,
Till each arrives at length.
Till each in heaven appears;
Oh glorious seat,
Where God our King
Shall shortly bring
Our willing feet.

5 God is our sun and shield,
Our light and our defence;
With gifts His hands are filled,
We draw our blessings thence;
Thrice happy he,
O God of hosts,
Whose spirit trusts
Alone in Thee.

Isaac Watts, 1674–1748
This hymn may also be sung to **Darwall**, No. 168

LUX EOI 87.87.D   A. S. SULLIVAN, 1842-1900

MIGHTY God, while angels bless Thee,
  May a mortal sing Thy name?
Lord of men as well as angels,
  Thou art every creature's theme,
Lord of every land and nation,
  Ancient of eternal days,
Sounded through the wide creation
  Be Thy just and endless praise.

2 For the grandeur of Thy nature,
  Grand beyond a seraph's thought;
For created works of power,
  Works with skill and kindness wrought;
For Thy providence that governs
  Through Thine empire's wide domain,
Wings an angel, guides a sparrow,
  Blessèd be Thy gentle reign.

3 But Thy rich, Thy free redemption,
  Dark through brightness all along,
Thought is poor, and poor expression,
  Who dare sing that wondrous song?
Brightness of the Father's glory,
  Shall Thy praise unuttered lie?
Break, my tongue, such guilty silence,
  Sing the Lord who came to die;

4 From the highest throne of glory,
  To the cross of deepest woe,
All to ransom guilty captives,
  Flow, my praise, for ever flow!
Wave the palm of conquest glorious,
  Strike thy loudest, sweetest chords:
Jesus died, and rose victorious,
  Sing, for thou art now the Lord's.

5 Saviour, Lord of life and glory,
  Silent I can never be;
For salvation's wondrous story,
  Praise, eternal praise to Thee.
Go, return, immortal Saviour,
  Leave Thy footstool, take Thy throne,
Thence return and reign for ever,
  Be the kingdom all Thine own!

Robert Robinson, 1735–90
and Thomas Robinson

This hymn may also be sung to **Austria,** No. 614

34

WESTMINSTER C.M.

J. TURLE, 1802-82

M^Y God, how wonderful Thou art,
 Thy majesty how bright!
How beautiful Thy mercy-seat,
 In depths of burning light!

2 How dread are Thine eternal years,
 O everlasting Lord,
By prostrate spirits day and night
 Incessantly adored!

3 How wonderful, how beautiful,
 The sight of Thee must be,
Thine endless wisdom, boundless
  power,
 And awful purity!

4 Oh, how I fear Thee, living God,
 With deepest, tenderest fears,
And worship Thee with trembling
  hope,
 And penitential tears!

5 Yet I may love Thee, too, O Lord,
 Almighty as Thou art,
For Thou hast stooped to ask of me
 The love of my poor heart.

6 No earthly father loves like Thee;
 No mother, e'er so mild,
Bears and forbears as Thou hast done
 With me, Thy sinful child.

7 Father of Jesus, love's reward,
 What rapture will it be,
Prostrate before Thy throne to lie
 And gaze and gaze on Thee!

Frederick William Faber, 1814–63

IRISH C.M.

Hymns and Sacred Poems, Dublin, 1749

M^Y God, I love Thee—not because
    I hope for heaven thereby,
Nor yet because who love Thee not
    Are lost eternally.

2 Thou, O my Jesus, Thou didst me
    Upon the cross embrace;
For me didst bear the nails and spear,
    And manifold disgrace.

3 And griefs and torments numberless,
    And sweat of agony,
And death itself—and all for me,
    Who was Thine enemy.

4 Then why, O blessèd Jesus Christ,
    Should I not love Thee well?
Not for the sake of winning heaven,
    Or of escaping hell;

5 Not with the hope of gaining aught;
    Not seeking a reward;
But as Thyself hast lovèd me,
    O ever-loving Lord.

6 E'en so I love Thee, and will love,
    And in Thy praise will sing;
Because Thou art my loving God
    And my eternal King.

Francis Xavier, c. 1506–52
tr. Edward Caswall, 1814–78

NUN DANKET 67.67.66.66

Adapted from a melody by
J. Crüger, 1598-1662

Now thank we all our God,
  With hearts, and hands, and
      voicès,
Who wondrous things hath done,
  In whom His world rejoices;
Who from our mothers' arms
  Hath blessed us on our way
With countless gifts of love,
  And still is ours to-day.

2 Oh may this bounteous God
  Through all our life be near us,
With ever-joyful hearts
  And blessèd peace to cheer us,
And keep us in His grace,
  And guide us when perplexed,
And free us from all ills
  In this world and the next.

3 All praise and thanks to God
  The Father now be given,
The Son, and Him who reigns
  With them in highest heaven,
The one eternal God,
  Whom earth and heaven adore;
For thus it was, is now,
  And shall be evermore.

Martin Rinckart, 1586–1649
tr. Catherine Winkworth, 1827–78

HOUGHTON 10.10.11.11 H. J. GAUNTLETT, 1805-76

O HEAVENLY King, look down from above;
Assist us to sing Thy mercy and love:
So sweetly o'erflowing, so plenteous the store,
Thou still art bestowing, and giving us more.

2 O God of our life, we hallow Thy name;
Our business and strife is Thee to proclaim.
Accept our thanksgiving for creating grace;
The living, the living shall show forth Thy praise.

3 Our Father and Lord, almighty art Thou;
Preserved by Thy word, we worship Thee now;
The bountiful donor of all we enjoy,
Our tongues, to Thine honour, and lives we employ.

4 But oh, above all Thy kindness we praise,
From sin and·from thrall which saves the lost race,
Thy Son Thou hast given the world to redeem,
And bring us to heaven whose trust is in Him.

5 Wherefore of Thy love we sing and rejoice,
With angels above we lift up our voice;
Thy love each believer shall gladly adore,
For ever and ever, when time is no more.

Charles Wesley, 1707–88

LAUDATE DOMINUM 55.55.65.65   C. H. H. PARRY, 1848-1918

OH praise ye the Lord!
  Praise Him in the height;
Rejoice in His word,
  Ye angels of light;
Ye heavens, adore Him
  By Whom ye were made,
And worship before Him,
  In brightness array'd.

2 Oh praise ye the Lord!
  Praise Him upon earth,
In tuneful accord,
  Ye sons of new birth;
Praise Him who hath brought you
  His grace from above,
Praise Him who hath taught you
  To sing of His love.

3 Oh praise ye the Lord,
  All things that give sound;
Each jubilant chord,
  Re-echo around;
Loud organs, His glory
  Forth tell in deep tone,
And sweet harp, the story
  Of what He hath done.

4 Oh praise ye the Lord!
  Thanksgiving and song
To Him be outpour'd
  All ages along:
For love in creation,
  For heaven restored,
For grace of salvation,
  Oh praise ye the Lord!

Henry Williams Baker, 1821–77

WAS LEBET, WAS SCHWEBET 12.10.12.10   Reinhardt MS., Uttingen, 1754

** for verses 1 & 5 only*

OH worship the Lord in the beauty of holiness!
Bow down before Him, His glory proclaim;
With gold of obedience, and incense of lowliness,
Kneel and adore Him; the Lord is His name.

2 Low at His feet lay thy burden of carefulness,
High on His heart He will bear it for thee,
Comfort thy sorrows, and answer thy prayerfulness,
Guiding thy steps as may best for thee be.

3 Fear not to enter His courts in the slenderness
Of the poor wealth thou wouldst reckon as thine;
Truth in its beauty, and love in its tenderness,
These are the offerings to lay on His shrine.

4 These, though we bring them in trembling and fearfulness,
He will accept for the Name that is dear;
Mornings of joy give for evenings of tearfulness,
Trust for our trembling, and hope for our fear.

5 Oh worship the Lord in the beauty of holiness,
Bow down before Him, His glory proclaim;
With gold of obedience, and incense of lowliness,
Kneel and adore Him; the Lord is His Name.

John Samuel Bewley Monsell, 1811–75

HANOVER 55.55.65.65
W. CROFT, 1678-1727

OH worship the King,
    All glorious above;
Oh gratefully sing
    His power and His love:
Our shield and defender,
    The ancient of days,
Pavilioned in splendour,
    And girded with praise.

2 Oh tell of His might,
    Oh sing of His grace,
Whose robe is the light,
    Whose canopy space;
His chariots of wrath
    The deep thunder-clouds form,
And dark is His path
    On the wings of the storm.

3 The earth with its store
    Of wonders untold.
Almighty, Thy power
    Hath founded of old,
Hath stablished it fast
    By a changeless decree,
And round it hath cast,
    Like a mantle, the sea.

4 Thy bountiful care
    What tongue can recite?
It breathes in the air,
    It shines in the light,
It streams from the hills,
    It descends to the plain,
And sweetly distils
    In the dew and the rain.

5 Frail children of dust,
    And feeble as frail,
In Thee do we trust,
    Nor find Thee to fail;
Thy mercies how tender,
    How firm to the end,
Our maker, defender,
    Redeemer, and friend!

6 Oh measureless might!
    Ineffable love!
While angels delight
    To hymn Thee above,
The humbler creation,
    Though feeble their lays,
With true adoration
    Shall lisp to Thy praise.

Robert Grant, 1779–1838

This hymn may also be sung to **Houghton,** No. 37

PRAISE MY SOUL   87.87.87   J. Goss, 1800-80

This hymn may also be sung to **Regent Square**, No. 5

HARMONY
2 Praise Him for His grace and fa - vour To our
3 Fa - ther - like- He tends and spares us; Well our
fa - thers in dis - tress; Praise Him still the same for
fee - ble frame He knows; In His hands He gent - ly
ev - er, Slow to chide, and swift to bless: Praise Him,
bears us, Res - cues us from all our foes; Praise Him,
praise Him, praise Him, praise Him, Glo - rious in His faith - ful - ness.
praise Him, praise Him, praise Him, Wide - ly as His mer - cy flows.

UNISON
4 An-gels, help us to a - dore Him, Ye be-hold Him
face to face; Sun and moon, bow down be - fore Him,
Dwell-ers all in time and space, Praise Him, praise Him,
praise Him, praise Him, Praise with us the God of grace.
H. F. Lyte, 1793-1847.

PHILIPPI 664.6664   J. G. EBELING, 1637-76

PRAISE God, ye seraphs bright,
Praise Him, ye sons of light,
Jesus adore!
What earthly choirs can swell,
What mortal tongues can tell,
Thy love, Immanuel,
God evermore.

2 Yet must we lisp Thy praise,
Though but in human lays,
Jesus most high!
Didst Thou not leave Thy Throne,
And to this world come down,
To bear our curse alone—
To bleed and die?

3 Come, saints, in God rejoice,
Lift up a mighty voice,
Sing to the Lamb;
For us His blood was shed,
For us He left the dead,
His foes discomfited;
Praise the I AM!

4 Soon shall we see His face,
Wearing no mournful trace—
Oh what a sight!
Soon shall we hear Him say,
"Come, waiting child, away;
Lo, now has dawned the day
That knows no night."

William Pennefather, 1816–73

This hymn may also be sung to **Malvern**, No. 220

LAUS DEO 87.87   R. REDHEAD, 1820-1901

PRAISE the Lord! Ye heavens, adore
   Him;
  Praise Him, angels in the height;
Sun and moon, rejoice before Him;
  Praise Him, all ye stars and light.

2 Praise the Lord, for He hath spoken;
  Worlds His mighty voice obeyed;
Laws, that never shall be broken,
  For their guidance He hath made.

3 Praise the Lord, for He is glorious;
  Never shall His promise fail:
God hath made His saints victorious;
  Sin and death shall not prevail.

4 Praise the God of our salvation;
  Hosts on high His power proclaim;
Heaven and earth, and all creation,
  Laud and magnify His name.

Anonymous: Foundling Hospital
Collection, 1796

CHORUS ANGELORUM C.M.   ARTHUR SOMERVELL, 1863-1937

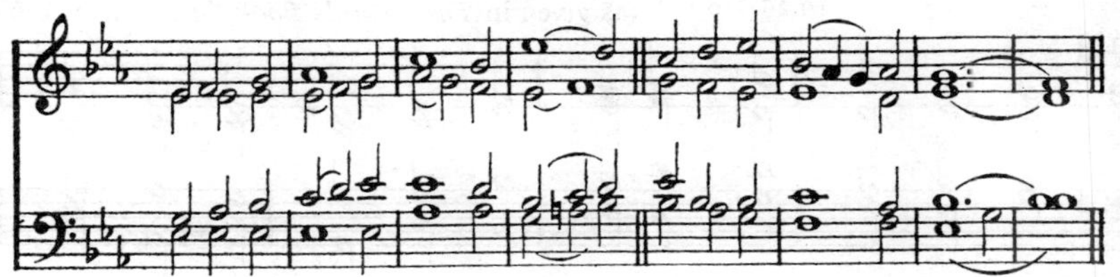

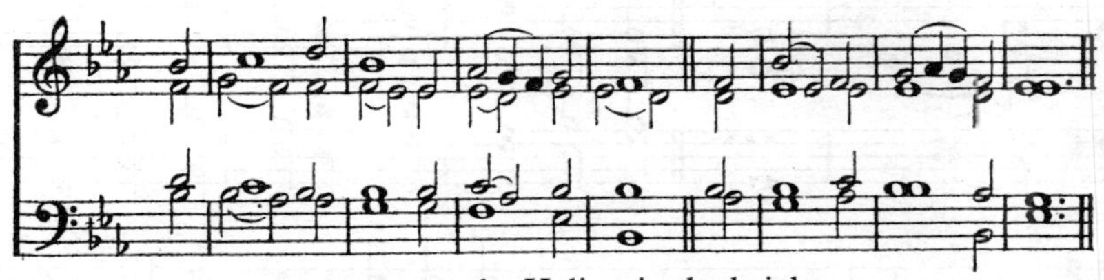

PRAISE to the Holiest in the height,
And in the depth be praise:
In all His words most wonderful,
Most sure in all His ways!

2 Oh loving wisdom of our God!
When all was sin and shame,
A second Adam to the fight
And to the rescue came.

3 Oh wisest love! that flesh and blood,
Which did in Adam fail,
Should strive afresh against the foe,
Should strive and should prevail;

4 And that a higher gift than grace
Should flesh and blood refine,
God's presence and His very self,
And essence all-divine.

5 Oh generous love! that He who smote
In man for man the foe,
The double agony in man
For man should undergo;

6 And in the garden secretly,
And on the cross on high,
Should teach His brethren and inspire
To suffer and to die.

7 Praise to the Holiest in the height,
And in the depth be praise;
In all His words most wonderful,
Most sure in all His ways!

John Henry Newman, 1801–90

This hymn may also be sung to **Gerontius**, No. 19

PRAISE to the Lord, the Almighty, the King of creation;
O my soul, praise Him, for He is thy health and salvation;
All ye who hear,
Brothers and sisters, draw near,
Praise Him in glad adoration.

2 Praise to the Lord, who o'er all things so wondrously reigneth,
Shelters thee under His wings, yea, so gently sustaineth:
Hast thou not seen?
All that is needful hath been
Granted in what He ordaineth.

3 Praise to the Lord, who doth prosper thy work, and defend thee!
Surely His goodness and mercy here daily attend thee:
Ponder anew
What the Almighty can do,
Who with His love doth befriend thee.

4 Praise to the Lord, who when darkness of sin is abounding,
Who, when the godless do triumph, all virtue confounding,
Sheddeth His light,
Chaseth the horrors of night,
Saints with His mercy surrounding.

5 Praise to the Lord! Oh let all that is in me adore Him!
All that hath life and breath come now with praises before Him!
Let the Amen
Sound from His people again:
Gladly for aye we adore Him.

Joachim Neander, 1650–80
tr. Catherine Winkworth, 1827–78 and others

O PERFECT LOVE   11.10.11.10

J. BARNBY, 1838-1896

PRAISE ye Jehovah! Praise the Lord most holy,
Who cheers the contrite, girds with strength the weak;
Praise Him, who will with glory crown the lowly,
And with salvation beautify the meek.

2 Praise ye the Lord for all His loving-kindness,
And all the tender mercies He has shown;
Praise Him who pardons all our sin and blindness,
And calls us sons, and seals us for His own.

3 Praise ye Jehovah, source of every blessing!
Before His gifts earth's richest boons are dim;
Resting in Him, His peace and joy possessing,
All things are ours, for we have all in Him.

4 Praise ye the Father, God the Lord who gave us,
With full and perfect love His only Son;
Praise ye the Son, who died Himself to save us;
Praise ye the Spirit, praise the Three in One!

Margaret Cockburn-Campbell, c. 1808-1841

This hymn may also be sung to **Strength and Stay**, No. 487

BRIDFORD MILLS 66.84

F. A. J. TONKIN, b. 1926

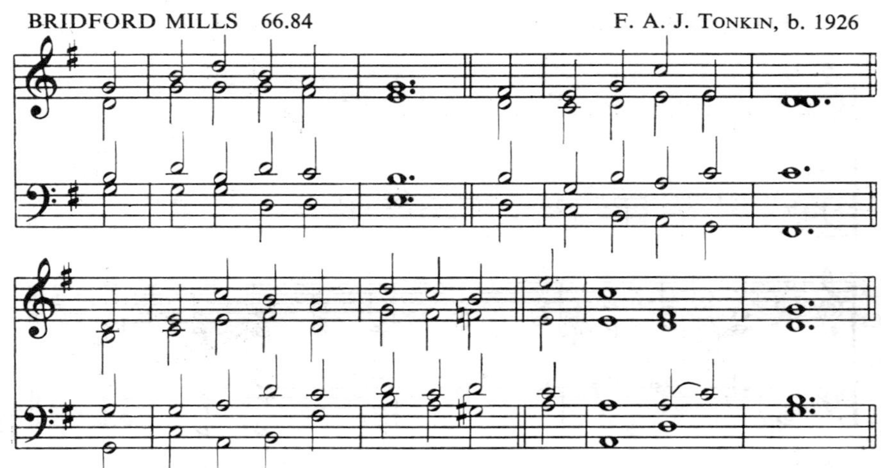

SALVATION to our God!
  Salvation to the Lamb!
The shedding of His precious blood
  Our only claim.

2 Our God salvation gives,
  And through the Lamb it flows;
Once slain for us—for us He lives,
  Our sole repose.

3 The Lamb once slain is seen
  On God's eternal throne;
And His redeemed are white and clean,
  Through Him alone.

4 Salvation's joyful sound
  Bursts from the blood-bought
    throng;
And holy angels all around
  Take up the song.

5 Our hearts are tuned for this,
  Their songs our tongues employ;
The Lamb the spring of all our bliss,
  And God our joy.

6 Salvation to our God,
  Thanksgiving, power, and might!
And to the Lamb who shed His blood,
  Our life and light!

Mary Bowly Peters, 1813–56

Words at foot of next page

49 CARLISLE S.M.

C. LOCKHART, 1745-1815

HOREB 77.77

J. H. RICHARDS, b. 1873

SONGS of praise the angels sang,
Heaven with hallelujahs rang,
When Jehovah's work begun,
When He spake, and it was done.

2 Songs of praise awoke the morn,
When the Prince of Peace was born;
Songs of praise arose when He
Captive led captivity.

3 Heaven and earth must pass away;
Songs of praise shall crown that day:
God will make new heavens and earth;
Songs of praise shall hail their birth.

4 And shall man alone be dumb
Till that glorious kingdom come?
No! the Church delights to raise
Psalms and hymns and songs of praise.

5 Saints below, with heart and voice,
Still in songs of praise rejoice;
Learning here, by faith and love,
Songs of praise to sing above.

6 Borne upon their latest breath,
Songs of praise shall conquer death;
Then, amidst eternal joy,
Songs of praise their powers employ!

James Montgomery, 1771–1854

This hymn may also be sung to **University College,** No. 584

Tune at foot of previous page

49

STAND up and bless the Lord,
Ye people of His choice;
Stand up, and bless the Lord your God
With heart, and soul, and voice.

2 Though high above all praise,
Above all blessing high,
Who would not fear His holy name,
And laud and magnify?

3 Oh for the living flame,
From His own altar brought,
To touch our lips, our minds inspire,
And wing to heaven our thought!

4 There with benign regard
Our praise He deigns to hear;
Though unrevealed to mortal sense,
The spirit feels Him near.

5 God is our strength and song,
And His salvation ours;
Then be His love in Christ proclaimed,
With all our ransomed powers.

6 Stand up, and bless the Lord,
The Lord your God adore;
Stand up, and bless His glorious name,
Henceforth for evermore.

James Montgomery, 1771–1854

50

ANTWERP L.M.

W. SMALLWOOD, 1831-97

SWEET is the work, my God, my King,
To praise Thy Name, give thanks
and sing;
To show Thy love by morning light,
And talk of all Thy truth at night.

2 Sweet is the day of sacred rest,
No mortal cares shall seize my breast;
Oh may my heart in tune be found
Like David's harp of solemn sound.

3 My heart shall triumph in my Lord,
And bless His works and bless His
word:
Thy works of grace, how bright they
shine:
How deep Thy counsels, how divine!

4 There shall I bear a glorious part,
When grace hath well refined my
heart,
And fresh supplies of joy are shed,
Like holy oil to cheer my head.

5 There shall I see and hear and know
All I desired or wished below;
And every power find sweet employ
In that eternal world of joy.

Isaac Watts, 1674–1748

This hymn may also be sung to **Duke St.**, No. 146

BIRMINGHAM   10.10.10.10

From Rev. F. CUNNINGHAM'S
A Selection of Psalm Tunes, 1834

SWEET is the work, O Lord Most High, to praise,
    And Thy great name for evermore to bless;
Praise for Thy kindness every morn to raise,
    And every night Thy faithfulness confess.

2 For Thou, Lord, through Thy work hast gladdened me,
    And in that work my triumph now I make;
Thy mighty arm hath brought salvation free,
    Which shall for ever joy and gladness wake.

3 The men of earth but seek their portion here,
    Nor ask Thy thoughts, nor seek Thy way to trace;
But Thou has ope'd our eye, and waked our ear,
    And on our head hast poured Thine oil of grace.

4 Thy saints, O Lord, shall flourish like the palm,
    Whose root lies deep beneath the desert soil;
There secret springs refresh; nor storm, nor calm
    Shall waste the fruit of Thy most patient toil.

5 Thus to hoar age may we Thy truth declare,
    Who faithful ever wast, and art to be;
Trophies of Thy redeeming grace we are,
    Thou art our Rock, beneath Thy shade we flee.

Author unknown

This hymn may also be sung to **Pax Dei,** No. 176

WOODLANDS 10.10.10.10   W. Greatorex, 1877-1949

TELL out, my soul, the greatness of the Lord!
Unnumbered blessings, give my spirit voice;
Tender to me the promise of His word;
In God my Saviour shall my heart rejoice.

2 Tell out, my soul, the greatness of His name!
Make known His might, the deeds His arm has done;
His mercy sure, from age to age the same;
His holy name—the Lord, the Mighty One.

3 Tell out, my soul, the greatness of His might!
Powers and dominions lay their glory by.
Proud hearts and stubborn wills are put to flight,
The hungry fed, the humble lifted high.

4 Tell out, my soul, the glories of His word!
Firm is His promise, and His mercy sure.
Tell out, my soul, the greatness of the Lord
To children's children and for evermore!

Timothy Dudley-Smith, b. 1926

LEONI   66.84.D

Adapted from a **Hebrew Melody**
by THOMAS OLIVERS, 1725-99

THE God of Abraham praise,
  Who reigns enthroned above,
Ancient of everlasting days,
  And God of love.
Jehovah! Great I AM!
  By earth and heaven confessed;
I bow, and bless the sacred Name,
  For ever blest.

2 The God of Abraham praise,
  At whose supreme command
From earth I rise, and seek the joys
  At His right hand:
I all on earth forsake,
  Its wisdom, fame, and power,
And Him my only portion make,
  My shield and tower.

3 The God of Abraham praise,
  Whose all-sufficient grace
Shall guide me all my happy days,
  In all my ways:
He calls a worm His friend,
  He calls Himself my God;
And He shall save me to the end,
  Through Jesu's blood.

4 He by Himself hath sworn,
  I on His oath depend:
I shall on eagles' wings upborne
  To heaven ascend:
I shall behold His face,
  I shall His power adore,
And sing the wonders of His grace,
  For evermore!

5 The whole triumphant host
  Give thanks to God on high:
"Hail, Father, Son, and Holy Ghost!"
  They ever cry:
Hail, Abraham's God, and mine!
  I join the heavenly lays;
All might and majesty are Thine,
  And endless praise!

Thomas Olivers, 1725–99

NIAGARA L.M.

R. JACKSON, 1842-1914

THE Lord is King! lift up thy voice,
O earth, and all ye heavens,
rejoice;
From world to world the joy shall ring,
"The Lord Omnipotent is King!"

2 The Lord is King! who then shall dare
Resist His will, distrust His care,
Or murmur at His wise decrees,
Or doubt His royal promises?

3 The Lord is King! child of the dust,
The Judge of all the earth is just;
Holy and true are all His ways:
Let every creature speak His praise.

4 He reigns! ye saints, exalt your strains;
Your God is King, your Father reigns;
And He is at the Father's side,
The Man of love, the Crucified.

5 Come, make your wants, your burdens
known;
He will present them at the throne;
And angel bands are waiting there
His messages of love to bear.

6 Oh, when His wisdom can mistake,
His might decay, His love forsake,
Then may His children cease to sing
"The Lord Omnipotent is King!"

Josiah Conder, 1789–1855

RHOSYMEDRE, 66.66.88 J. D. EDWARDS, 1805-85

THE Lord Jehovah reigns:
  His throne is built on high,
The garments He assumes
  Are light and majesty:
His glories shine with beams so bright,
No mortal eye can bear the sight.

2 The thunders of His hand
  Keep the wide world in awe;
His wrath and justice stand
  To guard His holy law;
And where His love resolves to bless,
His truth confirms and seals the grace.

3 Through all His mighty works
  Amazing wisdom shines,
Confounds the powers of hell,
  And breaks their dark designs;
Strong is His arm, and shall fulfil
His great decrees and sovereign will.

4 And will this sovereign King
  Of glory condescend?
And will He write His name
  My Father and my Friend?
I love His name, I love His word,
Join all my powers to praise the Lord.

Isaac Watts, 1674-1748

GODRE'R COED C.M. M. W. Davies

WHEN all Thy mercies, O my God,
My rising soul surveys,
Transported with the view, I'm lost
In wonder, love, and praise.

2 Unnumbered comforts to my soul
Thy tender care bestowed,
Before my infant heart conceived
From whence these comforts flowed.

3 When worn with sickness, oft hast
Thou
With health renewed my face;
And when in sin and sorrows sunk,
Revived my soul with grace.

4 Ten thousand thousand precious gifts
My daily thanks employ;
Nor is the least a cheerful heart
That tastes those gifts with joy.

5 Through every period of my life
Thy goodness I'll pursue;
And after death, in distant worlds,
The glorious theme renew.

6 Through all eternity, to Thee
A joyful song I'll raise;
But oh, eternity's too short
To utter all Thy praise!

Joseph Addison, 1672–1719

This hymn may also be sung to **Stracathro**, No. 88

YE holy angels bright,
  Who wait at God's right hand,
Or through the realms of light
  Fly at your Lord's command,
    Assist our song,
      Or else the theme
      Too high doth seem
    For mortal tongue.

2 Ye blessèd souls at rest,
  Who ran this earthly race,
And now, from sin released,
  Behold your Father's face,
    His praises sound,
      As in His light
      With sweet delight
    Ye do abound.

3 Ye saints, who toil below,
  Adore your heavenly King,
And onward as ye go
  Some joyful anthem sing;
    Take what He gives
      And praise Him still,
      Through good and ill,.
    Who ever lives.

4 My soul, bear thou thy part,
  Triumph in God above,
And with a well-tuned heart
  Sing thou the songs of love.
    Let all thy days
      Till life shall end,
      Whate'er He send,
    Be filled with praise.

Richard Baxter, 1615–91

This hymn may also be sung to **Croft's 136th,** No. 7

See also
  3 Father, in whom we live
62 My God, I thank Thee
67 Blest be the everlasting God
220 Glory to God on high, Let earth
411 Through all the changing scenes of life
534 Our Father, we would worship

EISENACH L.M.

J. H. SCHEIN, 1586-1630.
Arr. by J. S. BACH, 1685-1750

Ped.

FATHER of all! whose powerful voice
  Called forth this universal frame;
Whose mercies over all rejoice,
  Through endless ages still the same:

2 Thou by Thy word upholdest all;
  Thy bounteous love to all is showed,
Thou hear'st Thy every creature's call,
  And fillest every mouth with good.

3 Giver and Lord of life, whose power
  And guardian care for all are free,
To Thee, in fierce temptation's hour,
  From sin and Satan let us flee.

4 Thine, Lord, we are, and ours Thou
    art;
  In us be all Thy goodness showed.

Renew, enlarge, and fill our heart
  With peace, and joy, and heaven,
    and God.

5 Father, 'tis Thine each day to yield
  Thy children's wants a fresh supply;
Thou cloth'st the lilies of the field,
  And hearest the young ravens cry.

6 On Thee we cast our care; we live
  Through Thee, who know'st our
    every need:
Oh feed us with Thy grace, and give
  Our souls this day the living bread.

                        John Wesley, 1703-91

This hymn may also be sung to **Martham,** No. 59

59   MARTHAM L.M.

J. H. MAUNDER, 1858-1920

O LOVE of God, how strong and true;
Eternal, and yet ever new;
Uncomprehended and unbought,
Beyond all knowledge and all thought!

2 O heavenly Love, how precious still,
In days of weariness and ill,
In nights of pain and helplessness,
To heal, to comfort, and to bless.

3 O wide-embracing, wondrous Love;
We read thee in the sky above,
We read thee in the earth below,
In seas that swell and streams that flow.

4 We read thee best in Him who came
To bear for us the cross of shame,
Sent by the Father from on high,
Our life to live, our death to die.

5 We read thy power to bless and save
E'en in the darkness of the grave;
Still more in resurrection light
We read the fullness of thy might.

6 O love of God, our shield and stay
Through all the perils of our way;
Eternal Love, in thee we rest,
For ever safe, for ever blest!

Horatius Bonar, 1808–89

This hymn may also be sung to **Eisenach,** No. 58

NORICUM 77.77.77   F. JAMES, 1858-1922   60

FOR the beauty of the earth,
For the beauty of the skies,
For the love which from our birth
Over and around us lies,
Gracious God, to Thee we raise
This our sacrifice of praise.

2 For the beauty of each hour
Of the day and of the night,
Hill and vale, and tree and flower,
Sun and moon, and stars of light:

3 For the joy of ear and eye,
For the heart and mind's delight,
For the mystic harmony
Linking sense to sound and sight:

4 For the joy of human love,
Brother, sister, parent, child,
Friends on earth and friends above;
For all gentle thoughts and mild:

5 For each perfect gift of Thine
To our race so freely given,
Graces human and divine,
Flowers of earth and buds of heaven:

Folliott Sandford Pierpoint, 1835–1917

This hymn may also be sung to **England's Lane,** No. 110

CREDITON C.M.   T. CLARK, 1775-1859

I SING the almighty power of God,
   That made the mountains rise;
That spread the flowing seas abroad,
   And built the lofty skies.

2 I sing the wisdom that ordained
   The sun to rule the day:
The moon shines full at His command,
   And all the stars obey.

3 I sing the goodness of the Lord,
   That filled the earth with food;
He formed the creatures with His
     word,
   And then pronounced them good.

4 Lord, how Thy wonders are displayed,
   Where'er I turn my eye;
If I survey the ground I tread.
   Or gaze upon the sky.

5 There's not a plant or flower below,
   But makes Thy glories known;
And clouds arise, and tempests blow,
   By order from Thy throne.

6 God's hand is my perpetual guard;
   He keeps me with His eye:
Why should I then forget the Lord,
   Who is for ever nigh?

Isaac Watts, 1674-1748

This hymn may also be sung to **Byzantium,** No. 257

WENTWORTH 84.84.84

F. C. MAKER, 1844-1927

MY God, I thank Thee who hast made
  The earth so bright,
So full of splendour and of joy,
  Beauty and light;
So many glorious things are here,
  Noble and right.

2 I thank Thee, too, that Thou hast made
  Joy to abound,
So many gentle thoughts and deeds
  Circling us round,
That, in the darkest spot of earth
  Some love is found.

3 I thank Thee more, that all our joy
  Is touched with pain,
That shadows fall on brightest hours,
  That thorns remain;
So that earth's bliss may be our guide,
  And not our chain.

4 For Thou, who knowest, Lord, how soon
  Our weak heart clings,
Hast given us joys, tender and true,
  Yet all with wings,
So that we see, gleaming on high,
  Diviner things.

5 I thank Thee, Lord, that Thou hast kept
  The best in store:
We have enough, but not too much
  To long for more—
A yearning for a deeper peace
  Not known before.

6 I thank Thee, Lord, that here our souls,
  Though amply blest,
Can never find, although they seek,
  A perfect rest,
Nor ever shall, until they lean
  On Jesu's breast.

Adelaide Anne Procter, 1825–64

63

NUN DANKET ALL C.M.   J. Crüger, 1598-1662

ALL that I was—my sin, my guilt,
  My death—was all my own;
All that I am I owe to Thee,
  My gracious God, alone.

2 The evil of my former state
  Was mine, and only mine;
The good in which I now rejoice
  Is Thine, and only Thine.

3·The darkness of my former night,
  The bondage—all was mine;
The light of life in which I walk,
  The liberty is, Thine.

4 Thy grace first made me feel my sin,
  And taught me to believe;
Then, in believing, peace I found,
  And now I live, I live.

5 All that I am e'en here on earth,
  All that I hope to be—
When Jesus comes, and glory dawns,
  I owe it, Lord, to Thee.

Horatius Bonar, 1808–89
This hymn may also be sung to **Bedford,** No. 94

64 AMAZING GRACE C.M.   Composer unknown

AMAZING grace! How sweet the sound,
  That saved a wretch like me;
I once was lost, but now am found,
  Was blind but now I see.

2 'Twas grace that taught my heart to fear,
  And grace my fears relieved;
How precious did that grace appear
  The hour I first believed!

3 Through many dangers, toils and snares,
  I am already come;
'Tis grace hath brought me safe thus far,
  And grace will lead me home.

4 The Lord hath promised good to me,
  His word my hope secures;
He will my shield and portion be
  As long as life endures.

5 Yes, when this flesh and heart shall fail,
  And mortal life shall cease,
I shall possess within the veil
  A life of joy and peace.

6 When we've been there a thousand years,
  Bright shining as the sun,
We've no less days to sing God's praise
  Than when we first begun.

John Newton, 1725–1807

This hymn may also be sung to **Nun danket all,** No. 63

STROUDWATER C.M.   WILKINS' *Psalmody, c.* 1730   **65**

BEGIN, my tongue, some heavenly theme,
  And speak some boundless thing,
The mighty works or mightier name
  Of our eternal King.

2 Tell of His wondrous faithfulness,
  And sound His power abroad;
Sing the sweet promise of His grace
  And the fulfilling God.

3 Engraved as in eternal brass
  The mighty promise shines;
Nor can the powers of darkness raze
  Those everlasting lines.

4 His very word of grace is strong
  As that which built the skies;
The voice that rolls the stars along
  Speaks all the promises.

5 Oh might I hear Thy heavenly tongue
  But whisper, "Thou art Mine";
Those gentle words should raise my song
  To notes almost divine.

6 How would my leaping heart rejoice,
  And think my heaven secure!
I trust the all-creating voice,
  And faith desires no more.

Isaac Watts, 1674–1748

66

UNIVERSITY C.M.

C. COLLIGNON, 1725-85

BEHOLD the amazing gift of love
    The Father hath bestowed
On us, the sinful sons of men,
    To call us sons of God!

2 Concealed as yet this honour lies,
    By this dark world unknown—
A world that knew not when He came,
    E'en God's eternal Son.

3 High is the rank we now possess,
    But higher we shall rise,
Though what we shall hereafter be
    Is hid from mortal eyes.

4 Our souls, we know, when He appears,
    Shall bear His image bright;
For all His glory, full disclosed,
    Shall open to our sight.

5 A hope so great, and so divine,
    May trials well endure;
And purge the soul from sense and sin,
    As Christ Himself is pure.

Scottish Paraphrases, 1781
based on Isaac Watts, 1674–1748
This hymn may also be sung to **St. Stephen**, No. 67

67

ST. STEPHEN C.M.

WILLIAM JONES, 1726-1800

BLEST be the everlasting God,
The Father of our Lord!
Be His abounding mercy praised,
His majesty adored!

2 When from the dead He raised His
Son,
And called Him to the sky,
He gave our souls a lively hope
That they should never die:

3 That though our inbred sins require
Our flesh to see the dust;
Yet as the Lord our Saviour rose,
So all His followers must:

4 To an inheritance divine
Reserved against that day;
'Tis uncorrupted, undefiled,
And cannot fade away.

5 Saints by the power of God are kept,
Till the salvation come:
We walk by faith as strangers here,
Till Christ shall call us home.

Isaac Watts, 1674-1748
and *William Cameron, 1751-1811*
as in Scottish Paraphrases, 1781

NEWCASTLE 86.886

H. L. MORLEY, 1830-1916 **68**

ETERNAL Light! Eternal Light!
How pure the soul must be,
When, placed within Thy searching
sight,
It shrinks not, but with calm delight,
Can live, and look on Thee.

2 The spirits that surround Thy throne
May bear the burning bliss;
But that is surely theirs alone,
Since they have never, never known
A fallen world like this.

3 Oh how shall I, whose native sphere
Is dark, whose mind is dim,
Before the Ineffable appear,
And on my naked spirit bear
The uncreated beam?

4 There is a way for man to rise,
To that sublime abode,
An offering and a sacrifice,
A Holy Spirit's energies,
An Advocate with God.

5 These, these prepare us for the sight
Of majesty above;
The sons of ignorance and night
Can dwell in the eternal Light
Through the eternal Love.

This hymn may also be sung to **Rest,** No. 69

Thomas Binney, 1798-1874

REST 86.886   F. C. MAKER, 1844-1927

ETERNAL love! O mighty sea,
  That hath not bounds, or shore,
I gaze upon thy tideless waves,
I know the love that loving saves,
  I worship, and adore.

2 Eternal love, eternal love,
  That ever shall abide;
The love that saves, the love that
    keeps,
What vastness in Thy glorious deeps,
  O ocean deep and wide!

3 Eternal love that loveth me,
  And loving, made me love,
That brought my Saviour pain and
    loss,
The awful anguish of the cross,
  To lift my soul above!

4 Eternal love that bore the curse,
  That else must fall on me,
Now to the glory of Thy grace,
Mine eyes shall see the Saviour's face
  Through all eternity.

5 Eternal love, O Son of God,
  Glorious in all Thy ways!
Thou art enthroned in light divine,
The light in which Thy saints shall
    shine
Through everlasting days.

Samuel Trevor Francis, 1834–1925

This hymn may also be sung to **Newcastle,** No. 68

71   CHURCH TRIUMPHANT L.M.   J. W. ELLIOTT, 1833-1915

Words at foot of next page

EVAN C.M.   W. H. HAVERGAL, 1793-1870

FATHER, Thy name our souls would bless,
   As children taught by grace;
Lift up our hearts in righteousness,
   And joy before Thy face.

2 Sweet is the confidence Thou giv'st,
   Though high above our praise;
Our hearts resort to where Thou liv'st
   In heaven's unclouded rays.

3 There, in the purpose of Thy love,
   Our place is now prepared,
As sons, with Him who is above,
   Who all our sorrows shared.

4 Eternal ages shall declare
   The riches of Thy grace,
To those who, with Thy Son, shall share
   A son's eternal place.

5 We joy in Thee, Thy holy love
   Our endless portion is;
Like Thine own Son, with Him above,
   In brightest heavenly bliss:

6 His Father Thou and ours through grace,
   We taste the same delight—
Blest, in the brightness of Thy face,
   In heaven's unclouded light.

John Nelson Darby, 1800–82

This hymn may also be sung to **Richmond,** No. 18

71

Tune at foot of previous page

FATHER, whose everlasting love
   Thy only Son for sinners gave,
Whose grace to all did freely move,
   And sent Him down the world to save:

2 Help us Thy mercy to extol,
   Immense, unfathomed, unconfined;
To praise the Lamb who died for all,
   The general Saviour of mankind.

3 Thy undistinguishing regard
   Was cast on Adam's fallen race;
For all Thou hast in Christ prepared
   Sufficient, sovereign, saving grace.

4 The world He suffered to redeem;
   For all He hath the atonement made;
For those that will not come to Him
   The ransom of His life was paid.

5 Arise, O God, maintain Thy cause!
   The fullness of the Gentiles call;
Lift up the standard of Thy cross,
   And all shall own Thou diedst for all.

Charles Wesley, 1707–88

FIRST TUNE

RHYD-Y-GROES   88.88.88

T. D. EDWARDS, 1875-1930

GREAT God of wonders, all Thy ways
Are worthy of Thyself—divine!
But the fair glories of Thy grace
Beyond Thine other wonders shine:

Who is a pardoning God like Thee,
Or who has grace so rich and free?

2 Angels and men, resign your claim
    To pity, mercy, love, and grace;
These glories crown Jehovah's name
    With an incomparable blaze:

3 Crimes of such horror to forgive!
    Such guilty, daring worms to spare:
This is Thy grand prerogative,
    And in the honour none shall share.

Second Tune

SOVEREIGNTY 88.88.88

J. Newton, 1802-86

4 In wonder lost, with trembling joy,
    We take the pardon of our God;
Pardon for sins of deepest dye,
    A pardon bought with Jesu's blood:

5 Oh may this strange, this matchless
        grace
    This God-like miracle of love
Fill the wide earth with grateful praise,
    And all the angelic choirs above:

Samuel Davies, 1723–61

HEREFORD NEW   6.10.10:6   Composer unknown

BLESSED be God, our God!
  Who gave for us His well-belovèd
    Son,
The gift of gifts, all other gifts in one—
  Blessèd be God, our God!

2 What will He not bestow,
    Who freely gave this mighty gift
      unbought,
  Unmerited, unheeded, and un-
    sought—
  What will He not bestow?

3 He sparèd not His Son!
    'Tis this that silences each rising
      fear;
  'Tis this that bids the hard thought
    disappear—
  He sparèd not His Son!

4 Who shall condemn us now,
    Since Christ has died, and risen,
      and gone above,
  For us to plead at the right hand of
    Love,
  Who shall condemn us now?

5 'Tis God that justifies!
    Who shall recall the pardon or the
      grace,
  Or who the broken chain of guilt
    replace?
  'Tis God that justifies!

6 The victory is ours!
    For us in might came forth the
      Mighty One;
  For us He fought the fight, the
    triumph won—
  The victory is ours!

Horatius Bonar, 1808–89

74 CARLISLE S.M.   C. LOCKHART, 1745-1815

MY soul, repeat His praise
  Whose mercies are so great,
Whose anger is so slow to rise,
  So ready to abate.

2 High as the heavens are raised
  Above the ground we tread,
So far the riches of His grace
  Our highest thoughts exceed.

3 His power subdues our sins;
  And His forgiving love,
Far as the east is from the west,
  Doth all our guilt remove.

4 The pity of the Lord
  To those that fear His name,
Is such as tender parents feel;
  He knows our feeble frame.

5 Our days are as the grass,
  Or like the morning flower;
If one sharp blast sweep o'er the field,
  It withers in an hour.

6 But Thy compassions, Lord,
  To endless years endure,
And children's children ever find
  Thy words of promise sure.

Isaac Watts, 1674–1748

This hymn may also be sung to **St. Michael,** No. 529

ST. BERNARD C.M.   Adapted from *Tochter Sion,* 1741
by JOHN RICHARDSON, 1816-79 **75**

NOT all the outward forms on earth,
  Nor rites that God has given,
Nor will of man, nor blood, nor birth,
  Can raise a soul to heaven.

2 The sovereign will of God alone
  Creates the heirs of grace;
Born in the image of His Son,
  A new, peculiar race.

3 The Spirit, like some heavenly wind,
  Blows on the sons of flesh;
Implants a new, a heavenly mind,
  And forms the man afresh.

4 Baptized in Jesu's name, they own
  They died and live in Him;
Redemption by His blood alone,
  This, this is all their theme.

5 The Father, Son and Spirit's might
  Alone, the dead could raise;
And all the living, with delight,
  Jehovah's grace shall praise.

Isaac Watts, 1674–1748
This hymn may also be sung to **Irish,** No. 35

FRANCONIA S.M.

From a chorale in J. B. König's *Choralbuch*, 1738
Arr. by W. H. Havergal, 1793-1870

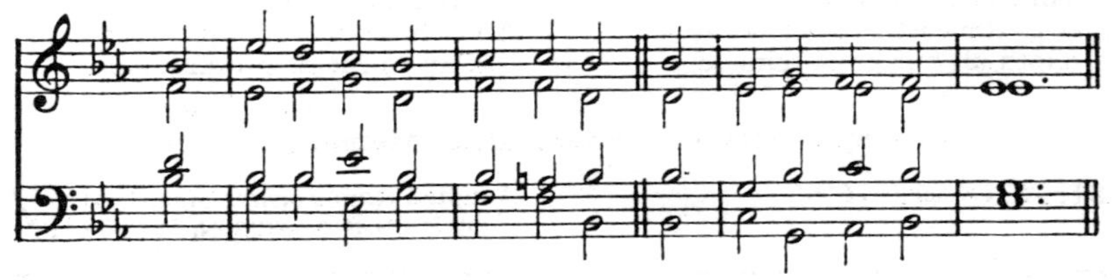

Not what these hands have done.
Could save my guilty soul;
Not what this toiling flesh has borne
Could make my spirit whole.

2 Not what I feel or do
Could give me peace with God;
Not all my prayers, and sighs, and
tears,
Could move my awful load.

3 Thy work alone, O Christ,
Removes my weight of sin;
Thy blood alone, O Lamb of God,
Doth give me peace within.

4 Thy love to me, O God,
Not mine, O Lord, to Thee,
Doth rid me of my dark unrest,
And set my spirit free.

5 Thy grace alone, O God,
To me doth pardon speak;
Thy power alone, O Son of God,
Doth my sore bondage break.

6 No other work save Thine,
No meaner blood will do;
No strength save that which is divine
Can bear me safely through.

Horatius Bonar, 1808–89

LAWES' PSALM 47   66.66.88

H. LAWES, 1596-1662

O BLESSED God! how kind
   Are all Thy ways to me,
Whose dark benighted mind
   Was enmity with Thee!
Yet now, subdued by sovereign grace,
My spirit joys in Thine embrace.

2 How precious are Thy thoughts,
   That o'er my spirit roll!
They rise above my doubts,
   And captivate my soul;
How great their sum, how high they
   rise,
Can ne'er be known beneath the skies.

3 Before Thy hands had made
   The sun to rule the day,
Or earth's foundation laid,
   Or fashioned Adam's clay,
What thoughts of peace and mercy
   flowed
From Thine own heart, my Lord and
   God!

4 A monument of grace,
   A sinner saved by blood,
The streams of love I trace
   Up to their source, O God,
And in Thy sacred counsels see
Eternal thoughts of love to me!

John Kent, 1766–1843

This hymn may also be sung to **Samuel,** No. 433

ST. ANNE C.M.

W. CROFT, 1678-1727

DESCANT

JOHN HUGHES, 1896-1968

O GOD, our help in ages past,
   Our hope for years to come,
Our shelter from the stormy blast,
   And our eternal home.

2 Under the shadow of Thy throne,
   Thy saints have dwelt secure,
Sufficient is Thine arm alone,
   And our defence is sure.

3 Before the hills in order stood,
   Or earth received her frame,
From everlasting Thou art God,
   To endless years the same.

4 A thousand ages in Thy sight
   Are like an evening gone;
Short as the watch that ends the night,
   Before the rising sun.

5 Time, like an ever-rolling stream,
   Bears all its sons away;
They fly forgotten as a dream
   Dies at the opening day.

6 O God, our help in ages past,
   Our hope for years to come!
Be Thou our guard while life shall last,
   And our eternal home.

Isaac Watts, 1674-1748

PORTLAND 888.4

ALMSGIVING 888.4

O LORD of heaven and earth and sea,
To Thee all praise and glory be:
How shall we show our love to Thee
Who givest all?

2 The golden sunshine, vernal air,
Sweet flowers and fruits, Thy love
declare:
Where harvests ripen, Thou art there,
Who givest all!

3 For peaceful homes and healthful days,
For all the blessings earth displays,
We owe Thee thankfulness and praise,
Who givest all!

4 Thou didst not spare Thine only Son,
But gav'st Him for a world undone,
And freely with that blessèd One
Thou givest all!

5 Thou giv'st the Holy Spirit's dower,
Spirit of life, and love, and power,
And dost His sevenfold graces shower
Upon us all!

6 For souls redeemed, for sins forgiven,
For means of grace, and hopes of
heaven,
Father, all praise to Thee be given,
Who givest all.

Christopher Wordsworth, 1807–85

MUNICH 76.76.D

Meiningen Gesangbuch, 1693

O GOD, the Rock of Ages,
  Who evermore hast been,
What time the tempest rages,
  Our dwelling-place serene:
Before Thy first creations,
  O Lord, the same as now,
To endless generations
  The Everlasting Thou!

2 Our years are like the shadows
   On sunny hills that lie,
Or grasses in the meadows
   That blossom but to die:
A sleep, a dream, a story
   By strangers quickly told,
An unremaining glory
   Of things that soon are old.

3 O Thou, who canst not slumber,
   Whose light grows never pale,
Teach us aright to number
   Our years before they fail.
On us Thy mercy lighten,
   On us Thy goodness rest,
And let Thy Spirit brighten,
   The hearts Thyself hast blest.

4 Lord, crown our faith's endeavour
   With beauty and with grace,
Till, clothed in light for ever,
   We see Thee face to face:
A joy no language measures;
   A fountain brimming o'er;
An endless flow of pleasures;
   An ocean without shore.

Edward Henry Bickersteth, 1825–1906

This hymn may also be sung to **Lancashire,** No. 489

ST. POLYCARP L.M.   From I. J. PLEYEL, 1757-1831

O LOVE, how deep, how broad, how high!
It fills the heart with ecstasy,
That God, the Son of God, should take
Our mortal form, for mortals' sake.

2 He sent no angel to our race,
Of higher or of lower place,
But wore the robe of human frame
Himself, and to this lost world came.

3 For us He was baptized and bore
His holy fast, and hungered sore;
For us temptation sharp He knew,
For us the tempter overthrew.

4 For us He prayed, for us He taught,
For us His daily works He wrought:
By words and signs and actions thus
Still seeking, not Himself, but us.

5 For us to wicked men betrayed,
Scourged, mocked, in purple robe arrayed,
He bore the shameful cross and death,
For us at length gave up His breath.

6 For us He rose from death again;
For us He went on high to reign;
For us He sent His Spirit here
To guide, to strengthen, and to cheer.

7 To Him whose boundless love has won
Salvation for us through His Son,
To God the Father, glory be,
Both now and through eternity.

Author unknown: From a 15th cent. MS.;
tr. and doxology by Benjamin Webb, 1820–85

This hymn may also be sung to **Mainzer**, No. 338

GOD THE FATHER:

NASHVILLE 888.D

M. Greiter, 1500-52

Thee will I praise with all my heart,
And tell mankind how good Thou art,
  How marvellous Thy works of grace;
Thy name I will in songs record,
And joy and glory in my Lord,
  Extolled above all thanks and praise.

2 The Lord will save His people here;
In times of need their help is near
  To all by sin and hell oppressed;
And they that know Thy name will trust
In Thee, who, to Thy promise just,
  Hast never left a soul distressed.

3 The Lord is by His judgments known;
He helps His poor afflicted one,
  His sorrows all He bears in mind;
The mourner shall not always weep,
Who sows in tears in joy shall reap,
  With grief who seeks with joy shall find.

4 A helpless soul that looks to Thee
Is sure at last Thy face to see,
  And all Thy goodness to partake;
The sinner who for Thee doth grieve,
And longs, and labours to believe,
  Thou never, never wilt forsake.

Charles Wesley, 1707–88

This hymn may also be sung to **Monmouth**, No. 25

GLASGOW C.M.

Moore's *Psalm-Singer's Pocket Companion*, 1756

THY ceaseless, unexhausted love,
  Unmerited and free,
Delights our evil to remove,
  And help our misery.

2 Thou waitest to be gracious still;
  Thou dost with sinners bear,
That, saved, we may Thy goodness
    feel,
  And all Thy grace declare.

3 Thy goodness and Thy truth to me,
  To every soul, abound,
A vast, unfathomable sea,
  Where all our thoughts are drowned.

4 Its streams the whole creation reach,
  So plenteous is the store,
Enough for all, enough for each,
  Enough for evermore.

5 Faithful, O Lord, Thy mercies are,
  A rock that cannot move:
A thousand promises declare
  The constancy of love.

6 Throughout the universe it reigns,
  Unalterably sure;
And while the truth of God remains,
  The goodness must endure.

Charles Wesley, 1707–88

This hymn may also be sung to **University**, No. 66

TO GOD BE THE GLORY 11.11.11.11 with refrain W. H. DOANE, 1832-1916

To God be the glory! great things
  He hath done!
So loved He the world that He gave
  us His Son,
Who yielded His life an atonement
  for sin,
And opened the life-gate that all may
  go in.

Praise the Lord! Praise the Lord!
  Let the earth hear His voice.
Praise the Lord! Praise the Lord!
  Let the people rejoice.
Oh come to the Father through
  Jesus the Son
And give Him the glory—great
  things He hath done!

2 Oh, perfect redemption, the purchase
    of blood!
  To every believer the promise of God;
  The vilest offender who truly believes,
  That moment from Jesus a pardon
    receives.

3 Great things He hath taught us, great
    things He hath done,
  And great our rejoicing through Jesus
    the Son:
  But purer and higher and greater will
    be
  Our wonder, our transport, when
    Jesus we see!

Frances Jane van Alstyne, 1820–1915

ELLACOMBE D.C.M.   *Mainz Gesangbuch, c. 1833*

To Thee, and to Thy Christ, O God,
 We sing, we ever sing;
For He the lonely wine-press trod,
 Our cup of joy to bring.
His glorious arm the strife main-
 tained,
 He marched in might from far:
His robes were with the vintage
 stained,
 Red with the wine of war.

2 To Thee, and to Thy Christ, O God,
 We sing, we ever sing;
For He invaded death's abode
 And robbed him of his sting.
The house of dust enthralls no more,
 For He, the strong to save,
Himself doth guard that silent door,
 Great Keeper of the grave.

3 To Thee, and to Thy Christ, O God,
 We sing, we ever sing;
For He hath crushed beneath His rod
 The world's proud rebel king.
He plunged in His imperial strength
 To gulfs of darkness down,
He brought His trophy up at length,
 The foiled usurper's crown.

4 To Thee, and to Thy Christ, O God,
 We sing, we ever sing;
For He redeem'd us with His blood
 From every evil thing.
Thy saving strength His arm upbore,
 The arm that set us free;
Glory, O God, for evermore
 Be to Thy Christ and Thee.

Anne Ross Cousin, 1824–1906

JERUSALEM C.M.

S. GROSVENOR, *c.* 1840

WHAT shall I do my God to love,
My loving God to praise?
The length, and breadth, and height
to prove,
And depth of sovereign grace?

2 Thy sovereign grace to all extends,
Immense and unconfined;
From age to age it never ends;
It reaches all mankind.

3 Throughout the world its breadth is
known,
Wide as infinity;
So wide it never passed by one,
Or it had passed by me.

4 My trespass was grown up to heaven;
But far above the skies,
In Christ abundantly forgiven,
I see Thy mercies rise.

5 The depth of all-redeeming love
What angel tongue can tell?
Oh may I to the utmost prove
The gift unspeakable.

6 Come quickly, gracious Lord, and
take
Possession of Thine own;
My longing heart vouchsafe to make
Thine everlasting throne.

Charles Wesley, 1707–88

87

OLD 148TH 66.66.88   Arr. John Roberts (Ieuan Gwyllt), 1822-77

WHAT was it, O our God,
 Led Thee to give Thy Son,
To yield Thy Well-beloved
 For us by sin undone?
'Twas love unbounded led Thee thus
To give Thy Well-beloved for us.

2 What led Thy Son, O God,
 To leave His throne on high,
To shed His precious blood,
 To suffer and to die?
'Twas love, unbounded love to us
Led Him to die and suffer thus.

3 What moved Thee to impart
 Thy Spirit from above,
Therewith to fill our heart
 With heavenly peace and love?
'Twas love, unbounded love to us,
Moved Thee to give Thy Spirit thus.

4 What love to Thee we owe,
 Our God, for all Thy grace!
Our hearts should overflow
 In everlasting praise.
Help us, O Lord, to praise Thee thus
For all Thy boundless love to us.

Ann Taylor, d. 1866

This hymn may also be sung to **St. John,** No. 57

WITH glorious clouds encompassed
    round,
  Whom angels dimly see,
Will the Unsearchable be found,
  Or God appear to me?

2 Will He forsake His throne above,
  Himself to me impart?
Answer, Thou Man of grief and love,
  And speak it to my heart!

3 In manifested love explain
  Thy wonderful design;
What meant the suffering Son of Man,
  The streaming blood divine?

4 Didst Thou not in our flesh appear,
  And live and die below,
That I may now perceive Thee near,
  And my Redeemer know?

5 Come then, and to my soul reveal
  The heights and depths of grace,
The wounds which all my sorrows
  heal,
That dear disfigured face.

6 I view the Lamb in His own light,
  Whom angels dimly see,
And gaze, transported at the sight,
  Through all eternity.

Charles Wesley, 1707–88

BONN (EBELING) 866.D

J. G. EBELING, 1637-76

ALL my heart this night rejoices,
    As I hear, far and near,
Sweetest angel voices;
"Christ is born!" their choirs are
    singing
Till the air everywhere
Now with joy is ringing.

2 Hark! a voice from yonder manger,
    Soft and sweet, doth entreat:
"Flee from woe and danger;
Brethren, come: from all that grieves
    you
You are freed: all you need
I will surely give you."

3 Come, then, let us hasten yonder;
    Here let all, great and small,
Kneel in awe and wonder;
Love Him who with love is yearning;
Hail the star that from far
Bright with hope is burning.

4 Thee, dear Lord, with heed I'll cherish,
    Live to Thee, and with Thee
Dying, shall not perish,
But shall dwell with Thee for ever
    Far on high, in the joy
That can alter never.

Paul Gerhardt, 1607–76
tr. Catherine Winkworth, 1827–78

IRIS   87.87 with refrain   French Carol Melody

ANGELS, from the realms of glory,
  Wing your flight o'er all the earth:
Ye who sang creation's story,
  Now proclaim Messiah's birth:
    Come and worship,
    Worship Christ, the new-born King.

2 Shepherds, in the field abiding,
  Watching o'er your flocks by night,
God with man is now residing,
  Yonder shines the Infant-Light:

3 Sages, leave your contemplations,
  Brighter visions beam afar;
Seek the great Desire of nations;
  Ye have seen His natal star:

4 Saints, before the altar bending,
  Watching long in hope and fear,
Suddenly the Lord descending
  In His temple shall appear:

James Montgomery, 1771–1854

This hymn may also be sung to **Blaencefn,** No. 244

CRADLE SONG 11.11.11.11   W. J. KIRKPATRICK, 1838-1921

AWAY in a manger, no crib for a bed,
The little Lord Jesus laid down His sweet head.
The stars in the bright sky looked down where He lay—
The little Lord Jesus asleep on the hay.

2 The cattle are lowing, the baby awakes,
But little Lord Jesus, no crying He makes.
I love Thee, Lord Jesus! look down from the sky,
And stay by my side until morning is nigh.

3 Be near me, Lord Jesus; I ask Thee to stay
Close by me for ever, and love me, I pray.
Bless all the dear children in Thy tender care,
And fit us for heaven to live with Thee there.

Author unknown

DIX   77.77.77   Adapted from a chorale by C. KOCHER, 1786-1872

As with gladness men of old
　Did the guiding star behold,
As with joy they hailed its light,
Leading onward, beaming bright;
So, most gracious Lord, may we
Evermore be led to Thee.

2 As with joyful steps they sped,
　Saviour, to Thy lowly bed,
There to bend the knee before
Thee whom heaven and earth adore;
So may we with willing feet
Ever seek Thy mercy-seat.

3 As they offered gifts most rare
　At Thy cradle rude and bare;
So may we with holy joy,
Pure, and free from sin's alloy,
All our costliest treasures bring,
Christ, to Thee, our heavenly King.

4 Holy Jesus, every day
　Keep us in the narrow way;
And, when earthly things are past,
Bring our ransomed souls at last
Where they need no star to guide,
Where no clouds Thy glory hide.

William Chatterton Dix, 1837–98

ST. BERNARD C.M.

Adapted from *Tochter Sion*, 1741
by JOHN RICHARDSON, 1816-79

BEHOLD the great Creator makes
   Himself a house of clay,
A robe of human flesh He takes
   Which He will wear for aye.

2 Hark, hark, the wise Eternal Word
   Like a weak infant cries!
In form of servant is the Lord,
   And God in cradle lies.

3 This wonder struck the world amazed,
   It shook the starry frame;
Squadrons of spirits stood and gazed,
   Then down in troops they came.

4 Glad shepherds ran to view this sight;
   A choir of angels sings;
And eastern sages with delight
   Adore the King of kings.

5 Join then, all hearts that are not stone,
   And all our voices prove,
To celebrate this Holy One,
   The God of peace and love.

Thomas Pestel, c. 1584–*c.* 1659.

This hymn may also be sung to **St. Saviour**, No. 94

FIRST TUNE

BEDFORD C.M.

W. WEALE, c. 1690-1727

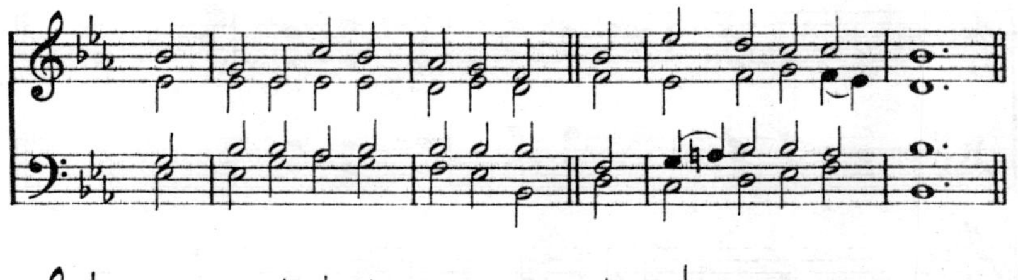

SECOND TUNE

ST. SAVIOUR C.M.

F. G. BAKER, 1837-1908

HARK, the glad sound! the Saviour comes,
The Saviour promised long;
Let every heart exult with joy,
And every voice be song.

2 On Him the Spirit, largely shed
Exerts His sacred fire;
Wisdom and might, and zeal and love
His holy breast inspire.

3 He comes, the prisoners to release,
In Satan's bondage held;
The gates of brass before Him burst,
The iron fetters yield.

4 He comes, from darkening scales of vice
To clear the inward sight;
And on the eyeballs of the blind
To pour celestial light.

5 He comes, the broken hearts to bind
The bleeding souls to cure;
And with the treasures of His grace
To enrich the humble poor.

6 Our glad hosannas, Prince of Peace,
Thy welcome shall proclaim;
And heaven's eternal arches ring
With Thy belovèd name.

*Philip Doddridge, 1702–51
and Scottish Paraphrases, 1781*

EPIPHANY HYMN　11.10.11.10　　　　　　　　J. F. Thrupp, 1827-67

Brightest and best of the sons of the morning,
Dawn on our darkness, and lend us thine aid!
Star of the east, the horizon adorning,
Guide where our infant Redeemer is laid!

2 Cold on His cradle the dewdrops are shining,
Low lies His head with the beasts of the stall;
Angels adore Him in slumber reclining—
Maker, and Monarch, and Saviour of all!

3 Say, shall we yield Him, in costly devotion,
Odours of Edom and offerings divine;
Gems of the mountain, and pearls of the ocean,
Myrrh from the forest, and gold from the mine!

4 Vainly we offer each ample oblation,
Vainly with gifts would His favour secure:
Richer by far is the heart's adoration;
Dearer to God are the prayers of the poor.

5 Brightest and best of the sons of the morning,
Dawn on our darkness, and lend us thine aid!
Star of the east, the horizon adorning,
Guide where our infant Redeemer is laid!

Reginald Heber, 1783–1826

This hymn may also be sung to **Broadwalk**, No. 501

CHILD in the manger,
  Infant of Mary;
Outcast and stranger,
  Lord of all!
Child who inherits
  All our transgressions,
All our demerits
  On Him fall.

2 Once the most holy
    Child of salvation
  Gently and lowly
    Lived below;
  Now as our glorious
    Mighty Redeemer,
  See Him victorious
    O'er each foe.

3 Prophets foretold Him,
    Infant of wonder;
  Angels behold Him
    On His throne;
  Worthy our Saviour
    Of all their praises;
  Happy for ever
    Are His own.

Mary Macdonald, 1817–c. 1890
tr. Lachlan Macbean, 1853–1931

YORKSHIRE   10.10.10.10.10.10   J. Wainwright, 1723-68

CHRISTIANS, awake, salute the happy
    morn,
Whereon the Saviour of mankind was
    born;
Rise to adore the mystery of love,
Which hosts of angels chanted from
    above;
With them the joyful tidings first
    begun
Of God Incarnate and the Virgin's
    Son.

2 Then to the watchful shepherds it
    was told,
Who heard the angelic herald's voice:
    "Behold,
I bring good tidings of a Saviour's
    birth
To you and all the nations upon earth:
This day hath God fulfilled His
    promised word
This day is born a Saviour, Christ the
    Lord."

3 He   spake: and   straightway   the
    celestial choir
In hymns of joy, unknown before,
    conspire;
The praises of redeeming love they
    sang,
And heaven's whole orb with alleluias
    rang;
God's highest glory was their anthem
    still,
Peace upon earth, and unto men good
    will.

4 Oh, may we keep and ponder in our
    mind,
God's wondrous love in saving lost
    mankind;
Trace we the Babe, who hath retrieved
    our loss,
From His poor manger, to His bitter
    cross;
Tread in His steps, assisted by His
    grace,
Till man's first heavenly state again
    takes place.

5 Then may we hope, the angelic hosts
    among,
  To sing, redeemed, a glad triumphal
    song;
  He that was born upon this joyful day
  Around us all His glory shall display;

Saved by His love, incessant we shall
    sing
Eternal praise to heaven's Almighty
  King.

John Byrom, 1692–1763

EVELYNS 65.65.D   W. H. MONK, 1823-89   **98**

FROM the eastern mountains
  Pressing on they come,
Wise men in their wisdom,
  To His humble home,
Stirred by deep devotion,
  Hasting from afar,
Ever journeying onward,
  Guided by a star.

2 There their Lord and Saviour
  Meek and lowly lay,
Wondrous light that led them
  Onward on their way,
Ever now to lighten
  Nations from afar,
As they journey homeward
  By that guiding star.

3 Thou who in a manger
  Once hast lowly lain,
Who dost now in glory
  O'er all kingdoms reign,

Gather in the heathen,
  Who in lands afar
Ne'er have seen the brightness
  Of Thy guiding star.

4 Gather in the outcasts,
  All who have gone astray,
Throw Thy radiance o'er them,
  Guide them on their way,
Those who never knew Thee,
  Those who have wandered far,
Guide them by the brightness
  Of Thy guiding star.

5 Onward through the darkness
  Of the lonely night,
Shining still before them
  With Thy kindly light,
Guide them, Jew and Gentile,
  Homeward from afar,
Young and old together,
  By Thy guiding star.

Godfrey Thring, 1823–1903

G ood Christian men, rejoice
With heart and soul and voice!
Give ye heed to what we say:
News! News!
Jesus Christ is born to-day.
Ox and ass before Him bow,
And He is in the manger now:
Christ is born to-day.

2 Good Christian men, rejoice
With heart and soul and voice!
Now ye hear of endless bliss:
Joy! Joy!
Jesus Christ was born for this.
He hath oped the heavenly door,
And man is blest for evermore.
Christ was born for this.

3 Good Christian men, rejoice
With heart and soul and voice!
Now ye need not fear the grave:
Peace! Peace!
Jesus Christ was born to save;
Calls you one, and calls you all,
To gain His everlasting hall.
Christ was born to save.

John Mason Neale, 1818–66

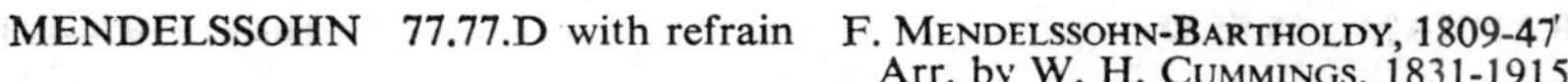

MENDELSSOHN 77.77.D with refrain   F. MENDELSSOHN-BARTHOLDY, 1809-47
Arr. by W. H. CUMMINGS, 1831-1915

HARK! the herald angels sing,
"Glory to the new-born King!
Peace on earth and mercy mild,
God and sinners reconciled."
Joyful, all ye nations rise,
Join the triumph of the skies;
With the angelic host proclaim,
"Christ is born in Bethlehem!"
Hark the herald angels sing,
"Glory to the new-born King!"

2 Christ, by highest heaven adored,
Christ, the everlasting Lord,
Late in time behold Him come,
Offspring of a virgin's womb!
Veiled in flesh the Godhead see;
Hail the incarnate Deity!
Pleased as man with man to dwell,
Jesus, our Immanuel.

3 Hail, the heaven-born Prince of Peace!
Hail the Sun of Righteousness!
Light and life to all He brings,
Risen with healing in His wings.
Mild He lays His glory by,
Born that man no more may die;
Born to raise the sons of earth,
Born to give them second birth.

4 Come, Desire of nations, come,
Fix in us Thy humble home:
Rise the woman's conquering seed,
Bruise in us the serpent's head:
Sing we then, with angels sing,
"Glory to the new-born King!
Glory in the highest heaven,
Peace on earth and sins forgiven."

Charles Wesley, 1707–88, and others

IOI

CRANHAM 65.65.D

G. HOLST, 1874-1934

*The metre of this hymn is irregular.   The music as printed is that of the first verse,
and can easily be adapted to the others.*

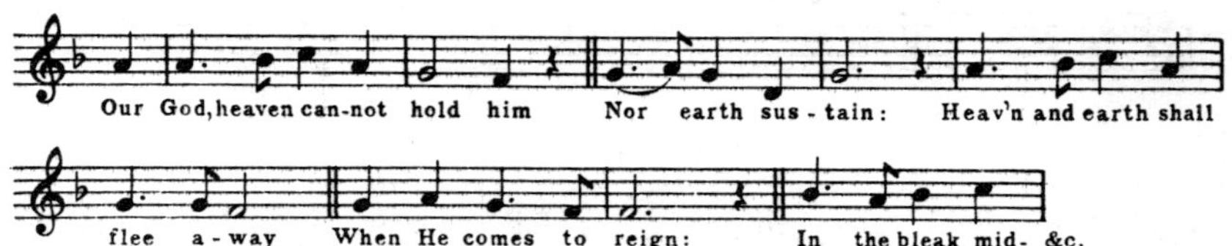

IN the bleak mid-winter,
    Frosty wind made moan,
Earth stood hard as iron,
    Water like a stone;
Snow had fallen, snow on snow,
    Snow on snow,
In the bleak mid-winter,
    Long ago.

2 Our God, heaven cannot hold Him,
    Nor earth sustain;
Heaven and earth shall flee away
    When He comes to reign:
In the bleak mid-winter
    A stable-place sufficed
The Lord God Almighty,
    Jesus.Christ.

3 Angels and archangels
    May have gathered there,
Cherubim and seraphim
    Throngèd the air;
But His mother only,
    In her maiden bliss,
Worshipped the Beloved
    With a kiss.

4 What can I give Him,
    Poor as I am?
If I were a shepherd,
    I would bring a lamb;
If I were a wise man,
    I would do my part;
Yet what I can I give Him—
    Give my heart.

Christina Georgina Rossetti, 1830-94

102

INFANT HOLY   447.447.44447

Polish Carol
arr. A. E. RUSBRIDGE, 1916-1969

INFANT holy,
Infant lowly,
For His bed a cattle stall;
Oxen lowing,
Little knowing
Christ the babe is Lord of all.
Swift are winging
Angels singing,
Nowells ringing,
Tidings bringing,
Christ the babe is Lord of all.

2 Flocks were sleeping,
Shepherds keeping
Vigil till the morning new
Saw the glory,
Heard the story,
Tidings of a gospel true.
Thus rejoicing,
Free from sorrow,
Praises voicing
Greet the morrow,
Christ the babe was born for you!

Polish; tr. Edith Margaret
Gellibrand Reed, 1885–1933

103

CAROL D.C.M.

R. S. WILLIS, 1819-1900

I^T came upon the midnight clear,
  That glorious song of old,
From angels bending near the earth
  To touch their harps of gold:
"Peace on the earth, goodwill to men
  From heaven's all-gracious King!"
The world in solemn stillness lay
  To hear the angels sing.

2 Still through the cloven skies they come
  With peaceful wings unfurled;
And still that heavenly music floats
  O'er all the weary world.
Above its sad and lowly plains
  They bend on hovering wing,
And ever o'er its Babel sounds
  The blessed angels sing.

3 Yet with the woes of sin and strife
  The world has suffered long;
Beneath the angel-strain have rolled
  Two thousand years of wrong;
And men, at war with men, hear not
  The love-song which they bring:
Oh hush the noise ye men of strife,
  And hear the angels sing.

4 For, lo, the days are hastening on,
  By prophet-bards foretold,
When with the ever circling years
  Comes round the age of gold;
When peace shall over all the earth
  Its ancient splendours fling,
And the whole world give back the song
  Which now the angels sing.

Edmund Hamilton Sears, 1810–76

ADORATION (ST. JOHN'S)   66.66.88   W. H. Havergal, 1793-1870

1 LET earth and heaven combine,
   Angels and men agree,
To praise in songs divine
   The incarnate Deity,
Our God contracted to a span,
Incomprehensibly made man.

2 He laid His glory by,
   He wrapped Him in our clay;
Unmarked by human eye,
   The latent Godhead lay;
Infant of days He here became,
And bore the mild Immanuel's name.

3 Unsearchable the love
   That hath the Saviour brought;
The grace is far above
   Or man or angel's thought:
Suffice for us that God, we know,
Our God, is manifest below.

4 He deigns in flesh to appear,
   Widest extremes to join;
To bring our vileness near,
   And make us all divine:
And we the life of God shall know,
For God is manifest below.

5 Made perfect first in love,
   And sanctified by grace,
We shall from earth remove,
   And see His glorious face:
Then shall His love be fully showed,
And man shall then be lost in God.

Charles Wesley, 1707–88

105

FOREST GREEN D.C.M.

English Traditional Melody
Arr. by R. VAUGHAN WILLIAMS, 1872–1958

O LITTLE town of Bethlehem,
　How still we see thee lie!
Above thy deep and dreamless sleep
　The silent stars go by:
Yet in thy dark streets shineth
　The everlasting Light;
The hopes and fears of all the years
　Are met in thee to-night.

2 For Christ is born of Mary;
　And, gathered all above,
While mortals sleep, the angels keep
　Their watch of wondering love.
O morning stars, together
　Proclaim the holy birth,
And praises sing to God the King,
　And peace to men on earth.

3 How silently, how silently,
　The wondrous gift is given!
So God imparts to human hearts
　The blessings of His heaven.
No ear may hear His coming;
　But in this world of sin,
Where meek souls will receive Him,
　　still
　The dear Christ enters in.

4 O holy child of Bethlehem,
　Descend to us, we pray;
Cast out our sin, and enter in;
　Be born in us to-day.
We hear the Christmas angels
　The great glad tidings tell;
O come to us, abide with us,
　Our Lord Immanuel.

Phillips Brooks, 1835–93

ADESTE FIDELES   Irregular   Probably by J. F. WADE, c. 1711-86

OH come, all ye faithful,
   Joyful and triumphant,
Oh come ye, oh come ye to Bethlehem;
   Come and behold Him
   Born the King of angels:
Oh come, let us adore Him, Christ the
   Lord.

2   True God of true God,
   Light of Light eternal,
Lo! He abhors not the Virgin's womb,
   Son of the Father,
   Begotten, not created:
Oh come, let us adore Him, Christ the
   Lord.

3   Sing, choirs of angels,
   Sing in exultation,
Sing, all ye citizens of heaven above,
   Glory to God
   In the highest:
Oh come, let us adore Him, Christ the
   Lord.

4   Yea, Lord, we greet Thee,
   Born this happy morning;
Jesus, to Thee be glory given,
   Word of the Father,
   Now in flesh appearing:
Oh come, let us adore Him, Christ the
   Lord.

Author unknown: Lat. 17th or 18th cent.
tr. Frederick Oakeley, 1802–80

IRBY   87.87.77   H. J. GAUNTLETT, 1805-76

ONCE in royal David's city
  Stood a lowly cattle-shed,
Where a mother laid her baby
  In a manger for His bed.
Mary was that mother mild,
Jesus Christ her little child.

2 He came down to earth from heaven,
  Who is God and Lord of all;
And His shelter was a stable,
  And His cradle was a stall:
With the poor and mean and lowly
Lived on earth our Saviour holy.

3 And through all His wondrous child-
    hood
  He would honour and obey,
Love, and watch the lowly mother
  In whose gentle arms He lay:
Christian children all must be
Mild, obedient, good as He.

4 For He is our childhood's pattern:
  Day by day like us He grew;
He was little, weak, and helpless,
  Tears and smiles like us He knew;
And He feeleth for our sadness,
And He shareth in our gladness.

5 And our eyes at last shall see Him,
  Through His own redeeming love;
For that child so dear and gentle
  Is our Lord in heaven above;
And He leads His children on
To the place where He is gone.

6 Not in that poor lowly stable,
  With the oxen standing by,
We shall see Him, but in heaven,
  Set at God's right hand on high,
When, like stars, His children crowned
All in white shall wait around.

Cecil Frances Alexander, 1818–95

HUMILITY. 77.77 with refrain

J. Goss, 1800-80

SEE, amid the winter's snow,
Born for us on earth below,
See, the Lamb of God appears,
Promised from eternal years.

Hail, thou ever-blessèd morn!
Hail, redemption's happy dawn!
Sing through all Jerusalem:
Christ is born in Bethlehem!

2 Lo, within a manger lies
He who built the starry skies,
He who, throned in height sublime,
Sits amid the cherubim.

3 Say, ye holy shepherds, say,
What your joyful news to-day;
Wherefore have ye left your sheep
On the lonely mountain steep?

4 As we watched at dead of night,
Lo, we saw a wondrous light:
Angels, singing peace on earth,
Told us of the Saviour's birth.

5 Sacred Infant, all divine,
What a tender love was Thine,
Thus to come from highest bliss
Down to such a world as this!

6 Teach, oh teach us, holy Child,
By Thy face so meek and mild,
Teach us to resemble Thee
In Thy sweet humility.

Edward Caswall, 1814-78

109

STILLE NACHT Irregular

Franz Gruber, 1787-1863
arr. by A. E. Rusbridge, 1916-1969

Silent night! Holy night!
All is calm, all is bright,
Round yon virgin and her child.
Holy Infant, so tender and mild,
Sleep in heavenly peace,
Sleep in heavenly peace.

2 Silent night! Holy night!
Shepherds quail at the sight;
Glories stream from heaven afar,
Heavenly hosts sing Alleluia!
Christ the Saviour is born,
Christ the Saviour is born.

3 Silent night! Holy night!
Son of God, love's pure light;
Radiant beams Thy holy face
With the dawn of saving grace,
Jesus, Lord, at Thy birth,
Jesus, Lord, at Thy birth.

Joseph Mohr, 1792-1848
tr. Anon., 1871

ENGLAND'S LANE 77.77.77

English Melody
adapted by GEOFFREY SHAW, 1879-1943

SING, oh sing, this blessèd morn!
Unto us a child is born,
Unto us a son is given,
God Himself comes down from heaven;

Sing, oh sing, this blessed morn,
Jesus Christ to-day is born!

2 God of God and Light of Light
Comes with mercies infinite,
Joining in a wondrous plan
Heaven to earth, and God to man:

3 God with us, Emmanuel,
Deigns for ever now to dwell;
He on Adam's fallen race
Sheds the fulness of His grace:

4 God comes down that man may rise,
Lifted by Him to the skies,
Christ is Son of Man, that we
Sons of God in Him may be:

5 Oh renew us, Lord, we pray,
With Thy Spirit day by day,
That we ever one may be,
With the Father and with Thee:

Christopher Wordsworth, 1807–85

This hymn may also be sung to **Noricum**, No. 60

PATER OMNIUM 88.88.88   H. J. E. HOLMES, 1852-1938

STUPENDOUS height of heavenly love,
  Of pitying tenderness divine;
It brought the Saviour from above,
  It caused the springing day to shine;
The sun of righteousness to appear,
And gild our gloomy hemisphere.

2 God did in Christ Himself reveal,
  To chase our darkness by His light,
Our sin and ignorance dispel,
  Direct our wandering feet aright;
And bring our souls, with pardon blest,
To realms of everlasting rest.

3 Come then, O Lord, Thy light impart,
  The faith that bids our terrors cease;
Into Thy love direct our heart,
  Into Thy way of perfect peace;
And cheer the souls of death afraid,
And guide them through the dreadful shade.

4 Answer Thy mercy's whole design,
  My God incarnated for me;
My spirit make Thy radiant shrine,
  My light and full salvation be;
And through the shades of death unknown
Conduct me to Thy dazzling throne.

Charles Wesley, 1707–88

THE great God of heaven is come down to earth,
His mother a Virgin, and sinless His birth;
The Father eternal His Father alone:
He sleeps in the manger; He reigns on the throne

2 A Babe on the breast of a Maiden He lies,
Yet sits with the Father on high in the skies;
Before Him their faces the Seraphim hide,
While Joseph stands waiting, unscared, by His side:

3 Lo! here is Emmanuel, here is the Child,
The Son that was promised to Mary so mild;
Whose power and dominion shall ever increase,
The Prince that shall rule o'er a kingdom of peace;

4 The Wonderful Counsellor, boundless in might,
The Father's own image, the beam of His light;
Behold Him now wearing the likeness of man,
Weak, helpless and speechless, in measure a span:

5 Oh wonder of wonders, which none can unfold:
The Ancient of days is an hour or two old;
The Maker of all things is made of the earth,
Man is worshipped by angels, and God comes to birth:

6 The Word in the bliss of the Godhead remains,
Yet in flesh comes to suffer the keenest of pains;
He is that He was, and for ever shall be,
But becomes that He was not, for you and for me.

Henry Ramsden Bramley, 1833-1917

II3

MARGARET Irregular

T. R. Matthews, 1826-1910

Thou didst leave Thy throne and
    Thy kingly crown,
When Thou camest to earth for me;
But in Bethlehem's home was there
    found no room
For Thy holy nativity.
    Oh come to my heart, Lord Jesus;
    There is room in my heart for Thee.

2 Heaven's arches rang when the angels
    sang,
    Proclaiming Thy royal degree:
But of lowly birth cam'st Thou, Lord,
    on earth,
And in great humility.

3 The foxes found rest, and the birds
    had their nest
In the shade of the forest tree;
But Thy couch was the sod, O Thou
    Son of God,
In the deserts of Galilee.

4 Thou camest, O Lord, with the living
    word,
    That should set Thy people free;
But with mocking scorn, and with
    crown of thorn,
They bore Thee to Calvary.
    Oh come to my heart, Lord Jesus!
    Thy cross is my only plea.

5 When heaven's arches shall ring, and
    her choirs shall sing,
    At Thy coming to victory,
Let Thy voice call me home, saying
    "Yet there is room.
There is room at My side for thee."
    And my heart shall rejoice, Lord Jesus,
    When Thou comest and callest for me!

        Emily Elliott, 1836–97

II4

FRAGRANCE 98.98.98 French Carol Melody arr. by C. H. KITSON, 1874-1944

THOU who wast rich beyond all
    splendour,
All for love's sake becamest poor;
Thrones for a manger didst surrender,
    Sapphire-paved courts for stable
      floor.
Thou who wast rich beyond all
    splendour,
All for love's sake becamest poor.

2 Thou who art God beyond all praising,
    All for love's sake becamest man;
Stooping so low, but sinners raising
    Heavenwards by Thine eternal plan.
Thou who art God beyond all praising,
    All for love's sake becamest man.

3 Thou who art love beyond all telling,
    Saviour and King, we worship Thee.
Immanuel, within us dwelling,
    Make us what Thou wouldst have
      us be.
Thou who art love, beyond all telling,
    Saviour and King, we worship Thee.

Frank Houghton, 1894-1972

115

DUNELM L.M.

C. VINCENT, 1852-1934

To us a Child of royal birth,
  Heir of the promises, is given;
The invisible appears on earth,
  The Son of Man, the God of heaven.

2 A Saviour born, in love supreme,
  He comes our fallen souls to raise,
He comes His people to redeem,
  With all the fulness of His grace.

3 The Christ, by raptured seers foretold,
  Filled with the eternal Spirit's power,
Prophet, and Priest, and King behold,
  And Lord of all the worlds adore.

4 The Lord of Hosts, the God most high,
  Who quits his throne on earth to live,
With joy we welcome from the sky,
  With faith into our hearts receive.

Charles Wesley, 1707–88

This hymn may also be sung to **Glanllyfnwy**, No. 381

116 PUER NOBIS Irregular

Melody from *Piae Cantiones*, 1582
harm. GEORGE HERBERT PALMER, 1846-1926

UNISON

U^{NTO} us a boy is born!
  King of all creation,
Came He to a world forlorn,
  The Lord of every nation.

2 Cradled in a stall was He
  With sleepy cows and asses;
But the very beasts could see
  That He all men surpasses.

3 Herod then with fear was filled:
  "A prince", he said, "in Jewry!"
All the little boys he killed
  At Bethlehem in his fury.

4 Now may Mary's Son, who came
  So long ago to love us,
Lead us all with hearts aflame
  Unto the joys above us.

5 Alpha and Omega He!
  Let the organ thunder,
While the choir with peals of glee
  Doth rend the air asunder!

German, 15th century;
tr. Percy Dearmer, 1867–1936

117

ST. MAGNUS C.M.   J. CLARK, 1670-1707

W^{HEN} came in flesh the incarnate Word,
  The heedless world slept on,
And only simple shepherds heard
  That God had sent His Son.

When comes the Saviour at the last,
  From east to west shall shine
The aweful pomp, and earth aghast
  Shall tremble at the sign.

3 Then shall the pure of heart be blest;
  As mild He comes to them,
As when upon the virgin's breast
  He lay at Bethlehem:

4 As mild to meek-eyed love and faith,
  Only more strong to save;
Strengthened by having bowed to death,
  By having burst the grave.

5 Lord, who could dare see Thee descend
  In state, unless he knew
Thou art the sorrowing sinner's friend.
  The gracious and the true.

6 Dwell in our hearts, O Saviour blest;
  So shall Thine advent's dawn
'Twixt us and Thee, our bosom-guest,
  Be but the veil withdrawn.

Joseph Anstice, 1808-36

This hymn may also be sung to **Dundee,** No. 130

II8

CREDO   88.88.88

WE saw Thee not when Thou didst
        come
   To this poor world of sin and death,
Nor e'er beheld Thy cottage-home
   In that despisèd Nazareth;
But we believe Thy footsteps trod
Its streets and plains, Thou Son of
   God.

2 We did not see Thee lifted high
   Amid that wild and savage crew,
Nor heard Thy meek imploring cry,
   "Forgive; they know not what they
        do":
Yet we believe the deed was done,
Which shook the earth and veiled the
   sun.

3 We stood not by the empty tomb
   Where late Thy sacred body lay,
Nor sat within that upper room,
   Nor met Thee in the open way;
But we believe that angels said,
"Why seek the living with the dead?"

4 We did not mark the chosen few,
   When Thou didst through the
        clouds ascend,
First lift to heaven their wondering
   view,
   Then to the earth all prostrate bend;
Yet we believe that mortal eyes
Beheld that journey to the skies.

5 And now that Thou dost reign on high,
   And thence Thy waiting· people
        bless,
No ray of glory from the sky
   Doth shine upon our wilderness;
But we believe Thy faithful Word,
And trust in our redeeming Lord.

John Hampden Gurney, 1802–62

NORTHROP C.M.   FIRST TUNE   A. NORTHROP, 1863-1938

WHILE shepherds watched their
    flocks by night,
All seated on the ground,
The angel of the Lord came down,
And glory shone around:

2 "Fear not!" said he (for mighty dread
    Had seized their troubled mind)
"Glad tidings of great joy I bring
    To you and all mankind.

3 "To you in David's town, this day
    Is born, of David's line,
A Saviour, who is Christ the Lord;
    And this shall be the sign:

4 "The heavenly babe you there shall
    find
To human view displayed,
All meanly wrapped in swaddling
    bands,
And in a manger laid."

5 Thus spake the seraph; and forthwith
    Appeared a shining throng
Of angels, praising God, who thus
    Addressed their joyful song:

6 "All glory be to God on high,
    And to the earth be peace;
Goodwill henceforth from heaven to
    men
Begin and never cease."

Nahum Tate, 1652-1715

SECOND TUNE

WINCHESTER OLD C.M.   *Este's Psalter, 1592*

120

LUX EOI 87.87.D

A. S. Sullivan, 1842–1900

Who is this so weak and helpless,
  Child of lowly Hebrew maid,
Rudely in a stable sheltered,
  Coldly in a manger laid?
'Tis the Lord of all creation,
  Who this wondrous path hath trod;
He is God from everlasting,
  And to everlasting God.

2 Who is this—a Man of Sorrows,
  Walking sadly life's hard way,
Homeless, weary, sighing, weeping
  Over sin and Satan's sway?
'Tis our God, our glorious Saviour,
  Who above the starry sky
Now for us a place prepareth,
  Where no tear can dim the eye.

3 Who is this—behold Him shedding
  Drops of blood upon the ground?
Who is this—despised, rejected,
  Mocked, insulted, beaten, bound?

'Tis our God, who gifts and graces
  On His Church now poureth down;
Who shall smite in righteous judgment
  All His foes beneath His throne.

4 Who is this that hangeth dying,
  While the rude world scoffs and
    scorns;
Numbered with the malefactors,
  Torn with nails, and crowned with
    thorns!
'Tis the God who ever liveth
  'Mid the shining ones on high,
In the glorious golden city
  Reigning everlastingly.

William Walsham How, 1823–97

See also
66 Behold the amazing gift of love
84 To God be the glory
123 Oh sing a song of Bethlehem
192 Come, Thou long-expected Jesus
266 Who is He in yonder stall
454 Love divine, all loves excelling

ARTAVIA 10.10.10.6   E. J. HOPKINS, 1818-1901

AND didst Thou love the race that
  loved not Thee?
And didst Thou take to heaven a
  human brow?
Dost plead with man's voice by the
  marvellous sea?
Art Thou his kinsman now?

2 O God, O kinsman loved, but not
  enough!
O Man, with eyes majestic after
  death!
Whose feet have toiled along our pathways rough,
Whose lips drawn human breath!

3 By that one likeness which is ours and
  Thine,
By that one nature which doth hold
  us kin,
By that high heaven where, sinless,
  Thou dost shine,
To draw us sinners in;

4 By Thy last silence in the judgement
  hall,
By long foreknowledge of the
  deadly tree,
By darkness, by the wormwood and
  the gall,
I pray Thee visit me.

5 Come, lest this heart should, cold
  and cast away,
Die e'er the Guest adored she
  entertain—
Lest eyes that never saw Thine
  earthly day
Should miss Thy heavenly reign.

Jean Ingelow, 1820–97

LOVE UNKNOWN　66.66.88　　　　　　　　　JOHN N. IRELAND, 1879-1962

My song is love unknown,
My Saviour's love to me;
Love to the loveless shown,
That they might lovely be.
Oh who am I,
That for my sake
My Lord should take
Frail flesh, and die?

2 He came from His blest throne
Salvation to bestow;
But men made strange, and none
The longed-for Christ would know:
But oh, my Friend,
My Friend indeed,
Who at my need
His life did spend.

3 Sometimes they strew His way,
And His sweet praises sing;
Resounding all the day
Hosannas to their King:
Then "Crucify!"
Is all their breath,
And for His death
They thirst and cry.

4 Why, what hath my Lord done?
What makes this rage and spite?
He made the lame to run,
He gave the blind their sight.

Sweet injuries!
Yet they at these
Themselves displease,
And 'gainst Him rise.

5 They rise and needs will have
My dear Lord made away;
A murderer they save,
The Prince of life they slay.
Yet cheerful He
To suff'ring goes,
That He His foes
From thence might free.

6 In life, no house, no home
My Lord on earth might have;
In death, no friendly tomb,
But what a stranger gave.
What may I say?
Heaven was His home;
But mine the tomb
Wherein He lay.

7 Here might I stay and sing,
No story so divine;
Never was love, dear King,
Never was grief like Thine.
This is my Friend,
In whose sweet praise
I all my days
Could gladly spend.

Samuel Crossman, 1624-84

FOREST GREEN D.C.M.

English Traditional Melody
Arr. by R. VAUGHAN WILLIAMS, 1872–1958

OH sing a song of Bethlehem,
Of shepherds watching there,
And of the news that came to them
From angels in the air;
The light that shone on Bethlehem
Fills all the world today;
Of Jesu's birth and peace on earth
The angels sing alway.

2 Oh sing a song of Nazareth,
Of sunny days of joy,
Oh sing of fragrant flowers' breath
And of the sinless Boy:
For now the flowers of Nazareth
In every heart may grow;
Now spreads the fame of His dear name
On all the winds that blow.

3 Oh sing a song of Galilee,
Of lake and woods and hill,
Of Him who walked upon the sea
And bade its waves be still:
For though like waves on Galilee,
Dark seas of trouble roll,
When faith has heard the Master's word,
Falls peace upon the soul.

4 Oh sing a song of Calvary,
Its glory and dismay;
Of Him who hung upon the tree,
And took our sins away:
For He who died on Calvary
Is risen from the grave,
And Christ our Lord, by heaven adored,
Is mighty now to save.

Louis Fitzgerald Benson, 1855–1930

ST. MATTHEW D.C.M.

Probably later form of melody
by WILLIAM CROFT, 1678-1727

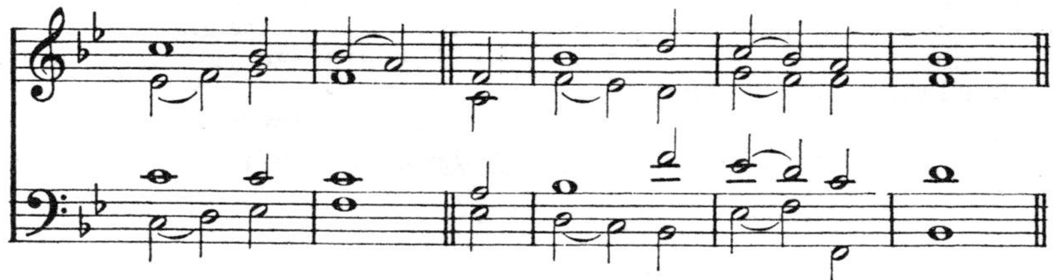

This hymn may also be sung to **Ellacombe**, No. 85

OH where is He that trod the sea?
 Oh where is He that spake,
And demons from their victims flee,
 The dead their slumbers break?
The palsied rise in freedom strong,
 The dumb men talk and sing,
And from blind eyes, benighted long,
 Bright beams of morning spring.

2 Oh where is He that trod the sea?
 Oh where is He that spake,
And piercing words of liberty
 The deaf ears open shake?
And mildest words arrest the haste
 Of fever's deadly fire;
And strong words heal the weak, who waste
 Their life in sad desire.

3 Oh where is He that trod the sea?
 'Tis only He can save;
To thousands hung'ring wearily
 A wondrous meal He gave:
The Word, who all the world had made,
 To His own creatures spake;
'Twas spring-tide when He blest the bread
 And harvest when He brake.

4 Oh where is He that trod the sea?
 My soul, the Lord is here!
Let all thy fears be hush'd in thee,
 Be thine to look, to hear;
Thy utmost needs He'll satisfy:
 Art thou diseased or dumb,
Or dost thou in thy hunger cry?
 "I come" saith Christ, "I come!"
Thomas Toke Lynch, 1818–71

125

ST. DROSTANE L.M.

J. B. DYKES, 1823-76

RIDE on! ride on in majesty!
 Hark! all the tribes "Hosanna!" cry;
O Saviour meek, pursue Thy road,
With palms and scattered garments strowed.

2 Ride on! ride on in majesty!
 In lowly pomp ride on to die:
 O Christ, Thy triumphs now begin
 O'er captive death and conquered sin.

3 Ride on! ride on in majesty!
 The wingèd squadrons of the sky
 Look down with sad and wondering eyes
 To see the approaching sacrifice.

4 Ride on! ride on in majesty!
 Thy last and fiercest strife is nigh:
 The Father on His sapphire throne;
 Awaits His own anointed Son.

5 Ride on! ride on in majesty!
 In lowly pomp ride on to die;
 Bow Thy meek head to mortal pain,
 Then take, O God, Thy power, and reign.

Henry Hart Milman, 1791–1868

This hymn may also be sung to **Winchester New,** No. 16

126

BROYAN D.C.M.

W. Cynon Evans, 1857-1943

THINE arm, O Lord, in days of old,
  Was strong to heal and save;
It triumphed o'er disease and death,
  O'er darkness and the grave.
To Thee they went—the blind, the dumb,
  The palsied, and the lame,
The leper with his tainted life,
  The sick with fevered frame.

2 And, lo! Thy touch brought life and health,
  Gave speech, and strength, and sight;
And youth renewed and frenzy calmed
  Owned Thee, the Lord of light:

And now, O Lord, be near to bless,
  Almighty as of yore,
In crowded street, by restless couch,
  As by Gennesaret's shore.

3 Be Thou our great Deliverer still,
  Thou Lord of life and death;
Restore and quicken, soothe and bless,
  With Thine almighty breath;
To hands that work and eyes that see
  Give wisdom's heavenly lore,
That whole and sick, that weak and strong,
  May praise Thee evermore.

Edward Hayes Plumptre, 1821–91

This hymn may also be sung to **St. Matthew**, No. 124

LLOYD   C.M.

C. HOWARD. 1856-1927

THOU art the Way: to Thee alone
From sin and death we flee:
And he who would the Father seek
Must seek Him, Lord, by Thee.

2 Thou art the Truth: Thy word alone
True wisdom can impart;
Thou only canst inform the mind,
And purify the heart.

3 Thou art the Life: the rending tomb
Proclaims Thy conquering arm;
And those who put their trust in Thee
Nor death nor hell shall harm.

4 Thou art the Way, the Truth, the Life:
Grant us that way to know,
That truth to keep, that life to win,
Whose joys eternal flow.

George Washington Doane, 1799–1859

This hymn may also be sung to **St. Fulbert**, No. 506

128

ABRIDGE C.M.

I. Smith, *c.* 1725-*c.* 1800

O BLESSED Saviour, is Thy love
So great, so full, so free?
Fain would we give our hearts, our minds,
Our lives, our all, to Thee.

2 We love Thee for the glorious worth
Which in Thyself we see;
We love Thee for that shameful cross
Endured so patiently.

3 No man of greater love can boast
Than for his friend to die;
Thou for Thine enemies wast slain!
What love with Thine can vie?

4 Though in the very form of God,
With heavenly glory crowned:
Thou didst a servant's form assume,
Beset with sorrows round.

5 Thou wouldst like wretched man be made,
In everything but sin,
That we as like Thee might become,
As we unlike had been.

6 Like Thee in faith, in meekness, love,
In every heavenly grace,
From glory unto glory changed,
Till we behold Thy face.

7 O Lord, we treasure in our souls
The memory of Thy love;
And ever shall Thy name to us
A grateful odour prove.

Joseph Stennett, 1663–1713

This hymn may also be sung to **Claremont,** No. 129

CLAREMONT C.M.

J. FOSTER, 1807-85

WHAT grace, O Lord, and beauty shone
Around Thy steps below!
What patient love was seen in all
Thy life and death of woe!

2 For ever on Thy burdened heart
A weight of sorrow hung,
Yet no ungentle, murmuring word,
Escaped Thy silent tongue.

3 Thy foes might hate, despise, revile,
Thy friends unfaithful prove:
Unwearied in forgiveness still,
Thy heart could only love.

4 Oh give us hearts to love like Thee,
Like Thee, O Lord, to grieve
Far more for others' sins, than all
The wrongs that we receive.

5 One with Thyself, may every eye
In us, Thy brethren, see
That gentleness and grace that spring
From union, Lord, with Thee!

Edward Denny, 1796–1889

This hymn may also be sung to **Abridge, No. 128**

See also
81 O love, how deep, how broad, how high
85 To Thee and to Thy Christ, O God
211 A Man there lived in Galilee
252 Oh perfect life of love!
437 Immortal love, for ever full
685 Dear Master, in whose life I see

130

DUNDEE C.M.

Scottish Psalter, 1615

A LAS! and did my Saviour bleed?
And did my Sovereign die?
Would He devote that sacred head
For such a worm as I?

2 Was it for crimes that I had done,
He groaned upon the tree?
Amazing pity! grace unknown!
And love beyond degree!

3 Well might the sun in darkness hide,
And shut his glories in.
When Christ, the mighty Maker, died
For man the creature's sin.

4 Well might I hide my blushing face
While His dear cross appears;
Dissolve my heart in thankfulness,
And melt mine eyes to tears.

5 But drops of grief can ne'er repay
The debt of love I owe;
Here, Lord, I give myself away:
'Tis all that I can do.

Isaac Watts, 1674–1748

131

ST. BRIDE S.M.

SAMUEL HOWARD, 1710-82

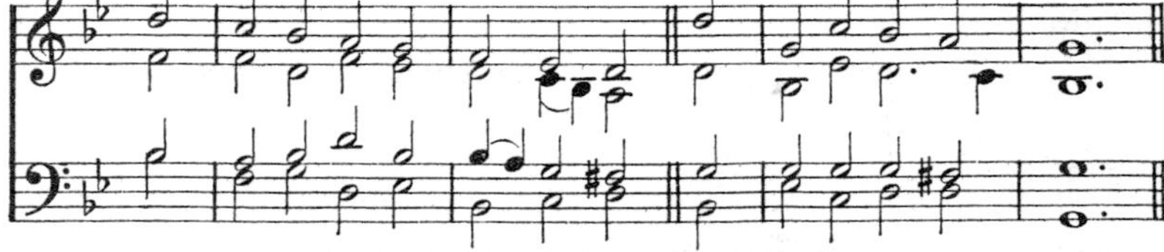

B EHOLD the amazing sight!
The Saviour lifted high:
The Son of God, His soul's delight,
Expire in agony.

2 For whom, for whom, my heart
Were all those sorrows borne?
Why did He feel that piercing smart,
And wear that crown of thorn?

3 For us in love He bled,
For us in anguish died;
'Twas love that bowed His sacred head,
And pierced His precious side.

4 We see, and we adore,
We trust that dying love;
We feel its strong attractive power
To lift our souls above.

5 Behold the amazing sight,
Nor trace His griefs alone,
But from the cross pursue our flight
To His triumphant throne.

Philip Doddridge, 1702–51

132

HARWICH 55.11.D

B. MILGROVE, *c.* 1731-1810

ALL ye that pass by,
To Jesus draw nigh;
To you is it nothing that Jesus should die?
Your ransom and peace,
Your surety He is:
Come, see if there ever was sorrow like His.

2 He dies to atone
For sins not His own;
Your debt He hath paid, and your work He hath done.
Ye all may receive
The peace He did leave,
Who made intercession: My Father, forgive!

3 For you and for me
He prayed on the tree:
The prayer is accepted, the sinner is free.
That sinner am I,
Who on Jesus rely,
And come for the pardon God cannot deny.

4 My pardon I claim;
For a sinner I am.
A sinner believing in Jesu's blest name.
He purchased the grace
Which now I embrace:
O Father, Thou know'st He hath died in my place.

Charles Wesley, 1707–88

133

WALDEN C.M.

J. E. JONES, 1866-1939

AND did the Holy and the Just,
The Sovereign of the skies,
Stoop down to man's estate and dust
That guilty worms might rise?

2 Yes, the Redeemer left the throne,
The radiant throne on high,
Surprising mercy, love unknown—
To suffer, bleed and die.

3 He took the guilty culprit's place
And suffered in his stead;
For man—oh, miracle of grace—
For man the Saviour bled.

4 Blest Lord, what heavenly wonders dwell
In Thine atoning blood!
By this are sinners saved from hell,
And rebels brought to God.

5 Jesus, my soul adoring bends
To love so full, so free;
Thy word declares that love extends
In saving power to me.

6 What glad returns can I impart,
For favour so divine?
Oh, take me, all, and fill my heart,
And make me wholly Thine.

Anne Steele, 1717–78

This hymn may also be sung to **Orlington,** No. 225

ST. CHRISTOPHER   76.86.86.86   F. C. Maker, 1844-1927

BENEATH the cross of Jesus
  I fain would take my stand,
The shadow of a mighty rock
  Within a weary land;
A home within the wilderness,
  A rest upon the way,
From the burning of the noontide heat
  And the burden of the day.

2 Oh safe and happy shelter!
  Oh refuge tried and sweet
Oh trysting-place, where heaven's love
  And heaven's justice meet!
As to the holy patriarch
  That wondrous dream was given,
So seems my Saviour's cross to me
  A ladder up to heaven.

3 There lies beneath its shadow,
  But on the farther side,
The darkness of an awful grave
  That gapes both deep and wide:
And there between us stands the cross,
  Two arms outstretched to save,
Like a watchman set to guard the way
  From that eternal grave.

4 Upon that cross of Jesus,
  Mine eye at times can see
The very dying form of One
  Who suffered there for me;
And from my smitten heart with tears,
  Two wonders I confess—
The wonder of His glorious love,
  And my own worthlessness.

5 I take, O cross, thy shadow,
  For my abiding place;
I ask no other sunshine than
  The sunshine of His face:
Content to let the world go by,
  To know no gain nor loss,—
My sinful self my only shame,
  My glory all the cross.

Elizabeth Cecilia Clephane, 1830–69

ST. GEORGE'S, BOLTON 76.76

JAMES WALCH, 1837-1901

No bone of Thee was broken,
  Thou spotless paschal Lamb!
Of life and peace a token,
  To us who know Thy name;
The Head, for all the members,
  The curse, the vengeance bore,
And God, our God remembers
  His people's sins no more.

2 We, Thy redeemed, are reaping
  What Thou didst sow in tears:
This feast which we are keeping
  Thy name to us endears:
It tells of justice hiding
  The face of God from Thee;
Proud men around deriding
  Thy sorrows on the tree.

3 Thy death of shame and sorrow
  Was like unto Thy birth,
Which would no glory borrow,
  No majesty from earth;
Thy pilgrims, we are hasting
  To our eternal home,
Its joy already tasting
  Of victory o'er the tomb.

4 Thy life and death reviewing,
  We tread the narrow way;
Our homeward path pursuing,
  We watch the dawn of day:
We eat and drink with gladness
  The living bread and wine,
And sing with sweetest sadness
  Our song of love divine.

Robert Cleaver Chapman, 1803-1902

This hymn may also be sung to **Passion Chorale**, No. 149

149

PASSION CHORALE 76.76.D

Melody by H. L. HASSLER, 1564-1612
Harmonised by J. S. BACH, 1685-1750

O HEAD, so full of bruises,
  So full of pain and scorn,
'Midst other sore abuses,
  Mocked with a crown of thorn!
O Head, ere now surrounded
  With brightest majesty;
In death once bowed and wounded,
  Accursèd on the tree.

2 Thou Countenance transcendent!
  Thou life-creating Sun
To worlds on Thee dependent,
  Yet bruised and spit upon!
O Lord, what Thee tormented
  Was our sins' heavy load;
We had the debt augmented,
  Which Thou didst pay in blood.

3 And oh, what consolation
  Fills the adoring breast,
When on Thy toil and passion,
  With wondering joy we rest.
Ah, should we, while thus musing
  On our Redeemer's cross,
E'en life itself be losing,
  Great gain would be that loss.

4 We give Thee thanks unfeignèd,
  Lord Jesus, Friend in need,
For what Thy soul sustainèd,
  When Thou for us didst bleed.
Grant us to lean unshaken
  Upon Thy faithfulness,
Until we hence are taken
  To see Thee face to face.

?Bernard of Clairvaux, 1091–1153
tr. Paul Gerhardt, 1607–76
John Gambold, 1711–71. J. C. Ryle, 1816–1900, and others
This hymn may also be sung to **St. George's Bolton,** No. 148

STELLA 88.88.88

Melody from *Easy Tunes for Catholic Schools*, 1852

O LOVE Divine, what hast Thou done!
The immortal God hath died for me!
The Father's co-eternal Son
Bore all my sins upon the tree;
The immortal God for me hath died!
My Lord, my Love is crucified!

2 Behold Him, all ye that pass by,
The dying Prince of Life and Peace!
Come, see, ye worms, your Maker die,
And say, was ever grief like His?
Come, feel with me His blood applied:
My Lord, my Love is crucified!

3 Is crucified for me and you,
To bring us rebels near to God;
Believe, believe the record true:
We all are bought with Jesu's blood;
Pardon for all flows from His side;
My Lord, my Love is crucified!

4 Then let us sit beneath His cross,
And gladly catch the healing stream,
All things for Him account but loss,
And give up all our hearts to Him;
Of nothing speak or think beside,
"My Lord, my Love is crucified!"

Charles Wesley, 1707–88

This hymn may also be sung to **St. Chrysostom**, No. 441

WEBER 77.77   C. M. F. E. VON WEBER, 1786-1826

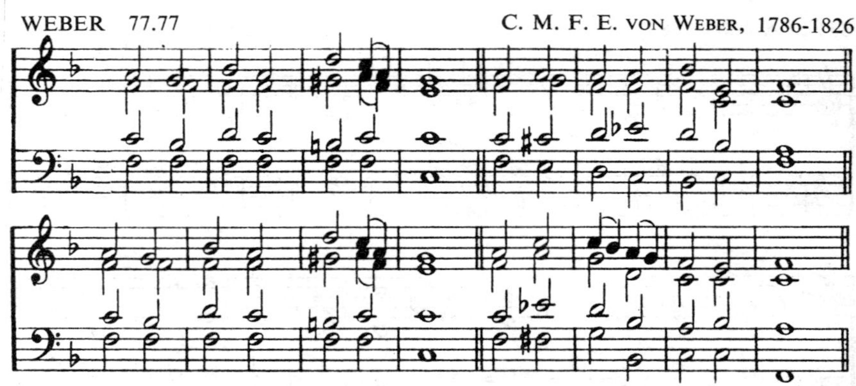

O MY Saviour, crucified,
  Near Thy cross would I abide,
There to look with steadfast eye,
On Thy dying agony.

2 Jesus bruised and put to shame
  Tells me all Jehovah's name;
God is love, I surely know
By the Saviour's depths of woe.

3 In His spotless soul's distress,
  I perceive my guiltiness;
Oh how vile my low estate,
Since my ransom was so great!

4 Dwelling on Mount Calvary,
  Contrite shall my spirit be;
Rest and holiness shall find,
Fashioned like my Saviour's mind.

Robert Cleaver Chapman, 1803–1902

This hymn may also be sung to **Nottingham**, No. 246

152

ARFRYN S.M.   W. J. EVANS, 1866-1947.

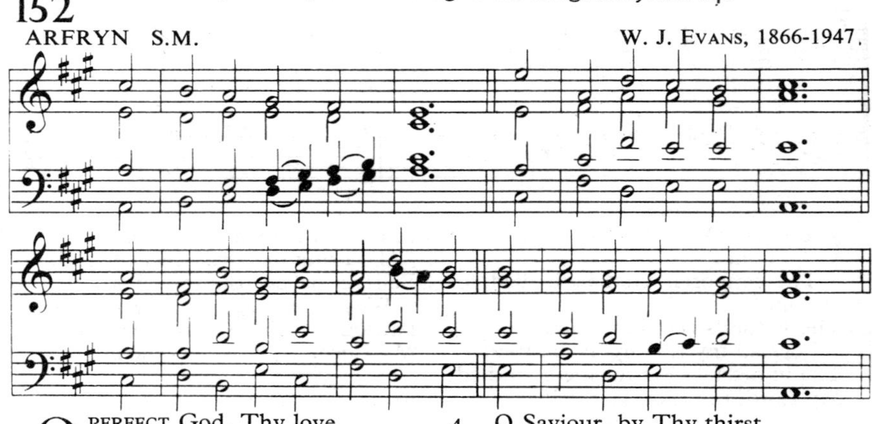

O PERFECT God, Thy love
  As perfect Man did share
Here upon earth each form of ill
  Thy fellow-man must bear.

2 Now from the tree of scorn
  We hear Thy voice again;
Thou who didst take our mortal flesh,
  Hast felt our mortal pain.

3 Thy body suffers thirst,
  Parched are Thy lips and dry:
How poor the offering man can bring
  Thy thirst to satisfy!

4 O Saviour, by Thy thirst
  Borne on the cross of shame,
Grant us in all our sufferings here
  To glorify Thy name;

5 That through each pain and grief
  Our souls may onward move
To gain more likeness to Thy life,
  More knowledge of Thy love.

Ada Rundall Greenaway, 1861–1937

This hymn may also be sung to
St. Bride, No. 131

Y WERN 76.76.D W. J. WILLIAMS, 1886-1962

OH, teach me what it meaneth—
  That cross uplifted high,
With One—the Man of Sorrows—
  Condemned to bleed and die!
Oh, teach me what it cost Thee
  To make a sinner whole;
And teach me, Saviour, teach me
  The value of a soul!

2 Oh, teach me what it meaneth—
  That sacred crimson tide—
The blood and water flowing
  From Thine own wounded side.
Teach me that if none other
  Had sinned, but I alone,
Yet still, Thy blood, Lord Jesus,
  Thine only, must atone.

3 Oh, teach me what it meaneth—
  Thy love beyond compare,
The love that reacheth deeper
  Than depths of self-despair!

Yea, teach me, till there gloweth
  In this cold heart of mine
Some feeble, pale reflection
  Of that pure love of Thine.

4 Oh, teach me what it meaneth,
  For I am full of sin;
And grace alone can reach me,
  And love alone can win.
Oh, teach me, for I need Thee—
  I have no hope beside,—
The chief of all the sinners
  For whom the Saviour died!

5 O Infinite Redeemer!
  I bring no other plea,
Because Thou dost invite me
  I cast myself on Thee.
Because Thou dost accept me
  I love and I adore;
Because Thy love constraineth,
  I'll praise Thee evermore!

Lucy Ann Bennett, 1850–1927

This hymn may also be sung to **Rutherford,** No. 479

154

EDEN L.M.

T. B. MASON, 1801-61

OH wondrous hour, when Jesus Thou
  Co-equal with the eternal God,
Beneath our sin vouchsafed to bow,
  And in our stead didst bear the rod.

2 On Thee, the Father's blessèd Son,
    Jehovah's utmost anger fell:
  That all was borne, that all was done,
    Thine agony, Thy cross can tell.

3 When most in angry Satan's power,
    Dear Lord, Thy suffering spirit seemed,
  Then, in that dark and fearful hour,
    Thine arm our guilty souls redeemed.

4 Thy cross! Thy cross! there, Lord we learn
    What Thou in all Thy fulness art;
  There through the darkening cloud discern
    The love of Thy devoted heart.

5 'Twas mighty love's constraining power
    That made Thee, blessèd Saviour, diė;
  'Twas love, in that tremendous hour,
    That triumphed in Thy parting sigh.

6 'Twas all for us—our life we owe,
    Our hope, our crown of joy to Thee;
  Thy sufferings in that hour of woe,
    Thy victory, Lord, have made us free.

Edward Denny, 1796–1889

155

AJALON 77.77.77

RICHARD REDHEAD, 1820-1901

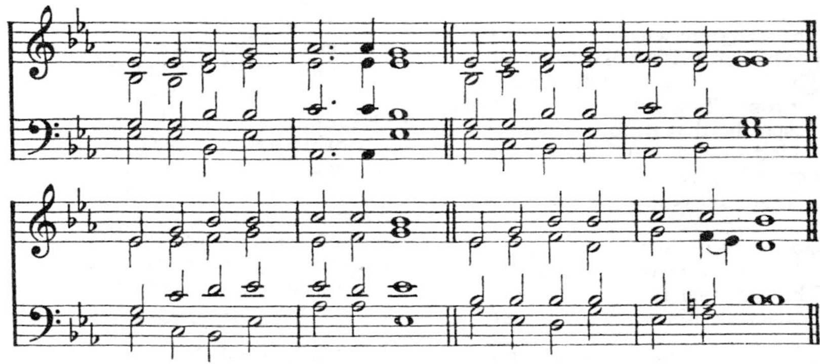

ROCK of Ages, cleft for me,
Let me hide myself in Thee:
Let the water and the blood
From Thy riven side which flowed,
Be of sin the double cure,
Cleanse me from its guilt and power.

2 Not the labour of my hands
Can fulfil Thy law's demands:
Could my zeal no respite know,
Could my tears for ever flow,
All for sin could not atone;
Thou must save, and Thou alone!

3 Nothing in my hand I bring;
Simply to Thy cross I cling;
Naked, come to Thee for dress;
Helpless, look to Thee for grace;
Foul, I to the fountain fly;
Wash me, Saviour, or I die.

4 While I draw this fleeting breath,
When my eyes shall close in death,
When I soar to worlds unknown,
See Thee on Thy judgment throne,
Rock of Ages, cleft for me.
Let me hide myself in Thee.

Augustus Montague Toplady, 1740–78

This hymn may also be sung to **Wells**, No. 161

156

WHITBURN L.M.   H. BAKER, 1835-1910

SHOW me Thy wounds, exalted Lord!
Thou hast the power and skill divine,
Since justice smote Thee with the sword,
To make my heart resemble Thine.

2 O grant me ever to behold,
With heavenly wisdom's piercing eye,
Thy pains of death, for they unfold
Thy name, Thou Son of God most high!

3 Show me Thy wounds, and by Thy skill
May I, my Saviour, be refined,
To do, like Thee, the Father's will,
And serve Him with a perfect mind.

Robert Cleaver Chapman, 1803–1902

157

NEWCASTLE 86.886

H. L. MORLEY, 1830-1916

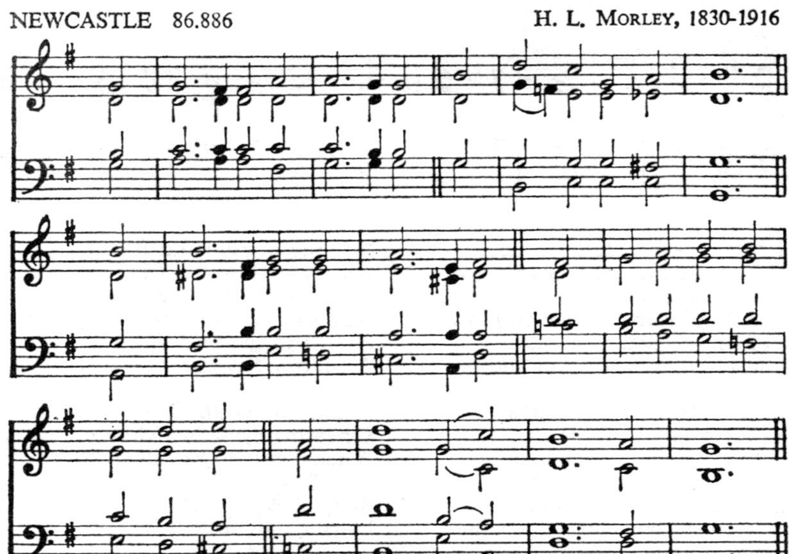

THE blood of Christ, Thy spotless Lamb,
O God, is all my plea;
Nought else could for my sin atone;
I have no merit of my own
Which I can bring to Thee.

2 No sacrifice save His who bore
My load upon the tree,
No other plea which lips could frame,
No other blood, no other name,
Accepted is by Thee.

3 Since Christ has entered by His blood
The holiest on high;
By that same hallowed, blood-stained track

Thou welcomest the wanderer back,
And biddest me draw nigh.

4 Oh wondrous cross! Oh precious blood!
Oh death by which I live!
The sinless One, for me made sin,
Doth now His wondrous heart within
Eternal refuge give!

5 By that blest cross, that cleansing blood,
I know His power to save;
The merits of His work confest,
I stand in Him completely blest,
A conqueror o'er the grave!

William Samuel Warren Pond, d. 1919

158 GREEN HILL   C.M.

A. L. PEACE, 1844-1912

THE Son of God, the Prince of life,
  Thrice in the garden prayed;
The sword was drawn to pierce the
    Man
  On whom our sins were laid.

2 He asked, if it were possible,
  The cup might pass away;
Made flesh for us, the Son of God
  A prostrate suppliant lay.

3 Strong crying, tears, and sweat of
    blood,
  Bespeak His agony;
Yet must He sink in deeper grief
  That we may never die.

4 The sword awakened cannot rest,
  Till God has slain His Son;
The Lord must die on Calvary,
  And thus for sin atone.

5 Go to Gethsemane, my soul,
  And watch with Jesus there;
Ponder His foretaste of the cup;
  Then to the cross repair.

Robert Cleaver Chapman, 1803–1902

This hymn may also be sung to **Horsley, No. 159**

159

HORSLEY C.M.   W. HORSLEY, 1774-1858

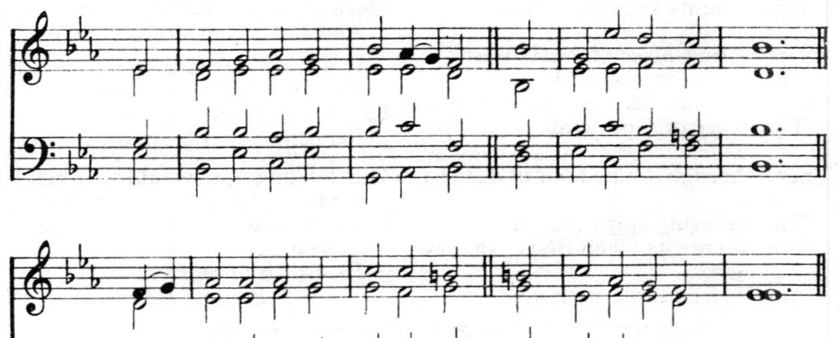

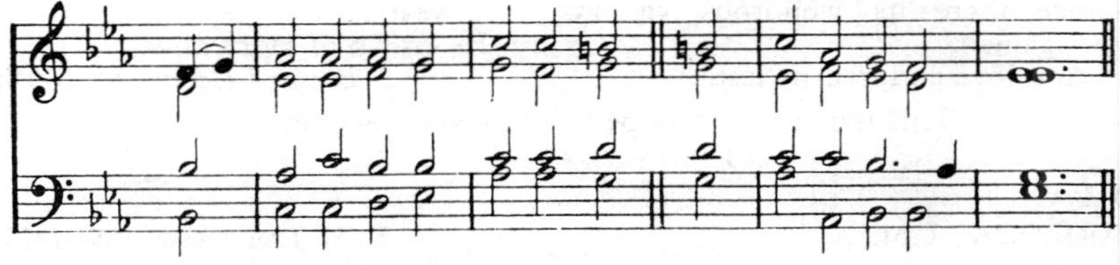

THERE is a green hill far away,
  Without a city wall,
Where the dear Lord was crucified,
  Who died to save us all.

2 We may not know, we cannot tell
  What pains He had to bear;
But we believe it was for us
  He hung and suffered there.

3 He died that we might be forgiven,
  He died to make us good,
That we might go at last to heaven,
  Saved by His precious blood.

4 There was no other good enough
  To pay the price of sin;
He only could unlock the gate
  Of heaven, and let us in.

5 Oh, dearly, dearly has He loved!
  And we must love Him too;
And trust in His redeeming blood,
  And try His works to do.

Cecil Frances Alexander, 1818–95

This hymn may also be sung to **Green Hill, No. 158**

160

DUNDEE C.M.

Scottish Psalter, 1615

To Calvary, Lord, in spirit now
  Our weary souls repair,
To dwell upon Thy dying love,
  And taste its sweetness there.

2 Sweet resting-place of every heart
  That feels the plague of sin,
Yet knows that deep mysterious joy,
  The peace of God within.

3 There, through Thine hour of deepest
    woe,
  Thy suffering spirit passed;
Grace there its wondrous victory
    gained,
  And love endured its last.

4 Dear suffering Lamb! Thy bleeding
    wounds,
  With cords of love divine,
Have drawn our willing hearts to Thee
  And linked our life with Thine.

5 Thy sympathies and hopes are ours:
  Dear Lord, we wait to see
Creation, all—below, above,
  Redeemed and blessed by Thee.

6 Our longing eyes would fain behold
  That bright and blessed brow,
Once wrung with bitterest anguish,
    wear
  Its crown of glory now.

Edward Denny, 1796–1889

This hymn may also be sung to **Stracathro**, No. 88

162

ARIZONA L.M.

Words at foot of next page

R. H. EARNSHAW, 1856-1929

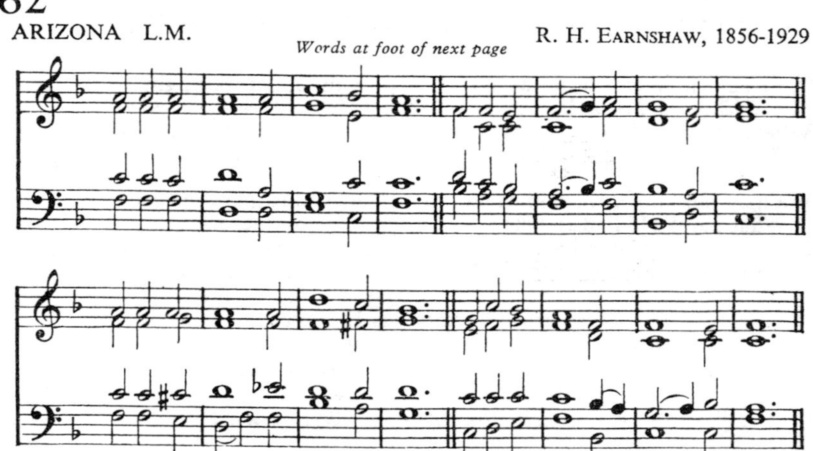

WELLS 77.77.77 — D. S. BORTNIANSKI, 1752-1825

THRONED upon the aweful tree,
  King of grief, I watch with Thee;
Darkness veils Thine anguished face,
None its lines of woe can trace,
None can tell what pangs unknown
Hold Thee silent and alone.

2 Silent through those three dread hours,
  Wrestling with the evil powers,
Left alone with human sin,
Gloom around Thee and within,
Till the appointed time is nigh,
Till the Lamb of God may die.

3 Hark the cry that peals aloud
Upward through the whelming cloud,
Thou, the Father's only Son,
Thou His own anointed One,
Thou dost ask Him—can it be?—
"Why hast Thou forsaken Me?"

4 Lord, should fear and anguish roll
Darkly o'er my sinful soul,
Thou, who once wast thus bereft
That Thine own might ne'er be left,
Teach me by that bitter cry
In the gloom to know Thee nigh.

John Ellerton, 1826–93

This hymn may also be sung to **Ajalon, No. 155**

Tune at foot of previous page

162

WE sing the praise of Him who died,
  Of Him who died upon the cross!
The sinner's hope—let men deride;
  For this we count the world but loss.

2 Inscribed upon the cross we see,
  In shining letters, "God is Love";
He bore our sins upon the tree,
  He brings us mercy from above.

3 The cross—it takes our guilt away;
  It holds the fainting spirit up;
It cheers with hope the gloomy day,
  And sweetens every bitter cup.

4 It makes the coward spirit brave,
  And nerves the feeble arm for fight;
It takes its terror from the grave,
  And gilds the bed of death with light.

5 The balm of life, the cure of woe,
  The measure and the pledge of love,
The sinner's refuge here below,
  The angels' theme in heaven above.

6 To Christ who won for sinners grace
  By bitter grief and anguish sore,
Be praise from all the ransomed race
For ever and for evermore.

Thomas Kelly, 1769–1855

LLEF L.M.

G. H. JONES, 1849-1919

WHEN I survey the wondrous cross,
On which the Prince of glory
died,
My richest gain I count but loss,
And pour contempt on all my pride.

2 Forbid it, Lord, that I should boast,
Save in the death of Christ my God!
All the vain things that charmed me
most,
I sacrifice them to His blood.

3 See from His head, His hands, His feet,
Sorrow and love flow mingled
down;
Did e'er such love and sorrow meet,
Or thorns compose so rich a crown?

4 His dying crimson like a robe,
Spreads o'er His body on the tree;
Then am I dead to all the globe,
And all the globe is dead to me.

5 Were the whole realm of nature mine,
That were an offering far too small;
Love so amazing, so divine,
Demands my soul, my life, my all.

Isaac Watts, 1674–1748

*The author's original version of verse 1,
line 2, was "Where the young Prince of
glory died."*

This hymn may also be sung to **Rockingham**, No. 564

ST. MATTHEW   D.C.M.

Probably later form of melody
by WILLIAM CROFT, 1678-1727

AWAKE, glad soul, awake, awake!
  Thy Lord hath risen long;
Go to His grave, and with thee take
  Both tuneful heart and song.
Where life is waking all around,
  Where love's sweet voices sing,
The first bright blossom may be found
  Of an eternal spring.

2 The shade and gloom of life are fled
  This resurrection day;
Henceforth in Christ are no more dead,
  The grave hath no more prey.

In Christ we live, in Christ we sleep,
  In Christ we wake and rise;
And the sad tears death makes us weep,
  He wipes from all our eyes.

3 Then wake, glad heart, awake, awake!
  And seek thy risen Lord;
Joy in His resurrection take,
  And comfort in His word.
And let thy life through all its ways
  One long thanksgiving be;
Its theme of joy, its song of praise—
  Christ died and rose for me.

John Samuel Bewley Monsell, 1811–75

165

STUTTGART 87.87

Melody by C. F. WITT, *c.* 1660-1716

CHRIST, above all glory seated!
  King triumphant, strong to save!
Dying, Thou hast death defeated;
  Buried, Thou hast spoiled the grave.

2 Thou art gone where now is given,
  What no mortal might could gain,
On the eternal throne of heaven,
  In Thy Father's power to reign.

3 There Thy kingdoms all adore Thee,
  Heaven above and earth below;
While the depths of hell before Thee
Trembling and defeated bow.

4 We, O Lord, with hearts adoring,
  Follow Thee above the sky;
Hear our prayers Thy grace imploring,
  Lift our souls to Thee on high.

5 So when Thou again in glory
  On the clouds of heaven shalt shine,
We Thy flock may stand before Thee,
  Owned for evermore as Thine.

6 Hail! all hail! In Thee confiding,
  Jesus, Thee shall all adore,
In Thy Father's might abiding
With one Spirit evermore!

Author unknown: c. 5th cent.
tr. James Russell Woodford, 1820–85

166

MORGENLIED   87.87.D with Refrain

F. C. MAKER, 1844-1927

CHRIST is risen! Hallelujah!
  Risen our victorious Head.
Sing His praises! Hallelujah!
  Christ is risen from the dead.
Gratefully our hearts adore Him,
  As His light once more appears,
Bowing down in joy before Him,
  Rising up from grief and tears.

Christ is risen! Hallelujah!
  Risen our victorious Head.
Sing His praises! Hallelujah!
  Christ is risen from the dead.

2 Christ is risen! All the sadness
  Of His earthly life is o'er,
Through the open gates of gladness
  He returns to life once more;
Death and hell before Him bending
  He doth rise, the Victor now,
Angels on His steps attending,
  Glory round His wounded brow.

3 Christ is risen! Henceforth never
  Death or hell shall us enthral,
We are Christ's, in Him for ever
  We have triumphed over all;
All the doubting and dejection
  Of our trembling hearts have ceased:
'Tis His day of resurrection,
  Let us rise and keep the feast.

John Samuel Bewley Monsell, 1811–75

This hymn may also be sung to **Lux Eoi,** No. **33**

FIRST TUNE

EASTER HYMN 77.77 **with Alleluias**

Adapted from a melody in
Lyra Davidica, 1708

CHRIST the Lord is risen to-day—
Alleluia!
Sons of men and angels say:
Raise your joys and triumphs high:
Sing, ye heavens; thou earth reply:

2 Love's redeeming work is done—
Fought the fight, the battle won;
Lo! our sun's eclipse is o'er;
Lo! He sets in blood no more.

3 Vain the stone, the watch, the seal—
Christ has burst the gates of hell:
Death in vain forbids Him rise—
Christ has opened paradise.

4 Lives again our glorious King!
Where, O death, is now thy sting?
Once He died our souls to save;
Where's thy vict'ry, boasting grave?

5 Soar we now where Christ has led,
Following our exalted Head:
Made like Him, like Him we rise;
Ours the cross, the grave, the skies:

6 King of glory! Soul of bliss!
Everlasting life is this,
Thee to know, Thy power to prove,
Thus to sing, and thus to love:

7 Hail, the Lord of earth and heaven!
Praise to Thee by both be given;
Thee we greet triumphant now;
Hail, the Resurrection Thou!

Charles Wesley, 1707-88

His Resurrection and Ascension

SECOND TUNE

LLANFAIR 77.77 with Alleluias

Melody by
R. WILLIAMS, *c*. 1781–1821

CHRIST the Lord is risen to-day—
Alleluia!
Sons of men and angels say:
Raise your joys and triumphs high:
Sing, ye heavens; thou earth reply:

2 Love's redeeming work is done—
Fought the fight, the battle won;
Lo! our sun's eclipse is o'er;
Lo! He sets in blood no more.

3 Vain the stone, the watch, the seal—
Christ has burst the gates of hell:
Death in vain forbids Him rise—
Christ has opened paradise.

4 Lives again our glorious King!
Where, O death, is now thy sting?
Once He died our souls to save;
Where's thy vict'ry, boasting grave?

5 Soar we now where Christ has led,
Following our exalted Head:
Made like Him, like Him we rise;
Ours the cross, the grave, the skies:

6 King of glory! Soul of bliss!
Everlasting life is this,
Thee to know, Thy power to prove,
Thus to sing, and thus to love:

7 Hail, the Lord of earth and heaven!
Praise to Thee by both be given;
Thee we greet triumphant now;
Hail, the Resurrection Thou!

Charles Wesley, 1707–88

168

ASCENSION   77.77 with Alleluias

Melody by W. H. MONK, 1823-89

HAIL the day that sees Him rise,
Alleluia!
Ravished from our wistful eyes!
Alleluia!
Christ, awhile to mortals given,
Alleluia!
Reascends His native heaven.
Alleluia!

2 There the pompous triumph waits:
Lift your heads, eternal gates;
Wide unfold the radiant scene;
Take the King of Glory in!

3 Him though highest heaven receives,
Still He loves the earth He leaves;
Though returning to His throne,
Still He calls mankind His own.

4 See! He lifts His hands above;
See! He shows the prints of love;
Hark! His gracious lips bestow
Blessings on His church below.

5 Master, parted from our sight
High above yon azure height,
Grant our hearts may thither rise,
Following Thee beyond the skies.

Charles Wesley, 1707–88

TORQUAY L.M.

W. YOUENS, 1834-1911

I know that my Redeemer lives:
What comfort this sweet sentence
    gives!
He lives, He lives, who once was dead;
He lives, my everlasting Head.

2 He lives, triumphant from the grave;
He lives, eternally to save;
He lives, all glorious in the sky;
He lives, exalted there on high.

3 He lives to bless me with His love;
He lives to plead for me above;
He lives my hungry soul to feed;
He lives to help in time of need.

4 He lives my kind, my faithful Friend,
He lives and loves me to the end,
He lives, and while He lives I'll sing,
He lives, my Prophet, Priest, and King.

5 He lives to bring me rich supply,
He lives to guide me with His eye,
He lives and grants me daily breath,
He lives, and I shall conquer death.

6 He lives my mansion to prepare,
He lives to bring me safely there,
He lives, all glory to His name,
Jesus, unchangeably the same!

Samuel Medley, 1738-99

This hymn may also be sung to **Church Triumphant**, No. 71

170

ST. ALBINUS   78.78. with Alleluia

H. J. GAUNTLETT, 1805-76

JESUS lives! thy terrors now
  Can, O death, no more appal us;
Jesus lives; by this we know
  Thou, O grave, canst not enthral us.
        Alleluia!

2 Jesus lives! henceforth is death
  But the gate of life immortal;
This shall calm our trembling breath
  When we pass its gloomy portal.
        Alleluia!

3 Jesus lives! for us He died:
  Then, alone to Jesus living,
Pure in heart may we abide,
  Glory to our Saviour giving.
        Alleluia!

4 Jesus lives! our hearts know well
  Nought from us His love shall sever;
Life, nor death, nor powers of hell
  Tear us from His keeping ever.
        Alleluia!

5 Jesus lives! to Him the throne
  Over all the world is given:
May we go where He is gone,
  Rest and reign with Him in heaven.
        Alleluia!

Christian Fürchtegott Gellert, 1715–69
tr. Frances Elizabeth Cox, 1812–97

CHRIST AROSE 65.64 with refrain

R. LOWRY, 1826-99

L ow in the grave He lay,
Jesus, my Saviour!
Waiting the coming day,
Jesus, my Lord!

Up from the grave He arose,
With a mighty triumph o'er His foes;
He arose a Victor from the dark domain,
And He lives for ever with His saints
to reign!
He arose! He arose!
Hallelujah! Christ arose!

2 Vainly they watch His bed,
Jesus, my Saviour!
Vainly they seal the dead,
Jesus, my Lord!

3 Death cannot keep his prey,
Jesus, my Saviour!
He tore the bars away,
Jesus, my Lord!

Robert Lowry, 1826–99

172

REX GLORIAE 87.87.D

HENRY SMART, 1813-79

See the Conqueror mounts in triumph,
  See the King in royal state
Riding on the clouds His chariot
  To His heavenly palace gate;
Hark! the choirs of angel voices
  Joyful hallelujahs sing,
And the portals high are lifted
  To receive their heavenly King.

2 Who is this that comes in glory,
  With the trump of jubilee?
Lord of battles, God of armies,
  He has gained the victory;
He who on the cross did suffer,
  He who from the grave arose,
He has vanquished sin and Satan,
  He by death has spoiled his foes.

3 Thou hast raised our human nature
  On the clouds to God's right hand;
There we sit in heavenly places,
  There with Thee in glory stand.
Jesus reigns, adored by angels,
  Man with God is on the throne,
Mighty Lord, in thine ascension
  We by faith behold our own.

4 Glory be to God the Father;
  Glory be to God the Son,
Dying, risen, ascending for us,
  Who the heavenly realm has won;
Glory to the Holy Spirit;
  To One God in Persons Three
Glory both in earth and heaven,
  Glory, endless glory be.

Christopher Wordsworth, 1807-85

This hymn may also be sung to **Bethany**, No. 8

EPHRAIM 77.77

First Tune

Henry Leslie, *c.* 1825-76

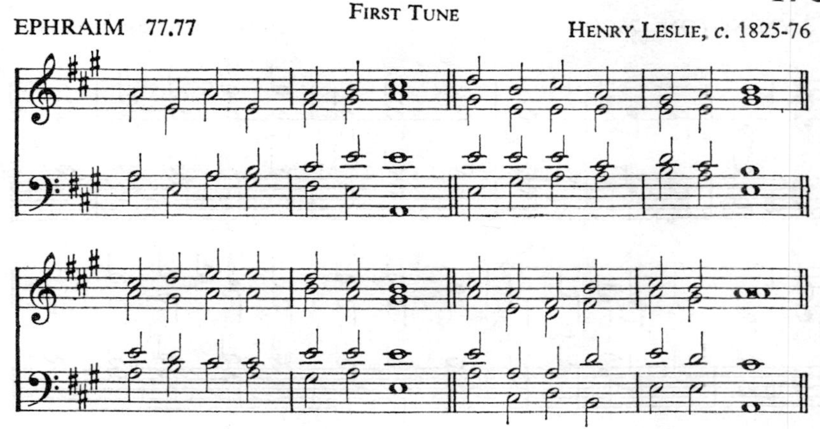

Second Tune

SHERBORNE 77.77

From F. Mendelssohn-Bartholdy, 1809-47

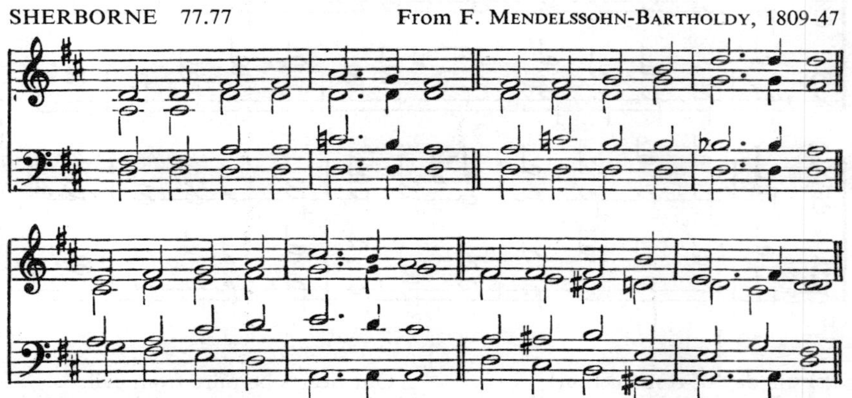

Son of God, exalted now,
Highest honours crown Thy brow,
On the Father's throne divine.
All the conqueror's triumphs Thine.

2 Here, Thy cup was grief and shame,
Here, despised Thy lowly name,
Hour of darkness—power of hell—
On Thy spotless soul it fell.

3 Now Thy travail all is o'er,
Thou shalt humbled be no more;
Joy to Thee shall ever flow,
From Thy toil and shame below.

4 Son of God, exalted now,
Thee we worship, bending low;
This the Father claims for Thee,
Reverent lips and bowèd knee.

5 Gather now full many a gem,
Saviour, for Thy diadem;
Trophies of Thy toil and love,
Meet to shine in courts above.

6 Speed the bright millennial day,
Call Thy Bride to come away;
Through the earth let joy and song
Thy glad triumphs roll along.

John Withy, 1809–92

174

LYMINGTON 76.76.D — ROBERT JACKSON, 1842-1914

THE day of resurrection!
  Earth, tell it out abroad;
The passover of gladness,
  The passover of God!
From death to life eternal,
  From earth unto the sky,
Our Christ hath brought us over
  With hymns of victory.

2 Our hearts be pure from evil,
  That we may see aright
The Lord in rays eternal
  Of resurrection light,
And, listening to His accents,
  May hear, so calm and plain,
His own "All hail!" and hearing,
  May raise the victor-strain.

3 Now let the heavens be joyful;
  Let earth her song begin;
The round world keep high triumph,
  And all that is therein;
Let all things seen and unseen,
  Their notes of gladness blend:
For Christ the Lord hath risen,
  Our Joy that hath no end.
        John of Damascus, 8th cent.
    tr. John Mason Neale, 1818–66

This hymn may also be sung to **Ellacombe**, No. 85

FRANCONIA S.M.

Arr. by W. H. HAVERGAL, 1793-1870
from a chorale in J. B. KÖNIG's *Choralbuch*, 1738

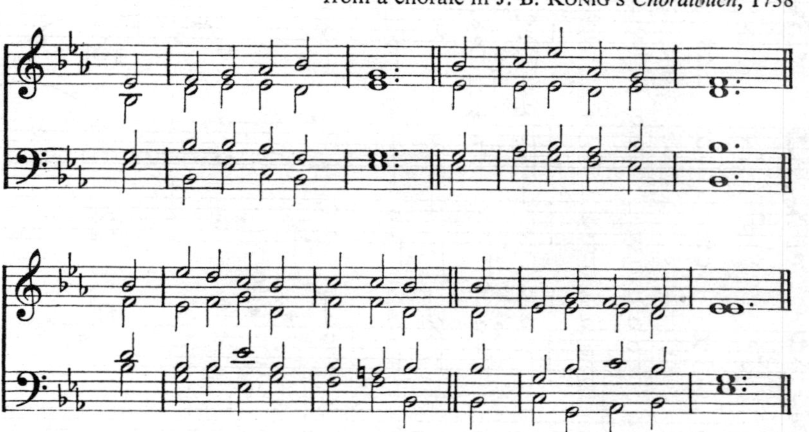

1. "THE Lord is risen indeed!"
    Now is His work performed;
The captive Surety now is freed,
    And death, our foe, disarmed.

2. "The Lord is risen indeed!"
    Then hell has lost his prey;
With Him is risen the ransomed seed
    To reign in endless day.

3. "The Lord is risen indeed!"
    Then justice asks no more,
Mercy and truth are now agreed,
    Which stood opposed before.

4. "The Lord is risen indeed!"
    This yields my soul a plea;
He bore the punishment decreed,
    And paid the debt for me.

5. "The Lord is risen indeed!"
    He lives, to die no more;
He lives, His people's cause to plead,
    Whose curse and shame He bore.

6. "The Lord is risen indeed!"
    Attending angels, hear!
Up to the courts of heaven with speed
    The joyful tidings bear.

7. Then take your golden lyres
    And strike each cheerful chord;
Join all ye bright celestial choirs,
    To sing our risen Lord.

Thomas Kelly, 1769–1855

This hymn may also be sung to **Huddersfield**, No. 328

176

PAX DEI 10.10.10.10

J. B. DYKES, 1823-76

THE Lord is risen; the Red Sea's judgment flood
Is passed, in Him who bought us with His blood;
The Lord is risen: we stand beyond the doom
Of all our sin, through Jesu's empty tomb.

2 The Lord is risen: with Him we also rose,
And in His grave see all our vanquished foes.
The Lord is risen: beyond the judgment land,
In Him in resurrection-life we stand.

3 The Lord is risen: shut in are we with God,
To tread the desert which His feet have trod.
The Lord is risen: the sanctuary's our place,
Where now we dwell before the Father's face.

4 The Lord is risen; the Lord is gone before;
We long to see Him, and to sin no more;
The Lord is risen: our triumph-shout shall be,
"Thou hast prevailed! Thy people Lord, are free."

William Paton Mackay, 1839-85

This hymn may also be sung to **Woodlands,** No. 52

VICTORY 888 with Alleluias

W. H. MONK, 1823-89
from G. P. DA PALESTRINA, 1525-94

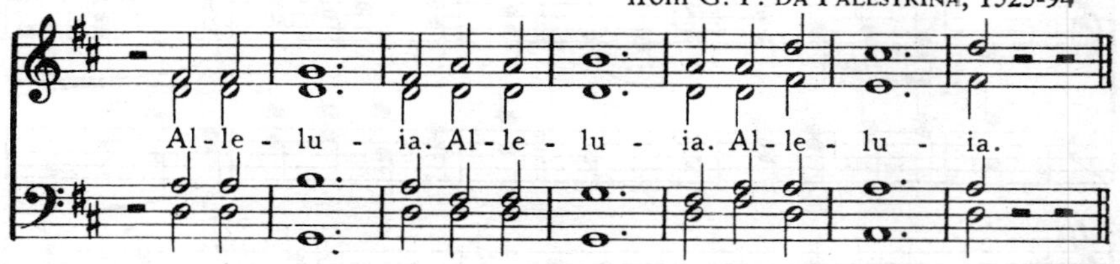

ALLELUIA! Alleluia! Alleluia!
The strife is o'er, the battle done;
The victory of life is won;
The song of triumph has begun.
    Alleluia!

2 The powers of death have done their
    worst,
But Christ their legions hath
    dispersed;
Let shouts of holy joy outburst.
    Alleluia!

3 The three sad days have quickly sped:
He rises glorious from the dead;
All glory to our risen Head!
    Alleluia!

4 He brake the bonds of death and hell;
The bars from heaven's high portals
    fell;
Let hymns of praise His triumph tell.
    Alleluia!

5 Lord, by the stripes which wounded
    Thee,
From death's dread sting Thy servants
    free,
That we may live, and sing to Thee;
    Alleluia!

Latin, 17th cent.
Francis Pott, 1832–1909

This hymn may also be sung to **Vulpius**, No. 377

178 VRUECHTEN 67.67.D with refrain
Dutch Melody, 17th cent. Arr. by GEOFFREY SHAW, 1879-1943

THIS joyful Eastertide
  Away with sin and sorrow!
My Love, the Crucified,
  Hath sprung to life this morrow.

Had Christ, that once was slain
Ne'er burst His three-days'
  prison
Our faith had been in vain;
But now hath Christ arisen,
Arisen, arisen, arisen.

2 My flesh in hope shall rest,
  And for a season slumber:
Till trump from east to west
  Shall wake the dead in number:

3 Death's flood hath lost his chill,
  Since Christ hath crossed the river;
Lover of souls, from ill
  My passing soul deliver.

George Ratcliffe Woodward, 1848–1934

179

MACCABÆUS 10.11.11.11 with refrain   G. F. HANDEL, 1685-1759

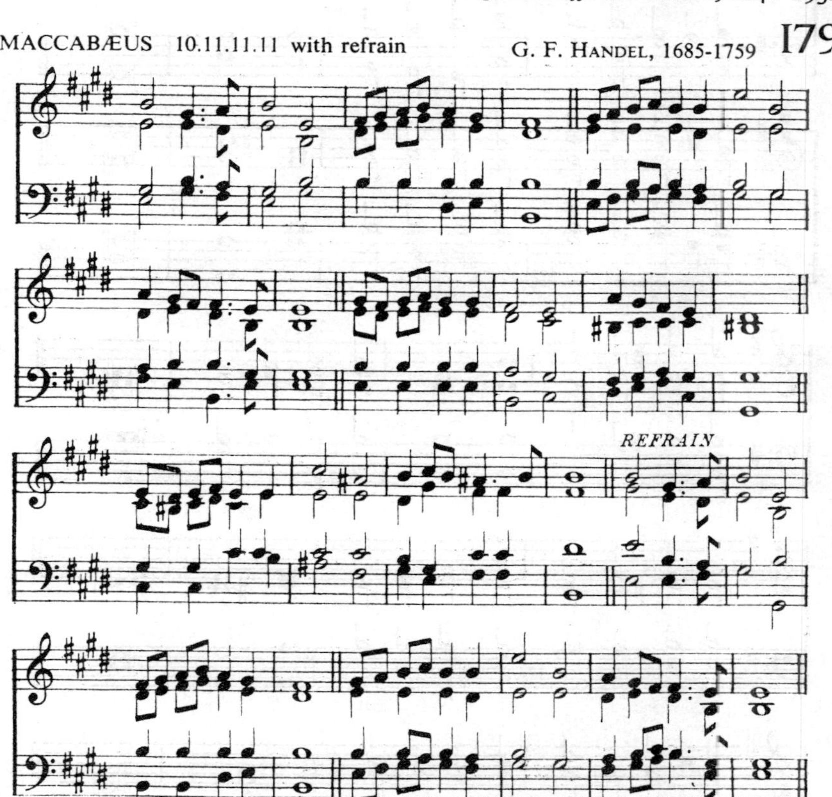

THINE be the glory, risen, conquering Son,
Endless is the victory Thou o'er death hast won;
Angels in bright raiment rolled the stone away,
Kept the folded grave-clothes, where Thy body lay.

  Thine be the glory, risen, conquering Son,
  Endless is the victory Thou o'er death hast won.

2 Lo! Jesus meets us, risen from the tomb;
Lovingly He greets us, scatters fear and gloom;
Let the church with gladness, hymns of triumph sing,
For her Lord now liveth, death hath lost its sting.

3 No more we doubt Thee, glorious Prince of life;
Life is nought without Thee: aid us in our strife;
Make us more than conquerers, through Thy deathless love:
Bring us safe through Jordan to Thy home above.

Edmond Louis Budry, 1854–1932
tr. Richard Birch Hoyle, 1875–1939

180

FORTUNATUS 11.11.11.11.11

A. S. SULLIVAN, 1842-1900

"WELCOME, happy morning!" age
   to age shall say;
Hell to-day is vanquished; heaven is
   won to-day!
Lo! the dead is living, God for
   evermore!
Him, their true creator, all His works
   adore.
   "Welcome, happy morning!" age
     to age shall say.

2 Maker and Redeemer, life and health
   of all,
Thou from heaven beholding human
   nature's fall,
Of the Father's Godhead true and only
   Son,
Manhood to deliver, manhood didst
   put on.
   "Welcome, happy morning!" age
     to age shall say.

3 Thou, of life the author, death didst
   undergo,
  Tread the path of darkness, saving
    strength to show:
  Come, then, true and faithful, now
    fulfil Thy word;
  'Tis Thine own third morning! Rise,
    O buried Lord!
    Hell to-day is vanquished; heaven
     is won to-day!

4 Loose the souls long prisoned, bound
   with Satan's chain;
  All that now is fallen raise to life
    again;
  Show Thy face in brightness, bid the
    nations see;
  Bring again our daylight: day returns
    with Thee!
    "Welcome, happy morning!" age
     to age shall say.

Venantius Fortunatus, 530–609
tr. John Ellerton, 1826–93

181

WETHERBY C.M.   S. S. WESLEY, 1810-76

Y E humble souls that seek the Lord,
   Chase all your fears away;
And bow with rapture down to see
  The place where Jesus lay.

2 Thus low the Lord of Life was
   brought,
  Such wonders love can do;
Thus cold in death that bosom lay,
  Which throbbed and bled for you.

3 But raise your eyes and tune your
   songs;
  The Saviour lives again:
Not all the bolts and bars of death
  The conqueror could detain.

4 High o'er the angelic bands He rears
  His once dishonoured head;
And through unnumbered years He
   reigns,
  Who dwelt among the dead.

5 With joy like His shall every saint
  His vacant tomb survey;
Then rise with his ascending Lord
  To realms of endless day.

Philip Doddridge, 1702–51
This hymn may also be sung to **Claremont,** No. 129

See also

182

FESTUS L.M.

Adapted from a melody in
FREYLINGHAUSEN's *Gesangbuch*, 1704

BEFORE the throne of God above
  I have a strong, a perfect plea;
A great High Priest, whose name is
    Love,
  Who ever lives and pleads for me.

2 My name is graven on His hands,
  My name is written on His heart;
I know that while in heaven He stands
  No tongue can bid me thence
    depart

3 When Satan tempts me to despair,
  And tells me of the guilt within,
Upward I look, and see Him there
  Who made an end of all my sin.

4 Because the sinless Saviour died,
  My sinful soul is counted free;
For God, the Just, is satisfied
  To look on Him and pardon me.

5 Behold Him there! the risen Lamb!
  My perfect, spotless righteousness,
The great unchangeable I AM,
  The King of glory and of grace!

6 One with Himself, I cannot die;
  My soul is purchased by His blood:
My life is hid with Christ on high,
  With Christ, my Saviour and my
    God.

Charitie Lees Bancroft, 1841–1923

This hymn may also be sung to **Wilton**, No. 469

183

PATER OMNIUM 88.88.88

H. J. E. HOLMES, 1852-1938

ENTERED the holy place above,
Covered with meritorious scars,
The tokens of His dying love
    Our great High-priest in glory
    bears;
He pleads His passion on the tree,
He shows Himself to God for me.

2 Before the throne my Saviour stands,
    My Friend and Advocate appears;
My name is graven on His hands,
    And Him the Father always hears:

While low at Jesu's cross I bow,
He hears the blood of sprinkling now.

3 This instant now I may receive
    The answer of His powerful prayer;
This instant now by Him I live,
    His prevalence with God declare;
And soon my spirit, in His hands,
Shall stand where my Forerunner
    stands.

Charles Wesley, 1707–88

MAGDALEN 88.88.88   JOHN STAINER, 1840-1901 **184**

O THOU eternal Victim, slain
A sacrifice for guilty man,
And by the eternal Spirit made
An offering in the sinner's stead,
Our everlasting Priest art Thou,
And plead'st Thy death for sinners
    now.

2 Thy offering still continues new,
Thy vesture keeps its crimson hue,
Thou stand'st the ever-slaughtered
    Lamb,

Thy priesthood still remains the same,
Thy years, O God, can never fail,
Nor Thy blest work within the veil.

3 Oh that our faith may never move,
But stand unshaken as Thy love!
Sure evidence of things unseen,
Now let it pass the years between,
View Thee again upon the tree,
My God, who dies for me, for me!

Charles Wesley, 1707–88

This hymn may also be sung to **Melita**, No. 503

185

KILMARNOCK C.M.

NEIL DOUGALL, 1776-1862

THE veil is rent, lo! Jesus stands
  Before the throne of grace;
And clouds of incense from His hands
  Fill all that glorious place.

2 His precious blood is sprinkled there,
  Before and on the throne;
And His own wounds in heaven
    declare
  His work on earth is done.

3 "'Tis finished!" on the cross He said,
  In agonies and blood;
"'Tis finished!" now He lives to plead,
  Before the face of God.

4 "'Tis finished!" Here our souls can
    rest,
  His work can never fail;
By Him, our Sacrifice and Priest,
  We enter through the veil.

5 Within the holiest of all,
  Cleansed by His precious blood,
Before Thy throne Thy children fall,
  And worship Thee, our God.

6 Boldly our hearts and voice we raise,
  His name, His blood, our plea:
Assured our prayers and songs of
    praise
  Ascend by Him to Thee.

James George Deck, 1802–84

This hymn may also be sung to **St. Stephen,** No. 67

GALILEE L.M.

P. ARMES, 1836-1908

WHERE high the heavenly temple stands,
The house of God not made with hands,
A great High Priest our nature wears,
The Saviour of mankind appears.

2 He who for men their surety stood,
And poured on earth His precious blood,
Pursues in heaven His mighty plan,
The Saviour and the Friend of man.

3 Though now ascended up on high.
He bends on earth a gracious eye;
Partaker of the human name,
He knows the frailty of our frame.

4 Our fellow-sufferer yet retains
A fellow-feeling of our pains;
And still remembers, in the skies,
His tears, His agonies and cries.

5 In every pang that rends the heart
The Man of Sorrows had a part;
He knows and feels our every grief,
And gives the suffering saint relief.

6 With boldness, therefore, at the throne,
Let us make all our sorrows known;
And seek His grace and heavenly power
To help us in the evil hour.

Michael Bruce, 1746–67
Scottish Paraphrases, 1781

HARINGTON C.M.   H. HARINGTON, 1727-1816

WITH joy we meditate the grace
  Of our High Priest above;
His heart is filled with tenderness,
  His very name is Love.

2 Touched with a sympathy within,
  He knows our feeble frame;
He knows what sore temptations
    mean;
  For He has felt the same.

3 But spotless, innocent, and pure,
  Our great Redeemer stood;
While Satan's fiery darts He bore,
  And did resist to blood.

4 He, in the days of feeble flesh,
  Poured out His cries and tears,
And, though exalted, feels afresh
  What every member bears.

5 He'll never quench the smoking flax,
  But raise it to a flame;
The bruised reed He never breaks,
  Nor scorns the meanest name.

6 Then boldly let our faith address
  His mercy and His power;
We shall obtain delivering grace,
  In the distressing hour.

7 He ever lives to intercede
  Before His Father's face;
Give Him, my soul, thy cause to plead,
  Nor doubt thy Father's grace.

Isaac Watts, 1674–1748

This hymn may also be sung to **Dublin,** No. 188

DUBLIN (HOWARD) C.M. Attributed to S. Howard, 1710-82

BEHOLD the Lamb with glory crowned!
To Him all power is given;
No place too high for Him is found,
No place too high in heaven.

2 He fills the throne—the throne above,
He fills it without wrong;
The object of His Father's love,
The theme of heaven's song.

3 Though high, yet He accepts the praise
His people offer here;
The faintest, feeblest cry they raise,
Will reach the Saviour's ear.

4 This song be ours, and this alone,
That celebrates the name
Of Him that sits upon the throne,
And that exalts the Lamb.

5 To Him whom men despise and slight,
To Him be glory given;
The crown is His, and His by right
The highest place in heaven.

Thomas Kelly, 1769–1855

189

ST. GEORGE'S, EDINBURGH
D.C.M. with Coda

A. M. Thomson, 1778-1831

CODA (after verse 4)

BEHOLD the glories of the Lamb,
   Amidst His Father's throne;
Prepare new honours for His name,
   And songs before unknown.
Lo! elders worship at His feet;
   The prayers of saints abound,
In vials full of odours rich,
   With harps of sweetest sound.

2 Hark how th' adoring hosts above
   With songs surround the throne!
Ten thousand thousand are their
     tongues;
   But all their hearts are one.
"Worthy the Lamb that died," they
     cry,
   "To be exalted thus;"
"Worthy the Lamb," let us reply,
   "For He was slain for us."

3 To Him be pow'r divine ascrib'd,
   And endless blessings paid;
Salvation, glory, joy, remain
   For ever on His head!
Thou hast redeem'd us with Thy
     blood,
   And set the pris'ners free;
Thou mad'st us kings and priests to
     God,
   And we shall reign with Thee.

4 From ev'ry kindred, ev'ry tongue,
   Thou brought'st Thy chosen race;
And distant lands and isles have shared
   The riches of Thy grace.
To Him that sits upon the throne,
   The God whom we adore,
And to the Lamb that once was slain,
   Be glory evermore.

Isaac Watts, 1674–1748

Coda
   Alleluia! Alleluia!
   Alleluia! Alleluia! Alleluia!
   Amen, Amen, Amen.

190

GLASGOW C.M.

MOORE'S *Psalm-Singer's Pocket Companion*, 1756

BEHOLD, the mountain of the Lord
  In latter days shall rise
On mountain-tops above the hills,
  And draw the wondering eyes.

2 To this the joyful nations round,
  All tribes and tongues, shall flow;
Up to the hill of God, they'll say,
  And to His house, we'll go.

3 The beam that shines from Zion's hill
  Shall lighten every land;
The King who reigns in Salem's towers
  Shall all the world command.

4 Among the nations He shall judge;
  His judgments truth shall guide;
His sceptre shall protect the just,
  And quell the sinner's pride.

5 No strife shall rage, nor hostile feuds
  Disturb those peaceful years;
To ploughshares men shall beat their swords,
  To pruning-hooks their spears.

6 Come then, O house of Jacob, come
  To worship at His shrine;
And, walking in the light of God,
  With holy beauties shine.

Michael Bruce, 1746–67

NEANDER 87.87.87

From Chorale *Unser Herrscher,*
by J. NEANDER, 1650-80

CHRIST is coming! let creation
  Bid her groans and travail cease;
Let the glorious proclamation
  Hope restore, and faith increase:
    Christ is coming!
  Come, Thou blessèd Prince of
  Peace.

2 Earth can now but tell the story
  Of Thy bitter cross and pain;
She shall yet behold Thy glory,
  When Thou comest back to reign:
    Christ is coming!
  Let each heart repeat the strain.

3 Through once cradled in a manger;
  Oft no pillow but the sod;
Here an alien and a stranger,
  Mocked of man, and bruised of
  God—
    All creation
  Yet shall own Thy kingly rod.

4 Long Thine exiles have been pining,
  Far from rest, and home, and Thee;
But in heavenly vesture shining,
  They shall soon Thy glory see:
    Christ is coming!
  Haste the joyous jubilee!

5 With that blessèd hope before us,
  Let no harp remain unstrung;
Let the mighty advent chorus
  Onward roll from tongue to tongue:
    Christ is coming!
  Come, Lord Jesus, quickly come!

John Ross Macduff, 1818–95

This hymn may also be sung to **Mannheim**, No. 389

LOVE DIVINE   87.87   J. STAINER, 1840-1901

COME, Thou long-expected Jesus,
    Born to set Thy people free,
From our fears and sins release us,
    Let us find our rest in Thee.

2 Israel's strength and consolation,
    Hope of all the earth Thou art;
Dear Desire of every nation,
    Joy of every longing heart.

3 Born Thy people to deliver,
    Born a child and yet a king,
Born to reign in us for ever,
    Now Thy gracious kingdom bring.

4 By Thine own eternal Spirit
    Rule in all our hearts alone;
By Thine all-sufficient merit
    Raise us to Thy glorious throne.

Charles Wesley, 1707–88

This hymn may also be sung to **All for Jesus,** No. 140

EDEN   D.S.M.   JOHN ROBERTS (IEUAN GWYLLT), 1822-77

CROWN Him with many crowns,
The Lamb upon His throne;
Hark! how the heavenly anthem drowns
All music but its own.
Awake, my soul, and sing
Of Him who died for thee,
And hail Him as thy matchless King
Through all eternity.

2   Crown Him, the Lord of Love!
Behold His hands and side,
Rich wounds, yet visible above
In beauty glorified:
No angel in the sky
Can fully bear that sight,
But downward bends his burning eye
At mysteries so bright.

3   Crown Him the Lord of life,
Who triumphed o'er the grave,
And rose victorious in the strife
For those He came to save:
His glories now we sing
Who died, and rose on high;
Who died eternal life to bring,
And lives that death may die.

4   Crown Him, the Lord of Peace;
Whose power a sceptre sways
From pole to pole, that wars may cease
And all be prayer and praise:
His reign shall know no end,
And round His piercèd feet,
Fair flowers of paradise extend
Their fragrance ever sweet.

5   Crown Him the Lord of years,
The Potentate of time,
Creator of the rolling spheres,
Ineffably sublime.
All hail, Redeemer, hail!
For Thou hast died for me;
Thy praise shall never, never fail
Throughout eternity.

Matthew Bridges, 1800–94 and Godfrey Thring, 1823–1903
This hymn may also be sung to **Diademata,** No. 3

194

HENRY LESLIE, *c.* 1825-76

EARTH, rejoice, our Lord is King!
Sons of men, His praises sing;
Sing ye in triumphant strains,
Jesus the Messiah reigns!

2 Power is all to Jesus given,
Lord of hell, and earth, and heaven,
Every knee to Him shall bow;
Satan, hear, and tremble now!

3 Angels and archangels join,
All triumphantly combine,
All in Jesu's praise agree,
Carrying on His victory.

4 Though the sons of night blaspheme,
More there are with us than them;
God with us, we cannot fear;
Fear, ye fiends, for Christ is here!

5 Lo! to faith's enlightened sight,
All the mountain flames with light;
Hell is nigh, but God is nigher,
Circling us with hosts of fire.

6 Christ the Saviour is come down,
Points us to the victor's crown,
Bids us take our seats above,
More than conquerors in His love.

Charles Wesley, 1707–88

CRÜGER 76.76.D

Adapted by W. H. MONK, 1823-89,
from a chorale by J. CRÜGER, 1598-1662

HAIL to the Lord's Anointed,
  Great David's greater Son!
Hail in the time appointed,
  His reign on earth begun!
He comes to break oppression,
  To set the captive free,
To take away transgression,
  And rule in equity.

2 He comes with succour speedy
  To those who suffer wrong;
To help the poor and needy,
  And bid the weak be strong;
To give them songs for sighing,
  Their darkness turn to light,
Whose souls, condemned and dying,
  Were precious in His sight.

3 He shall come down like showers
  Upon the fruitful earth;
And love, joy, hope, like flowers,
  Spring in His path to birth:
Before Him on the mountains,
  Shall peace the herald go,
And righteousness in fountains
  From hill to valley flow.

4 Arabia's desert ranger
  To Him shall bow the knee;
The Ethiopian stranger
  His glory come to see;
With offerings of devotion
  Ships from the isles shall meet,
To pour the wealth of ocean
  In tribute at His feet.

5 Kings shall fall down before Him,
  And gold and incense bring!
All nations shall adore Him,
  His praise all people sing;
For He shall have dominion
  O'er river, sea, and shore,
Far as the eagle's pinion
  Or dove's light wing can soar.

6 O'er every foe victorious,
  He on His throne shall rest;
From age to age more glorious,
  All-blessing and all-blest;
The tide of time shall never
  His covenant remove;
His name shall stand for ever,
  His changeless name of Love.

James Montgomery, 1771–1854

This hymn may also be sung to **Munich,** No. 80

196

THANKSGIVING   77.77.D

W. B. Gilbert, 1829-1910

Hark! the song of jubilee,
  Loud as mighty thunders' roar:
Or the fullness of the sea,
  When it breaks upon the shore.
Hallelujah! for the Lord
  God Omnipotent shall reign:
Hallelujah! let the word
  Echo round the earth and main.

2 Hallelujah! hark! the sound,
  From the depths unto the skies,
Wakes above, beneath, around,
  All creation's harmonies:
See Jehovah's banner furled:
  Sheathed His sword; He speaks—
    'tis done:
And the kingdoms of this world
  Are the kingdoms of His Son.

3 He shall reign from pole to pole
  With illimitable sway:
He shall reign, when, like a scroll,
  Yonder heavens have passed away;
Then the end—beneath His rod
  Man's last enemy shall fall;
Hallelujah! Christ in God,
  God in Christ, is all in all.

James Montgomery, 1771–1854

This hymn may also be sung to **St. George's, Windsor**, No. 621

FIRST TUNE

RIMINGTON L.M.   F. DUCKWORTH, 1862-1941

SECOND TUNE

TRURO L.M.   *Psalmodia Evangelica*, 1789

JESUS shall reign where'er the sun
Does its successive journeys run;
His kingdom stretch from shore to shore,
Till moons shall wax and wane no more.

2 For Him shall endless prayer be made,
And praises throng to crown His head;
His name like sweet perfume shall rise
With every morning sacrifice.

3 People and realms of every tongue
Dwell on His love with sweetest song;
And infant voices shall proclaim
Their early blessings on His name.

4 Blessings abound where'er He reigns;
The prisoner leaps to lose his chains;
The weary find eternal rest,
And all the sons of want are blest.

5 Where He displays His healing power,
Death and the curse are known no more;
In Him the sons of Adam boast
More blessings than their father lost.

6 Let every creature rise and bring
Peculiar honours to our King;
Angels descend with songs again,
And earth repeat the loud Amen.

Isaac Watts, 1674-1748

BEATITUDO C.M.   J. B. Dykes, 1823-76

L IGHT of the lonely pilgrim's heart!
      Star of the coming day!
Arise, and with Thy morning beams
    Chase all our griefs away.

2 Come, blessèd Lord! bid every shore
      And answering island sing
The praises of Thy royal name,
      And own Thee as their King.

3 Bid the whole earth, responsive now
      To the bright world above,
Break forth in rapturous strains of joy,
      In memory of Thy love.

4 O Lord, Thy fair creation groans,
      The earth, the air, the sea,
In unison with all our hearts,
      And calls aloud for Thee.

5 Come, then, with all Thy quickening
            power,
      With one awakening smile,
And bid the serpent's trail no more
      Thy beauteous realms defile.

6 Thine was the cross, with all its fruit
      Of grace and peace divine;
Be Thine the crown of glory now,
      The palm of victory Thine!

                    Edward Denny, 1796–1889

HELMSLEY 87.87.47

English Melody, 18th cent

Lo! He comes with clouds descend-
  ing,
  Once for favoured sinners slain;
Thousand thousand saints attending,
  Swell the triumph of His train!
    Hallelujah!
God appears on earth to reign.

2 Now redemption, long expected,
  See in solemn pomp appear;
All His saints, by man rejected,
  Now shall meet Him in the air.
    Hallelujah!
See the day of God appear!

3 Every eye shall now behold Him,
  Robed in glorious majesty;
Those who set at naught and sold
  Him,
Pierced and nailed Him to the tree,
    Deeply wailing,
Shall the true Messiah see.

4 Those dear tokens of His passion
  Still His dazzling body bears,
Cause of endless exultation
  To His ransomed worshippers;
    With what rapture
Gaze we on those glorious scars!

5 Yea, Amen! let all adore Thee,
  High on Thine eternal throne;
Saviour, take the power and glory,
  Claim the kingdom for Thine own;
    Oh come quickly!
Hallelujah! come, Lord, come!

John Cennick, 1718–1755 Martin Madan, 1726–1790 Charles Wesley, 1707–1788

200

CROWN HIM 87.87.47   Arr. by G. C. Stebbins, 1846-1945

LOOK, ye saints, the sight is glorious;
　See the Man of Sorrows now;
From the fight returned victorious,
　Every knee to Him shall bow:
　　Crown Him! crown Him!
　Crowns become the Victor's brow.

2 Crown the Saviour, angels crown Him;
　Rich the trophies Jesus brings;
In the seat of power enthrone Him,
　While the vault of heaven rings;
　　Crown Him! crown Him!
　Crown the Saviour King of kings.

3 Sinners in derision crowned Him,
　Mocking thus the Saviour's claim:
Saints and angels crowd around Him,
　Own His title, praise His name:
　　Crown Him! crown Him!
　Spread abroad the Victor's fame.

4 Hark, those bursts of acclamation!
　Hark, those loud triumphant chords!
Jesus takes the highest station!
　Oh what joy the sight affords!
　　Crown Him! crown Him!
　King of kings, and Lord of lords!

Thomas Kelly, 1769–1855

This hymn may also be sung to **Triumph,** No. 625

GOPSAL 66.66.88

G. F. HANDEL, 1685-1759

REJOICE! the Lord is King,
   Your Lord and King adore;
Mortals, give thanks and sing,
   And triumph evermore:
Lift up your heart, lift up your voice:
Rejoice; again I say, rejoice.

2 Jesus the Saviour reigns,
   The God of truth and love;
When He had purged our stains,
   He took His seat above:
Lift up your heart, lift up your voice:
Rejoice; again I say, rejoice.

3 His kingdom cannot fail:
   He rules o'er earth and heaven;
The keys of death and hell
   Are to our Jesus given:
Lift up your heart, lift up your voice:
Rejoice; again I say, rejoice.

4 He sits at God's right hand
   Till all His foes submit,
And bow to His command
   And fall beneath His feet.
Lift up your heart, lift up your voice:
Rejoice; again I say, rejoice.

5 Rejoice in glorious hope:
   Jesus Himself shall come,
And take His servants up
   To their eternal home:
We soon shall hear the archangel's
     voice;
The trump of God shall sound,
   Rejoice!

Charles Wesley, 1707–88

This hymn may also be sung to **Adoration,** No. 104

202

THE GLORY SONG 10.10.10.10 with refrain C. H. GABRIEL, 1856-1932

SING we the King who is coming to
reign,
Glory to Jesus, the Lamb that was
slain,
Life and salvation His empire shall
bring,
Joy to the nations when Jesus is King.
> *Come let us sing: Praise to our
> King,*
> *Jesus our King, Jesus our King:*
> *This is our song, who to Jesus
> belong:*
> *Glory to Jesus, to Jesus our King.*

2 Souls shall be saved from the burden
of sin,
Doubt shall not darken His witness
within,
Hell hath no terrors, and death hath
no sting;
Love is victorious when Jesus is King.

3 All men shall dwell in His marvellous
light,
Races long severed His love shall unite.
Justice and truth from His sceptre
shall spring,
Wrong shall be ended when Jesus is
King.

4 All shall be well in His kingdom of
peace,
Freedom shall flourish and wisdom
increase,
Foe shall be friend when His triumph
we sing,
Sword shall be sickle when Jesus is
King.

5 Kingdom of Christ, for thy coming
we pray,
Hasten, O Father, the dawn of the day
When this new song Thy creation
shall sing,
Satan is vanquished and Jesus is King.

Charles Silvester Horne, 1865–1914

203

ST. MAGNUS C.M.

J. CLARK, 1670-1707

THE head that once was crowned
   with thorns
Is crowned with glory now:
A royal diadem adorns
   The mighty victor's brow!

2 The highest place that heaven affords
   Is His, is His by right;
The King of kings, and Lord of lords,
   And heaven's eternal light.

3 The joy of all who dwell above,
   The joy of all below
To whom He manifests His love,
   And grants His name to know.

4 To them, the cross, with all its shame,
   With all its grace is given;
Their name an everlasting name,
   Their joy the joy of heaven.

5 They suffer with their Lord below,
   They reign with Him above;
Their profit and their joy to know
   The mystery of His love.

6 The cross He bore is life and health,
   Though shame and death to Him;
His people's hope, His people's wealth,
   Their everlasting theme.

Thomas Kelly, 1769–1855

THE race that long in darkness pined
Have seen a glorious light;
The people dwell in day, who dwelt
In death's surrounding night.

2 To hail Thy rise, Thou better sun,
The gathering nations come,
Joyous as when the reapers bear
The harvest-treasures home.

3 To us a child of hope is born,
To us a son is given;
Him shall the tribes of earth obey,
Him all the hosts of heaven.

4 His name shall be the Prince of peace,
For evermore adored,
The Wonderful, the Counsellor,
The great and mighty Lord.

5 His power increasing still shall spread;
His reign no end shall know:
Justice shall guard His throne above,
And peace abound below.

Scottish Paraphrases, 1781

205

THERE'S A LIGHT UPON THE MOUNTAINS   15.15.15.15

M. L. WOSTENHOLM, b. 1887

THERE'S a light upon the mountains,
  and the day is at the spring,
When our eyes shall see the beauty
  and the glory of the King;
Weary was our heart with waiting,
  and the night-watch seemed so long;
But His triumph-day is breaking,
  and we hail it with a song.

2 In the fading of the starlight we can
    see the coming morn;
  And the lights of men are paling
    in the splendours of the dawn:
  For the eastern skies are glowing
    as with light of hidden fire,
  And the hearts of men are stirring
    with the throbs of deep desire.

3 There's a hush of expectation, and a
    quiet in the air;
  And the breath of God is moving
    in the fervent breath of prayer:

For the suffering, dying Jesus is the
  Christ upon the throne,
And the travail of our spirit is the
  travail of His own.

4 He is breaking down the barriers,
    He is casting up the way;
  He is calling for His angels to build
    up the gates of day:
  But His angels here are human,
    not the shining hosts above;
  For the drum-beats of His army
    are the heart-beats of our love.

5 Hark! we hear a distant music,
    and it comes with fuller swell:
  'Tis the triumph-song of Jesus,
    of our King, Immanuel:
  Zion, go ye forth to meet Him;
    and, my soul, be swift to bring
  All thy sweetest and thy dearest
    for the triumph of our King!

Henry Burton, 1840–1930

ST. CECILIA 66.66   L. G. HAYNE, 1836-83

THY kingdom come, O God;
  Thy rule, O Christ, begin;
Break with Thine iron rod
  The tyrannies of sin.

2 Where is Thy reign of peace
  And purity and love?
When shall all hatred cease,
  As in the realms above?

3 When comes the promised time
  That war shall be no more,
And lust, oppression, crime,
  Shall flee Thy face before?

4 We pray Thee, Lord, arise,
  And come in Thy great might;
Revive our longing eyes,
  Which languish for Thy sight.

5 Men scorn Thy sacred name,
  And wolves devour Thy fold;
By many deeds of shame
  We learn that love grows cold.

6 O'er heathen lands afar
  Thick darkness broodeth yet;
Arise, O Morning Star,
  Arise and never set.

Lewis Hensley, 1824–1905

This hymn may also be sung to **Quam Dilecta**, No. 539

2O7

ST. GEORGE'S, EDINBURGH
D.C.M. with Coda

A. M. THOMSON, 1778-1831

CODA (after verse 2)

Y^E gates, lift up your heads on high;
  Ye doors that last for aye,
Be lifted up, that so the King
  Of glory enter may!
But who of glory is the King?
  The mighty Lord is this,
E'en that same Lord that great in
    might
  And strong in battle is.

2 Ye gates, lift up your heads; ye doors,
  Doors that do last for aye,
Be lifted up, that so the King
  Of glory enter may!
But who is He that is the King
  The King of glory? who is this?
The Lord of hosts, and none but He,
  The King of glory is.

Francis Rous, 1579–1659
William Barton, 1597–1678

Coda
  Alleluia! Alleluia!
  Alleluia! Alleluia! Alleluia!
  Amen, Amen, Amen.

See also
165 Christ above all glory seated
580 Thou art coming, O my Saviour
610 Let the song go round the earth
635 Hark, ten thousand voices crying
644 Ten thousand times ten thousand
645 The countless multitude on high
699 Lord, when Thy Kingdom comes,
    remember me

208

HALLELUJAH 87.87.D

S. S. WESLEY, 1810-76

ALLELUIA! sing to Jesus!
  His the sceptre, His the throne;
Alleluia! His the triumph,
  His the victory alone.
Hark, the songs of holy Zion
  Thunder like a mighty flood:
"Jesus out of every nation
  Hath redeemed us by His blood."

2 Alleluia! not as orphans
  Are we left in sorrow now;
Alleluia! He is near us,
  Faith believes, nor questions how.
Though the clouds from sight received
    Him
  When the forty days were o'er,
Shall our hearts forget His promise,
  "I am with you evermore"?

3 Alleluia! Bread of heaven,
  Thou on earth our food, our stay;
Alleluia! here the sinful
  Flee to Thee from day to day.
Intercessor, Friend of sinners,
  Earth's Redeemer, plead for me
Where the songs of all the sinless
  Sweep across the crystal sea.

4 Alleluia! King eternal,
  Thee the Lord of Lords we own;
Alleluia! born of Mary,
  Earth Thy footstool, heaven Thy
    throne:
Thou within the veil hast entered,
  Our High Priest and Surety Thou.
Alleluia! at Thy coming
  Every knee to Thee shall bow!

William Chatterton Dix, 1837–98

This hymn may also be sung to **Mead House,** No. 607

His Glory, Name and Praise

FIRST TUNE

DIADEM   C.M.

J. ELLOR, 1819-99

ALL hail the power of Jesu's name,
   Let angels prostrate fall;
Bring forth the royal diadem,
   And crown Him Lord of all.

2 Crown Him, ye martyrs of our God,
   Who from the altar call;
Extol the Stem of Jesse's rod,
   And crown Him Lord of all.

3 Ye seed of Israel's chosen race,
   Ye ransomed from the fall,
Hail Him who saves you by His grace,
   And crown Him Lord of all.

4 Sinners! whose love can ne'er forget
   The wormwood and the gall;
Go, spread your trophies at His feet,
   And crown Him Lord of all.

5 Let every kindred, every tribe,
   On this terrestrial ball,
To Him all majesty ascribe,
   And crown Him Lord of all.

6 Oh that with yonder sacred throng,
   We at His feet may fall;
Join in the everlasting song,
   And crown Him Lord of all.

Edward Perronet, 1726–92
alt. John Rippon, 1751–1836

209

LADYWELL D.C.M.

SECOND TUNE

W. H. FERGUSON, 1874-1950

ALL hail the power of Jesu's name,
  Let angels prostrate fall;
Bring forth the royal diadem,
  And crown Him Lord of all.

2 Crown Him, ye martyrs of our God,
  Who from the altar call;
Extol the Stem of Jesse's rod,
  And crown Him Lord of all.

3 Ye seed of Israel's chosen race,
  Ye ransomed from the fall,
Hail Him who saves you by His grace,
  And crown Him Lord of all.

4 Sinners! whose love can ne'er forget
  The wormwood and the gall;
Go, spread your trophies at His feet,
  And crown Him Lord of all.

5 Let every kindred, every tribe,
  On this terrestrial ball,
To Him all majesty ascribe,
  And crown Him Lord of all.

6 Oh that with yonder sacred throng,
  We at His feet may fall;
Join in the everlasting song,
  And crown Him Lord of all.

Edward Perronet, 1726–92
alt. John Rippon, 1751–1836

TYROLESE 76.76.D

Tyrolese Carol
Arr. by R. VAUGHAN WILLIAMS, 1872–1958

A MAN there lived in Galilee
  Unlike all men before,
For He alone from first to last
  Our flesh unsullied wore;
A perfect life of perfect deeds
  Once to the world was shown,
That all mankind might mark His
    steps
  And in them plant their own.

2 A Man there died on Calvary
  Above all others brave;
His fellow-men He saved and blessed,
  Himself He scorned to save.
No thought can gauge the weight of
    woe
  On Him, the sinless, laid;
We only know that with His blood
  Our ransom-price was paid.

3 A Man there reigns in Glory now,
  Divine, yet human still;
That human which is all divine
  Death sought in vain to kill.
All power is His; supreme He rules
  The realms of time and space;
Yet still our human cares and needs
  Find in His heart a place.

Somerset Corry Lowry, 1855–1932

211

SINE NOMINE 10.10.10.4

R. VAUGHAN WILLIAMS, 1872-1958

ALL praise to Thee, for Thou, O King divine,
Didst yield the glory that of right was Thine,
That in our darkened hearts Thy grace might shine:
    Hallelujah!

2 Thou cam'st to us in lowliness of thought;
By Thee the outcast and the poor were sought,
And by Thy death was God's salvation wrought:
    Hallelujah!

3 Let this mind be in us which was in Thee,
Who wast a servant that we might be free,
Humbling Thyself to death on Calvary:
    Hallelujah!

4 Wherefore, by God's eternal purpose, Thou
Art high exalted o'er all creatures now,
And given the name to which all knees shall bow:
    Hallelujah!

5 Let every tongue confess with one accord,
In heaven and earth, that Jesus Christ is Lord;
And God the Father be by all adored:
    Hallelujah!

Francis Bland Tucker, b. 1895

212

FIRST TUNE

MOMENT BY MOMENT   10.10.10.10 Dactylic

MARY W. MOODY

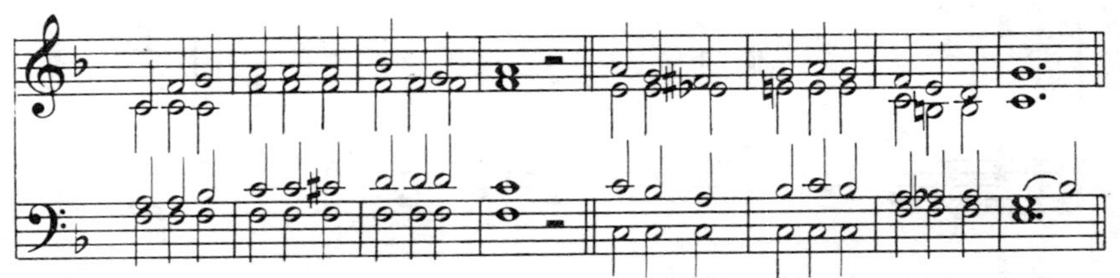

SECOND TUNE

TRISAGION   10.10.10.10 Dactylic

H. SMART, 1813-1879

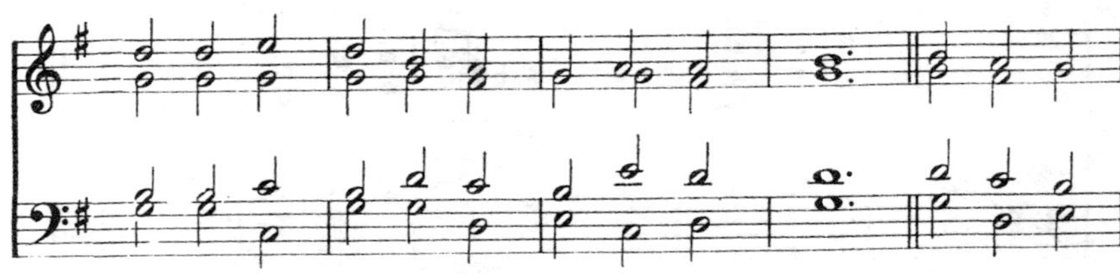

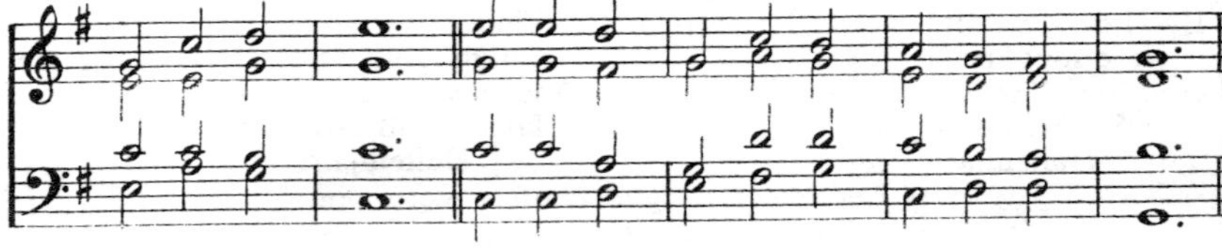

Blessing and honour and glory and
    power,
Wisdom and riches and strength
    evermore
Give ye to Him who our battle hath
    won,
Whose are the kingdom, the crown,
    and the throne.

2 Into the heav'n of the heav'ns hath
    He gone;
Sitteth He now in the joy of the
    throne;
Weareth He now of the kingdom the
    crown;
Singeth He now the new song with
    His own.

3 Soundeth the heav'n of the heav'ns
    with His name;
Ringeth the earth with His glory and
    fame;

Ocean and mountain, stream, forest,
    and flower
Echo His praises and tell of His power.

4 Ever ascendeth the song and the joy;
Ever descendeth the love from on
    high;
Blessing and honour and glory and
    praise,
This is the theme of the hymns that
    we raise.

5 Give we the glory and praise to the
    Lamb;
Take we the robe and the harp and
    the palm;
Sing we the song of the Lamb that
    was slain,
Dying in weakness, but rising to reign.

Horatius Bonar, 1808–89

213

INNOCENTS 77.77   Anon., *Parish Choir*, 1850

Brethren, let us join to bless
    Christ, the Lord our Righteous-
    ness;
Let our praise to Him be given,
High at God's right hand in heaven.

2 Son of God, to Thee we bow:
Thou art Lord, and only Thou;
Thou the woman's promised seed;
Thou who didst for sinners bleed.

3 Thee the angels ceaseless sing,
Thee we praise, our Priest and King;
Worthy is Thy name of praise,
Full of glory, full of grace.

4 Thou hast the glad tidings brought
Of salvation by Thee wrought;
Wrought to set Thy people free;
Wrought to bring our souls to Thee.

5 May we follow and adore
    Thee, our Saviour, more and more;
    Guide and bless us with Thy love,
    Till we see Thy face above.

John Cennick, 1718–55

214

TRUMPET 66.66.88

L. Edson, 1748-1820

Come, every joyful heart
  That loves the Saviour's name,
Your noblest powers exert,
  To celebrate His fame;
Tell all above and all below,
The debt of love to Him you owe.

2 He left His starry crown,
    And laid His robes aside,
  On wings of love came down,
    And wept, and bled, and died:
  What He endured no tongue can tell,
  To save our souls from death and hell.

3 From the dark grave He rose,
    The mansion of the dead;
  And thence His mighty foes
    In glorious triumph led;
  Up through the sky the Conqueror rode,
  And lives on high, the Saviour God.

4 Thence will He quickly come—
    His chariot will not stay—
  And bear His people home
    To realms of endless day;
  There shall we see His lovely face,
  And ever be in His embrace.

5 O Lord, we ne'er can pay
    The debt of love we owe;
  Yet grant us day by day
    Our gratitude to show;
  Our life, our all, to Thee we give,
  To Thee, by whom alone we live.

Samuel Stennett, 1727–95

This hymn may also be sung to **Darwall,** No. 168

NATIVITY C.M.

H. LAHEE, 1825-1912

COME, let us join our cheerful songs
    With all around the throne;
Ten thousand thousand are their
    tongues,
    But all their joys are one.

2 "Worthy the Lamb that died," they
        cry,
    "To be exalted thus;"
"Worthy the Lamb," our lips reply,
    "For He was slain for us."

3 Jesus is worthy to receive
    Honour and power divine;
And blessings, more than we can give,
    Be, Lord, for ever Thine!

4 Let all that dwell above the sky,
    And air, and earth, and seas,
Conspire to lift Thy glories high,
    And speak Thine endless praise.

5 The whole creation join in one,
    To bless the sacred name
Of Him who sits upon the throne,
    And to adore the Lamb.

Isaac Watts, 1674–1748

216

CASTLE STREET (LUTHER'S CHANT)   L.M.   H. C. ZEUNER, 1795-1857

COME, let us sing the song of songs,
  The saints in heaven began the
    strain,
The homage which to Christ belongs:
"Worthy the Lamb, for He was slain!"

2 Slain to redeem us by His blood,
  To cleanse from every sinful stain,
  And make us kings and priests to God;
  "Worthy the Lamb, for He was slain!"

3 To Him who suffered on the tree,
  Our souls, at His soul's price, to gain,
  Blessing and praise and glory be:
  "Worthy the Lamb, for He was slain!"

4 To Him, enthroned by filial right,
  All power in heaven and earth
    proclaim,
  Honour and majesty and might:
  "Worthy the Lamb, for He was slain!"

5 Long as we live, and should we die,
  And while in heaven with Him we
    reign,
  This song our song of songs shall be:
  "Worthy the Lamb, for He was slain!"

                    James Montgomery, 1771-1854

NORMANDY 87.87.D   C. Bost, 1790-1874

Come, Thou Fount of every bless-
    ing!
  Tune my heart to sing Thy grace;
Streams of mercy never ceasing
  Call for songs of loudest praise.
Teach me, Lord, some rapturous
    measure,
  Sung by ransomed hosts above;
Oh the vast, the boundless treasure
  Of my God's unchanging love.

2 Here I raise my Ebenezer,
  Hither by Thy help I'm come;
And I hope, by Thy good pleasure,
  Safely to arrive at home.
Jesus sought me when a stranger,
  Wandering from the fold of God;
He, to rescue me from danger,
  Interposed His precious blood.

3 Oh to grace how great a debtor
    Daily I'm constrained to be!
  Let that grace, Lord, like a fetter,
    Bind my wandering heart to Thee.
  Prone to wander, Lord, I feel it,
    Prone to leave the God I love—
  Here's my heart, Lord, take and seal it,
    Seal it from Thy courts above.

Robert Robinson, 1735–90
This hymn may also be sung to **Lux Eoi**, No. 33

GREENLAND 76.76.D

From J. M. HAYDN, 1737-1806

ERE God had built the mountains,
  Or raised the fruitful hills,
Before He filled the fountains
  That feed the running rills;
In Thee, from everlasting,
  The wonderful "I AM"
Found pleasures never wasting,
  And Wisdom is Thy name.

2 When, like a tent to dwell in,
  He spread the skies abroad;
And swathed about the swelling
  Of ocean's mighty flood:
He wrought by weight and measure;
  And Thou wast with Him then:
Thyself the Father's pleasure,
  And Thine, the sons of men.

3 Thus Wisdom's works discover
  Thy glory and Thy grace,
Thou everlasting Lover
  Of our unworthy race!
Thy gracious eye surveyed us
  Ere stars were seen above:
In wisdom Thou hast made us,
  And died for us in love.

4 And couldst Thou be delighted
  With creatures such as we,
Who, when we saw Thee, slighted
  And nailed Thee to a tree?
Unfathomable wonder!
  And mystery divine!
The voice that speaks in thunder,
  Says, "Sinner, I am thine."

William Cowper, 1731-1800

This hymn may also be sung to **Aurelia,** No. 588

BEAUMARIS 87.87   Composer unknown

GAZING on Thee, Lord, in glory,
    While our hearts in worship bow,
There we read the wondrous story
    Of the cross—its shame and woe.

2 Every mark of dark dishonour
      Heaped upon the thorn-crown'd
          brow,
  All the depths of Thy heart's sorrow
      Told in answering glory now.

3 On that cross alone—forsaken—
      Where no pitying eye was found;
  Now to God's right hand exalted,
      With Thy praise the heavens
          resound.

4 Did Thy God e'en then forsake Thee,
      Hide His face from Thy deep need?
  In Thy face once marr'd and smitten,
      All His glory now we read.

5 Gazing on it we adore Thee,
      Blessed, precious, holy Lord;
  Thou, the Lamb, alone art worthy—
      This be earth's and heaven's accord.

6 Rise our hearts, and bless the Father,
      Ceaseless song e'en here begun,
  Endless praise and adoration
      To the Father and the Son.

                    Centra Thompson, 1822–1909

This hymn may also be sung to **St. Oswald**, No. 560

220

MALVERN 664.6664

The Hallelujah, 1849

GLORY to God on high!
Let earth and skies reply,
  "Praise ye His name!"
Angels His love adore,
Who all our sorrows bore,
And saints cry evermore,
  "Worthy the Lamb!"

2 Jesus, our Lord and God,
Bore sin's tremendous load,
  "Praise ye His name!"
Tell what His arm hath done,
What spoils from death He won,
Sing His great Name alone:
  "Worthy the Lamb!"

3 All they around the throne
Cheerfully join in one,
  Praising His name:
Now we, who know His blood
Hath made our peace with God,
Would sound His praise abroad,
  "Worthy the Lamb!"

4 Join, all the ransomed race,
Our Lord and God to bless;
  "Praise ye His name!"
In Him we will rejoice,
And make a cheerful noise,
Shouting with heart and voice.
  "Worthy the Lamb!"

5 Let all the hosts above
Join in one song of love,
  Praising His name.
To Him ascribed be,
Honour and majesty,
Through all eternity:
  "Worthy the Lamb!"

James Allen, 1734-1804

This hymn may also be sung to **Philippi**, No. 42

MOSCOW 664.6664

Adapted from F. Giardini, 1716-96

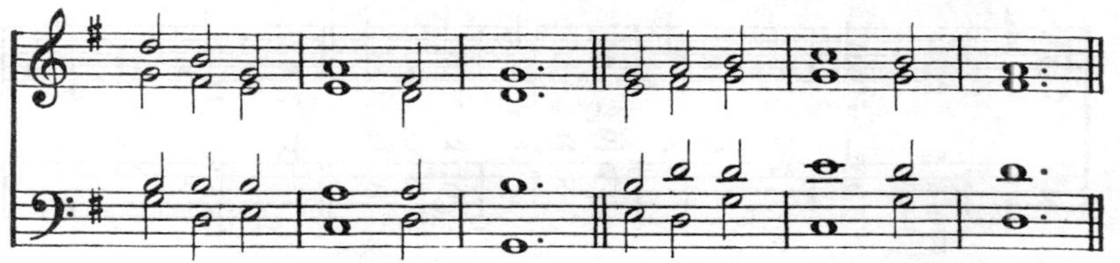

Glory to God on high!
Peace upon earth and joy,
  Goodwill to man.
We, who His blessing prove,
Join with the host above,
Praising His wondrous love,
  Too vast to scan.

2 Mercy and truth unite,
This is a wondrous sight,
  All sights above!
Jesus the curse sustains,
Bitter the cup He drains,
Nothing for us remains—
  Nothing but love.

3 Love that no tongue can teach,
Love that no thought can reach—
  No love like His.
God is its blessed source,
Death could not stop its course,
Nothing can stay its force,
  Matchless it is.

4 Blest in this love we sing,
To God our praise we bring;
  All sin forgiven.
Jesus, our Lord, to Thee,
Honour and majesty
Now and for ever be,
  Here and in heaven.

Thomas Kelly, 1769–1855

This hymn may also be sung to **Malvern**, No. 220

222

HYFRYDOL 87.87.D

Melody by R. H. Prichard, 1811-87

Hail, Thou once despisèd Jesus,
  Hail, Thou Galilean King;
Thou didst suffer to release us,
  Thou didst free salvation bring.
Hail, Thou agonizing Saviour,
  Bearer of our sin and shame,
By Thy merits we find favour;
  Life is given through Thy name.

2 Paschal Lamb, by God appointed,
  All our sins on Thee were laid:
By almighty love anointed,
  Thou hast full atonement made.
All Thy people are forgiven,
  Through the virtue of Thy blood:
Opened is the gate of heaven,
  Peace is made 'twixt man and God.

3 Jesus, hail! enthroned in glory,
  There for ever to abide;
All the heavenly hosts adore Thee,
  Seated at Thy Father's side:
There for sinners Thou art pleading,
  There Thou dost our place prepare,
Ever for us interceding,
  Till in glory we appear.

4 Worship, honour, power, and blessing
  Thou art worthy to receive:
Loudest praises, without ceasing,
  Meet it is for us to give:
Help, ye bright angelic spirits,
  Bring your sweetest, noblest lays;
Help to sing our Saviour's merits,
  Help to chant Immanuel's praise.

John Bakewell, 1721–1819

This hymn may also be sung to **Sanctus**, No. 13

GOSHEN 77.87.D Adapted from F. J. HAYDN, 1732-1809

HEAD of Thy Church triumphant,
  We joyfully adore Thee,
    Till Thou appear,
    Thy members here
  Shall sing like those in glory.
We lift our hearts and voices
  With blest anticipation,
    And cry aloud,
    And give to God
  The praise of our salvation.

2 The name we still acknowledge
  That burst our bonds in sunder,
    And loudly sing
    Our conquering King,
  In songs of joy and wonder.

In every day's deliverance
  His mercies we discover;
    'Tis He, 'tis He
    That smote the sea,
  And led us safely over!

3 By faith we see the glory
  To which Thou shalt restore us;
    The cross despise
    For that high prize
  Which Thou hast set before us.
We sing Thy praise, exulting
  In Thine almighty favour;
    The love divine
    Which made us Thine
  Shall keep us Thine for ever.

Charles Wesley, 1707–88

224

CUDDESDON 65.65.D

FIRST TUNE

W. H. FERGUSON, 1874-1950

IN the name of Jesus
  Every knee shall bow,
Every tongue confess Him
  King of Glory now.
'Tis the Father's pleasure
  We should call Him Lord,
Who from the beginning
  Was the mighty word.

2 At His voice creation
  Sprang at once to sight,
All the angel faces,
  All the hosts of light,
Thrones and dominations,
  Stars upon their way,
All the heavenly orders
  In their great array.

3 Humbled for a season
  To receive a name
From the lips of sinners
  Unto whom He came,
Faithfully He bore it
  Spotless to the last,
Brought it back victorious,
  When from death He passed.

4 Name Him, brothers, name Him,
  With love strong as death,
But with awe and wonder,
  And with bated breath:
He is God the Saviour,
  He is Christ the Lord,
Ever to be worshipped,
  Trusted and adored.

5 In your hearts enthrone Him:
  There let Him subdue
All that is not holy,
  All that is not true:
Crown Him as your Captain
  In temptation's hour,
Let His will enfold you
  In its light and power.

6 Brothers, this Lord Jesus
  Shall return again,
With His Father's glory,
  With His angel-train;
For all wreaths of empire
  Meet upon His brow,
And our hearts confess Him
  King of glory now.

Caroline Maria Noel, 1817-77

His Glory, Name and Praise

ORLINGTON C.M.   J. Campbell, 1807-1860

How sweet the name of Jesus sounds
In a believer's ear.
It soothes his sorrows, heals his
wounds,
And drives away his fear.

2 It makes the wounded spirit whole,
And calms the troubled breast;
'Tis manna to the hungry soul,
And to the weary rest.

3 Dear name! the rock on which I
build;
My shield and hiding-place;
My never-failing treasury, filled
With boundless stores of grace.

4 Jesus my Shepherd, Saviour, Friend,
My Prophet, Priest and King,
My Lord, my Life, my Way, my End,
Accept the praise I bring.

5 Weak is the effort of my heart,
And cold my warmest thought;
But when I see Thee as Thou art,
I'll praise Thee as I ought.

6 Till then I would Thy love proclaim
With every fleeting breath;
And may the music of Thy name
Refresh my soul in death.

John Newton, 1725-1807

This hymn may also be sung to **Lloyd, No. 127**

CONSTANCE 87.87.D Iambic A. S. SULLIVAN, 1842-1900

I'VE found a Friend, oh such a Friend!
  He loved me ere I knew Him;
He drew me with the cords of love,
  And thus He bound me to Him;
And round my heart still closely twine
  Those ties which nought can sever,
For I am His, and He is mine,
  For ever and for ever.

2 I've found a Friend, oh such a Friend!
  He bled, He died to save me;
And not alone the gift of life,
  But His own self He gave me.
Nought that I have my own I call,
  I hold it for the Giver:
My heart, my strength, my life, my all,
  Are His, and His for ever.

3 I've found a Friend, oh such a Friend!
  All power to Him is given,
To guard me on my onward course,
  And bring me safe to heaven.
Th' eternal glories gleam afar,
  To nerve my faint endeavour:
So now to watch! to work! to war!
  And then—to rest for ever!

4 I've found a Friend, oh such a Friend!
  So kind, and true, and tender,
So wise a Counsellor and Guide,
  So mighty a Defender.
From Him, who loves me now so well,
  What power my soul can sever?
Shall life, or death, or earth, or hell?
  No; I am His for ever!

James Grindlay Small, 1817–88

227

ABERYSTWYTH 77.77.D

JOSEPH PARRY, 1841-1903

JESU, Lover of my soul,
  Let me to Thy bosom fly,
While the nearer waters roll,
  While the tempest still is high:
Hide me, O my Saviour, hide,
  Till the storm of life be past;
Safe into the haven guide,
  Oh receive my soul at last.

2 Other refuge have I none;
  Hangs my helpless soul on Thee;
Leave, ah! leave me not alone,
  Still support and comfort me:
All my trust on Thee is stayed,
  All my help from Thee I bring;
Cover my defenceless head
  With the shadow of Thy wing.

3 Thou, O Christ, art all I want;
  More than all in Thee I find;
Raise the fallen, cheer the faint,
  Heal the sick, and lead the blind:
Just and holy is Thy name,
  I am all unrighteousness;
False and full of sin I am,
  Thou art full of truth and grace.

4 Plenteous grace with Thee is found,
  Grace to cover all my sin;
Let the healing streams abound,
  Make and keep me pure within:
Thou of life the fountain art,
  Freely let me take of Thee,
Spring Thou up within my heart,
  Rise to all eternity.

Charles Wesley, 1707-88

This hymn may also be sung to **Hollingside**, No. 455

DISMISSAL 87.87.87

W. L. VINER, 1790-1867

1. JESUS came—the heavens adoring—
   Came with peace from realms on high;
Jesus came for man's redemption,
   Lowly came on earth to die:
   Alleluia! Alleluia!
   Came in deep humility.

2. Jesus comes to hearts rejoicing,
   Bringing news of sins forgiven;
Jesus comes in sounds of gladness,
   Leading souls redeemed to heaven;
   Alleluia! Alleluia!
   Now the gate of death is riven.

3. Jesus comes again in mercy,
   When our hearts are bowed with care:
Jesus comes again in answer
   To our earnest heart-felt prayer;
   Alleluia! Alleluia!
   Comes to save us from despair.

4. Jesus comes on clouds triumphant,
   When the heavens shall pass away;
Jesus comes again in glory;
   Let us then our homage pay,
   Alleluia! ever singing
   Till the dawn of endless day.

Godfrey Thring, 1823–1903

This hymn may also be sung to **Regent Square**, No. 5

229

EAGLEY C.M.

J. WALCH, 1837-1901

JESUS, how much Thy name unfolds
  To every opened ear;
The pardoned sinner's memory holds
  None other half so dear.

2 Thy name encircles every grace
  That God as man could show;
There only can the Spirit trace
  A perfect life below.

3 Jesus—it speaks a life of love,
  And sorrows meekly borne;
It tells of sympathy above,
  Whatever makes us mourn.

4 It speaks of righteousness complete,
  Of holiness to God;
And to our ears no tale so sweet
  As Thine atoning blood.

5 Jesus—the One who knew no sin,
  Made sin to make us just;
Worthy art Thou our love to win
  Worthy of all our trust.

6 The mention of Thy name shall bow
  Our hearts to worship Thee;
The chiefest of ten thousand Thou,
  The chief of sinners we.

Mary Bowly Peters, 1813–56

This hymn may also be sung to **St. Peter,** No. 230

230

ST. PETER C.M.

A. R. REINAGLE, 1799-1877

J ESUS, in Thee our eyes behold
A thousand glories more
Than the rich gems and polished gold,
The sons of Aaron wore.

2 They first their own sin-offering
brought,
To purge themselves from sin;
Thy life was pure, without a spot,
And all Thy nature clean.

3 Fresh blood, as constant as the day,
Was on their altars spilt;
But Thy one offering took away
For ever all our guilt.

4 Their priesthood ran through several
hands,
For mortal was their race;
Thy never-changing office stands
Eternal as Thy days.

5 Once in the circuit of a year,
With blood, but not his own,
Aaron within the veil appears,
Before the golden throne.

6 But Christ, by His own precious blood,
Ascends above the skies,
And, in the presence of our God,
Shows His own sacrifice.

Isaac Watts, 1674–1748

This hymn may also be sung to **Evan**, No. 70

231

ST. BEES   77.77   J. B. DYKES, 1823-76

" J ESUS!"—name of wondrous love;
Name all other names above,
Unto which must every knee
Bow in deep humility.

2 "Jesus!"—name of priceless worth
To the fallen sons of earth,
For the promise that it gave—
"Jesus shall His people save."

3 "Jesus!"—name of mercy mild,
Given to the Holy Child
When the cup of human woe
First He tasted here below.

4 "Jesus!"—only name that's given
Under all the mighty heaven
Whereby man, to sin enslaved,
Bursts his fetters, and is saved.

5 "Jesus!"—name of wondrous love;
Human name of God above;
Pleading only this, we flee,
Helpless, O our God, to Thee.

William Walsham How, 1823–97

GOD THE SON:

FIRST TUNE

ONE DAY 11.10.11.10 with refrain

C. H. MARSH, 1886-1956

SECOND TUNE

WAS LEBET   11.10.11.10

Reinhardt MS., Üttingen, 1754

With this tune, the refrain is sung as a fifth verse, using the tied notes in bar 2.

JESUS our Lord, with what joy we adore Thee,
   Chanting our praise to Thyself on the throne!
Blest in Thy presence, we worship before Thee,
   Own Thou art worthy, and worthy alone:
   Lord, Thou art worthy; Lord, Thou art worthy;
   Lord, Thou art worthy and worthy alone!
   Blest in Thy presence, we worship before Thee
   Own Thou art worthy, and worthy alone.

2 Verily God, yet become truly human—
   Lower than angels—to die in our stead;
How hast Thou, long promised "seed of the woman,"
   Trod on the serpent, and bruisèd his head!

3 How didst Thou humble Thyself to be taken,
   Led by Thy creatures, and nailed to the cross!
Hated of men, and of God, too, forsaken,
   Shunning not darkness, the curse, and the loss!

4 How hast Thou triumphed, and triumphed with glory,
   Battled death's forces, rolled back every wave!
Can we refrain, then, from telling the story?
   Lord, Thou art victor o'er death and the grave!

Henry D'Arcy Champney, 1854–1942

233

LYDIA C.M.

T. Phillips, 1735-1807

Jesus! the name high over all,
    In hell, or earth, or sky:
Angels and men before it fall,
    And devils fear and fly.

2 Jesus! the name to sinners dear,
    The name to sinners given;
It scatters all their guilty fear,
    It turns their hell to heaven.

3 Jesus! the prisoner's fetters breaks,
    And bruises Satan's head;
Power into strengthless souls it speaks,
    And life into the dead.

4 Oh, that the world might taste and see
    The riches of His grace!
The arms of love that compass me
    Would all mankind embrace.

5 His only righteousness I show,
    His saving truth proclaim:
'Tis all my business here below,
    To cry Behold the Lamb!

6 Happy, if with my latest breath
    I might but gasp His name:
Preach Him to all, and cry in death
    Behold, behold the Lamb!

Charles Wesley, 1707–88

235 ST. AGNES C.M.   *Words at foot of next page*   J. B. Dykes, 1823-76

TRENTHAM S.M.

R. JACKSON, 1842-1914

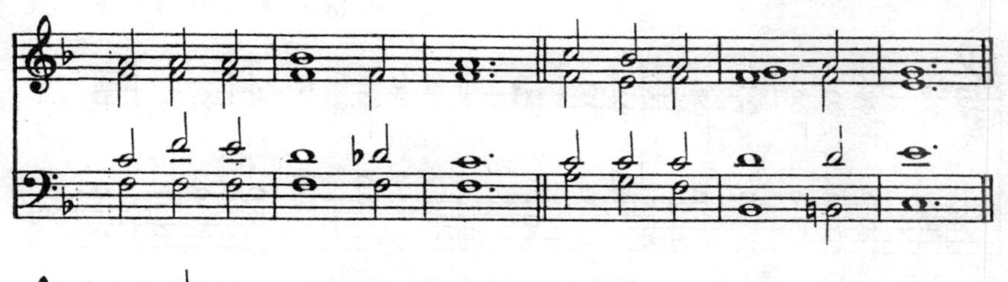

Jesus, the sinner's Friend,
We hide ourselves in Thee!
God looks upon Thy sprinkled blood;
It is our only plea.

2 He hears Thy precious name;
We claim it as our own;
The Father must accept and bless
His well-belovèd Son.

3 He sees Thy precious blood;
It cleanses all our sin;
The golden gates have welcomed
Thee,
And we may enter in.

4 Jesus, the sinner's Friend,
We cannot speak Thy praise,
No mortal voice can sing the song
That ransomed hearts would raise.

5 But when before the throne,
Upon the glassy sea,
Clothed in our blood-bought robes of
white,
We stand complete in Thee;

6 Jesus, we'll give Thee then
Such praises as are meet,
And cast ten thousand golden crowns
Adoring at Thy feet!

Catherine Pennefather, d. 1893

Tune at foot of previous page **235**

Jesus, the very thought of Thee
With sweetness fills my breast;
But sweeter far Thy face to see,
And in Thy presence rest.

2 Nor voice can sing, nor heart can
frame,
Nor can the memory find
A sweeter sound than Thy blest
name,
O Saviour of mankind!

3 O hope of every contrite heart,
O joy of all the meek,
To those who fall, how kind Thou art,
How good to those who seek!

4 But what to those who find? Ah, this
Nor tongue nor pen can show;
The love of Jesus what it is,
None but His loved ones know.

5 O Jesus, light of all below,
Fountain of life and love,
Surpassing all the joys we know
And all we seek above:

6 Jesus, our only joy be Thou,
As Thou our crown wilt be;
Jesus, be Thou our glory now,
And through eternity!

Bernard of Clairvaux, 1090–1153
tr. Edward Caswall, 1814–78

This hymn may also be sung to **Mendip**, No. 415

236

HEMBURY FORT L.M.

B. H. MUDDITT, b. 1906
Arr. by F. A. J. TONKIN, b. 1926

J ESUS, Thou joy of loving hearts,
Thou fount of life, Thou light of men,
From the best bliss that earth imparts,
We turn, unfilled, to Thee again.

2 Thy truth unchanged hath ever stood;
Thou savest those that on Thee call;
To them that seek Thee, Thou art good,
To them that find Thee, all in all.

3 We taste Thee, O Thou living bread,
And long to feast upon Thee still;
We drink of Thee, the fountain-head,
And thirst our souls from Thee to fill.

4 Our restless spirits yearn for Thee,
Where'er our changeful lot is cast;
Glad when Thy gracious smile we see,
Blest when our faith can hold Thee fast.

5 Lord Jesus, ever with us stay,
Make all our moments calm and bright;
Chase the dark night of sin away,
Shed o'er the world Thy holy light!

Bernard of Clairvaux, 1090–1153
tr. Ray Palmer, 1808–87

This hymn may also be sung to **Maryton,** No. 31

DARWALL 66.66.88

J. DARWALL, 1731-89

PART I

JOIN all the glorious names
    Of wisdom, love, and power,
That mortals ever knew,
    That angels ever bore:
All are too mean to speak His worth,
Too mean to set my Saviour forth.

2 But oh what gentle terms,
    What condescending ways,
Doth our Redeemer use
    To teach His heavenly grace:
Mine eyes with joy and wonder see
What forms of love He bears for me.

3 Great Prophet of my God,
    My tongue would bless Thy
      name;
By Thee the joyful news
    Of our salvation came:
The joyful news of sins forgiven,
Of hell subdued and peace with
      heaven.

4 Be Thou my Counsellor,
    My Pattern and my Guide;
And through this desert land
    Still keep me near Thy side;
Oh let my feet ne'er run astray,
Nor rove, nor seek the crooked way.

5 I love my Shepherd's voice,
    His watchful eye shall keep
My wandering soul among
    The thousands of His sheep:
He feeds His flock, He calls their
      names,
His bosom bears the tender lambs.

6 My dear Almighty Lord,
    My Conqueror and my King,
Thy sceptre and Thy sword,
    Thy reigning grace I sing.
Thine is the power: behold I sit
In willing bonds before Thy feet.

Isaac Watts, 1674-1748

238

TRUMPET 66.66.88

L. EDSON, 1748-1820

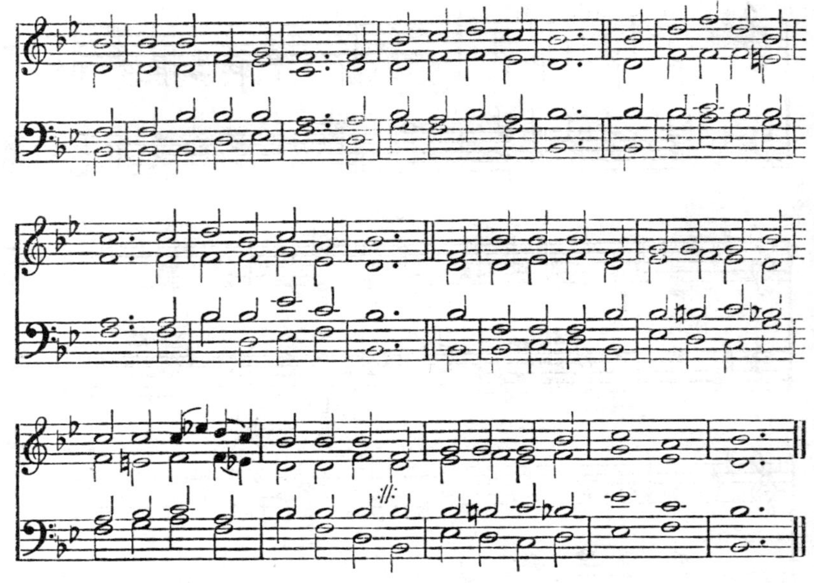

PART II

JOIN all the glorious names
  Of wisdom, love, and power,
That mortals ever knew,
  That angels ever bore:
All are too mean to speak His worth,
Too mean to set my Saviour forth.

2 Jesus, my great High Priest,
  Offered His blood and died:
My guilty conscience seeks
  No sacrifice beside:
His powerful blood did once atone,
And now it pleads before the throne.

3 To this dear Surety's hand
  Will I commit the cause;
He answers, and fulfils
  His Father's broken laws:
Behold my soul at freedom set!
My Surety paid the dreadful debt.

4 My Advocate appears
  For my defence on high;
The Father bows His ears
  And lays His thunder by:
Not all that hell or sin can say
Shall turn His heart, His love away.

5 Now let my soul arise
  And tread the tempter down;
My Captain leads me forth
  To conquest and a crown.
The feeblest saint shall win the day,
Though death and hell obstruct the
    way.

6 Should all the hosts of death
  And powers of hell unknown,
Put their most dreadful forms
  Of rage and mischief on,
I shall be safe, for Christ displays
Superior power, and guardian-grace.

Isaac Watts, 1674–1748

This hymn may also be sung to **St. John**, No. 57

His Glory, Name and Praise

MILLENNIUM 66.66.88

Source unknown

1. L ET earth and heaven agree,
   Angels and men be joined,
To celebrate with me
   The Saviour of mankind;
To adore the all-atoning Lamb,
And bless the sound of Jesu's name.

2. Jesus, transporting sound!
   The joy of earth and heaven;
No other help is found,
   No other name is given,
By which we can salvation have;
But Jesus came the world to save.

3. His name the sinner hears,
   And is from sin set free;
'Tis music in his ears,
   'Tis life and victory;
New songs do now his lips employ,
And dances his glad heart for joy.

4. Stung by the scorpion sin,
   My poor expiring soul
The healing sound drinks in,
   And is at once made whole:
See there my Lord upon the tree!
I hear, I feel, He died for me.

5. Oh for a trumpet voice,
   On all the world to call!
To bid their hearts rejoice
   In Him who died for all;
For all my Lord was crucified,
For all, for all my Saviour died.

Charles Wesley, 1770–88

240

RHUDDLAN 87.87.87.

Welsh Traditional Melody

240

Lord, enthroned in heavenly splen-
 dour,
 First-begotten from the dead,
Thou alone, our strong defender,
 Liftest up Thy people's head.
  Alleluia, Alleluia,
 Jesus, true and living bread!

2 Prince of life, for us Thou livest,
 By Thy body souls are healed;
Prince of peace, Thy peace Thou
 givest,
 By Thy blood is pardon sealed;
  Alleluia, Alleluia,
 Word of God, in flesh revealed.

3 Paschal Lamb! Thine offering
 finished,
 Once for all, when Thou wast slain,
In its fulness undiminished

Shall for evermore remain,
 Alleluia, Alleluia,
Cleansing souls from every stain.

4 Great High Priest of our profession,
 Through the veil Thou enteredst in;
By Thy mighty intercession
 Grace and mercy Thou dost win:
  Alleluia, Alleluia,
 Only sacrifice for sin.

5 Life-imparting heavenly manna,
 Stricken rock, with streaming side,
Heaven and earth, with loud hosanna,
 Worship Thee, the Lamb who died;
  Alleluia, Alleluia,
 Risen, ascended, glorified!

George Hugh Bourne, 1840–1925

This hymn may also be sung to **Westminster Abbey**, No. 619

241

Tune at foot of next page

Lord Jesus, to tell of Thy love,
 Our souls shall for ever delight;
And join with the blessèd above
 In praises by day and by night.

2 Wherever we follow Thee, Lord,
 Admiring, adoring, we see
That love which was stronger than
 death,
 Flow out without limit, and free.

3 Descending from glory on high,
 With men Thy delight was to dwell;
Contented, our Surety to die,
 By dying to save us from hell;

4 Enduring the grief and the shame,
 And bearing our sins on the cross,
Oh who would not boast of this love,
 And count the world's glory but
 loss!

Thomas Haweis, 1733–1820

ASCALON 668.D

Silesian Melody

My heart and voice I raise,
  To spread Messiah's praise;
Messiah's praise let all repeat;
  The universal Lord,
  By whose almighty word
Creation rose in form complete.

2 A servant's form He wore,
  And in His body bore
Our dreadful curse on Calvary:
  He like a victim stood,
  And poured His sacred blood,
To set the guilty captives free.

3 But soon the victor rose
  Triumphant o'er His foes,
And led the vanquished host in
    chains:
  He threw their empire down,
  His foes compelled to own
O'er all the great Messiah reigns.

4 Hail, Saviour, Prince of Peace!
  Thy kingdom shall increase,
Till all the world Thy glory see,
  And righteousness abound
  As the great deep profound,
And fill the earth with purity.

Benjamin Rhodes, 1743–1815

Words at foot of previous page

CELESTE 88.88

Lancashire Sunday School Songs. 1857 241

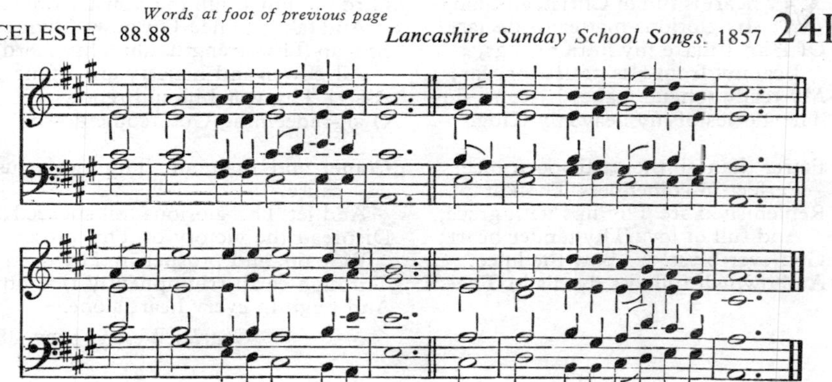

CAREY (SURREY)   88.88.88   Melody by H. CAREY, *c.* 1692-1743

MY heart is full of Christ, and longs
   Its glorious matter to declare!
Of Him I make my loftier songs,
   I cannot from His praise forbear;
My ready tongue makes haste to sing
The glories of my heavenly King.

2 Fairer than all the earth-born race,
   Perfect in comeliness Thou art;
Replenished are Thy lips with grace,
   And full of love Thy tender heart;
God ever blest! we bow the knee,
And own all fullness dwells in Thee.

3 Gird on Thy thigh the Spirit's sword,
   And take to Thee Thy power divine;
Stir up Thy strength, almighty Lord,
   All power and majesty are Thine:
Assert Thy worship and renown;
O all-redeeming God, come down!

4 Come, and maintain Thy righteous
     cause,
   And let Thy glorious toil succeed;
Dispread the victory of Thy cross,
   Ride on, and prosper in Thy deed;
Through earth triumphantly ride on,
And reign in every heart alone.

Charles Wesley, 1707–88

BLAENCEFN 87.87.47

J. THOMAS, 1839-1921

MY Redeemer, oh what beauties
  In that lovely name appear;
None but Jesus, in His glories,
  Shall the honoured title wear:
    My Redeemer,
  Thou hast my salvation wrought.

2 Sunk in ruin, sin, and misery,
  Bound by Satan's captive chain,
Guided by his artful treachery,
  Hurrying on to endless pain;
    My Redeemer
  Plucked me as a brand from hell.

3 Mine by covenant, mine for ever,
  Mine by oath, and mine by blood,
Mine—nor time the bond shall sever,
  Mine as an unchanging God:
    My Redeemer!
  Oh, how sweet to call Thee mine!

4 When in heaven I see Thy glory,
  When before Thy throne I bow,
Perfectly I shall be like Thee,
  Fully Thy redemption know:
    My Redeemer
  Then shall hear me shout His praise.

Author unknown

This hymn may also be sung to **Cwm Rhondda**, No. 383

245

TAL-Y-LLYN 76.76.D

Welsh Hymn Melody

MY song shall be of Jesus;
  His mercy crowns my days,
He fills my cup with blessings,
  And tunes my heart to praise:
My song shall be of Jesus,
  The precious Lamb of God,
Who gave Himself my ransom,
  And bought me with His blood.

2 My song shall be of Jesus,
  When, sitting at His feet,
I call to mind His goodness,
  In meditation sweet:

My song shall be of Jesus,
  Whatever ill betide;
I'll sing the grace that saves me,
  And keeps me at His side.

3 My song shall be of Jesus,
  While pressing on my way
To reach the blissful region
  Of pure and perfect day:
And when my soul shall enter
  The gate of Eden fair,
A song of praise to Jesus
  I'll sing for ever there.

Frances Jane van Alstyne, 1820–1915

246 NOTTINGHAM 77.77

School of MOZART

NAME of Jesus! highest name!
  Name that earth and heaven
    adore;
From the heart of God it came,
  Leads me to God's heart once more:

2 Name of Jesus! living tide!
  Days of drought for me are past;
How much more than satisfied
  Are the thirsty lips at last.

3 Name of Jesus! dearest name!
  Bread of heaven, and balm of love;
Oil of gladness, surest claim
  To the treasures stored above.

4 Jesus gives forgiveness free,
  Jesus cleanses all my stains;
Jesus gives His life to me,
  Jesus always He remains.

5 Only Jesus! fairest name!
  Life, and rest, and peace, and bliss;
Jesus, evermore the same,
  He is mine and I am His.

Gerhard Tersteegen, 1697–1769
tr. Emma Frances Bevan, 1827–1909

This hymn may also be sung to **Innocents,** No. 213

ELLASGARTH   8.10.10.4   PEGGY SPENCER PALMER, b. 1900   247

NONE other Lamb, none other name,
  None other hope in heaven or
    earth or sea,
None other hiding-place from guilt
    and shame,
    None beside Thee.

2 My faith burns low, my hope burns
    low;
  Only my heart's desire cries out in
    me,
By the deep thunder of its want and
    woe,
    Cries out to Thee.

3 Lord, Thou art life, though I be dead,
  Love's fire Thou art, however cold
    I be:
Nor heaven have I, nor place to lay
    my head,
    Nor home, but Thee.

Christina Georgina Rossetti, 1830–94

LYNTON C.M.   A. J. Jamouneau, 1865–1927

O BLESSED Lord, what hast Thou
    done!
How vast a ransom paid!
Who could conceive God's only Son
    Upon the altar laid?

2 Thy Father, in His gracious love,
    Did spare Thee from His side;
And Thou didst stoop to bear above,
    At such a cost, Thy Bride.

3 Lord! while our souls in faith repose
    Upon thy precious blood,
Peace, like an even river, flows,
    And mercy, like a flood.

4 But boundless joy shall fill our hearts,
    When, gazing on Thy face,
We fully see what faith imparts,
    And glory crowns Thy grace.

5 Unseen, we love Thee—dear Thy
    name,
But when our eyes behold,
With joyful wonder we'll exclaim,
    "The half had not been told!"

6 For thou exceedest all the fame
    Our ears have ever heard;
How happy we who know Thy name,
    And trust Thy faithful word!

Mary Bowly Peters, 1813–56

ARIEL 886.D

L. MASON, 1792-1872

OH, could I speak the matchless worth,
Oh, could I sound the glories forth
  Which in my Saviour shine:
I'd soar, and touch the heavenly strings,
And vie with Gabriel while he sings
  In notes almost divine.

2 I'd sing the precious blood He spilt,
My ransom from the dreadful guilt
  Of sin, and wrath divine.
I'd sing His glorious righteousness,
In which all-perfect, heavenly dress
  My soul shall ever shine.

3 I'd sing the characters He bears,
And all the forms of love He wears,
  Exalted on His throne.
In loftiest songs of sweetest praise,
I would to everlasting days
  Make all His glories known.

4 Soon the delightful day will come,
When my dear Lord will take me home
  And I shall see His face;
Then, with my Saviour, Lord and Friend,
A blest eternity I'll spend,
  Triumphant in His grace!

Samuel Medley, 1738–99

250

FIRST TUNE
GODRE'R COED   C.M.
M. W. DAVIES
SECOND TUNE
LYNGHAM   C.M.
T. JARMAN, 1776-1861

OH for a thousand tongues to sing
  My great Redeemer's praise;
The glories of my God and King,
  The triumphs of His grace.

2 My gracious Master and my God,
    Assist me to proclaim,
  To spread through all the earth
    abroad
  The honours of Thy name.

3 Jesus! the name that charms our fears,
    That bids our sorrows cease;
  'Tis music in the sinner's ears,
    'Tis life, and health, and peace.

4 He speaks, and, listening to His voice,
    New life the dead receive,
  The mournful, broken hearts rejoice,
    The humble poor believe.

5 Hear Him, ye deaf; His praise, ye
      dumb,
    Your loosened tongues employ;
  Ye blind, behold your Saviour come;
    And leap, ye lame, for joy.

6 He breaks the power of cancelled sin,
    He sets the prisoner free:
  His blood can make the foulest clean,
    His blood avails for me.

Charles Wesley, 1707–88

This hymn may also be sung to **Lydia**, No. 233

251

WARWICK C.M.   S. STANLEY, 1767-1822

O JESUS, King most wonderful,
    Thou conqueror renowned,
Thou sweetness most ineffable,
  In whom all joys are found!

2 When once Thou visitest the heart,
    Then truth begins to shine,
  Then earthly vanities depart,
    Then kindles love divine.

3 Jesus, Thy mercies are untold
    Through each returning day;
  Thy love exceeds a thousandfold
    The best that we can say.

4 May every heart confess Thy name,
    And ever Thee adore;
  And, seeking Thee, itself inflame
    To seek Thee more and more.

5 Thee may our tongues for ever bless,
    Thee may we love alone;
  And ever in our lives express
    The image of Thine own!

6 Grant us, while here on earth we stay,
    Thy love to feel and know;
  And when from hence we pass away,
    To us Thy glory show.

(attrib. to) Bernard of Clairvaux, 1091–1153 *tr. Edward Caswall,* 1814–78

This hymn may also be sung to **Abridge**, No. 128

252

GWENGAR S.M.

J. PARRY, 1841-1903

O PERFECT life of love!
　　All, all is finished now,
All that He left His Throne above
　　To do for us below.

2　No work is left undone
　　Of all the Father willed;
His toil, His sorrows, one by one,
　　The Scriptures have fulfilled.

3　No pain that we can share
　　But He has felt its smart;
All forms of human grief and care
　　Have pierced His tender heart.

4　And on His thorn-crowned head,
　　And on His sinless soul,
Our sins in all their guilt were laid
　　That He might make us whole.

5　In perfect love He dies;
　　For me He dies, for me;
O all-atoning Sacrifice,
　　I cling by faith to Thee.

6　In every time of need,
　　Before the judgment-throne,
Thy work, O Lamb of God, I'll plead,
　　The merits, not my own.

7　Yet work, O Lord, in me
　　As Thou for me hast wrought;
And let my love the answer be
　　To grace Thy love has brought.

Henry Williams Baker, 1821–77

253

DALEHURST C.M.

A. COTTMAN, 1841-79

O SACRED name! O name of power!
  What grace therein doth shine;
I'll treasure with each passing hour,
  Its memories sublime.

2 It tells of the Unchangeable,
  The Faithful and the True,
Incarnate God, Immanuel—
  Oh wonder ever new.

3 It tells me of the sinner's Friend,
  Whose blood has set me free;
But never can I comprehend
  His deep, deep love for me.

4 It tells me of the risen Lord,
  Who now in heaven appears;
And by His Spirit and His Word,
  Calms all my doubts and fears.

5 It tells me of the Advocate,
  Who pleads before the Throne
My cause, though dark and intricate,
  As though it were His own.

6 It tells me of eternal rest,
  Beneath a cloudless sky;
Oh happy souls, divinely blest,
  With Jesus ever nigh!

Charles Russell Hurditch, b. 1840

ST. SAVIOUR C.M.   F. G. BAKER, 1840-1919 **254**

O SAVING name! O name of power!
  The very soul of rest!
Our claim upon Jehovah's heart—
  We plead Thee, and are blest.

2 O name of peace—mysterious name;
  In Thee doth conflict end;
Mercy and truth, in Thee agreed,
  Eternally do blend.

3 O name of balm, where conscience finds
  A cure for every woe;
Where healing ointments aye are found,
  And cleansing waters flow.

4 O fragrant name, for ever full
  Of odours rare and choice,
Where God doth find such incense sweet
  As makes His heart rejoice.

5 Name of renown, the psalm of heaven,
  The very soul of rest!
Jesus, Thy name adoringly
  We plead, and we are blest.

Author unknown

GLORIA   76.76.D   J. H. BURKE

O SAVIOUR, precious Saviour,
  Whom yet unseen we love,
O name of might and favour,
  All other names above,
    We worship Thee, we bless Thee,
      To Thee alone we sing;
    We praise Thee, and confess Thee
    Our holy Lord and King!

2 O bringer of salvation,
  Who wondrously hast wrought,
Thyself the revelation
  Of love beyond our thought,
    We worship Thee, we bless Thee,
      To Thee alone we sing;
    We praise Thee, and confess Thee
    Our gracious Lord and King!

3 In Thee all fullness dwelleth,
  All grace and power divine;
The glory that excelleth,
  O Son of God, is Thine,
    We worship Thee, we bless Thee,
      To Thee alone we sing;
    We praise Thee, and confess Thee
    Our glorious Lord and King!

4 Oh, grant the consummation
  Of this our song above
In endless adoration
  And everlasting love!
    Then shall we praise and bless Thee
    Where perfect praises ring,
    And evermore confess Thee
    Our Saviour and our King!

Frances Ridley Havergal, 1836–79

His Glory, Name and Praise

BODMIN L.M.

ALFRED SCOTT-GATTY, 1847-1918

O THOU my soul forget no more
  The Friend who all thy misery
bore;
Let every idol be forgot,
But, O my soul, forget Him not.

2 Jesus for thee a body takes,
Thy guilt assumes, thy fetters breaks,
Discharging all thy dreadful debt;
And canst thou e'er such love forget?

3 Renounce thy works and ways with
  grief,
And cleave to this most sure relief;
Nor Him forget who left His throne,
And for thy life gave up His own.

4 Infinite truth and mercy shine
In Him, and He Himself is thine;
And canst thou then, with sin beset,
Such charms, such matchless charms,
  forget?

5 Ah no, till life itself depart,
His name shall cheer and warm my
  heart;
And shouting this from earth I'll rise,
And join the chorus of the skies.

Krishna Pal, 1764–1822
tr. Joshua Marshman, 1768–1837

This hymn may also be sung to **Abends,** No. 297

257

BYZANTIUM C.M.

T. Jackson, 1715-81

"PRAISE ye the Lord," again, again,
   The Spirit strikes the chord;
Nor toucheth He our hearts in vain;
   We praise, we praise the Lord.

2 "Rejoice in Him," again, again,
   The Spirit speaks the word;
And faith takes up the happy strain;
   Our joy is in the Lord.

3 "Stand fast in Christ;" ah, yet again,
   He teaches all the band;
Since human efforts are in vain,
   In Christ it is we stand.

4 "Clean every whit;" Thou saidst it,
    Lord;
   Shall one suspicion lurk?
Thine, surely, is a faithful word,
   And Thine a finished work.

5 For ever be the glory given
   To Thee, O Lamb of God!
Our every joy on earth, in heaven,
   We owe it to Thy blood.

Mary Bowly Peters, 1813–56

This hymn may also be sung to **St. Saviour**, No. 94

LÜBECK 77.77   FREYLINGHAUSEN's *Gesangbuch*, 1704

SWEETER sounds than music knows,
    Charm me in Immanuel's name;
All her hopes my spirit owes
    To His birth, and cross, and shame.

2 When He came, the angels sung,
    "Glory be to God on high:"
Lord, unloose my stammering tongue;
    Who should louder sing than I?

3 Did the Lord a man become
    That He might the law fulfil,
Bleed and suffer in my room—
    And canst thou, my tongue, be still!

4 No! I must my praises bring,
    Though they worthless are and
        weak;
For should I refuse to sing,
    Sure the very stones would speak.

5 O my Saviour, Shield, and Sun,
    Shepherd, Prophet, Priest and
        Friend!
Every precious name in one;
    I will love Thee without end.

John Newton, 1725–1807

This hymn may also be sung to **Monkland**, No. 29

259

SARON C.M.

T. HUGHES, 1870-1910

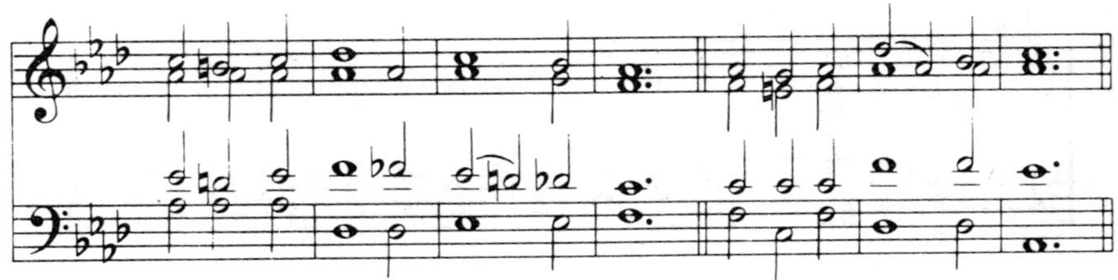

THERE is a name I love to hear,
I love to speak its worth;
It sounds like music in mine ear,
The sweetest name on earth.

2 It tells me of a Saviour's love,
Who died to set me free;
It tells me of His precious blood,
The sinner's perfect plea.

3 It tells me of a Father's smile
Beaming upon His child;
It cheers me through "this little
while,"
Through desert, waste, and wild.

4 It tells of One whose loving heart
Can feel my smallest woe;
Who in each sorrow bears a part,
That none can bear below.

5 It bids my trembling soul rejoice,
It dries each rising tear;
It tells me, in a "still small voice,"
To trust and never fear.

6 Jesus! the name I love so well,
The name I love to hear;
No saint on earth its worth can tell,
No heart conceive how dear.

Frederick Whitfield, 1829–1904

This hymn may also be sung to **St. Botolph,** No. 428

ALLHALLOWS C.M. *Attributed to S. Webbe, 1740-1816*

THERE is a name—one only name,
  On which the soul can rest;
The trusting heart makes this its claim,
  And is for ever blest.

2 There is a name, the sweetest name;
  Let us in this draw nigh;
The veil is rent, the way is made
  To God beyond the sky.

3 There is a name—it is our plea
  Before the Father's throne;
Of all His gifts, this is the key
  Which makes them all our own.

4 No burning mount, no thunder's roar,
  Shall fright one soul away;
No foe can shut that open door,
  Since Jesus is the way.

5 Oh plead His name, His precious
    name,
  With boldness at the throne;
For all He has, and all we need,
  Himself has made our own.

Author unknown

261

SUPREMACY 86.86.88

FIRST TUNE

NORMAN TOMBLIN b. 1907

His Glory, Name and Praise

PALMYRA 86.86.88   Second Tune   Joseph Summers, 1843-1916

Thou art the Everlasting Word,
  The Father's only Son,
God manifestly seen and heard,
  And heaven's belovèd One.
Worthy, O Lamb of God, art Thou,
That every knee to Thee should bow.

2 In Thee most perfectly expressed
  The Father's glories shine,
Of the full deity possessed,
  Eternally divine!

3 True image of the infinite,
  Whose essence is concealed;
Brightness of uncreated light,
  The heart of God revealed.

4 But the high mysteries of Thy name
  An angel's grasp transcend;
The Father only (glorious claim!)
  The Son can comprehend.

5 Yet loving Thee, on whom His love
  Ineffable doth rest,
Thy members all, in Thee—above,
  As one with Thee are blest!

6 Throughout the universe of bliss
  The centre Thou, and sun,
The eternal theme of praise is this,
  To Heaven's belovèd one.

Josiah Conder, 1789-1855

262

BROTHER JAMES' AIR   C.M.

Arr. by F. A. J. Tonkin, b. 1926

THOU dear Redeemer, dying Lamb!
  We love to sing of Thee;
No music's like Thy charming name,
  Nor half so sweet can be.

2 Our Jesus shall be still our theme,
    While in this world we stay;
  We'll sing our Jesu's lovely name,
    When all things else decay.

3 When we appear in yonder cloud,
    With all the favoured throng,
  Then will we sing more sweet, more
      loud,
    And Christ shall be our song.

John Cennick, 1718–55

This hymn may also be sung to **Hensbury,** No. 417

His Glory, Name and Praise

263

STELLA   88.88.88

Melody from *Easy Tunes for Catholic Schools*, 1852

THOU hidden Source of calm repose,
  Thou all-sufficient love divine,
My help and refuge from my foes,
  Secure I am, if Thou art mine;
From sin and grief, from guilt and
    shame,
  I hide me, Jesus, in Thy name.

2 Thy mighty name salvation is,
  And keeps my happy soul above:
Comfort it brings, and power and
    peace,
  And joy and everlasting love:
To me, with Thy dear name are given
  Pardon and holiness and heaven.

3 Jesus, my all in all Thou art,
  My rest in toil, mine ease in pain;
The medicine of my broken heart;
  In war, my peace; in loss, my gain;
My smile beneath the tyrant's frown;
  In shame, my glory and my crown.

4 In want, my plentiful supply;
  In weakness, my almighty power;
In bonds, my perfect liberty;
  My light in Satan's darkest hour;
My help and stay whene'er I call,
  My life in death, my heaven, my all.

Charles Wesley, 1707–88

264

MANOAH C.M.

G. A. Rossini, 1792-1868

To Christ the Lord let every tongue
    Its noblest tribute bring;
Himself the subject of our song,
    What joy it is to sing!

2 Behold the beauties of His face,
    And on His glories dwell;
Think of the wonders of His grace,
    And all His triumphs tell.

3 Majestic sweetness sits enthroned
    Upon the Saviour's brow;
His head with radiant glories crowned,
    His lips with grace o'erflow.

4 No mortal can with Him compare
    Among the sons of men;
Fairer is He than all the fair
    That fill the heavenly train.

5 He saw me plunged in deep distress,
    He flew to my relief;
For me He bore the shameful cross,
    And carried all my grief.

6 To Him I owe my life and breath,
    And all the joys I have;
He makes me triumph over death,
    He saves me from the grave.

7 To heaven, the place of His abode,
    He brings my weary feet;
Shows me the glories of my God,
    And makes my joy complete.

8 Since from His bounty I receive
    Such proofs of love divine,
Had I a thousand hearts to give,
    Lord, they should all be Thine!

Samuel Stennett, 1727–95

His Glory, Name and Praise

CHRISTCHURCH 66.66.88

C. STEGGALL, 1826-1905

WE come, O Christ, to Thee,
  True Son of God and man,
By whom all things consist,
  In whom all life began:
In Thee alone we live and move,
And have our being in Thy love.

2 Thou art the.Way to God,
  Thy blood our ransom paid;
In Thee we face our Judge
  And Maker unafraid.
Before the throne absolved we stand:
Thy love has met Thy law's demand.

3 Thou art the living Truth!
  All wisdom dwells in Thee,
Thou source of every skill,
  Eternal verity!
Thou great I AM! In Thee we rest,
True answer to our every quest.

4 Thou only art true Life,
  To know Thee is to live
The more abundant life
  That earth can never give:
O risen Lord! We live in Thee
And Thou in us eternally!

5 We worship Thee, O Christ,
  Our Saviour and our King,
To Thee our youth and strength
  Adoringly we bring:
So fill our hearts that men may see
Thy life in us and turn to Thee!

E. Margaret Clarkson, b. 1915

WHO IS HE? 77. and refrain

B. R. HANBY, 1833-67

WHO is He in yonder stall,
At whose feet the shepherds fall?
'Tis the Lord! Oh wondrous story!
'Tis the Lord, the King of Glory!
At His feet we humbly fall—
Crown Him, crown Him, Lord of all!

2 Who is He in deep distress,
Fasting in the wilderness?

3 Who is He to whom they bring
All the sick and sorrowing?

4 Who is He who stands and weeps
At the grave where Lazarus sleeps?

5 Who is He the gathering throng
Greet with loud triumphant song?

6 Lo! at midnight, who is He
Prays in dark Gethsemane?

7 Who is He on yonder tree
Dies in grief and agony?

8 Who is He who from the grave
Comes to succour, help, and save?

9 Who is He who from His throne
Rules through all the worlds alone?

Benjamin Russell Hanby, 1833–67

DOWN AMPNEY 66.11.D   R. VAUGHAN WILLIAMS, 1872-1958

COME down, O Love Divine,
　Seek Thou this soul of mine,
And visit it with Thine own ardour
　glowing;
　O Comforter, draw near,
　Within my heart appear,
And kindle it, Thy holy flame
　bestowing.

2　O let it freely burn,
　Till earthly passions turn
To dust and ashes, in its heat con-
　suming;
　And let Thy glorious light
　Shine ever on my sight,
And clothe me round, the while my
　path illuming.

3　Let holy charity
　Mine outward vesture be,
And lowliness become mine inner
　clothing;
　True lowliness of heart,
　Which takes the humbler part,
And o'er its own shortcomings weeps
　with loathing.

4　And so the yearning strong,
　With which the soul will long,
Shall far outpass the power of human
　telling;
　For none can guess its grace,
　Till he become the place
Wherein the Holy Spirit makes His
　dwelling.

Bianco da Siena, d. 1434
tr. Richard Frederick Littledale,
1833-90

268

BOD ALWYN S.M.

DAVID JENKINS, 1848–1915

B REATHE on me, Breath of God,
  Fill me with life anew,
That I may love what Thou dost love,
  And do what Thou wouldst do.

2 Breathe on me, Breath of God,
  Until my heart is pure;
Until with Thee I will one will,
  To do and to endure.

3 Breathe on me, Breath of God,
  Till I am wholly Thine;
Until this earthly part of me
  Glows with Thy fire divine.

4 Breathe on me, Breath of God,
  So shall I never die,
But live with Thee the perfect life
  Of Thine eternity.

Edwin Hatch, 1835–89

269

HOLYROOD S.M.

JAMES WATSON, 1816-1880
Adaptation by ROBIN SHELDON, b. 1932

LORD God the Holy Ghost,
  In this accepted hour,
As on the day of Pentecost,
  Descend in all Thy power.

2 We meet with one accord
  In our appointed place,
And wait the promise of our Lord,
  The Spirit of all grace.

3 Like mighty rushing wind
  Upon the waves beneath,
Move with one impulse every mind,
  One soul, one feeling, breathe.

4 The young, the old, inspire
  With wisdom from above;
And give us hearts and tongues of fire.
  To pray and praise and love.

5 Spirit of light, explore,
  And chase our gloom away—
With lustre shining more and more,
  Unto the perfect.day.

6 Spirit of truth, be Thou
  In life and death our guide;
O Spirit of adoption, now
  May we be sanctified.

James Montgomery, 1771–1854

270

ST. STEPHEN   C.M.

WILLIAM JONES, 1726-1800

COME, Holy Ghost, our hearts
  inspire;
  Let us Thine influence prove,
Source of the old prophetic fire,
  Fountain of light and love.

2 Come, Holy Ghost, for moved by
  Thee
  The prophets wrote and spoke;
Unlock the truth, Thyself the key,
  Unseal the sacred Book.

3 Expand Thy wings, celestial Dove,
  Brood o'er our nature's night;
On our disordered spirits move,
  And let there now be light.

4 God, through Himself, we then shall
  know
  If Thou within us shine;
And sound, with all Thy saints below,
  The depths of love divine.

Charles Wesley, 1707–88

271

ABERGELE C.M.

J. AMBROSE LLOYD, 1815-74

SPIRIT divine, attend our prayers
   And make this house Thy home;
Descend with all Thy gracious powers,
   Oh, come, great Spirit, come!

2 Come as the light: to us reveal
   Our emptiness and woe;
And lead us in those paths of life
   Where all the righteous go.

3 Come as the fire, and purge our
     hearts
   Like sacrificial flame;
Let our whole soul an offering be
   To our Redeemer's name.

4 Come as the dew, and sweetly bless
   This consecrated hour;
May barrenness rejoice to own
   Thy fertilizing power.

5 Come as the dove, and spread Thy
     wings,
   The wings of perfect love;
And let Thy church on earth become
   Blest as the church above.

6 Spirit divine, attend our prayers;
   Make a lost world Thy home;
Descend with all Thy gracious powers.
   Oh, come, Great Spirit, come!

Andrew Reed, 1787–1862

272

ROCHESTER C.M.

C. H. STEWART, 1884-1932

SPIRIT of holiness, do Thou
  Dwell in this soul of mine;
Possess my heart and make me know
  A sanctity divine.

2 Spirit of truth, Thy Word reveal,
  Its treasures open wide;
Lead me to see my Father's will,
  And in that will abide.

3 Spirit of Jesus, glorify
  The Master's name in me;
Whether I live or if I die,
  Let Christ exalted be.

4 Spirit of love, Thy best of gifts
  Upon Thy servant pour;
Love, which another's burden lifts
  And serves God every hour.

James Holroyde, b. 1850

GALILEE L.M.   P. ARMES, 1836-1908 273

COME, gracious Spirit, heavenly dove,
With light and comfort from above;
Be Thou our guardian, Thou our guide,
O'er every thought and step preside.

2 Conduct us safe, conduct us far
  From every sin and hurtful snare;
Lead to Thy Word, which rules must give,
  And teach us lessons how to live.

3 The light of truth to us display,
  And make us know and choose Thy way;
Plant holy fear in every heart,
  That we from God may ne'er depart.

4 Lead us to Christ, the living Way,
  Nor let us from His pastures stray;
Lead us to holiness, the road
  That we must take to dwell with God.

5 Lead us to heaven, that we may share
  Fullness of joy for ever there;
Lead us to God, our final rest,
  To be with Him for ever blest.

Simon Browne, c. 1680–1732, and others

274

CALM L.M.

J. B. Dykes, 1823-76

O BREATH of God, breathe on us now,
And move within us while we pray;
The spring of our new life art Thou,
The very light of our new day.

2 Oh strangely art Thou with us, Lord,
Neither in height nor depth to seek;
In nearness shall Thy voice be heard;
Spirit to spirit Thou dost speak.

3 Christ is our Advocate on high;
Thou art our Advocate within;
Oh plead the truth, and make reply
To every argument of sin.

4 But ah, this faithless heart of mine!
The way I know; I know my guide:
Forgive me, O my Friend divine,
That I so often turn aside.

5 Be with me when no other friend
The mystery of my heart can share;
And be Thou known, when fears transcend,
By Thy best name of Comforter.

Alfred Henry Vine, 1845-1917

276 STUTTGART 87.87

Melody by C. F. Witt, c. 1660-1716

Words at foot of next page

HEREFORD L.M.

S. S. WESLEY, 1810-76

O THOU who dost direct my feet
    To right or left where path-
ways part,
Wilt Thou not, faithful Paraclete,
    Direct the journeying of my heart?

2 Into the love of God, I pray,
    Deeper and deeper let me press,
Exploring all along the way
    Its secret strength and tenderness.

3 Into the steadfastness of One
    Who patiently endured the cross,
Of Him who, though He were a Son,
    Came to His crown through bitter
    loss.

4 This is the road of my desire—
    Learning to love as God loves me,
Ready to pass through flood or fire
    With Christ's unwearying con-
    stancy.

Frank Houghton, 1894–1972

Tune at foot of previous page

276

COME, Thou everlasting Spirit,
    Bring to every thankful mind
All the Saviour's dying merit,
    All His sufferings for mankind:

2 True Recorder of His passion,
    Now the living faith impart,
Now reveal His great salvation,
    Preach His gospel to our heart.

3 Come, Thou Witness of His dying;
    Come, Remembrancer divine,
Let us feel Thy power, applying
    Christ to every soul, and mine.

Charles Wesley, 1707–88

This hymn may also be sung to **Sicilian Mariners,** No. 372

277

BUCKLAND 77.77   FIRST TUNE   L. G. HAYNE, 1836-83

HOLY Spirit, Truth divine,
Dawn upon this soul of mine;
Word of God, and inward light,
Wake my spirit, clear my sight,

2 Holy Spirit, Love divine,
Glow within this heart of mine,
Kindle every high desire,
Perish self in Thy pure fire.

3 Holy Spirit, Power divine,
Fill and nerve this will of mine:
By Thee may I strongly live,
Bravely bear, and nobly strive.

4 Holy Spirit, Law divine,
Reign within this soul of mine;
Be my law, and I shall be
Firmly bound, for ever free.

5 Holy Spirit, Peace divine,
Still this restless heart of mine,
Speak to calm this tossing sea,
Stayed in Thy tranquility.

6 Holy Spirit, Joy divine,
Gladden Thou this heart of mine;
In the desert ways I'll sing:
Spring, O well, for ever spring!

Samuel Longfellow, 1819–92

SECOND TUNE

CULBACH 77.77   SCHEFFLER'S *Heilige Seelenlust*, 1657

CAREY (SURREY) 88.88.88   Melody by H. CAREY, *c.* 1692-1743

CREATOR Spirit, by whose aid
The world's foundations first
 were laid,
Come, visit every waiting mind,
Come, pour Thy joys on human kind;
From sin and sorrow set us free
And make Thy temples worthy Thee.

2 O Source of uncreated light,
 The Father's promised Paraclete,
 Thrice holy fount, thrice holy fire,
 Our hearts with heavenly love inspire;
 Come, and Thy sacred unction bring,
 To sanctify us while we sing.

3 Plenteous of grace, descend from high,
 Rich in Thy sevenfold energy:
 Thou strength of His almighty hand
 Whose power doth heaven and earth
  command,
 Give us Thyself, that we may see
 The Father and the Son by Thee.

4 Immortal honour, endless fame,
 Attend the almighty Father's name;
 The Saviour Son be glorified,
 Who for lost man's redemption died;
 And equal adoration be,
 Eternal Paraclete, to Thee!

Latin Hymn, 9th cent.
tr. John Dryden, 1631-1700

This hymn may also be sung to **Melita**, No. 503

279

SHREWSBURY 86.84

J. E. HUNT, 1903-1958

OUR blest Redeemer, ere He breathed
  His tender last farewell,
A Guide, a Comforter, bequeathed
  With us to dwell.

2 He came in semblance of a dove,
    With sheltering wings outspread,
  The holy balm of peace and love
    On earth to shed.

3 He came in tongues of living flame,
    To teach, convince, subdue;
  All-powerful as the wind he came,
    As viewless too.

4 He comes sweet influence to impart,
    A gracious, willing guest,
  Where He can find one humble heart
    Wherein to rest.

5 And His that gentle voice we hear,
    Soft as the breath of even
  That checks each fault, that calms
    each fear,
    And speaks of heaven.

6 And ev'ry virtue we possess,
    And ev'ry victory won,
  And ev'ry thought of holiness,
    Are His alone.

7 Spirit of purity and grace,
    Our weakness pitying see;
  Oh make our hearts thy dwelling-
    place,
  And worthier Thee.

Henriette Auber, 1773-1862

This hymn may also be sung to **St. Cuthbert**, No. 135

SPIRITUS VITAE 98.98

O BREATH of Life, come sweeping
through us,
Revive Thy church with life and
power;
O Breath of Life, come, cleanse,
renew us,
And fit Thy church to meet this
hour.

2 O Wind of God, come bend us, break
us,
Till humbly we confess our need;
Then in Thy tenderness remake us,
Revive, restore; for this we plead.

3 O Breath of Love, come breathe
within us,
Renewing thought and will and
heart:
Come, Love of Christ, afresh to win
us,
Revive Thy church in every part.

4 Revive us, Lord! Is zeal abating
While harvest fields are vast and
white?
Revive us, Lord, the world is waiting,
Equip Thy church to spread the
light.

Bessie Porter Head, 1850–1936

DIADEMATA D.S.M.

G. J. ELVEY, 1816-93

1. SPIRIT of faith, come down,
Reveal the things of God;
And make to us the Godhead known,
And witness with the blood.
'Tis thine the blood to apply,
And give us eyes to see
Who did for every sinner die
Hath surely died for me.

2. No man can truly say
That Jesus is the Lord,
Unless Thou take the veil away,
And breathe the living word;
Then, only then, we feel
Our interest in His blood,
And cry, with joy unspeakable:
Thou art my Lord, my God!

3. Oh that the world might know
The all-atoning Lamb!
Spirit of faith, descend, and show
The virtue of His name;
The grace which all may find,
The saving power impart;
And testify to all mankind,
And speak in every heart.

4. Inspire the living faith,
Which whosoe'er receives,
The witness in himself he hath,
And consciously believes;
That faith that conquers all,
And doth the mountain move,
And saves whoe'er on Jesus call,
And perfects them in love.

Charles Wesley, 1707–88

This hymn may also be sung to **Ascension, No. 15**

HURDLE END 10.10.10.10

B. H. MUDDITT, b. 1906
Arr. by F. A. J. TONKIN, b. 1926

BREAK Thou the bread of life,
   Dear Lord, to me,
As Thou didst break the loaves
   Beside the sea;
Beyond the sacred page
   I seek Thee, Lord;
My spirit pants for Thee,
   Thou living Word!

2 Thou art the bread of life,
   O Lord, to me,
Thy holy Word the truth
   That saveth me.
Give me to eat and live
   With Thee above;
Teach me to love Thy truth,
   For Thou art love.

3 Oh send Thy Spirit, Lord,
   Now unto me;
That He may touch my eyes
   And make me see,
Show me the truth concealed
   Within Thy Word,
And in Thy book revealed
   I see Thee, Lord.

4 Bless Thou the truth, dear Lord,
   To me, to me,
As Thou didst bless the loaves
   By Galilee;
Then shall all bondage cease,
   All fetters fall;
And I shall find my peace,
   My All in all.

Mary Artemisia Lathbury, 1841–1913
v. 3 by Alexander Groves, 1842–1909

283

SOUTHWELL C.M.

H. S. IRONS, 1834-1905

FATHER of mercies in Thy word
    What endless glory shines!
For ever be Thy name adored
    For these celestial lines.

2 Here springs of consolation rise
    To cheer the fainting mind;
And thirsty souls receive supplies,
    And sweet refreshment find.

3 Here the Redeemer's welcome voice
    Spreads heavenly peace around;
And life and everlasting joys
    Attend the blissful sound.

4 Oh may these hallowed pages be
    My ever dear delight!
And still new beauties may I see,
    And still increasing light.

5 Divine Instructor, gracious Lord,
    Be Thou for ever near;
Teach me to love Thy sacred word,
    And view my Saviour there.

Anne Steele, 1717–78

This hymn may also be sung to **Beatitudo**, No. 198

285 ROCHESTER C.M.

Words at foot of next page

C. H. STEWART, 1884-1932

JAZER C.M.　　　　　　　　　　　　　　　A. E. TOZER. 1857-1910

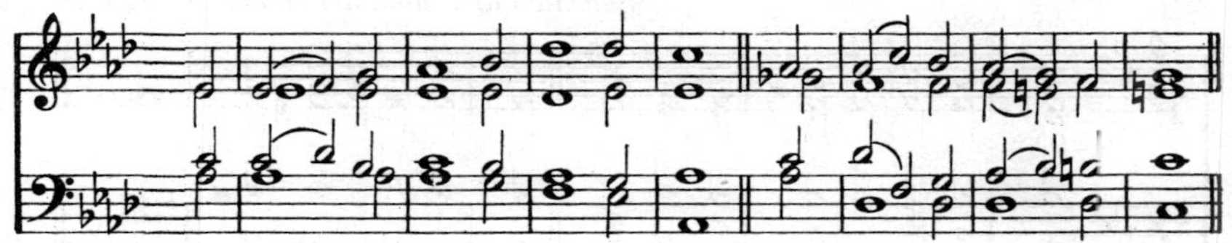

LAMP of our feet, whereby we trace
　　Our path when wont to stray;
Stream, from the fount of heavenly
　　　grace;
　　Brook, by the traveller's way:

2 Bread of our souls, whereon we feed;
　　True manna from on high;
Our guide and chart, wherein we read
　　Of realms beyond the sky:

3 Pillar of fire, through watches dark,
　　And radiant cloud by day:
When waves would whelm our tossing
　　　bark,
　　Our anchor and our stay:

4 Word of the everlasting God,
　　Will of His glorious Son,
Without thee how could earth be trod,
　　Or heaven itself be won?

5 Yet to unfold thy hidden worth,
　　Thy mysteries to reveal,
That Spirit which first gave thee
　　　forth,
　　Thy volume must unseal.

6 Lord, grant that we aright may learn
　　The wisdom it imparts,
And to its heavenly teaching turn,
　　With simple, childlike hearts.

Bernard Barton. 1784-1849

This hymn may also be sung to **Evan,** No. 70

Tune at foot of previous page　　　　285

JESUS, Thou source of true delight,
　　Whom we, unseen, adore,
Unveil our souls to all Thy light,
　　That we may love Thee more.

2 Thy glory o'er creation shines,
　　But in the sacred word
We read in fairer, brighter lines
　　The glories of our Lord.

3 'Tis here, whene'er our comforts
　　　droop,
　　And sins and sorrows rise,
Thy love, with cheerful beams of
　　　hope,
　　Each fainting heart supplies.

4 Jesus, our Lord, our life, our light,
　　Oh come with blissful ray,
Break through the gloomy shades of
　　　night,
　　And bring the looked-for day!

5 Then shall each soul with rapture
　　　trace
The wonders of Thy love,
And the full glories of Thy face
As known to those above.

Anne Steele, 1717-78

TIVERTON C.M.

GRIGG, in JOHN RIPPON'S
Selection of Psalm and Hymn Tunes, 1796

THE Spirit breathes upon the word,
  And brings the truth to sight;
Precepts and promises afford
  A sanctifying light.

2 A glory gilds the sacred page,
  Majestic, like the sun;
It gives a light to every age;
  It gives, but borrows none.

3 The hand that gave it still supplies
  The gracious light and heat;
His truths upon the nations rise;
  They rise, but never set.

4 Let everlasting thanks be Thine,
  For such a bright display,
As makes a world of darkness shine
  With beams of heavenly day.

5 My soul rejoices to pursue
  The steps of Him I love,
Till glory breaks upon my view,
  In brighter worlds above.

William Cowper, 1731–1800

This hymn may also be sung to **Holy Trinity**, No. 523

288

Words at foot of next page

LIEBSTER JESU 78.78.88

Later form of melody by J. R. AHLE, 1625-73

ST. MATTHIAS 88.88.88

W. H. MONK, 1823-89

INSPIRER of the ancient seers,
  Who wrote from Thee the sacred page,
The same through all succeeding years,
  To us, in our degenerate age,
The Spirit of Thy word impart,
And breathe Thy life into our heart.

2 Come, O Thou Prophet of the Lord,
  Thou great Interpreter divine,
Explain Thine own transmitted word;
  To teach and to inspire is Thine;
Thou only canst Thyself reveal,
Open the book, and loose the seal.

3 While now Thine oracles we read,
  With earnest prayer and strong desire,
Thy Spirit now from Thee proceed,
  Our souls to awaken and inspire,
Our weakness help, our darkness chase,
And guide us by the light of grace!

4 Lord Jesus, now the veil remove,
  The folly of our darkened heart;
Unfold the wonders of Thy love,
  The knowledge of Thyself impart;
Our ear, our inmost soul we bow:
Speak, Lord, Thy servants hearken now.   *Charles Wesley*, 1707–88

This hymn may also be sung to **Melita**, No. 503

Tune at foot of previous page

288

LORD and Saviour, at Thy word
  We are gathered now to hear Thee;
Let our minds and wills be stirred
  Thus to seek and love and fear Thee;
By Thy teachings true and holy
Drawn from earth to love Thee solely.

2 All our knowledge, sense and sight
  Lie in deepest darkness shrouded,
Till Thy Spirit banish night
  With the beams of truth unclouded;
Thou alone to God canst win us,
Thou must work all good within us.

3 Glorious Lord, Thyself impart,
  Light of light, from God proceeding,
Open Thou each mind and heart,
  Help us by the Spirit's pleading.
Hear the song Thy people raise:
Lord, accept our prayer and praise.

  Tobias Clausnitzer, 1619–84
  tr. Catherine Winkworth, 1827–78

289

RAVENSHAW 66.66 Trochaic

MICHAEL WEISSE, 1480-1534
Arr. by W. H. MONK, 1823-89

LORD, Thy word abideth,
  And our footsteps guideth;
Who its truth believeth
Light and joy receiveth.

2 When our foes are near us,
  Then Thy word will cheer us.
  Word of consolation,
  Message of salvation.

3 When the storms are o'er us,
  And dark clouds before us,
  Then its light directeth,
  And our way protecteth.

4 Who can tell the pleasure,
  Who recount the treasure,
  By Thy word imparted
  To the simple-hearted?

5 Word of mercy, giving
  Succour to the living;
  Word of life, supplying
  Comfort to the dying.

6 Oh that we discerning
  Its most holy learning,
  Lord, may love and fear Thee,
  Evermore be near Thee.

Henry Williams Baker, 1821–77

ST. ETHELWALD S.M.

W. H. MONK, 1823-89

None teacheth, Lord, like Thee,
None can such truth impart,
Such treasures from Thy word un-
fold,
Nor so impress the heart.

2 How blest Thy servants were,
When, with them on their way,
Thou did'st commune, and sweetly
chase
Their sorrows all away.

3 So now to us draw near,
And speak to every heart;
Our light in darkness, joy in grief,
And all in all, Thou art.

4 Open to us Thy word,
Thy precious thoughts reveal,
Thy purposes and ways explain,
And teach us all Thy will.

5 So shall our doubt, and fear,
And care, and grief subside,
And each enraptured heart exclaim,
"O Lord, with us abide!"

D. Webley

MANNA 886.D

Adapted from J. G. SCHICHT, 1753-1823

Not far beyond the sea nor high
Above the heavens, but very nigh
  Thy voice, O God, is heard.
For each new step of faith we take
Thou hast more truth and light to
    break
  Forth from Thy holy Word.

2 The babe in Christ Thy Scriptures
    feed
With milk sufficient for his need,
  The nurture of the Lord.
Beneath life's burden and its heat
The full-grown man finds stronger
    meat
  In Thy unfailing Word.

3 Rooted and grounded in Thy love,
With saints on earth and saints above
  We join in full accord,
To grasp the breadth, length, depth,
    and height,
The crucified and risen might
  Of Christ, the Incarnate Word.

4 Help us to press toward that mark,
And, though our vision now is dark,
  To live by what we see.
So, when we see Thee face to face,
Thy truth and light our dwelling-
    place
  For evermore shall be.

George Bradford Caird, b. 1917

BENTLEY 76.76.D · JOHN HULLAH, 1812-84

O WORD of God incarnate,
  O wisdom from on high,
O truth unchanged, unchanging,
  O light of our dark sky,
We praise Thee for the radiance,
  That from the hallowed page,
A lantern to our footsteps,
  Shines on from age to age.

2 The church from her dear Master
  Received the gift divine,
And still that light she lifteth
  O'er all the earth to shine:
It is the golden casket
  Where gems of truth are stored;
It is the heaven-drawn picture
  Of Christ, the living Word.

3 It floateth like a banner
  Before God's host unfurled;
It shineth like a beacon
  Above the darkling world:
It is the chart and compass
  That o'er life's surging sea,
Mid mists and rocks and quicksands
  Still guide, O Christ, to Thee.

4 Oh make Thy church, dear Saviour,
  A lamp of burnished gold,
To bear before the nations
  Thy true light as of old;
Oh teach Thy wandering pilgrims
  By this their path to trace,
Till, clouds and darkness ended,
  They see Thee face to face!

William Walsham How, 1823-97

This hymn may also be sung to **Ewing,** No. 534

KINGLEY VALE 87.87.47   H. P. ALLEN, 1869-1946

UNISON

THANKS to God whose Word was spoken
In the deed that made the earth.
His the voice that called a nation,
  His the fires that tried her worth.
    God has spoken:
  Praise Him for His open Word.

2 Thanks to God whose Word incarnate
  Glorified the flesh of man.
Deeds and words and death and rising
  Tell the grace in heaven's plan.
    God has spoken:
Praise Him for His open Word.

3 Thanks to God whose Word was written
  In the Bible's sacred page,
Record of the revelation
  Showing God to every age.
    God has spoken:
  Praise Him for His open Word.

4 Thanks to God whose Word is published
  In the tongues of every race.
See its glory undiminished
  By the change of time or place.
    God has spoken:
  Praise Him for His open Word.

5 Thanks to God whose Word is answered
  By the Spirit's voice within.
Here we drink of joy unmeasured,
  Life redeemed from death and sin.
    God is speaking:
  Praise Him for His open Word.

Richard Thomas Brooks, b. 1918

This hymn may also be sung to **Regent Square**, No. 5

WARRINGTON L.M.

R. HARRISON, 1748-1810

THE heavens declare Thy glory, Lord,
  In every star Thy wisdom shines;
But when our eyes behold Thy Word,
  We read Thy name in fairer lines.

2 The rolling sun, the changing light,
    And night and day, Thy power confess;
  But the blest volume Thou hast writ
    Reveals Thy justice and Thy grace.

3 Sun, moon, and stars convey Thy praise
    Round the whole earth, and never stand;
  So when Thy truth began its race,
    It touched and glanced on every land.

4 Nor shall Thy spreading gospel rest
    Till through the world Thy truth has run;
  Till Christ has all the nations blest,
    That see the light or feel the sun.

5 Great Sun of Righteousness, arise,
    Bless the dark world with heavenly light:
  Thy gospel makes the simple wise;
    Thy laws are pure, Thy judgements right.

6 Thy noblest wonders here we view,
    In souls renewed, and sins forgiven;
  Lord, cleanse my sins, my soul renew,
    And make Thy Word my guide to heaven.

Isaac Watts, 1674–1748

295

PETERSHAM D.C.M.

C. W. POOLE, 1828-1924

W^E limit not the truth of God
    To our poor reach of mind,
By notions of our day and sect,
    Crude, partial, and confined;
No, let a new and better hope
    Within our hearts be stirred:
      The Lord hath yet more light and
        truth
      To break forth from His word.

2 Who dares to bind to his dull sense
    The oracles of heaven,
 For all the nations, tongues, and
    climes,
    And all the ages given?
That universe, how much unknown!
    That ocean unexplored!—

3 Darkling our great forefathers went
    The first steps of the way;
'Twas but the dawning, yet to grow
    Into the perfect day.
And grow it shall; our glorious Sun
    More fervid rays afford:

4 O Father, Son and Spirit, send
    Us increase from above;
Enlarge, expand all Christian souls
    To comprehend Thy love:
And make us to go on to know,
    With nobler powers conferred,
      The Lord hath yet more light and
        truth
      To break forth from His word.

George Rawson, 1807-89

COMPANION   88.88.88   R. S. Newman, 1850-1927

When quiet in my house I sit,
    Thy Book be my companion still,
My joy Thy sayings to repeat,
    Talk o'er the records of Thy will,
And search the oracles divine,
Till every heartfelt word be mine.

2 Oh may the gracious words divine
    Subject of all my converse be!
So will the Lord His follower join,
    And walk and talk Himself with me;
So shall my heart His presence prove,
And burn with everlasting love.

3 Oft as I lay me down to rest,
    Oh may the reconciling word
Sweetly compose my weary breast!
    While, on the bosom of my Lord,
I sink in blissful dreams away,
And visions of eternal day.

4 Rising to sing my Saviour's praise,
    Thee may I publish all day long;
And let Thy precious word of grace
    Flow from my heart, and fill my tongue;
Fill all my life with purest love,
And join me to the church above.

Charles Wesley, 1707-88

See also
270   Come, Holy Ghost, our hearts inspire
352   How firm a foundation
598   Lord Jesus, Thy disciples see
603   Talk with us, Lord

ABENDS L.M. H. S. OAKELEY, 1830-1903

BEHOLD, a Stranger at the door!
He gently knocks, has knocked
before,
Has waited long, is waiting still:
You treat no other friend so ill.

2 But will He prove a friend indeed?
He will! the very friend you need!
The Man of Nazareth, 'tis He,
With garments dyed at Calvary.

3 Admit Him; for the human breast
Ne'er entertained so kind a guest:
No mortal tongue their joys can tell,
With whom He condescends to dwell.

4 Yet know, nor of the terms complain,
When Jesus comes He comes to reign,
To reign, and with no partial sway;
Thoughts must be slain that disobey.

5 Sovereign of souls, Thou Prince of
Peace,
Oh may Thy gentle reign increase:
Throw wide the door, each willing
mind;
And be His empire all mankind.

Joseph Grigg, 1728–68

MOUNT ZION 88.88.88

I. J. PLEYEL, 1757-1831

BEHOLD, the Lamb of God, who bears
The sins of all the world away!
A servant's form He meekly wears,
He sojourns in a house of clay;
His glory is no longer seen,
But God with God is man with men.

2 See where the God incarnate stands,
And calls His wandering creatures home!
He all day long spreads out His hands,
Come, weary souls, to Jesus come!
Ye all may hide you in My breast;
Believe, and I will give you rest.

3 Sinners, believe the gospel word,
Jesus is come your souls to save!
Jesus is come, your common Lord;
Pardon ye all through Him may have,
May now be saved, whoever will;
This Man receiveth sinners still.

Charles Wesley, 1707–88

This hymn may also be sung to **Carey (Surrey)**, No. 243

299

WONDERFUL LOVE 10.4.10.7.4.10

F. L. WISEMAN, 1858-1944

C OME let us sing of a wonderful love,
  Tender and true;
Out of the heart of the Father above,
  Streaming to me and to you:
  Wonderful love
Dwells in the heart of the Father
  above.

2 Jesus, the Saviour, this gospel to tell,
    Joyfully came;
  Came with the helpless and hopeless
      to dwell,
    Sharing their sorrow and shame;
    Seeking the lost,
  Saving, redeeming at measureless cost.

3 Jesus is seeking the wanderers yet;
    Why do they roam?
  Love only waits to forgive and forget;
    Home! weary wanderer, home!
    Wonderful love
  Dwells in the heart of the Father
    above.

4 Come to my heart, O Thou wonderful
      love,
    Come and abide,
  Lifting my life till it rises above
    Envy and falsehood and pride;
    Seeking to be
  Lowly and humble, a learner of Thee.

Robert Walmsley, 1831–1905

COME UNTO ME 76.76.D

J. B. DYKES, 1823-76

"Come unto Me, ye weary,
And I will give you rest."
Oh blessed voice of Jesus,
Which comes to hearts oppressed!
It tells of benediction,
Of pardon, grace and peace,
Of joy that hath no ending,
Of love which cannot cease.

2 "Come unto Me, ye wand'rers,
And I will give you light."
Oh loving voice of Jesus,
Which comes to cheer the night!
Our hearts were filled with sadness,
And we had lost our way,
But He has brought us gladness,
And songs at break of day.

3 "Come unto Me, ye fainting,
And I will give you life."
Oh cheering voice of Jesus,
Which comes to aid our strife!
The foe is stern and eager,
The fight is fierce and long:
But He has made us mighty,
And stronger than the strong.

4 "And whosoever cometh,
I will not cast him out."
Oh welcome voice of Jesus,
Which drives away our doubt,
Which calls us, very sinners,
Unworthy though we be
Of love so free and boundless,
To come, dear Lord, to Thee.

William Chatterton Dix, 1837–98

301

BRYN ABER 87.87.47

D. VAUGHAN THOMAS, 1873-1934

1. COME, ye sinners, poor and needy,
   Weak and wounded, sick and sore;
   Jesus ready stands to save you,
   Full of pity, love, and power;
   He is able,
   He is willing; doubt no more.

2. Come, ye needy, come and welcome;
   God's free bounty glorify:
   True belief and true repentance—
   Every grace that brings you nigh—
   Without money,
   Come to Jesus Christ and buy.

3. Come, ye weary, heavy-laden,
   Bruised and broken by the Fall;
   If you tarry till you're better,
   You will never come at all:
   Not the righteous—
   Sinners, Jesus came to call.

4. Let not conscience make you linger,
   Nor of fitness fondly dream;
   All the fitness He requireth
   Is to feel your need of Him:
   This He gives you—
   'Tis the Spirit's rising beam.

5. Lo! the incarnate God, ascended,
   Pleads the merit of His blood;
   Venture on Him, venture wholly,
   Let no other trust intrude;
   None but Jesus
   Can do helpless sinners good.

Joseph Hart, 1712-68

CAIRNBROOK 85.83   EBENEZER PROUT, 1835-1909

PROVE Him! An almighty Saviour
Is the Saviour still;
Prove that He can save you fully—
Can and will.

2 Prove Him! He is God eternal,
An unchanging Friend,
With a love that never knoweth
Bound or end.

3 Boundless is His love as ocean,
Wide as heaven's own roof,
Put the riches of His mercy
Now to proof.

4 Prove Him now—for now you need
Him;
Life is poor indeed
Lacking His great love that filleth
All our need.

5 Prove Him—now the time of mercy,
'Tis the Saviour's day;
Make it yours, nor let it sadly
Die away.

6 Prove Him—with your sin and sorrow,
Come; He longs to give
Pardon, freedom, with all gladness,
Joys that live!

7 Heaven within you, heaven above you,
Then your heart will raise
Glad thanksgiving for His mercies,
Songs of praise!

Author unknown

303

PILOT 77.77.77

J. E. GOULD, 1822-75

SINNERS Jesus will receive;
  Sound this word of grace to all
Who the heavenly pathway leave,
  All who linger, all who fall;
This can bring them back again:
Christ receiveth sinful men.

2 Come, and He will give you rest,
  Sorrow-stricken, sin-defiled—
He can make the sinfullest,
  God the Father's blessèd child:
Trust Him, trust His word again:
Christ receiveth sinful men.

3 Sick, and sorrowful, and blind,
  I with all my sins draw nigh—
O my Saviour, Thou canst find
  Help for sinners such as I.
Speak that word of love again:
Christ receiveth sinful men.

4 Now my heart condemns me not,
  Pure before the law I stand;
He who cleansed me from all spot,
  Satisfied its last demand.
Hear the word of peace again:
Christ receiveth sinful men.

5 Christ receiveth sinful men,
  Even me with all my sin;
Purged from every spot and stain,
  Heaven with Him I enter in.
Death hath no more sting or pain:
Christ receiveth sinful men.

Erdmann Neumeister, 1671–1756
tr. Emma Frances Bevan, 1827–1909

ST. MABYN 87.87   A. H. BROWN, 1830-1926

SOULS of men, why will ye scatter
   Like a crowd of frightened sheep?
Foolish hearts, why will ye wander
   From a love so true and deep?

2 Was there ever kindest shepherd
   Half so gentle, half so sweet
As the Saviour who would have us
   Come and gather round His feet?

3 There's a wideness in God's mercy,
   Like the wideness of the sea;
There's a kindness in His justice
   Which is more than liberty.

4 For the love of God is broader
   Than the measures of man's mind;
And the heart of the Eternal
   Is most wonderfully kind.

5 There is plentiful redemption
   In the blood that has been shed;
There is joy for all the members
   In the sorrows of the Head.

6 If our love were but more simple,
   We should take Him at His word,
And our lives would be all sunshine
   In the sweetness of our Lord.

          Frederick William Faber, 1814–63

This hymn may also be sung to **Cross of Jesus**, No. 143

305

FIRST TUNE

THE OLD, OLD STORY 76.76.D with refrain W. H. DOANE, 1832-1916

The Call of God

SECOND TUNE

REMEMBRANCE 76.76 without refrain

JOSIAH BOOTH, 1852-1930

TELL me the old, old story
  Of unseen things above,
Of Jesus and His glory,
  Of Jesus and His love.
Tell me the story simply,
  As to a little child,
For I am weak and weary,
  And helpless and defiled.
    Tell me the old, old story,
    Of Jesus and His love!

2 Tell me the story slowly,
  That I may take it in—
That wonderful redemption,
  God's remedy for sin.
Tell me the story often,
  For I forget so soon:
The "early dew" of morning
  Has passed away at noon.

3 Tell me the story softly,
  With earnest tones and grave;
Remember! I'm the sinner
  Whom Jesus came to save.
Tell me the story always,
  If you would really be,
In any time of trouble,
  A comforter to me.

4 Tell me the same old story,
  When you have cause to fear
That this world's empty glory
  Is costing me too dear.
Yes, and when *that* world's glory
  Is dawning on my soul,
Tell me the old, old story:
  "Christ Jesus makes thee whole."

Arabella Catherine Hankey, 1834–1911

306

THE Lord is rich and merciful,
  The Lord is very kind;
Oh come to Him, come now to Him
  With a believing mind;
His comforts, they shall strengthen thee,
  Like flowing waters cool;
And He shall for thy spirit be
  A fountain ever full.

2 The Lord is glorious and strong,
  Our God is very high;
Oh trust in Him, trust now in Him,
  And have security;
He shall to thee be like the sea,
  And thou shalt surely feel
His wind, that bloweth healthily,
  Thy sicknesses to heal.

3 The Lord is wonderful and wise,
  As all the ages tell;
Oh learn of Him, learn now of Him,
  When with thee it is well;
And with His light thou shalt be blest,
  Therein to work and live;
And He shall be to thee a rest
  When evening hours arrive.

Thomas Toke Lynch, 1818–71.

The Call of God

307

GREENLAND 76.76.D

From J. M. HAYDN, 1737-1806

TO-DAY Thy mercy calls us
  To wash away our sin,
However great our trespass,
  Whatever we have been:
However long from mercy
  Our hearts have turned away,
Thy precious blood can cleanse us
  And make us white to-day.

2 To-day Thy gate is open,
  And all who enter in
Shall find a Father's welcome,
  And pardon for their sin.
The past shall be forgotten,
  A present joy be given,
A future grace be promised,
  A glorious crown in heaven.

3 To-day our Father calls us;
  His Holy Spirit waits;
The blessèd angels gather
  Around the heavenly gates:
No question will be asked us
  How often we have come;
Although we oft have wandered,
  It is our Father's home!

4 Oh, all-embracing mercy!
  Oh, ever open door!
What should we do without thee
  When heart and eye run o'er?
When all things seem against us,
  To drive us to despair,
We know one gate is open,
  One ear will hear our prayer!

Oswald Allen, 1816–78

308

SAGINA 88.88.88

T. CAMPBELL, 1825-76

And can it be that I should gain
 An interest in the Saviour's blood?
Died He for me, who caused His pain?
 For me, who Him to death pursued?
Amazing love! how can it be
That Thou, my God, shouldst die for me?

2 'Tis mystery all! The Immortal dies!
 Who can explore His strange design!
In vain the first-born seraph tries
 To sound the depths of love divine!
'Tis mercy all! let earth adore,
Let angel minds inquire no more.

3 He left His Father's throne above—
 So free, so infinite His grace—
Emptied Himself of all but love,
 And bled for Adam's helpless race
'Tis mercy all, immense and free;
For, O my God, it found out me.

4 Long my imprisoned spirit lay
  Fast bound in sin and nature's
    night;
Thine eye diffused a quickening ray,
  I woke, the dungeon flamed with
    light;
My chains fell off, my heart was free;
I rose, went forth, and followed Thee.

5 No condemnation now I dread;
  Jesus, and all in Him, is mine!
Alive in Him, my living Head,
  And clothed in righteousness
    divine,
Bold I approach the eternal throne,
And claim the crown, through Christ
  my own.

Charles Wesley, 1707–88

MILLENNIUM 66.66.88   Source unknown **309**

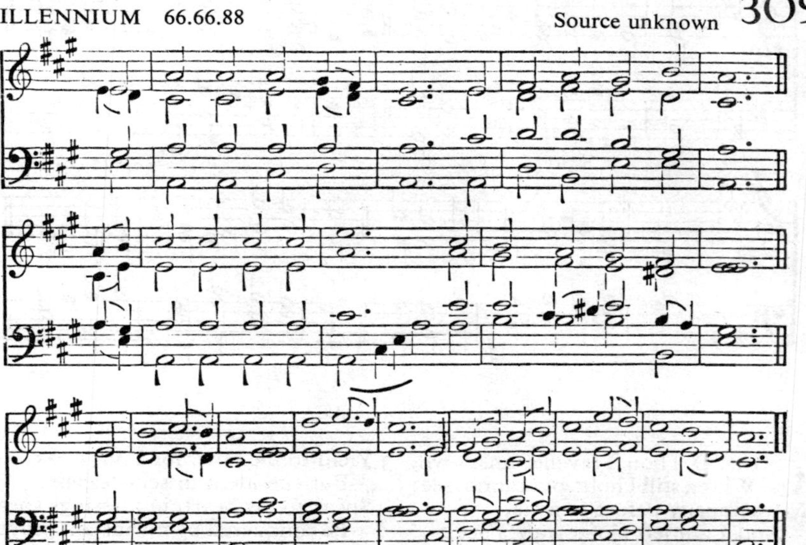

A RISE, my soul, arise,
  Shake off thy guilty fears;
Th'atoning Sacrifice
  In my behalf appears:
Before the throne my Surety stands;
My name is written on His hands.

2 He ever lives above,
  For me to intercede,
His all-redeeming love,
  His precious blood, to plead;
His blood atoned for all our race,
And sprinkles now the throne of grace.

3 Five open wounds He bears,
  Received on Calvary:
They pour effectual prayers,
  They strongly speak for me:
Forgive him, oh forgive! they cry,
Nor let that ransomed sinner die!

4 The Father hears Him pray,
  His dear Anointed One;
He cannot turn away
  The presence of His Son:
His Spirit answers to the blood,
And tells me I am born of God.

5 My God is reconciled,
  His pardoning voice I hear;
He owns me for His child,
  I can no longer fear;
With confidence I now draw nigh,
And Father, Abba, Father! cry.

Charles Wesley, 1707–88

3IO

COLCHESTER 88.88.88

S. S. WESLEY, 1810-76

COME, O Thou Traveller unknown,
  Whom still I hold, but cannot see;
My company before is gone,
  And I am left alone with Thee;
With Thee all night I mean to stay,
And wrestle till the break of day.

2 In vain Thou strugglest to get free;
  I never will unloose my hold!
Art Thou the Man that died for me?
  The secret of Thy love unfold:
Wrestling, I will not let Thee go,
Till I Thy name, Thy nature know.

3 Yield to me now, for I am weak,
  But confident in self-despair:
Speak to my heart, in blessings speak,
  Be conquered by my instant prayer;
Speak, or Thou never hence shalt move,
And tell me if Thy Name is Love?

4 'Tis Love, 'tis Love, Thou diedst for me;
  I hear Thy whisper in my heart;
The morning breaks, the shadows flee,
  Pure universal Love Thou art;
To me, to all, Thy mercies move;
Thy nature, and Thy Name, is Love.

5 I know Thee, Saviour, who Thou art,
  Jesus, the feeble sinner's friend;
Nor wilt Thou with the night depart,
  But stay, and love me to the end;
Thy mercies never shall remove;
Thy nature, and Thy Name, is Love.

Charles Wesley, 1707–88

This hymn may also be sung to **Pater omnium**, No. III

KEDRON C.M.

Arr. by F. A. J. TONKIN, b. 1926

COME, let us to the Lord our God
  With contrite hearts return;
Our God is gracious, nor will leave
  The desolate to mourn.

2 His voice commands the tempest
    forth,
  And stills the stormy wave;
 And though His arm be strong to
    smite,
  'Tis also strong to save.

3 Long hath the night of sorrow
    reigned;
  The dawn shall bring us light:
 God shall appear, and we shall rise
  With gladness in His sight.

4 Our hearts, if God we seek to know,
  Shall know Him and rejoice;
 His coming like the morn shall be,
  Like morning songs His voice.

5 As dew upon the tender herb,
  Diffusing fragrance round;
 As showers that usher in the spring,
  And cheer the thirsty ground.

6 So shall His presence bless our souls,
  And shed a joyful light;
 That hallowed morn shall chase away
  The sorrows of the night.

John Morison, 1750–98

This hymn may also be sung to **Byzantium**, No. 257

312

WEBER 77.77

C. M. F. E. VON WEBER, 1786-1826

DEPTH of mercy! can there be
   Mercy still reserved for me?
Can my God His wrath forbear?
Me, the chief of sinners, spare?

2 I have long withstood His grace,
Long provoked Him to His face;
Would not hearken to His calls,
Grieved Him by a thousand falls.

3 Whence to me this waste of love?
Ask my Advocate above!
See the cause in Jesu's face,
Now before the throne of grace.

4 There for me the Saviour stands,
Shows His wounds, and spreads His
      hands;
God is love, I know, I feel;
Jesus weeps, and loves me still.

5 Jesus, answer from above;
Is not all Thy nature love?
Wilt Thou not the wrong forget?
Suffer me to kiss Thy feet?

6 If I rightly read Thy heart,
If Thou all compassion art,
Bow Thine ear, in mercy bow,
Pardon and accept me now!

Charles Wesley, 1707–88

314 MARTYRDOM C.M.
Words at foot of next page

H. WILSON, 1766-1824
adapted by R. A. SMITH, 1780-1829

RIVAULX L.M.   J. B. DYKES, 1823-76

FATHER of heaven, whose love profound
A ransom for our souls hath found,
Before Thy throne we sinners bend,
To us Thy pardoning love extend.

2 Almighty Son, Incarnate Word,
Our Prophet, Priest, Redeemer, Lord,
Before Thy throne we sinners bend,
To us Thy saving grace extend.

3 Eternal Spirit, by whose breath
The soul is raised from sin and death,
Before Thy throne we sinners bend,
To us Thy quickening power extend.

4 Almighty Father, Spirit, Son;
Mysterious Godhead, Three in One,
Before Thy throne we sinners bend,
Grace, pardon, life to us extend.

Edward Cooper, 1770–1833

Tune at foot of previous page   314

FOR ever here my rest shall be,
Close to Thy wounded side;
This all my hope, and all my plea,
For me the Saviour died.

2 My dying Saviour, and my God,
Fountain for guilt and sin,
Sprinkle me ever with Thy blood,
And cleanse, and keep me clean.

3 Wash me, and make me thus Thine own,
Wash me, and mine Thou art,
Wash me, but not my feet alone,
My hands, my head, my heart.

4 The atonement of Thy blood apply,
Till faith to sight improve,
Till hope in full fruition die,
And all my soul be love.

Charles Wesley, 1707–88

315

ABENDS L.M.

H. S. Oakeley, 1830-1903

God calling yet! Shall I not hear?
Earth's pleasures shall I still hold dear?
Shall life's swift passing years all fly,
And still my soul in slumber lie?

2 God calling yet! Shall I not rise?
Can I His loving voice despise,
And basely His kind care repay?
He calls me still; can I delay?

3 God calling yet! And shall He knock,
And I my heart the closer lock?
He still is waiting to receive,
And shall I dare His Spirit grieve?

4 God calling yet! And shall I give
No heed, but still in bondage live?
I wait, but He does not forsake;
He calls me still; my heart, awake!

5 God calling yet! I cannot stay;
My heart I yield without delay:
Vain world, farewell, from thee I part;
The voice of God hath reached my heart.

Gerhard Tersteegen, 1697–1769
tr. Sarah Findlater, 1823–1907 and others

317

DALEHURST C.M.   *Words at foot of next page*   A. Cottman, 1841-79

NOTTINGHAM 77.77 — School of MOZART

Hark, my soul; it is the Lord;
'Tis thy Saviour, hear His word;
Jesus speaks, and speaks to thee:
"Say, poor sinner, lov'st thou Me?

3 Can a woman's tender care
Cease towards the child she bare!
Yes, she may forgetful be,
Yet will I remember thee!

2 I delivered thee when bound,
And when bleeding healed thy wound;
Sought thee wandering, set thee right,
Turned thy darkness into light.

4 Mine is an unchanging love,
Higher than the heights above,
Deeper than the depths beneath,
Free and faithful, strong as death.

5 Thou shalt see My glory soon,
When the work of grace is done;
Partner of My throne shalt be:
Say, poor sinner, lov'st thou Me?

6 Lord, it is my chief complaint,
That my love is weak and faint;
Yet I love Thee, and adore,
Oh for grace to love Thee more!

William Cowper, 1731–1800

317

Tune at foot of previous page

Heal us, Immanuel; hear our prayer;
We wait to feel Thy touch:
Deep-wounded souls to Thee repair;
And, Saviour, we are such.

2 Our faith is feeble, we confess;
We faintly trust Thy word:
But wilt Thou pity us the less?
Be that far from Thee, Lord,.

3 Remember him who once applied
With trembling for relief;
Lord, I believe! with tears he cried,
Oh help my unbelief!

4 She, too, who touched Thee in the press,
And healing virtue stole,
Was answered: Daughter, go in peace,
Thy faith hath made thee whole.

5 Like her, with hopes and fears we come,
To touch Thee, if we may:
Oh send us not despairing home,
Send none unhealed away.

William Cowper, 1731–1800

This hymn may also be sung to Bedford, No. 94

318

EWHURST 888.7

C. J. ALLEN, 1886-1973

I AM not skilled to understand
  What God hath willed, what God
    hath planned;
I only know at His right hand
  Stands one who is my Saviour.

2 I take God at His word and deed;
  "Christ died to save me," this I read;
And in my heart I find a need
  Of Him to be my Saviour.

3 And was there then no other way
  For God to take?—I cannot say;
I only bless Him, day by day,
  Who saved me through my Saviour.

4 That He should leave His place on
    high
  And come for sinful man to die,
You count it strange?—so do not I,
  Since I have known my Saviour.

5 And oh that He fulfilled may see
  The travail of His soul in me,
And with His work contented be,
  As I with my dear Saviour!

6 Yea, living, dying, let me bring
  My strength, my solace, from this
    spring,
That He who lives to be my King
  Once died to be my Saviour.

Dora Greenwell, 1821–82

GOD HOLDS THE KEY   84.884

G. C. STEBBINS, 1846-1945

I COME, O blessed Lord, to Thee
  I come to-day;
I am no longer satisfied
  To stay away.

2 I will not wait until my life
    Like Thine shall grow;
  I'll come at once—I know I've
      sinned:
    I'll tell Thee so.

3 It is enough for me to know,
    Thou wilt receive
  And cleanse my heart from ev'ry sin
    If I believe.

4 Help me that I forget myself
    In loving Thee;
  And let Thine image on my heart
    Reflected be.

5 Oh, take me, Saviour crucified,
    And let me prove
  That those who most have been
      forgiven
    Have most of love.

Ellen K. Bradford

English Traditional Melody
Arr. by R. VAUGHAN WILLIAMS, 1872–1958

KINGSFOLD D.C.M.

I HEARD the voice of Jesus say,
  "Come unto Me and rest;
Lay down, thou weary one, lay down
  Thy head upon My breast."
I came to Jesus as I was,
  Weary, and worn, and sad,
I found in Him a resting-place,
  And He has made me glad.

2 I heard the voice of Jesus say,
  "Behold, I freely give
The living water,—thirsty one,
  Stoop down, and drink, and live."

I came to Jesus, and I drank
  Of that life-giving stream,
My thirst was quenched, my soul
    revived,
  And now I live in Him.

3 I heard the voice of Jesus say,
  "I am this dark world's light!
Look unto Me, thy morn shall rise,
  And all thy day be bright."
I looked to Jesus, and I found
  In Him my Star, my Sun;
And in that light of life I'll walk
  Till travelling days are done.

Horatius Bonar, 1808–89

This hymn may also be sung to **Forest Green,** No. 105

RUTH   65.65.D   S. Smith, 1821-1917

Jesus, I will trust Thee,
  Trust Thee with my soul;
Guilty, lost, and helpless,
  Thou canst make me whole.
There is none in heaven
  Or on earth like Thee;
Thou hast died for sinners—
  Therefore, Lord, for me.

2 Jesus, I must trust Thee,
  Pondering Thy ways,
Full of love and mercy
  All Thine earthly days;
Sinners gathered round Thee,
  Lepers sought Thy face;
None too vile or loathsome
  For a Saviour's grace.

3 Jesus, I can trust Thee,
  Trust Thy written Word,
Though Thy voice of pity
  I have never heard.
When Thy Spirit teacheth,
  To my taste how sweet!
Only may I hearken
  Sitting at Thy feet.

4 Jesus, I do trust Thee,
  Trust Thee without doubt;
Whosoever cometh
  Thou wilt not cast out,
Faithful is Thy promise,
  Precious is Thy blood;
These my soul's salvation,
  Thou my Saviour God.

Mary Jane Walker, 1816–78

322

TRUST 888.6

FIRST TUNE

G. W. TORRANCE, 1835-1907

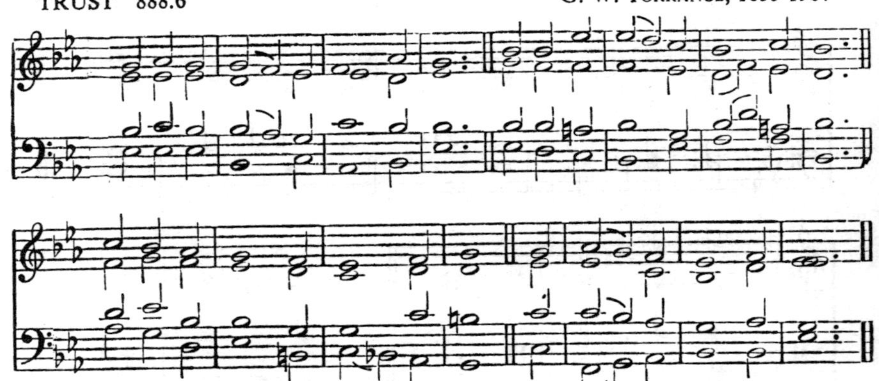

DRAWN to the cross which Thou hast blessed
With healing gifts for souls distressed,
To find in Thee my life, my rest:
Christ crucified, I come!

2 Stained with the sins which I have wrought
In word and deed and secret thought,
For pardon which Thy blood hath bought:

3 Weary of selfishness and pride,
False pleasures gone, vain hopes denied,
Deep in Thy wounds my shame to hide:

4 Thou knowest all my griefs and fears,
Thy grace abused, my misspent years;
Yet now to Thee, for cleansing tears:

5 I would not, if I could, conceal
The ills which only Thou canst heal,
So to the cross, where sinners kneel:

6 Wash me, and take away each stain,
Let nothing of my sin remain;
For cleansing, though it be through pain:

7 To be what Thou wouldst have me be,
Accepted, sanctified in Thee,
Through what Thy grace shall work in me:
Christ crucified, I come!

Genevieve Mary Irons, 1855-1928

SECOND TUNE

MISERICORDIA 888.6

HENRY SMART, 1813-79

WALFORD 888.6   FIRST TUNE   G. T. THALBEN-BALL, 1896-

JUST as I am—without one plea,
But that Thy blood was shed for
  me,
And that Thou bidd'st me come to
  Thee,
   O Lamb of God, I come!

2 Just as I am—and waiting not
To rid my soul of one dark blot,
To Thee, whose blood can cleanse
  each spot,
   O Lamb of God, I come!

3 Just as I am—though tossed about
With many a conflict, many a doubt,
Fightings and fears, within, without,
   O Lamb of God, I come!

4 Just as I am—poor, wretched,
  blind,—
Sight, riches, healing of the mind,
Yea, all I need, in Thee to find,
   O Lamb of God, I come!

5 Just as I am—Thou wilt receive,
Wilt welcome, pardon, cleanse, re-
  lieve;
Because Thy promise I believe,
   O Lamb of God, I come!

6 Just as I am—Thy love unknown
Has broken every barrier down;
Now to be Thine, yea, Thine alone,
   O Lamb of God, I come!

7 Just as I am—of that free love
The breadth, length, depth and
  height to prove—
Here for a season, then above—
   O Lamb of God, I come!
    Charlotte Elliott, 1789-1871

This hymn may also be sung to **Saffron Walden**, No. 532

JUST AS I AM 888.6   SECOND TUNE   JOSEPH BARNBY, 1838-96

LLEDROD L.M.   Welsh Hymn Melody

LORD, I was blind! I could not see
In Thy marred visage any grace;
But now the beauty of Thy face
In radiant vision dawns on me.

2 Lord, I was deaf! I could not hear
The thrilling music of Thy voice;
But now I hear Thee and rejoice,
And all Thine uttered words are dear.

3 Lord, I was dumb! I could not speak
The grace and glory of Thy name;
But now, as touched with living
flame,
My lips Thine eager praises wake.

4 Lord, I was dead! I could not stir
My lifeless soul to come to Thee;
But now, since Thou hast quick-
ened me,
I rise from sin's dark sepulchre.

5 For Thou hast made the blind to see,
The deaf to hear, the dumb to
speak,
The dead to live; and lo, I break
The chains of my captivity!

William Tidd Matson, 1833–99

This hymn may also be sung to **Bodmin,** No. 21

BETHEL 664.6664

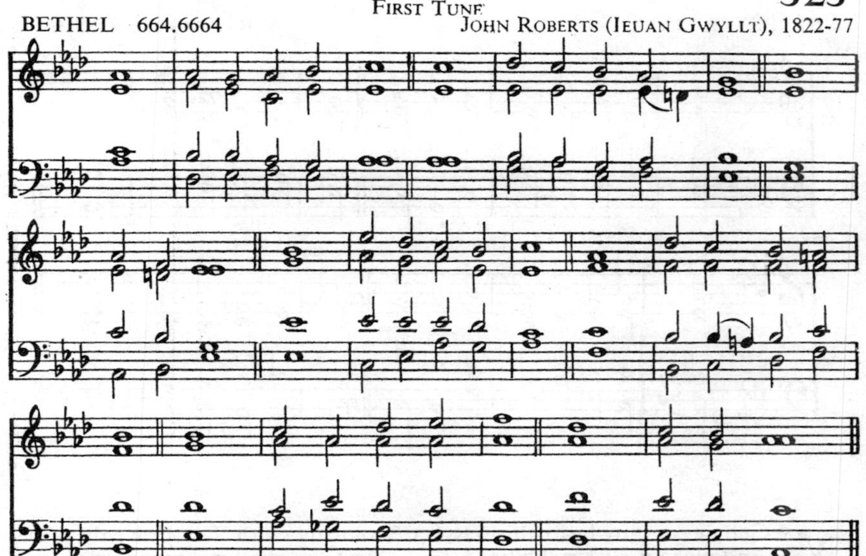

MY faith looks up to Thee,
Thou Lamb of Calvary,
Saviour Divine:
Now hear me while I pray,
Take all my guilt away,
Oh, let me from this day
Be wholly Thine!

2 May Thy rich grace impart
Strength to my fainting heart,
My zeal inspire;
As Thou hast died for me,
Oh, may my love to Thee
Pure, warm, and changeless be,
A living fire!

3 When life's dark maze I tread,
And griefs around me spread,
Be Thou my Guide;
Bid darkness turn to day,
Wipe sorrow's tears away,
Nor let me ever stray
From Thee aside.

4 When ends life's transient dream,
When death's cold, sullen stream
Shall o'er me roll;
Blest Saviour, then in love
Fear and distrust remove;
Oh, bear me safe above,
A ransomed soul.

Ray Palmer, 1808–87

OLIVET 664.6664

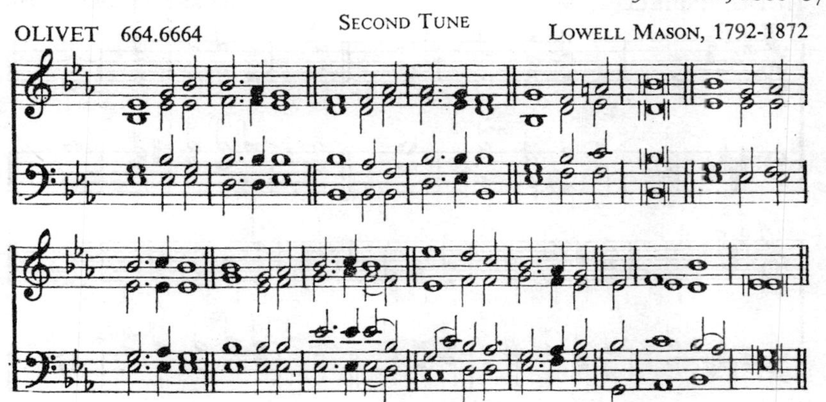

MY God, accept my heart this day,
And make it always Thine,
That I from Thee no more may stray,
No more from Thee decline.

2 Before the cross of Him who died,
Behold, I prostrate fall;
Let every sin be crucified,
And Christ be all in all.

3 Anoint me with Thy heavenly grace,
And seal me for Thine own;
That I may see Thy glorious face,
And worship near Thy throne.

4 Let every thought and work and word
To Thee be ever given:
Then life shall be Thy service, Lord,
And death the gate of heaven.

Matthew Bridges, 1800–94

328

Words at foot of next page

HUDDERSFIELD S.M.   WILLIAMS' *Psalmody*, 1770

HIRAETH   64.64.664   J. P. HULLAH, 1812-84

No, not despairingly
  Come I to Thee;
No; not distrustingly
  Bend I the knee.
Sin hath gone over me,
Yet is this still my plea,
  Jesus hath died.

2 Lord, I confess to Thee
  Sadly my sin;
All I am tell I Thee,
  All I have been.
Purge Thou my sin away,
Wash Thou my soul this day,
  Lord, make me clean.

3 Faithful and just art Thou,
  Forgiving all;
Low at Thy piercèd feet,
  Saviour, I fall:
Oh, let the cleansing blood,
Blood of the Lamb of God,
  Pass o'er my soul!

4 Then all is peace and light
  This soul within:
Thus shall I walk with Thee
  The loved Unseen,
Leaning on Thee, my God,
Guided along the road,
  Nothing between.

Horatius Bonar, 1808–89

Tune at foot of previous page

328

Not all the blood of beasts
  On Jewish altars slain
Could give the guilty conscience
    peace
  Or wash away its stain.

2 But Christ, the heavenly Lamb,
  Takes all our guilt away;
A sacrifice of nobler name,
  And richer blood than they.

3 My faith would lay her hand
  On that dear head of Thine,
While like a penitent I stand,
  And there confess my sin.

4 My soul looks back to see
  The burden Thou didst bear,
When hanging on the accursèd tree,
  And knows her guilt was there.

5 Believing, we rejoice
  To see the curse remove;
We bless the Lamb with cheerful
    voice,
  And sing redeeming love.   *Isaac Watts, 1674–1748*

MEIRIONNYDD   76.76.D   WILLIAM LLOYD, 1786-1852

O JESUS, Thou art standing,
  Outside the fast-closed door,
In lowly patience waiting
  To pass the threshold o'er:
Shame on us, Christian brothers,
  His name and sign who bear;
Oh, shame, thrice shame upon us,
  To keep Him standing there!

2 O Jesus, Thou art knocking,
  And lo! that hand is scarred,
And thorns Thy brow encircle,
  And tears Thy face have marred:
Oh, love that passeth knowledge,
  So patiently to wait!
Oh, sin that hath no equal,
  So fast to bar the gate!

3 O Jesus, Thou art pleading
  In accents meek and low;
"I died for you, My children,
  And will ye treat Me so?"
O Lord, with shame and sorrow
  We open now the door:
Dear Saviour, enter, enter,
  And leave us nevermore.

William Walsham How, 1823-97

This hymn may also be sung to **Pearsall**, No. 406

RHYS   11.10.11.10   W. J. Evans, 1866-1947

OH word of pity, for our pardon
  pleading,
  Breathed in the hour of loneliness
  and pain;
Oh voice, which through the ages
  interceding
  Calls us to fellowship with God
  again!

2 Oh word of comfort, through the
  silence stealing,
  As the dread act of sacrifice began;
Oh infinite compassion, still revealing
  The infinite forgiveness won for
  man!

3 Oh word of hope to raise us nearer
  heaven,
  When courage fails us and when
  faith is dim!
The souls for whom Christ prays to
  Christ are given,
  To find their pardon and their joy
  in Him.

4 O Intercessor, who art ever living
  To plead for dying souls that they
  may live,
Teach us to know our sin which needs
  forgiving,
  Teach us to know Thy love which
  does forgive.

Ada Rundall Greenaway, 1861–1937

This hymn may also be sung to **O Perfect Love**, No. 46

331

ST. CATHERINE 88.88.88

Melody by H. F. Hemy 1818-88

SAVIOUR from sin, I wait to prove
  That Jesus is Thy healing name;
To lose, when perfected in love,
  Whate'er I have, or can, or am.
I stay me on Thy faithful word:
The servant shall be as his Lord.

2 Answer that gracious end in me
  For which Thy precious life was
    given;
Redeem from all iniquity;
  Restore, and make me meet for
    heaven:
Unless Thou purge my every stain,
Thy suffering and my faith are vain.

3 Didst Thou not die that I might live
  No longer to myself, but Thee,
Might body, soul, and spirit give
  To Him who gave Himself for me?
Come then, my Master and my God,
Take the dear purchase of Thy blood.

4 Thy own peculiar servant claim,
  For Thy own truth and mercy's
    sake;
Hallow in me Thy glorious name;
  Me for Thine own this moment
    take,
And change, and throughly purify;
Thine only may I live and die.

Charles Wesley, 1707–88

GLENFINLAS 65.65

K. G. FINLAY, 1882-1974

O MY Saviour, lifted
    From the earth for me,
Draw me, in Thy mercy,
    Nearer unto Thee.

2 Lift my earth-bound longings,
    Fix them, Lord, above;
Draw me with the magnet
    Of Thy mighty love.

3 And I come, Lord Jesus;
    Dare I turn away?
No! Thy love hath conquered,
    And I come to-day.

4 Bringing all my burdens,
    Sorrow, sin and care;
At Thy feet I lay them,
    And I leave them there.

William Walsham How, 1823-97

This hymn may also be sung to **Quietude**, No. 536

333

CROSS OF JESUS 87.87

J. STAINER, 1840-1901

"STRICKEN, smitten and afflicted,"
    See Him dying on the tree!
'Tis the Christ, by man rejected,
    Yes, my soul, 'tis He! 'tis He!

2 Many hands were raised to wound
        Him,
    None would interpose to save;
But the awful stroke that found Him,
    Was the stroke that justice gave.

3 Ye who think of sin but lightly,
    Nor suppose the evil great,
Here may view its nature rightly,
    Here its guilt may estimate.

4 Mark the sacrifice appointed!
    See *who* bears the awful load!
'Tis the Word, the Lord's Anointed,
    Son of man, and Son of God.

5 Here we have a firm foundation;
    Here's the refuge of the lost:
Christ's the rock of our salvation;
    His the name of which we boast.

6 Lamb of God, for sinners wounded,
    Sacrifice to cancel guilt,
None shall ever be confounded,
    Who on Him their hope have built.

Thomas Kelly, 1769-1855

334

TREWEN 88.88.D Anapaestic

D. Emlyn Evans, 1843-1913

A DEBTOR to mercy alone,
  Of covenant mercy I sing;
Nor fear, with Thy righteousness on,
  My person and offering to bring.
The terrors of Law and of God
  With me can have nothing to do;
My Saviour's obedience and blood
  Hide all my transgressions from view.

2 The work which His goodness began,
  The arm of His strength will complete;
His promise is Yea and Amen,
  And never was forfeited yet.
Things future, nor things that are now,
  Not all things below nor above,
Can make Him His purpose forgo,
  Or sever my soul from His love.

3 My name from the palms of His hands
  Eternity will not erase:
Impressed on His heart it remains,
  In marks of indelible grace.
Yes, I to the end shall endure,
  As sure as the earnest is given;
More happy, but not more secure,
  The glorified spirits in heaven.

Augustus Montague Toplady, 1740-78

EIN' FESTE BURG   87.87.66.667   Melody by M. LUTHER, 1483-1546

A MIGHTY fortress is our God,
    A bulwark never failing;
Our helper He, amid the flood
    Of mortal ills prevailing;
        For still our ancient foe
        Doth seek to work his woe;
        His craft and power are great,
        And arm'd with cruel hate—
            On earth is not his equal.

2 Did we in our own strength confide,
    Our striving would be losing,
Were not the right Man on our side,
    The man of God's own choosing.
        Dost ask who that may be?
        Christ Jesus, it is He!
        Lord Sabaoth is His name,
        From age to age the same:
            And He must win the battle.

3 And though this world, with devils
        filled,
    Should threaten to undo us,
We will not fear; for God hath willed
    His truth to triumph through us.
        Let goods and kindred go,
        This mortal life also;
        The body they may kill:
        God's truth abideth still,
            His kingdom is for ever.

Martin Luther, 1483–1546
tr. Frederick Henry Hedge, 1805–90

336

GROESWEN 87.87.67

J. A. LLOYD, 1815-74

ALL my hope on God is founded;
    He doth still my trust renew,
Me through change and chance He
        guideth,
    Only good and only true.
        God unknown,
        He alone
    Calls my heart to be His own.

2 Pride of man and earthly glory,
    Sword and crown betray his trust:
What with care and toil he buildeth,
    Tower and temple, fall to dust.
        But God's power,
        Hour by hour,
    Is my temple and my tower.

3 God's great goodness aye endureth,
    Deep His wisdom, passing thought:
Splendour, light, and life attend Him,
    Beauty springeth out of nought.
        Evermore
        From His store
    New-born worlds rise and adore.

4 Daily doth the Almighty Giver
    Bounteous gifts on us bestow.
His desire our soul delighteth,
    Pleasure leads us where we go.
        Love doth stand
        At His hand;
    Joy doth wait on His command.

5 Still from man to God eternal
    Sacrifice of praise be done,
High above all praises praising
    For the gift of Christ His Son.
        Christ doth call
        One and all:
    Ye who follow shall not fall.

Robert Seymour Bridges, 1844–1930
based on Joachim Neander, 1650–80

SENNEN COVE C.M.

W. H. HARRIS, 1883-1973

A MIND at "perfect peace" with
    God;
Oh what a word is this!
A sinner reconciled through blood;
    This, this indeed is peace!

2 By nature and by practice far—
    How very far from God!
Yet now by grace brought nigh to Him,
    Through faith in Jesu's blood.

3 So nigh, so very nigh to God,
    I cannot nearer be;
For in the Person of His Son
    I am as near as He.

4 So dear, so very dear to God,
    More dear I cannot be;
The love wherewith He loves the
        Son—
Such is His love to me!

5 Why should I ever careful be,
    Since such a God is mine?
He watches o'er me night and day,
    And tells me "Mine is thine."

Catesby Paget

This hymn may also be sung to **St. Bernard**, No. 75

MAINZER L.M.   JOSEPH MAINZER, 1801-51

AUTHOR of faith, eternal Word,
  Whose Spirit breathes the active
     flame;
Faith, like its Finisher and Lord,
  To-day as yesterday the same:

2 To Thee our humble hearts aspire,
  And ask the gift unspeakable;
Increase in us the kindled fire,
  In us the work of faith fulfil.

3 By faith we know Thee strong to save;
  Save us, a present Saviour Thou!
Whate'er we hope, by faith we have,
  Future, and past subsisting now.

4 To him that in Thy name believes
  Eternal life with Thee is given;
Into himself he all receives,
  Pardon, and holiness, and heaven.

5 The things unknown to feeble sense,
  Unseen by reason's glimmering ray,
With strong, commanding evidence
  Their heavenly origin display.

6 Faith lends its realizing light,
  The clouds disperse, the shadows
     fly;
The Invisible appears in sight,
  And God is seen by mortal eye.

Charles Wesley, 1707–88

This hymn may also be sung to **Winchester New**, No. 16

339

RHODES S.M.   C. W. JORDAN, 1840-1909

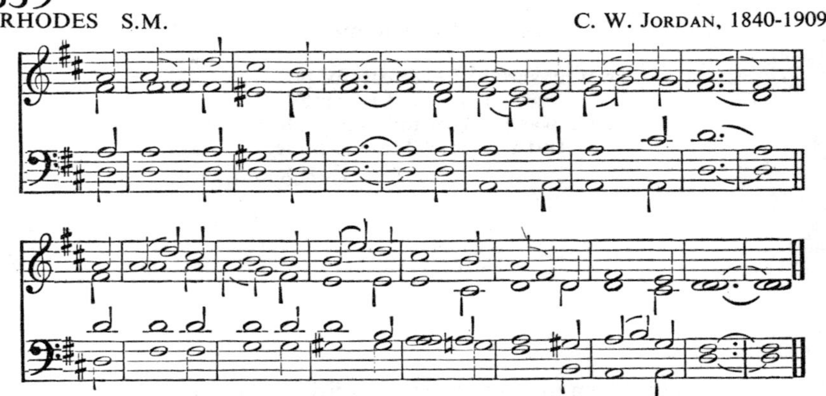

A WAKE, and sing the song
    Of Moses and the Lamb.
Wake every heart and every tongue,
    To praise the Saviour's Name.

2 Sing of His dying love;
    Sing of His rising power;
Sing how He intercedes above
    For us whose sins He bore.

3 Sing on your heavenly way,
    Ye ransomed sinners, sing;
Sing on, rejoicing every day
    In Christ, the eternal King.

4 Soon shall we hear Him say,
    "Ye blessed children, come!"
Soon will He call us hence away,
    To our eternal home.

5 There shall our raptured tongues
    His endless praise proclaim;
And sweeter voices swell the song
    Of Moses and the Lamb.

William Hammond, 1718/19–83

340

SAMSON L.M.
G. F. HANDEL, 1685-1759

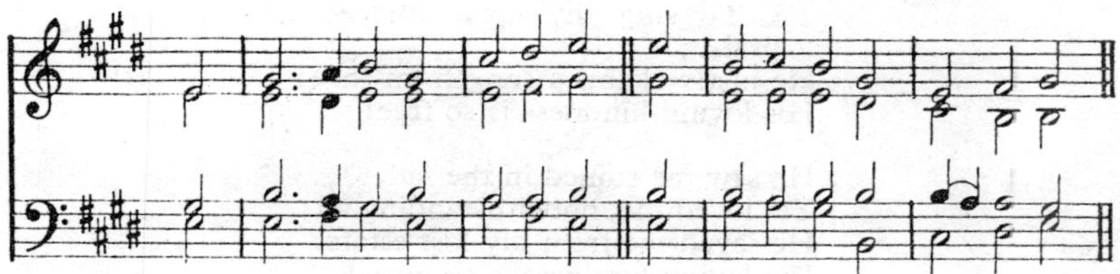

A WAKE, my soul, awake and raise
    Thy tribute to Jehovah's praise;
His glorious name adoring bless,
"According to His righteousness."

2 High as the highest mountain's head
From the deep ocean's deepest bed,
And ever steadfast, strong and sure—
So doth His righteousness endure.

3 Thy righteousness is "very high,"
Yet Thou, O God, hast brought it
    nigh;
And now with joy my lips confess
Jehovah as my righteousness.

4 What though temptations strong
    assail?
He who is stronger shall prevail!
What though their waves as mountains
    rise?
My righteousness is in the skies!

5 Sing on, my soul; thy song of praise
Shall last through time and endless
    days,
For e'en when with Him thou shalt
    bless
Jesus, "the Lord our righteousness."

William Samuel Warren Pond, d.1919

341

MAINZER L.M.

JOSEPH MAINZER, 1801-51

A WAKE, my soul, in joyful lays
  To sing thy great Redeemer's
praise;
He justly claims a song from thee:
His loving-kindness is so free!

2 He saw me ruined in the fall,
Yet loved me, notwithstanding all;
He saved me from my lost estate:
His loving-kindness is so great!

3 When I was Satan's easy prey,
And deep in debt and bondage lay,
He paid His life for my discharge:
His loving-kindness is so large!

4 Through mighty hosts of cruel foes
Where earth and hell my way oppose
He safely leads my soul along:
His loving-kindness is so strong!

5 Often I feel my sinful heart
Prone from my Saviour to depart;
But though I oft have Him forgot,
His loving-kindness changes not.

6 So when I pass death's gloomy vale,
And life and mortal powers shall fail,
Then may I while He gives me breath
His loving-kindness sing in death!

7 Then shall I mount, and soar away
To the bright world of endless day;
There shall I sing, with sweet
  surprise,
His loving-kindness in the skies!

Samuel Medley, 1738–99

HOUGHTON 10.10.11.11   H. J. GAUNTLETT, 1805-76

BEGONE, unbelief, my Saviour is near,
And for my relief will surely appear;
By prayer let me wrestle, and He will perform;
With Christ in the vessel, I smile at the storm.

2 Determined to save, He watched o'er my path,
When, Satan's blind slave, I sported with death;
And can He have taught me to trust in His name,
And thus far have brought me, to put me to shame?

3 His love in time past forbids me to think
He'll leave me at last in trouble to sink;
Each sweet Ebenezer I have in review,
Confirms His good pleasure to help me quite through.

4 Why should I complain of want or distress,
Temptation or pain? He told me no less;
The heirs of salvation, I know from His word,
Through much tribulation must follow their Lord.

5 Since all that I meet shall work for my good,
The bitter is sweet, the medicine food;
Though painful at present, 'twill cease before long,
And then, oh how pleasant the conqueror's song!

John Newton, 1725–1807
This hymn may also be sung to **Hanover,** No. 40

343

IRISH C.M.

Hymns and Sacred Poems, Dublin, 1749

G OD moves in a mysterious way
  His wonders to perform;
He plants His footsteps in the sea,
  And rides upon the storm.

2 Deep in unfathomable mines
  Of never-failing skill,
He treasures up His bright designs,
  And works His sovereign will.

3 Ye fearful saints, fresh courage take;
  The clouds ye so much dread
Are big with mercy, and shall break
  In blessings on your head.

4 Judge not the Lord by feeble sense,
  But trust Him for His grace;
Behind a frowning providence
  He hides a smiling face.

5 His purposes will ripen fast,
  Unfolding every hour;
The bud may have a bitter taste,
  But sweet will be the flower.

6 Blind unbelief is sure to err,
  And scan His work in vain;
God is His own interpreter,
  And He will make it plain.

William Cowper, 1731–1800

UNDE ET MEMORES 10.10.10.10.10.10   W. H. MONK, 1823-89

B^E still, my soul: the Lord is on thy side;
   Bear patiently the cross of grief or pain;
Leave to thy God to order and provide;
   In every change He faithful will remain.
Be still, my soul: thy best, thy heavenly Friend
Through thorny ways leads to a joyful end.

2 Be still, my soul: thy God doth undertake
   To guide the future as He has the past.
Thy hope, thy confidence let nothing shake;
   All now mysterious shall be bright at last.
Be still, my soul: the waves and winds still know
His voice who ruled them while He dwelt below.

3 Be still, my soul: the hour is hastening on
   When we shall be forever with the Lord,
When disappointment, grief, and fear are gone,
   Sorrow forgot, love's purest joys restored.
Be still, my soul: when change and tears are past,
All safe and blessèd we shall meet at last.

Katharina von Schlegel, b. 1697
tr. Jane Laurie Borthwick, 1813–97
This hymn may also be sung to Song 1, No. 451

MEIRIONNYDD   76.76.D

By Thee, O God! invited,
  We look unto the Son,
In whom Thy soul delighted,
  Who all Thy will hath done;
And by the one chief treasure
  Thy bosom freely gave,
Thine own pure love we measure,
  Thy willing mind to save.

2 O God of mercy—Father!
  The one unchanging claim,
The brightest hopes we gather
  From Christ's most precious name,
That always sounds so sweetly
  In Thine unwearied ear,
And frees our souls completely
  From all our sinful fear.

3 The trembling sinner feareth
  That God can ne'er forget;
But one full payment cleareth
  His memory of all debt.
When naught beside could ease us,
  Or set our souls at large,
Thy holy work, Lord Jesus,
  Secured a full discharge.

4 No wrath God's heart retaineth,
  To usward who believe;
No dread in ours remaineth,
  As we His love receive;
Returning sons He kisses,
  And with His robe invests;
His perfect love dismisses
  All terror from our breasts.

Mary Bowly Peters, 1813-56

This hymn may also be sung to **Missionary**, No. 470

TRENTHAM S.M.

R. JACKSON, 1842-1914

Come and rejoice with me!
For once my heart was poor,
And I have found a treasury
Of love, a boundless store.

2 Come and rejoice with me!
I, once so sick at heart,
Have met with One who knows my case,
And knows the healing art.

3 Come and rejoice with me!
For I was wearied sore,
And I have found a mighty arm
Which holds me evermore.

4 Come and rejoice with me!
My feet so wide did roam,
And One has sought me from afar,
And beareth me safe home.

5 Come and rejoice with me!
For I have found a Friend
Who knows my heart's most secret depths
Yet loves me without end.

6 I knew not of His love,
And He had loved so long,
With love so faithful and so deep,
So tender and so strong.

7 And now I know it all,
Have heard and known His voice,
And hear it still from day to day,—
Can I enough rejoice?

Elisabeth Rundle Charles, 1828–96

This hymn may also be sung to **Huddersfield**, No. 328

ST. GODRIC 66.66.88   J. B. DYKES, 1823-76

D ONE is the work that saves!
   Once and for ever done;
Finished the righteousness
   That clothes the unrighteous one.
The love that blesses us below
Is flowing freely to us now.

2   The sacrifice is o'er
     The veil is rent in twain,
   The mercy-seat is red
     With blood of victim slain.
  Why stand we then without, in fear?
  The blood of Christ invites us near.

3   The gate is open wide;
     The new and living way
  Is clear, and free, and bright
     With love, and peace, and day.
  Into the holiest now we come,
  Our present and our endless home.

4   Before the mercy-seat
     The High Priest stands within,
  The blood is in His hand
     Which makes and keeps us clean.
  With boldness let us now draw near;
  That blood has banished every fear.

5   Then to the Lamb once slain
     Be glory, praise, and power,
  Who died and lives again,
     Who liveth evermore;
  Who loved and washed us in His
     blood,
  Who made us kings and priests to
     God.

Horatius Bonar, 1808–89

This hymn may also be sung to **Trumpet**, No. 214

PRAISE 886.D

A. RADIGER, 1749-1817

FROM whence this fear and unbelief,
Since God, my Father, put to grief
His spotless Son for me?
Can He, the righteous Judge of men,
Condemn me for that debt of sin
Which, Lord, was charged on Thee?

2 Complete atonement Thou hast made,
And to the utmost farthing paid
Whate'er Thy people owed;
How, then, can wrath on me take place,
If sheltered in Thy righteousness,
And sprinkled by Thy blood?

3 If Thou hast my discharge procured,
And freely in my place endured
The whole of wrath divine;
Payment God will not twice demand,
First at my Surety's piercèd hand,
And then again at mine.

4 Turn then, my soul, unto thy rest;
The merits of thy great High Priest
Speak peace and liberty;
Trust in His efficacious blood,
Nor fear thy banishment from God,
Since Jesus died for thee.

Augustus Montague Toplady, 1740–78

349

GOD HOLDS THE KEY 84.884   G. C. STEBBINS, 1846-1945

G OD holds the key of all unknown,
    And I am glad;
If other hands should hold the key,
Of if He trusted it to me,
    I might be sad.

2 What if to-morrow's cares were here
    Without its rest?
I'd rather He unlocked the day,
And, as the hours swing open, say,
    "My will is best."

3 The very dimness of my sight
    Makes me secure;
For, groping in my misty way,
I feel His hand, I hear Him say,
    "My help is sure."

4 I cannot read His future plans;
    But this I know:
I have the smiling of His face,
And all the refuge of His grace,
    While here below.

5 Enough; this covers all my wants;
    And so I rest!
For what I cannot, He can see,
And in His care I saved shall be,
    For ever blest.

Joseph Parker, 1830–1902

FAITHFULNESS   11.10.11.10 with refrain   W. M. RUNYAN, 1870-1957

GREAT is Thy faithfulness, O God
   my Father,
   There is no shadow of turning with
      Thee:
Thou changest not, Thy compassions,
   they fail not,
   As Thou hast been, Thou for ever
      wilt be.

*Great is Thy faithfulness! Great is Thy
   faithfulness!*
*Morning by morning new mercies
   I see;*
*All I have needed Thy hand hath
   provided,*
*Great is Thy faithfulness, Lord,
   unto me.*

2 Summer and winter, and springtime
     and harvest,
   Sun, moon and stars in their
      courses above,
   Join with all nature in manifold
      witness
   To Thy great faithfulness, mercy
      and love.

3 Pardon for sin and a peace that
     endureth;
   Thine own dear presence to cheer
      and to guide;
   Strength for to-day and bright hope
      for to-morrow:
   Blessings all mine, with ten thou-
      sand beside!

Thomas O. Chisholm, 1866–1960

351

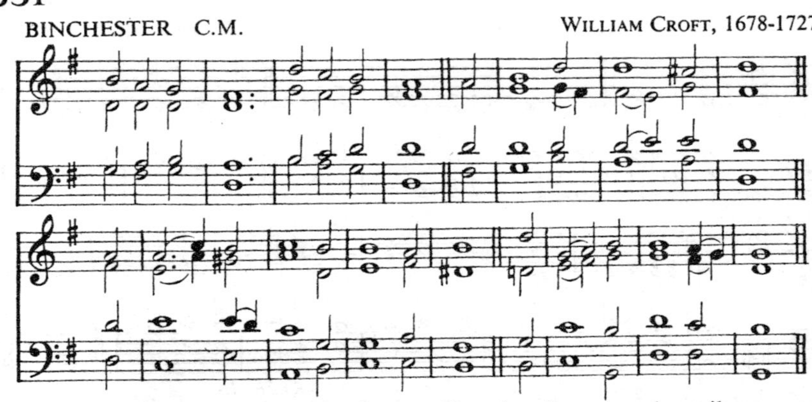

HAPPY are they, they that love God,
  Whose hearts have Christ confest,
Who by His cross have found their life,
  And 'neath His yoke their rest.

2 Glad is the praise, sweet are the songs,
  When they together sing;
And strong the prayers that bow the ear
  Of heaven's eternal King.

3 Christ to their homes giveth His peace,
  And makes their loves His own;
But ah, what tares the evil one
  Hath in His garden sown.

4 Sad were our lot, evil this earth,
  Did not its sorrows prove
The path whereby the sheep may find
  The fold of Jesu's love.

5 Then shall they know, they that love Him,
  How all their pain is good;
And death itself cannot unbind
  Their happy brotherhood.

Charles Coffin, 1676–1749
tr. Robert Seymour Bridges, 1844–1930

352 ADDOLIAD 11.11.11.11 — FIRST TUNE — D. GRIFFITHS, 1851-1932

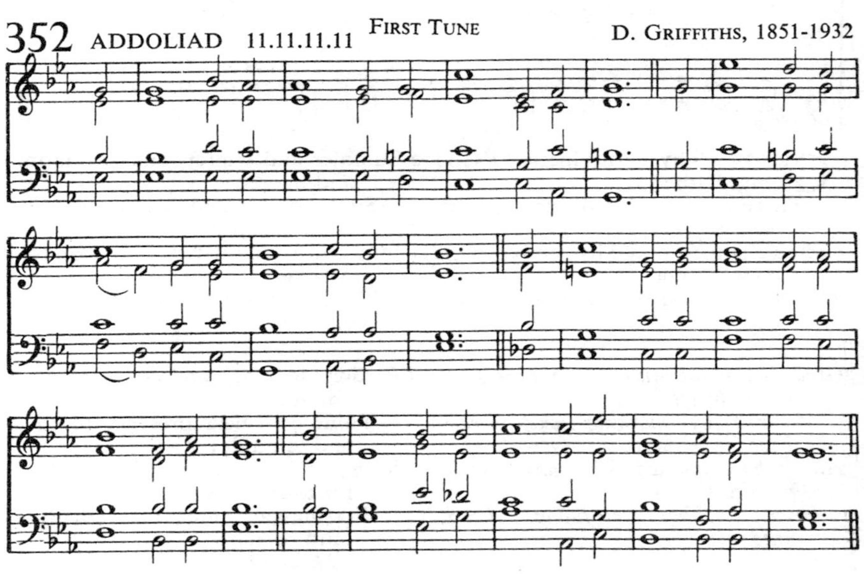

Second Tune

MONTGOMERY 11.11.11.11

Probably by Samuel Jarvis,
first published 1762

How firm a foundation, ye saints of
  the Lord,
Is laid for your faith in His excellent
  word!
What more can He say, than to you
  He hath said,
You, who unto Jesus for refuge have
  fled!

2 In every condition, in sickness, in
  health,
In poverty's vale, or abounding in
  wealth,
At home or abroad, on the land or the
  sea,
As thy days may demand, shall thy
  strength ever be.

3 Fear not, I am with thee; O be not
  dismayed,
For I am thy God, and will still give
  thee aid;
I'll strengthen thee, help thee, and
  cause thee to stand,
Upheld by My righteous, omnipotent
  hand.

4 When through the deep waters I call
  thee to go,
The rivers of grief shall not thee
  overflow;
For I will be with thee, thy troubles to
  bless,
And sanctify to thee thy deepest
  distress.

5 When through fiery trials thy pathway
  shall lie,
My grace all-sufficient shall be thy
  supply;
The flame shall not hurt thee; I only
  design
Thy dross to consume, and thy gold
  to refine.

6 The soul that on Jesus hath leaned
  for repose,
I will not, I will not, desert to its foes;
That soul, though all hell should endeavour to shake,
I'll never—no, never—no, never
  forsake.

Richard Keen, in Rippon's Selection, 1787

353

CRANBROOK S.M.

T. Clark, 1775-1859

GRACE! 'tis a charming sound,
Harmonious to the ear;
Heaven with the echo shall resound,
And all the earth shall hear.

2 Grace first contrived the way
To save rebellious man;
And all the steps that grace display,
Which drew the wondrous plan.

3 'Twas grace that wrote my name
In life's eternal book;
'Twas grace that gave me to the
Lamb,
Who all my sorrows took.

4 Grace led my wandering feet
To tread the heavenly road;
And new supplies each hour I meet,
While pressing on to God.

5 Grace taught my soul to pray,
And made my eyes o'erflow;
'Tis grace has kept me to this day,
And will not let me go.

6 Grace all the work shall crown
Through everlasting days;
It lays in heaven the topmost stone,
And well deserves the praise.

Philip Doddridge, 1702–51

This hymn may also be sung to **Silchester**, No. 491

354

GWENGAR S.M.

J. PARRY, 1841–1903

I BLESS the Christ of God;
I rest on love divine;
And with unfaltering lip and heart,
I call this Saviour mine.

2 His cross dispels each doubt;
I bury in His tomb
Each thought of unbelief and fear,
Each lingering shade of gloom.

3 I praise the God of grace;
I trust His truth and might;
He calls me His, I call Him mine,
My God, my joy, my light.

4 In Him is only good,
In me is only ill;
My ill but draws His goodness forth,
And me He loveth still.

5 'Tis He who saveth me,
And freely pardon gives,
I love because He loveth me,
I live because He lives.

6 My life with Him is hid,
My death has passed away,
My clouds have melted into light,
My midnight into day.

Horatius Bonar, 1808–89

355

HUDDERSFIELD S.M.   WILLIAMS' *Psalmody*, 1770

I HEAR the words of love,
  I gaze upon the blood,
I see the mighty sacrifice,
  And I have peace with God.

2   'Tis everlasting peace!
    Sure as Jehovah's name,
'Tis stable as His steadfast throne,
    For evermore the same.

3   The clouds may go and come,
    And storms may sweep my sky,
This blood-sealed friendship changes
       not,
    The cross is ever nigh.

4   My love is ofttimes low,
    My joy still ebbs and flows,
But peace with Him remains the
       same,
    No change Jehovah knows.

5   That which can shake the cross
    May shake the peace it gave,
Which tells me Christ has never died,
    Or never left the grave!

6   Till then my peace is sure,
    It will not, cannot yield,
Jesus, I know, has died and lives—
    On this firm rock I build.

7   I change, He changes not,
    The Christ can never die;
His love, not mine, the resting place,
    His truth, not mine, the tie.

Horatius Bonar, 1808–89

This hymn may also be sung to **St. Michael**, No. 529

HYFRYDOL 87.87.D

Melody by R. H. PRICHARD, 1811-87

I WILL sing the wondrous story
  Of the Christ who died for me;
How He left His home in glory,
  For the cross on Calvary.
I was lost: but Jesus found me—
  Found the sheep that went astray;
Threw His loving arms around me,
  Drew me back into His way.

2 I was bruised: but Jesus healed me—
  Faint was I from many a fall;
Sight was gone, and fears possessed
    me;
  But He freed me from them all.
Days of darkness still come o'er me;
  Sorrow's paths I often tread:
But the Saviour still is with me,
  By His hand I'm safely led.

3 He will keep me till the river
  Rolls its waters at my feet:
Then He'll bear me safely over,
  Where the loved ones I shall meet.
Then I'll sing the wondrous story
  Of the Christ who died for me –
Sing it with the saints in glory,
  Gathered by the crystal sea.

Francis Harold Rowley, 1854–1952

357

UNIVERSITY C.M.

C. COLLIGNON, 1725-85

I'M not ashamed to own my Lord,
Or to defend His cause;
Maintain the honour of His word,
The glory of His cross.

2 Jesus, my God, I know His name,
His name is all my trust;
Nor will He put my soul to shame,
Nor let my hope be lost.

3 Firm as His throne His promise
stands,
And He can well secure
What I've committed to His hands
Till the decisive hour.

4 Then will He own my worthless name
Before His Father's face,
And in the New Jerusalem
Appoint my soul a place.

Isaac Watts, 1674–1748

PENLAN 76.76.D

David Jenkins, 1848-1915

IN heavenly love abiding,
  No change my heart shall fear;
And safe is such confiding,
  For nothing changes here.
The storm may roar without me;
  My heart may low be laid;
But God is round about me:
  And can I be dismayed?

2 Wherever He may guide me,
  No want shall turn me back;
My Shepherd is beside me,
  And nothing can I lack:
His wisdom ever waketh,
  His sight is never dim!
He knows the way He taketh,
  And I will walk with Him.

3 Green pastures are before me,
  Which yet I have not seen;
Bright skies will soon be o'er me,
  Where dark the clouds have been.
My hope I cannot measure,
  My path to life is free;
My Saviour has my treasure,
  And He will walk with me.

Anna Laetitia Waring, 1820-1910
This hymn may also be sung to **Pen-yr-yrfa**, No. 571

LLEDROD L.M.   Welsh Hymn Melody

JESUS, Thy blood and righteousness
My beauty are, my glorious dress!
'Midst flaming worlds, in these arrayed,
With joy shall I lift up my head.

2 Bold shall I stand in that great day,
For who aught to my charge shall lay?
Fully through these absolved I am
From sin and fear, from guilt and shame.

3 Thus Abraham, the friend of God,
Thus all the saints redeemed with blood,
Saviour of sinners Thee proclaim,
And all their boast is in Thy name.

4 This spotless robe the same appears,
When ruined nature sinks in years;
No age can change its glorious hue:
The robe of Christ is ever new.

5 When from the dust of death I rise
To claim my mansion in the skies,
E'en then shall this be all my plea—
"Jesus hath lived, hath died for me."

6 Oh let the dead now hear Thy voice,
Now bid Thy banished ones rejoice,
Their beauty this, their glorious dress,
"Jesus, the Lord our righteousness."

Nicolaus Ludwig von Zinzendorf, 1700–60
tr. John Wesley, 1703–91

This hymn may also be sung to **Winchester New**, No. 16

ANTWERP L.M.

W. SMALLWOOD, 1831-97

JESUS, Thy far-extended fame
  My drooping soul exults to hear;
Thy name, Thy all-restoring name,
  Is music in a sinner's ear.

2 Sinners of old Thou didst receive
  With comfortable words and kind,
Their sorrows cheer, their wants
    relieve,
  Heal the diseased, and cure the
    blind.

3 And art Thou not the Saviour still,
  In every place and age the same?
Hast Thou forgot Thy gracious skill,
  Or lost the virtue of Thy name?

4 Faith in Thy changeless name I have;
  The good, the kind physician, Thou
Art able now our souls to save,
  Art willing to restore them now.

5 Wouldst Thou the body's health
    restore,
  And not regard the sin-sick soul?
The sin-sick soul Thou lov'st much
    more,
  And surely Thou shalt make it
    whole.

6 All my disease, my every sin,
  To Thee, Lord Jesus, I confess;
In pardon, Lord, my cure begin,
  And perfect it in holiness.

Charles Wesley, 1707-88

This hymn may also be sung to **Whitburn,** No. 156

CREDO 88.88.88

J. Stainer, 1840–1901

M^Y hope is built on nothing less
Than Jesu's blood and
righteousness;
I dare not trust the sweetest frame,
But wholly lean on Jesu's name:
On Christ, the solid rock, I stand;
All other ground is sinking sand.

2 When darkness seems to veil His
face,
I rest on His unchanging grace;
In every high and stormy gale,
My anchor holds within the veil.

3 His oath, His covenant, and blood,
Support me in the 'whelming flood;
When all around my soul gives way,
He then is all my hope and stay.

4 When the last trumpet's voice shall
sound
Oh may I then in Him be found
Clothed in His righteousness alone
Faultless to stand before His throne.

Edward Mote, 1797–1874, and others

This hymn may also be sung to **St. Catherine**, No. 331

KELSO 66.86.10.12 — Composer unknown

1. No blood, no altar now,
     The sacrifice is o'er;
   No flame, no smoke ascends on
       high,
     The Lamb is slain no more.
   But richer blood has flowed from
       nobler veins,
   To purge the soul from guilt, and
       cleanse the reddest stains.

2. We thank Thee for the blood,
     The blood of Christ, Thy Son;
   The blood by which our peace is
       made,
     Our victory is won:
   Great victory o'er hell, and sin, and
       woe,
   That needs no second fight, and
       leaves no second foe.

3. We thank Thee for the grace,
     Descending from above,
   That overflows our widest guilt,
     The eternal Father's love.
   Love of the Father's everlasting Son,
   Love of the Holy Ghost, Jehovah,
       three in one.

4. We thank Thee for the hope,
     So glad, and sure, and clear;
   It holds the drooping spirit up
     Till the long dawn appear;
   Fair hope! with what a sunshine
       does it cheer
   Our roughest path on earth, our
       dreariest desert here!

5. We thank Thee for the crown
     Of glory and of life;
   'Tis no poor withering wreath of
       earth,
     Man's prize in mortal strife:
   'Tis incorruptible as is the throne,
   The kingdom of our God and His
       incarnate Son.

Horatius Bonar, 1808–89

363

NUN DANKET ALL C.M.

J. CRÜGER, 1598-1662

"No condemnation!" O my soul,
'Tis God that speaks the word;
Perfect in comeliness art thou
In Christ thy glorious Lord.

2 In heaven His blood for ever speaks
In God the Father's ear;
His Church the jewels on His heart,
Jesus will ever bear.

3 "No condemnation," precious word—
Consider it, my soul.
Thy sins were all on Jesus laid;
His stripes have made thee whole.

4 Teach us, O God, to fix our eyes
On Christ the spotless Lamb;
So shall we love Thy gracious will,
And glorify Thy name.

Robert Cleaver Chapman, 1803–1902

This hymn may also be sung to **Lynton**, No. 248

MADRID 88.88.88

W. MATTHEWS, 1759-1830

Now I have found the ground,
    wherein
  Sure my soul's anchor may remain:
The wounds of Jesus, for my sin
  Before the world's foundation slain:
Whose mercy shall unshaken stay,
When heaven and earth are fled away.

2 O love, thou bottomless abyss,
    My sins are swallowed up in thee!
  Covered is my unrighteousness,
    Nor spot of guilt remains on me,
  While Jesu's blood, through earth and
      skies,
  Mercy, free, boundless mercy, cries!

3 By faith I plunge me in this sea,
    Here is my hope, my joy, my rest;
  Hither, when hell assails, I flee,
    I look into my Saviour's breast;
  Away, sad doubt, and anxious fear!
  Mercy is all that's written there.

4 Though waves and storms go o'er my
      head,
  Though strength, and health, and
      friends be gone,
  Though joys be withered all and dead,
  Though every comfort be with-
      drawn,
  On this my steadfast soul relies—
  Father, Thy mercy never dies!

5 Fixed on this ground will I remain,
    Though my heart fail, and flesh
        decay;
  This anchor shall my soul sustain,
    When earth's foundations melt
        away;
  Mercy's full power I then shall prove
  Loved with an everlasting love!

*Johann Andreas Rothe, 1688-1758
    tr. John Wesley, 1703-91*

This hymn may also be sung to **St. Matthias**, No. 287

365

DUKE STREET L.M.

J. Hatton, *d.* 1793

O HAPPY day, that fixed my choice
  On Thee, my Saviour and my God!
Well may this glowing heart rejoice,
  And tell its raptures all abroad.

2 'Tis done! the great transaction's done;
  I am my Lord's, and He is mine;
He drew me, and I followed on,
  Charmed to confess the voice divine.

3 Now rest, my long-divided heart;
  Fixed on this blissful centre, rest;
Nor ever from thy Lord depart,
  In Him of every good possessed.

4 High heaven, that heard the solemn vow,
  That vow renewed shall daily hear:
Till in life's latest hour I bow,
  And bless in death a bond so dear.

Philip Doddridge, 1702–51

This hymn may also be sung to **Festus,** No. 17

367

KELLY 88.85

Words at foot of next page

Composer unknown

SONG 46   10.10   ORLANDO GIBBONS, 1583-1625

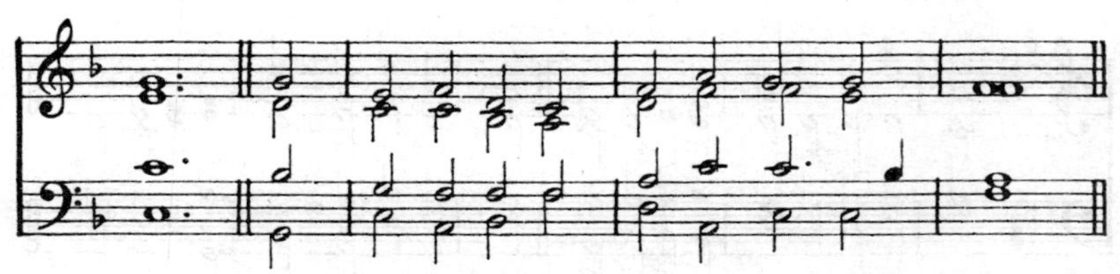

PEACE, perfect peace, in this dark
  world of sin?
The blood of Jesus whispers peace
  within.

2 Peace, perfect peace, by thronging
    duties pressed?
  To do the will of Jesus, this is rest.

3 Peace, perfect peace, with sorrows
    surging round?
  On Jesu's bosom nought but calm is
    found.

4 Peace, perfect peace, with loved ones
    far away?
  In Jesu's keeping we are safe, and
    they.

5 Peace, perfect peace, our future all
    unknown?
  Jesus we know, and He is on the
    throne.

6 Peace, perfect peace, death shadowing
    us and ours?
  Jesus has vanquished death and all its
    powers.

7 It is enough: earth's struggles soon
    shall cease,
  And Jesus call us to heaven's perfect
    peace.

Edward Henry Bickersteth, 1825–1906

367

Tune at foot of previous page

PRAISE the Saviour, ye who know
  Him!
Who can tell how much we owe Him?
Gladly let us render to Him
  All we have and are.

2 Jesus is the name that charms us,
  He for conflict fits and arms us,
  Nothing moves, and nothing harms us.
    When we trust in Him.

3 Trust in Him, ye saints, for ever;
  He is faithful, changing never;
  Neither force nor guile can sever
    Those He loves from Him.

4 Keep, us, Lord, oh, keep us cleaving
  To Thyself, and still believing,
  Till the hour of our receiving
    Promised joys in heaven.

5 Then we shall be where we would be,
  Then we shall be what we should be,
  Things which are not now, nor could
    be,
  Then shall be our own.

Thomas Kelly, 1769–1855

368

KENT L.M.

J. F. LAMPE, 1703-51

REJOICE, ye saints, rejoice and praise
The blessings of redeeming
grace;
Jesus, your everlasting tower,
Mocks at the angry tempest's power.

2 His love's a refuge ever nigh,
His watchfulness, a mountain high;
His name's a rock, which winds above
And waves below can never move.

3 His covenant, for ever sure,
To endless ages will endure;
His perfect work will ever prove
The depth of His unchanging love.

4 While all things change, He changes
not,
He ne'er forgets, though oft forgot;
His love's unchangeably the same,
And as enduring as His name.

5 Rejoice, ye saints, rejoice, and praise
The blessings of this wondrous grace;
Jesus, your everlasting tower,
Can bear unmoved the tempest's
power.

James Harrington Evans, 1785–1849

This hymn may also be sung to **Mainzer**, No. 338

369

BEAUMARIS   87.87

Composer unknown

RISE, my soul! behold 'tis Jesus,
  Jesus fills thy wond'ring eyes;
See Him now in glory seated,
  Where thy sins no more can rise.

2 There, in righteousness transcendent,
  Lo! He doth in heaven appear,
Shows the blood of His atonement
  As thy title to be there.

3 All thy sins were laid upon Him,
  Jesus bore them on the tree;
God who knew them laid them on
    Him,
  And, believing, thou art free.

4 God now brings thee to His dwelling,
  Spreads for thee His feast divine,
Bids thee welcome, ever telling
  What a portion there is thine.

5 In that circle of God's favour
  (Circle of the Father's love),
All is rest—and rest for ever—
  All is perfectness above.

6 Blessèd, glorious word, "for ever"!
  Yea, "for ever" is the word;
Nothing can the ransomed sever,
  Naught divide them from the Lord.

Joseph Denham Smith, 1817–89

MIT FREUDEN ZART   87.87.887   370
UNISON   Hymn melody of the *Bohemian Brethren*, 1566

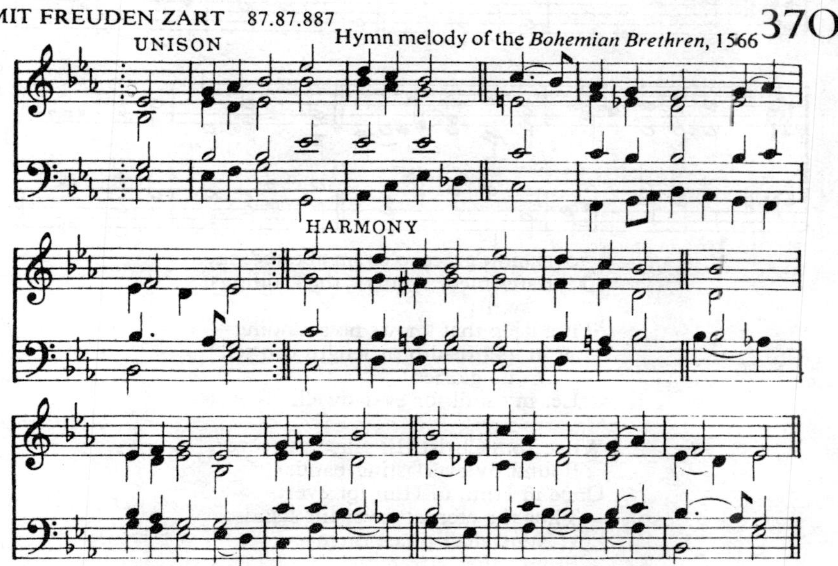

SING praise to God who reigns above,
  The God of all creation,
The God of power, the God of love,
  The God of our salvation;
With healing balm my soul He fills,
And every faithless murmur stills:
  To God all praise and glory.

2 What God's almighty power hath
    made,
  His gracious mercy keepeth;
By morning glow or evening shade
  His watchful eye ne'er sleepeth;
Within the kingdom of His might,
Lo! all is just and all is right:
  To God all praise and glory.

3 The Lord is never far away,
  But, through all grief distressing,
An ever-present help and stay,
  Our peace, and joy, and blessing;
As with a mother's tender hand,
He leads His own, His chosen band:
  To God all praise and glory.

4 Thus, all my toilsome way along,
  I sing aloud Thy praises,
That men may hear the grateful song
  My voice unwearied raises;
Be joyful in the Lord, my heart,
Both soul and body bear your part:
  To God all praise and glory.

Johann Jakob Schultz, 1640–90
tr. Frances Elizabeth Cox, 1812–97

This hymn may also be sung to **Castle Street**, No. 216

RHUDDLAN 87.87.87.   Welsh Traditional Melody

SOVEREIGN grace, o'er sin abounding,
Ransomed souls the tidings swell;
'Tis a deep that knows no sounding—
Who its breadth or length can tell?
On its glories
Let my soul for ever dwell.

2 What from Christ His saints can sever,
Bound by everlasting bands?
Once in Him, in Him for ever,
Thus the eternal covenant stands;
None shall pluck them
From the Strength of Israel's hands.

3 Heirs of God, joint heirs with Jesus,
Long ere time its course begun;
To His name eternal praises!
See what wonders love has done!
One with Jesus;
By eternal union one.

4 On such love, my soul, still ponder—
Love so great, so rich, so free!
Say, while lost in holy wonder,
Why, O Lord, such love to me?
Hallelujah!
Grace shall reign eternally.

John Kent, 1766–1843
This hymn may also be sung to **Cwm Rhondda**, No. 383

SICILIAN MARINERS 87.87   W. TATTERSALL's *Psalmody*, 1794

SWEET the moments, rich in blessing,
Which before the cross we spend,
Life, and health, and peace possessing,
From the sinner's dying Friend.

2 Here we rest, in wonder viewing
All our sins on Jesus laid,
And a full redemption flowing
From the sacrifice He made.

3 Here we find the dawn of heaven,
While upon the cross we gaze,
See our trespasses forgiven,
And our songs of triumph raise.

4 Oh that, near the cross abiding,
We may to the Saviour cleave!
Naught with Him our hearts dividing,
All for Him content to leave.

5 May we still, the cross discerning,
There for peace and comfort go;
There new wonders daily learning,
All the depths of mercy know.

James Allen, 1734–1804
and William Walter Shirley, 1725–86

AR HYD Y NOS   84.84.8884   Welsh Melody

THROUGH the love of God our Saviour,
    All will be well.
Free and changeless is His favour;
    All, all is well.
Precious is the blood that healed us,
Perfect is the grace that sealed us,
Strong the hand stretched forth to shield us,
    All must be well.

2 Though we pass through tribulation,
    All will be well.
Ours is such a full salvation,
    All, all is well.
Happy, still in God confiding,
Fruitful, if in Christ abiding,
Holy, through the Spirit's guiding,
    All must be well.

3 We expect a bright to-morrow,
    All will be well.
Faith can sing through days of sorrow,
    All, all is well.
On our Father's love relying,
Jesus every need supplying,
Or in living, or in dying,
    All must be well.

Mary Bowly Peters, 1813–56

GOSHEN 77.87.D

Adapted from F. J. HAYDN, 1732-1809

THY name we bless, Lord Jesus!
  That name all names excelling:
How great Thy love, all praise above,
  Should every tongue be telling.
  The Father's loving-kindness
  In giving Thee was shown us;
Now by Thy blood redeemed to God,
  As children He doth own us.

2 From that eternal glory
  Thou hadst with God the Father,
He gave His Son, that He in one
  His children all might gather.
  Our sins were all laid on Thee,
  God's wrath Thou hast endurèd;
It was for us Thou suffer'dst thus,
  And hast our peace securèd.

3 Thou from the dead wast raisèd,
  And from all condemnation
The church is free, as risen in Thee,
  Head of the new creation!
  On high Thou hast ascended
  To God's right hand in heaven;
The Lamb once slain, alive again,
  To Thee all power is given.

4 Thou hast bestowed the earnest
  Of that we shall inherit;
Till Thou shalt come to take us home,
  We're sealed by God the Spirit.
  We wait for Thine appearing,
  When we shall know more fully
The grace divine that made us Thine,
  Thou Lamb of God most holy!

Samuel Prideaux Tregelles, 1813-75

HANOVER   55.55.65.65

W. CROFT, 1678-1727

YE servants of God,
  Your Master proclaim,
And publish abroad
  His wonderful name;
The name all-victorious
  Of Jesus extol;
His kingdom is glorious,
  And rules over all.

2 God ruleth on high,
  Almighty to save;
And still He is nigh,
  His presence we have.
The great congregation
  His triumph shall sing,
Ascribing salvation
  To Jesus our King.

3 Salvation to God,
  Who sits on the throne;
Let all cry aloud,
  And honour the Son;
The praises of Jesus
  The angels proclaim,
Fall down on their faces,
  And worship the Lamb.

4 Then let us adore
  And give Him His right;
All glory and power,
  All wisdom and might;
All honour and blessing,
  With angels above;
And thanks never-ceasing,
  And infinite love.

Charles Wesley, 1707–88

DOLWYDDELAN 66.84.D

German Melody, 1693

W^E are by Christ redeemed;
   The cost—His precious blood:
Be nothing by our souls esteemed
   Like this great good.
Were the vast world our own,
   With all its varied store,
And Thou, Lord Jesus, wert un-
     known
   We still were poor.

2 No more we blindly grope
   Where true light doth not shine,
By faith we fix our every hope
   On One divine.
Thou art our Shepherd, Lord!
   We can no good thing want;
The blessings promised in Thy word
   Thou'lt freely grant.

3 Our earthen vessels break,
   The world itself grows old;
But Thou our precious dust wilt take,
   And freshly mould:
Wilt give these bodies vile
   A fashion like Thine own;
Wilt bid the whole creation smile,
   And hush its groan.

4 Thus far, by grace preserved,
   Each moment speeds us on;
The crown and kingdom are reserved
   Where Christ is gone.
When cloudless morning shines,
   We shall His glory share;
In pleasant places are the lines,
   The home how fair!

Mary Bowly Peters, 1813–56

This hymn may also be sung to **Leoni,** No. 53

VULPIUS (GELOBT SEI GOTT) 888 with Alleluias

Melody by MELCHIOR VULPIUS, *c.* 1560-1616

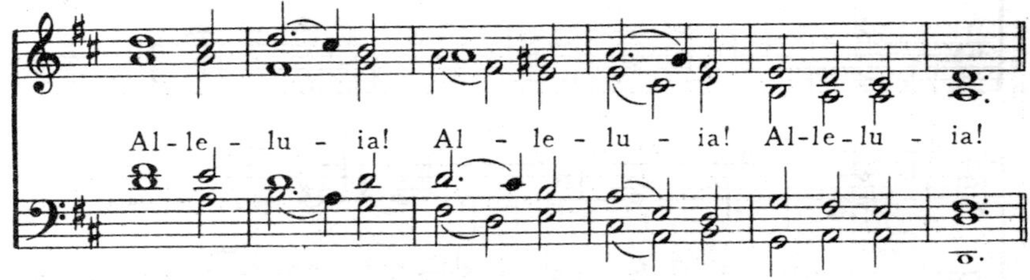

WHY should I fear the darkest hour,
Or tremble at the tempter's power?
Jesus vouchsafes to be my tower.
Alleluia!

2 Though hot the fight, why quit the field?
Why should I either flee or yield,
Since Jesus is my mighty shield?

3 I know not what may soon betide,
Or how my wants shall be supplied:
But Jesus knows, and will provide.

4 Though sin should fill me with distress,
The throne of grace I can address;
For Jesus is my righteousness.

5 Though faint my prayers, and cold my love,
My steadfast hope shall not remove
While Jesus intercedes above.

6 Against me earth and hell combine;
But on my side is power divine:
Jesus is all, and He is mine.

John Newton, 1725–1807

This hymn may also be sung to **Victory, No.** 177

ST. ISHMAEL D.S.M. CHARLES VINCENT, 1852-1934

ALONG the shining road
  That leads to life so free,
I tread with glad and glowing heart,
  For Jesus leadeth me;
Though long ago He passed
  Beyond our mortal sight,
The very pathway that He went
  Still shines with heavenly light.

2 I know that but for Him
  The road would darkened be,
And shapes and shadows dark and dread
  Might gather threateningly;
But He has trodden first
  The long, the changeful way,
And left His light upon it all
  To turn the night to day.

3 The shining road may seem
  To lose itself in night;
The valley mist, the winter cloud
  May hide it from my sight.
I know full well it winds,
  Until, or soon or late,
It finds upon the hills of God
  His shining City gate.

Frederic Goldsmith French, 1867-1947

This hymn may also be sung to **Nearer Home**, No. 632

SAMSON L.M.

G. F. HANDEL, 1685-1759

AWAKE our souls, away our fears,
  Let every trembling thought be gone;
Awake, and run the heavenly race,
  And put a cheerful courage on.

2 True, 'tis a strait and thorny road,
  And mortal spirits tire and faint;
But they forget the mighty God
  Who feeds the strength of every saint.

3 Thee, mighty God, whose matchless power
  Is ever new and ever young,
And firm endures while endless years
  Their everlasting circles run.

4 From Thee, the overflowing spring,
  Our souls shall drink a fresh supply;
While such as trust their native strength
  Shall melt away, and droop, and die.

5 Swift as an eagle cuts the air,
  We'll mount aloft to Thine abode:
On wings of love our souls shall fly,
  Nor tire along the heavenly road.

Isaac Watts, 1674–1748

381

Words at foot of next page

GLANLLYFNWY L.M.

E. DAVIES, b. 1870

MONKLAND 77.77

Arr. by J. B. WILKES, 1785-1869

CHILDREN of the heavenly King,
   As ye journey, sweetly sing;
Sing your Saviour's worthy praise,
Glorious in His works and ways.

2 Glory be to Jesu's name,
   Glory be to Christ, the Lamb;
Through His blood you are redeemed,
You who justly were condemned.

3 Shout, ye little flock, and blest,
   You on Jesu's throne shall rest;
There your seat is now prepared,
There your kingdom and reward.

4 Lift your eyes, ye sons of light,
   Zion's city is in sight;
There our endless home shall be,
There our Lord we soon shall see.

5 Fear not, brethren; joyful stand
   On the borders of your land;
Christ your Lord, the Father's Son,
Bids you undismayed go on.

6 Lord, obediently we go,
   Gladly leaving all below;
Only Thou our leader be,
And we still will follow Thee.

John Cennick, 1718–55

This hymn may also be sung to **Ephraim**, No. 173

381

Tune at foot of previous page

FIGHT the good fight with all thy
   might,
Christ is thy strength, and Christ thy
   right;
Lay hold on life, and it shall be
Thy joy and crown eternally.

2 Run the straight race through God's
      good grace,
Lift up thine eyes, and seek His face;
Life with its way before thee lies,
Christ is the path, and Christ the
   prize.

3 Cast care aside, lean on thy Guide;
His boundless mercy will provide;
Lean, and thy trusting soul shall prove,
Christ is its life, and Christ its love.

4 Faint not, nor fear, His arms are near,
He changeth not, and thou art dear;
Only believe, and thou shalt see
That Christ is all in all to thee.

John Samuel Bewley Monsell, 1811–75

This hymn may also be sung to **Duke Street**, No. 146

LLANLLYFNI D.S.M.

JOHN JONES (Talysarn), 1786-1857
Arr. by DAVID JENKINS, 1848-1915

GIVE to the winds thy fears;
Hope, and be undismayed;
God hears thy sighs and counts thy
tears,
God shall lift up thy head;
Through waves and clouds and
storms,
He gently clears thy way;
Wait thou His time, so shall this night
Soon end in joyous day.

2　He everywhere hath sway,
And all things serve His might,
His every act pure blessing is,
His path unsullied light:
When He makes bare His arm,
What shall His work withstand?
When He His people's cause defends.
Who, who shall stay His hand?

3　Leave to His sovereign sway
To choose and to command,
With wonder filled thou then shalt own
How wise, how strong His hand:
Thou comprehend'st Him not,
Yet earth and heaven both tell,
God sits as sovereign on the throne,
He ruleth all things well.

4　Thou seest our weakness, Lord;
Our hearts are known to Thee;
Oh lift Thou up the sinking hand,
Confirm the feeble knee!
Let us, in life, in death,
Thy steadfast truth declare,
And publish with our latest breath
Thy love and guardian care.

Paulus Gerhardt, 1607-1676
tr. John Wesley, 1703-1791

This hymn may also be sung to **From Strength to Strength**, No. 405

CWM RHONDDA 87.87.47   JOHN HUGHES (Pontypridd), 1873-1932

G UIDE me, O Thou great Jehovah,
  Pilgrim through this barren
    land;
I am weak, but Thou art mighty;
  Hold me with Thy powerful hand:
    Bread of heaven,
  Feed me now and evermore.

2 Open now the crystal fountain,
  Whence the healing waters flow;
Let the fiery, cloudy pillar,
  Lead me all my journey through:
    Strong Deliverer,
  Be Thou still my strength and
    shield.

3 When I tread the verge of Jordan,
  Bid my anxious fears subside;
Death of death and hell's destruction,
  Land me safe on Canaan's side:
    Songs of praises
  I will ever give to Thee.

William Williams, 1717–91
tr. Peter Williams, 1722–96
This hymn may also be sung to **Bryn Calfaria**, No. 138

MONKS GATE 65.65.66.65

English Traditional Melody
Arr. by R. VAUGHAN WILLIAMS, 1872–1958

HE who would valiant be
  'Gainst all disaster,
Let him in constancy
  Follow the Master.
There's no discouragement
Shall make him once relent
His first avowed intent
  To be a pilgrim.

2 Who so beset him round
  With dismal stories,
Do but themselves confound—
  His strength the more is.
No foes shall stay his might,
Though he with giants fight:
He will make good his right
  To be a pilgrim.

3 Since, Lord, thou dost defend
  Us with Thy Spirit,
We know we at the end
  Shall life inherit.
Then fancies flee away!
I'll fear not what men say,
I'll labour night and day
  To be a pilgrim.

adapted from John Bunyan, 1628–88

HOLD THOU MY HAND   11.10.11.10   H. P. MAIN, 1839-1925

H OLD Thou my hand! so weak I am,
  and helpless,
    I dare not take one step without
      Thy aid;
Hold Thou my hand! for then O
    loving Saviour,
    No dread of ill shall make my soul
      afraid.

2 Hold Thou my hand! and closer,
    closer draw me
    To Thy dear self—my hope, my
      joy, my all:
  Hold Thou my hand, lest haply I
    should wander;
    And missing Thee my trembling
      feet should fall.

3 Hold Thou my hand! the way is dark
    before me
    Without the sunlight of Thy face
      divine:
  But when by faith I catch its radiant
    glory,
    What heights of joy, what rapturous
      songs are mine!

4 Hold Thou my hand! that when I
    reach the margin
    Of that lone river Thou didst cross
      for me,
  A heavenly light may flash along its
    waters,
    And every wave like crystal bright
      shall be.

Frances Jane van Alstyne, 1820–1915

This hymn may also be sung to **Strength and Stay**, No. 487

386

DRAW NEAR 66.86.44

R. HARKNESS, 1880-1961

JESUS Himself drew near
And joined them as they walked,
And soon their hearts began to burn,
As of Himself He talked:
Draw near, O Lord.

2 Jesus Himself drew near,
They were no longer sad;
When He was walking at their side,
How could they but be glad?
Draw near, O Lord.

3 Jesus Himself drew near,
And all their doubts were solved;
He showed them why Christ came to
die
And what that death involved.
Draw near, O Lord.

4 Jesus Himself drew near,
And at the journey's end
They could not let Him leave them
thus,
The stranger was their friend.
Draw near, O Lord.

Ada R. Habershon, 1861–1918

PILOT   77.77.77

J. E. GOULD, 1822-75

JESUS, Saviour, pilot me
  Over life's tempestuous sea;
Unknown waves before me roll,
Hiding rock and treacherous shoal;
Chart and compass come from Thee:
Jesus, Saviour, pilot me!

2 As a mother stills her child,
  Thou canst hush the ocean wild;
Boisterous waves obey Thy will
When Thou say'st to them, "Be still!"
Wondrous Sovereign of the sea—
Jesus, Saviour, pilot me!

3 When at last I near the shore,
  And the fearful breakers roar
'Twixt me and the peaceful rest—
Then, while leaning on Thy breast,
May I hear Thee say to me—
"Fear not, I will pilot thee!"

Edward Hopper, 1818–88

388

SPIRE (ARNSTADT) 55.88.55   Original melody by A. DRESE, 1620-1701

JESUS, still lead on,
   Till our rest be won,
And, although the way be cheerless,
We will follow, calm and fearless:
   Guide us by Thy hand
   To our Fatherland.

2   If the way be drear,
    If the foe be near,
  Let not faithless fears o'ertake us,
  Let not love and hope forsake us,
    For, through many a foe,
    To our home we go.

3   When we seek relief
    From a long-felt grief,
  When oppressed by new temptations,
  Lord increase and perfect patience:
    Show us that bright shore
    Where we weep no more.

4   When sweet earth and skies
    Fade before our eyes;
  When through death · we look to
    heaven,
  And our sins are all forgiven,
    From Thy bright abode,
    Call us home to God.

5   Jesus, still lead on,
    Till our rest be won;
  Heavenly Leader, still direct us,
  Still support, console, protect us,
    Till we safely stand
    In our Fatherland.

Nicolaus Ludwig von Zinzendorf,
1700–60
tr. Jane Laurie Borthwick, 1813–97

MANNHEIM 87.87.87   Altered from Chorale by F. FILITZ, 1804-76

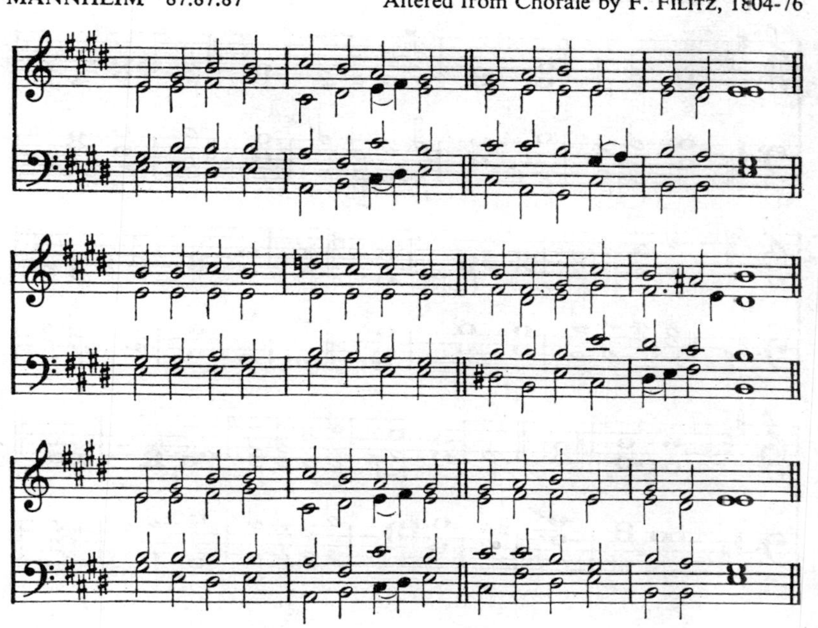

LEAD us, heavenly Father, lead us
    O'er the world's tempestuous sea;
Guard us, guide us, keep us, feed us,
    For we have no help but Thee;
Yet possessing every blessing,
    If our God our Father be.

2 Saviour, breathe forgiveness o'er us;
    All our weakness Thou dost know;
Thou didst tread this earth before us,
    Thou didst feel its keenest woe;
Lone and dreary, faint and weary,
    Through the desert Thou didst go.

3 Spirit of our God, descending,
    Fill our hearts with heavenly joy;
Love with every passion blending,
    Pleasure that can never cloy:
Thus provided, pardoned, guided,
    Nothing can our peace destroy.

James Edmeston, 1791–1867

390

ALL SOULS 10.10.10.10

John Yoakley, 1860-1932

Lead us, O Father, in the paths of peace;
Without Thy guiding hand we go astray,
And doubts appal, and sorrows still increase;
Lead us through Christ, the true and living way.

2 Lead us, O Father, in the paths of truth;
Unhelped by Thee, in error's maze we grope,
While passion stains and folly dims our youth,
And age comes on uncheered by faith and hope.

3 Lead us, O Father, in the paths of right;
Blindly we stumble when we walk alone,
Involved in shadows of a darksome night,
Only with Thee we journey safely on.

4 Lead us, O Father, to Thy heavenly rest,
However rough and steep the path may be,
Through joy or sorrow, as Thou deemest best,
Until our lives are perfected in Thee.

William Henry Burleigh, 1812–71

BARTON   10.4.10.4.10.10

J. T. LIGHTWOOD, 1856-1944

LIGHT of the world, faint were our weary feet
   With wandering far;
But Thou didst come our lonely hearts to greet,
   O Morning Star;
And Thou didst bid us lift our gaze on high,
To see the glory of the glowing sky.

2 In days long past we missed our homeward way;
   We could not see;
Blind were our eyes, our feet were bound to stray;
   How blind to Thee!
But Thou didst pity, Lord, our gloomy plight;
And Thou didst touch our eyes, and give them sight.

3 Now hallelujahs rise along the road
   Our glad feet tread;
Thy love hath shared our sorrow's heavy load;
   There's light o'erhead:
Glory to Thee whose love hath led us on,
Glory for all the great things Thou hast done.

4 Where is death's sting, where, grave, thy victory,
   Where all the pain,
Now that thy King the veil that hung o'er thee
   Hath rent in twain?
Light of the world, we hear Thee bid us come
To light and love in Thine eternal home.

Laura Ormiston Chant, 1848–1923

392

DISMISSAL 87.87.87

W. L. Viner, 1790-1867

Lord dismiss us with Thy blessing,
　Fill our hearts with joy and peace;
Let us each, Thy love possessing,
　Triumph in redeeming grace:
　　Oh, refresh us!
　Travelling through this wilderness.

2 Thanks we give, and adoration,
　For the gospel's joyful sound;
May the fruits of Thy salvation
In our hearts and lives abound;
　May Thy presence
With us, evermore, be found.

3 So, whene'er the signal's given
　Us from earth to call away;
Borne on angels' wings to heaven
　Glad the summons to obey,
　　May we ever
Reign with Thee in endless day.

John Fawcett, 1740-1817

393 ALBANO C.M.

Vincent Novello, 1781-1861

Lord, it belongs not to my care
　Whether I die or live;
To love and serve Thee is my share,
　And this Thy grace must give.

2 If life be long, I will be glad
　That I may long obey;
If short, yet why should I be sad
　To soar to endless day?

3 Christ leads me through no darker
      rooms
   Than He went through before;
 He that into God's kingdom comes
   Must enter by this door.

4 Come, Lord, when grace has made me
      meet
   Thy blessed face to see;
 For if Thy work on earth be sweet,
   What will Thy glory be?

5 Then shall I end my sad complaints,
   And weary, sinful days,
 And join with the triumphant saints
   That sing Jehovah's praise.

6 My knowledge of that life is small,
   The eye of faith is dim;
 But 'tis enough that Christ knows all,
   And I shall be with Him.

Richard Baxter, 1615–91

This hymn may also be sung to **Holy Trinity**, No. 523

INTEGER VITAE (FLEMMING)   11.11.11.5   F. F. FLEMMING, 1778-1813   **394**

LORD of our life, and God of our
   salvation,
 Star of our night, and hope of every
   nation,
 Hear and receive Thy church's
   supplication,
   Lord God Almighty!

2 See round Thine ark the hungry
   billows curling;
 See how Thy foes their banners are
   unfurling;
 Lord, while their darts envenomed
   they are hurling,
   Thou canst preserve us.

3 Lord, Thou canst help when earthly
   armour faileth,
 Lord, Thou canst save when sin itself
   assaileth,

Lord, o'er Thy church nor death nor
   hell prevaileth;
   Grant us Thy peace, Lord.

4 Peace in our hearts our evil thoughts
   assuaging,
 Peace in Thy church where brothers
   are engaging,
 Peace when the world its busy war is
   waging,
   Calm Thy foes' raging.

5 Grant us Thy help till backward they
   are driven,
 Grant them Thy truth, that they may
   be forgiven,
 Grant peace on earth, and after we
   have striven,
   Peace in Thy heaven.

Matthaus Appelles von Löwenstern, 1594–1648   *free tr. Philip Pusey*, 1799–1855

395

TENETE 85.85.D

Philipp Bliss, 1838-76

'MIDST the darkness, storm, and sorrow,
  One bright gleam I see;
Well I know the blessèd morrow
  Christ will come for me.
'Midst the light and peace and glory
  Of the Father's home,
Christ for me is watching, waiting,
  Waiting till I come.

2 There amidst the songs of heaven
    Sweeter to His ear
  Is the footfall through the desert,
    Ever drawing near.
  There, made ready are the mansions
    Radiant, bright, and fair;
  But the Bride the Father gave Him
    Still is wanting there.

3 Who is this who comes to meet me
    On the desert way,
  As the Morning Star foretelling
    God's unclouded day?
  He it is who came to win me.
    On the cross of shame;
  In His glory well I know Him,
    Evermore the same.

4 Oh the blessed joy of meeting,
    All the desert past!
  Oh the wondrous words of greeting
    He shall speak at last!
  He and I together entering
    Those bright courts above:
  He and I together sharing
    All the Father's love.

5 He who in His hour of sorrow
   Bore the curse alone;
I who through the lonely desert
   Trod where He had gone:

He and I in that bright glory,
   One deep joy shall share;
Mine, to be for ever with Him;
   His, that I am there.

Emma Frances Bevan, 1827–1909

This hymn may also be sung to **Pater Meus**, No. 472

LEONI (66.84.D)   Adapted from a Hebrew Melody 396
by THOMAS OLIVERS, 1725-99

MY Shepherd is the Lamb,
   The living Lord, who died;
With all things good I ever am
   By Him supplied;
He richly feeds my soul
   With blessings from above;
And leads me where the rivers roll
   Of endless love.

2 My soul He doth restore
   Whene'er I go astray;
He makes my cup of joy run o'er
   From day to day;
His love, so full, so free,
   Anoints my head with oil;
Mercy and goodness follow me,—
   Fruit of His toil.

3 When faith and hope shall cease,
   And love abides alone,
I then shall see Him face to face,
   And know as known.
Still shall I lift my voice;
   His praise my song shall be;
And I will in His love rejoice
   Who died for me.

James Beaumont, d. 1750

397

SWABIA S.M.

Arr. by W. H. HAVERGAL, 1793-1870,
from a melody in J. M. SPIESS' *Gesangbuch*, 1745

MY times are in Thy hand;
My God, I wish them there!
My life, my soul, my all I leave
Entirely to Thy care.

2 My times are in Thy hand;
Whatever they may be,
Pleasing or painful, dark or bright,
As best may seem to Thee.

3 My times are in Thy hand;
Why should I doubt or fear?
My Father's hand will never cause
His child a needless tear.

4 My times are in Thy hand,
Jesus the Crucified!
The hand my many sins had pierced
Is now my guard and guide.

5 My times are in Thy hand,
Jesus my advocate!
Nor can that hand be stretched in vain,
For me to supplicate.

6 My times are in Thy hand;
I'll always trust in Thee,
Till I have left this weary land,
And all Thy glory see.

William Freeman Lloyd, 1791–1853

This hymn may also be sung to **Rhodes,** No. 339

398

SOUTHWELL C.M.

H. S. IRONS, 1834-1905

O^H for a faith that will not shrink
  Though pressed by many a foe;
That will not tremble on the brink
  Of poverty or woe:

2 That will not murmur nor complain
  Beneath the chastening rod,
But in the hour of grief or pain
  Can lean upon its God:

3 A faith that shines more bright and
    clear
  When tempests rage without;
That when in danger knows no fear,
  In darkness feels no doubt;

4 A faith that keeps the narrow way
  Till life's last spark is fled,
And with a pure and heavenly ray
  Lights up a dying bed.

5 Lord, give me such a faith as this,
  And then, whate'er may come,
I'll taste e'en here the hallowed bliss
  Of an eternal home.

William Hiley Bathurst, 1796–1877

This hymn may also be sung to Irish, No. 35

399

ST. COLUMBA   C.M.

Irish Traditional Melody
Arr. BY C. V. STANFORD 1852-1924

O G^{OD} of Bethel, by whose hand
  Thy people still are fed;
Who through this weary pilgrimage
  Hast all our fathers led:

2 Our vows, our prayers, we now present
  Before Thy throne of grace:
God of our fathers, be the God
  Of their succeeding race.

3 Through each perplexing path of life
  Our wandering footsteps guide:
Give us, each day, our daily bread,
  And raiment fit provide.

4 Oh spread Thy covering wings around
  Till all our wanderings cease,
And at our Father's loved abode,
  Our souls arrive in peace.

Philip Doddridge, 1702–51   and John Logan, 1748–88

This hymn may also be sung to Martyrdom, No. 314, or Salzburg, No. 445

400

ALSTONE L.M.

C. E. WILLING, 1830-1904

OH grant us light, that we may know
   The wisdom Thou alone
     canst give;
That truth may guide where'er we go
   And virtue bless where'er we live.

2 Oh grant us light, that we may see,
   Where error lurks in human lore,
And turn our doubting minds to
     Thee,
   And love Thy simple word the
     more.

3 Oh grant us light, that we may learn
   How dead is life from Thee apart;
How sure is joy for all who turn
   To Thee an undivided heart.

4 Oh grant us light, in grief and pain,
   To lift our burdened hearts above,
And count the very cross a gain,
   And bless our Father's hidden love.

5 Oh grant us light, when soon or late
   All earthly scenes shall pass away,
In Thee to find the open gate
   To deathless home and endless day.

Lawrence Tuttiett, 1825–97

ST. ANSELM 76.76.D

J. BARNBY, 1838-1896

O HAPPY band of pilgrims,
　If onward ye will tread
With Jesus as your Fellow,
　To Jesus as your Head!
Oh, happy, if ye labour
　As Jesus did for men:
Oh, happy, if ye hunger
　As Jesus hungered then!

2 The faith by which ye see Him,
　The hope in which ye yearn,
The love that through all troubles
　To Him alone will turn:
What are they but His heralds
　To lead you to His sight?
What are they save the effluence
　Of uncreated light?

3 The trials that beset you,
　The sorrows ye endure,
The manifold temptations
　That death alone can cure:
What are they but His jewels
　Of right celestial worth?
What are they but the ladder
　Set up to heaven on earth?

4 The cross that Jesus carried,
　He carried as your due;
The crown that Jesus weareth,
　He weareth it for you.
O happy band of pilgrims,
　Look upward to the skies,
Where such a light affliction
　Shall win you such a prize!

John Mason Neale, 1818–66; based on Joseph the Hymnographer, 9th cent.

INVOCATION D.C.M. extended   R. A. SMITH, 1780-1829

OH send Thy light forth and Thy
truth;
Let them be guides to me,
And bring me to Thine holy hill,
E'en where Thy dwellings be.

2 Then will I to God's altar go,
To God my chiefest joy;
Yea, God, my God, Thy name to
praise
My harp I will employ.

3 Why art thou then cast down, my soul?
What should discourage thee?
And why with vexing thoughts art
thou
Disquieted in me?

4 Still trust in God; for Him to praise
Good cause I yet shall have;
He of my count'nance is the health,
My God that doth me save.

Robert Archibald Smith, 1780–1829

This hymn may also be sung to **St. Matthew**, No. 124

403

OMBERSLEY L.M.

W. H. GLADSTONE, 1840-91

O^H, walk with Jesus, would'st thou
    know
How deep, how wide His love can
    flow!
They only fail His love to prove
Who in the ways of sinners rove.

2 Walk thou with Him; that way is
    light,
All other pathways end in night:
Walk thou with Him; that way is rest,
All other pathways are unblest.

3 Oh, walk with Jesus! to thy view
He will make all things sweet and
    new;
Will bring new fragrance from each
    flower,
And hallow every passing hour.

4 Jesus, a great desire have we
To walk life's troubled path with
    Thee:
Come to us now, in converse stay;
And oh, walk with us day by day.

Edwin Paxton Hood, 1820–85

SHARON 87.87

WILLIAM BOYCE, 1710-79

RISE, my soul! thy God directs thee;
  Stranger hands no more impede:
Pass thou on, His hand protects
    thee—
  Strength that has the captive freed.

2 Is the wilderness before thee—
  Desert lands where drought abides?
Heavenly springs shall there restore
    thee,
  Fresh from God's exhaustless tides.

3 Light divine surrounds thy going;
  God Himself shall mark thy way:
Secret blessings, richly flowing,
  Lead to everlasting day.

4 In the desert, God will teach thee
  What the God that thou hast found;
Patient, gracious, powerful, holy—
  All His grace shall there abound.

5 Though thy way be long and dreary,
  Eagle strength He'll still renew:
Garments fresh and foot unweary
  Tell how God hath brought thee
    through.

6 When to Canaan's long-loved
    dwelling,
  Love divine thy foot shall bring,
There, with shouts of triumph
    swelling,
  Zion's songs, in rest, to sing:

7 There no stranger-God shall meet
    thee,
  Stranger thou in courts above!
He who to His rest shall greet thee,
  Greets thee with a well-known love.

John Nelson Darby, 1800–82

This hymn may also be sung to **Beaumaris,** No. 219

FROM STRENGTH TO STRENGTH D.S.M. E. W. NAYLOR, 1867-1934

SOLDIERS of Christ, arise,
And put your armour on,
Strong in the strength which God
supplies
Through His eternal Son;
Strong in the Lord of hosts,
And in His mighty power,
Who in the strength of Jesus trusts
Is more than conqueror.

2 Stand then in His great might,
With all His strength endued,
And take, to arm you for the fight,
The panoply of God;
That having all things done,
And all your conflicts past,
Ye may o'ercome through Christ
alone,
And stand entire at last.

3 To keep your armour bright,
Attend with constant care,
Still walking in your Captain's sight,
And watching unto prayer.
Go to His temple, go,
Nor from His altar move;
Let every house His worship know,
And every heart His love.

4 Pray, without ceasing pray,
(Your Captain gives the word,)
His summons cheerfully obey,
And call upon the Lord;
To God your every want
In instant prayer display,
Pray always; pray, and never faint,
Pray, without ceasing pray.

5 From strength to strength go on,
Wrestle and fight and pray,
Tread all the powers of darkness
down,
And win the well-fought day;
Still let the Spirit cry
In all His soldiers, "Come,"
Till Christ the Lord descends from
high,
And takes the conquerors home.

Charles Wesley, 1707–88

This hymn may also be sung to **St. Ethelwald**, No. 290

406

PEARSALL 76.76.D

R. L. DE PEARSALL, 1795-1856

SOMETIMES a light surprises
  The Christian while he sings:
It is the Lord who rises
  With healing in His wings
When comforts are declining,
  He grants the soul again
A season of clear shining,
  To cheer it after rain.

2 In holy contemplation,
  We sweetly then pursue
The theme of God's salvation,
  And find it ever new:
Set free from present sorrow,
  We cheerfully can say,
E'en let the unknown morrow
  Bring with it what it may.

3 It can bring with it nothing
  But He will bear us through;
Who gives the lilies clothing,
  Will clothe His people too:
Beneath the spreading heavens
  No creature but is fed,
And He who feeds the ravens,
  Will give His children bread.

4 Though vine nor fig tree neither
  Their wonted fruit should bear,
Though all the field should wither,
  Nor flocks nor herds be there,
Yet God, the same abiding,
  His praise shall tune my voice;
For, while in Him confiding,
  I cannot but rejoice.

William Cowper, 1731–1800

GLANHAFREN 64.64.66.64

Welsh melody

TEACH me Thy way, O Lord,
    Teach me Thy way!
Thy gracious aid afford,
    Teach me Thy way!
Help me to walk aright,
More by faith, less by sight;
Lead me with heavenly light:
    Teach me Thy way!

2 When doubts and fears arise,
    Teach me Thy way!
When storms o'erspread the skies,
    Teach me Thy way!
Shine through the cloud and rain,
Through sorrow, toil, and pain;
Make Thou my pathway plain:
    Teach me Thy way!

3 Long as my life shall last,
    Teach me Thy way!
Where'er my lot be cast,
    Teach me Thy way!
Until the race is run,
Until the journey's done,
Until the crown is won,
    Teach me Thy way!

Benjamin Mansell Ramsey, 1849–1923

408

FIRST TUNE

DOMINUS REGIT ME   87.87 Iambic

J. B. DYKES, 1823-76

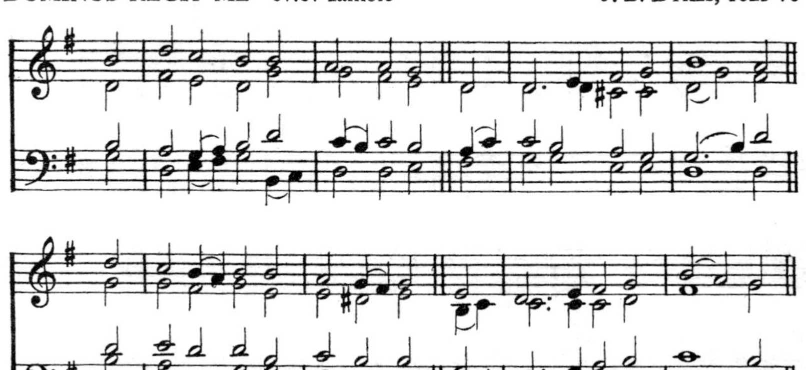

SECOND TUNE

DEGANWY   87.87, Iambic

B. WILLIAMS, 1839-1918

THE King of love my Shepherd is,
  Whose goodness faileth never:
I nothing lack if I am His,
  And He is mine, for ever.

2 Where streams of living waters flow
  My ransomed soul He leadeth,
And, where the verdant pastures grow
  With food celestial feedeth.

3 Perverse and foolish oft I strayed,
  But yet in love He sought me,
And on His shoulder gently laid,
  And home rejoicing brought me.

4 In death's dark vale I fear no ill
  With Thee, dear Lord, beside me,
Thy rod and staff my comfort still,
  Thy cross before to guide me.

5 Thou spread'st a table in my sight;
  Thy unction grace bestoweth;
And oh what transport of delight
  From Thy pure chalice floweth.

6 And so, through all the length of days,
  Thy goodness faileth never:
Good Shepherd, may I sing Thy praise
  Within Thy house for ever.

Henry Williams Baker, 1821–77

CRIMOND C.M.

Melody by JESSIE S. IRVINE, 1836-87

THE Lord's my Shepherd, I'll not
    want:
He makes me down to lie
In pastures green; He leadeth me
    The quiet waters by.

2 My soul He doth restore again;
    And me to walk doth make
Within the paths of righteousness,
    E'en for His own name's sake.

3 Yea, though I walk in death's dark
    vale,
    Yet will I fear none ill:
For Thou art with me; and Thy rod
    And staff me comfort still.

4 My table Thou has furnishèd
    In presence of my foes;
My head Thou dost with oil anoint,
    And my cup overflows.

5 Goodness and mercy all my life
    Shall surely follow me;
And in God's house for evermore
    My dwelling-place shall be.

William Whittingham, c. 1524–79
Francis Rous, 1579–1659, and others

This hymn may also be sung to Orlington, No. 225

410

NEWINGTON 77.77

W. D. MACLAGAN, 1826-1910

THINE for ever: God of love,
  Hear us from Thy throne above;
Thine for ever may we be,
Here and in eternity.

2 Thine for ever: Lord of life,
  Shield us through our earthly strife;
Thou the Life, the Truth, the Way,
Guide us to the realms of day.

3 Thine for ever: oh, how blest
  They who find in Thee their rest;
Saviour, Guardian, heavenly Friend,
Oh, defend us to the end!

4 Thine for ever: Shepherd, keep
  These Thy frail and trembling sheep;
Safe alone beneath Thy care,
Let us all Thy goodness share.

5 Thine for ever: Thou our Guide,
  All our wants by Thee supplied,
All our sins by Thee forgiven,
Lead us, Lord, from earth to heaven.

Mary Fawler Maude, 1819–1913

411

WILTSHIRE C.M.

G. T. SMART, 1776-1867

Through all the changing scenes of
   life
  In trouble and in joy,
The praises of my God shall still
  My heart and tongue employ.

2 Of His deliverance I will boast,
  Till all that are distressed
From my example comfort take,
  And charm their griefs to rest.

3 Oh magnify the Lord with me,
  With me exalt His name;
When in distress to Him I called,
  He to my rescue came.

4 The hosts of God encamp around
  The dwellings of the just;
Deliverance He affords to all
  Who on His succour trust.

5 Oh make but trial of His love!
  Experience will decide
How blest are they, and only they,
  Who in His truth confide.

6 Fear Him, ye saints, and you will then
  Have nothing else to fear;
Make you His service your delight—
  Your wants shall be His care.

Nahum Tate, 1652–1715
and Nicholas Brady, 1659–1726

412

MARCHING   87.87   Martin Shaw, 1875-1958

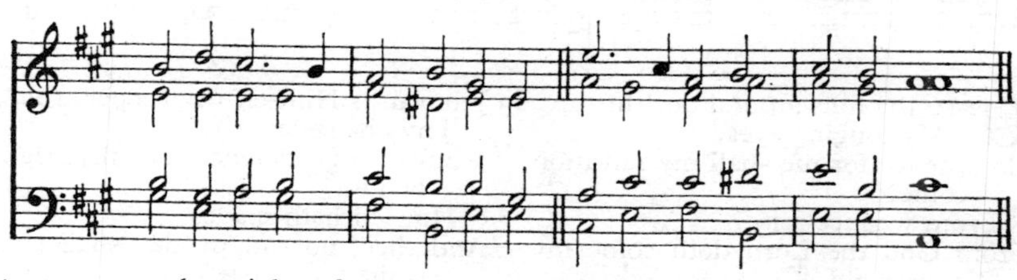

Through the night of doubt and
   sorrow
  Onward goes the pilgrim band,
Singing songs of expectation,
  Marching to the promised land.

2 Clear before us through the darkness
  Gleams and burns the guiding light;
Brother clasps the hand of brother,
  Stepping fearless through the night.

3 One the light of God's own presence
  O'er His ransomed people shed,
Chasing far the gloom and terror,
  Brightening all the path we tread;

4 One the object of our journey,
  One the faith that never tires,
One the earnest looking forward,
  One the hope our God inspires;

5 One the strain that lips of thousands
  Lift as from the heart of one;
One the conflict, one the peril,
  One the march in God begun;

6 One the gladness of rejoicing
  On the far eternal shore,
Where the one almighty Father
  Reigns in love for evermore.

Bernhardt Severin Ingemann, 1789–1862 ; *tr. Sabine Baring-Gould, 1834–1924*

4I3

ALBERTA 10.4.10.4.10.10

W. H. HARRIS, 1883-1973

UNTO the hills around do I lift up
  My longing eyes,
Oh whence for me shall my salvation
  come,
  From whence arise?
From God the Lord doth come my
  certain aid,
From God the Lord, who heaven and
  earth hath made.

2 He will not suffer that thy foot be
  moved;
  Safe shalt thou be.
No careless slumber shall His eyelids
  close,
  Who keepeth thee.
Behold our God, the Lord, He
  slumbereth ne'er,
Who keepeth Israel in His holy care.

3 Jehovah is Himself thy keeper true,
  Thy changeless shade;
Jehovah thy defence on thy right
  hand
  Himself hath made.
And thee, no sun by day shall ever
  smite,
No moon shall harm thee in the silent
  night.

4 From every evil shall He keep thy
  soul,
  From every sin;
Jehovah shall preserve thy going out,
  Thy coming in.
Above thee watching, He, whom we
  adore,
Shall keep thee henceforth, yea, for
  evermore.

John Douglas Sutherland Campbell, 1845–1914

This hymn may also be sung to **Sandon,** No. 570

NOX PRAECESSIT C.M.   J. Baptiste Calkin, 1827-1905

WALK in the light, so shalt thou
    know
That fellowship of love,
His Spirit only can bestow,
    Who reigns in light above.

2 Walk in the light, and sin abhorred
    Shall ne'er defile again;
The blood of Jesus Christ thy Lord
    Shall cleanse from every stain.

3 Walk in the light, and thou shalt find
    Thy heart made truly His,
Who dwells in cloudless light en-
    shrined,
    In whom no darkness is.

4 Walk in the light, and thou shalt own
    Thy darkness passed away,
Because that Light hath on thee
    shone,
    In which is perfect day.

5 Walk in the light, and e'en the tomb
    No fearful shade shall wear;
Glory shall chase away its gloom,
    For Christ hath conquered there.

6 Walk in the light and thine shall be
    A path, though thorny, bright;
For God, by grace, shall dwell in thee
    And God Himself is light.

Bernard Barton, 1784-1849

415

MENDIP C.M.

English Traditional Melody
Arr. by R. VAUGHAN WILLIAMS, 1872–1958

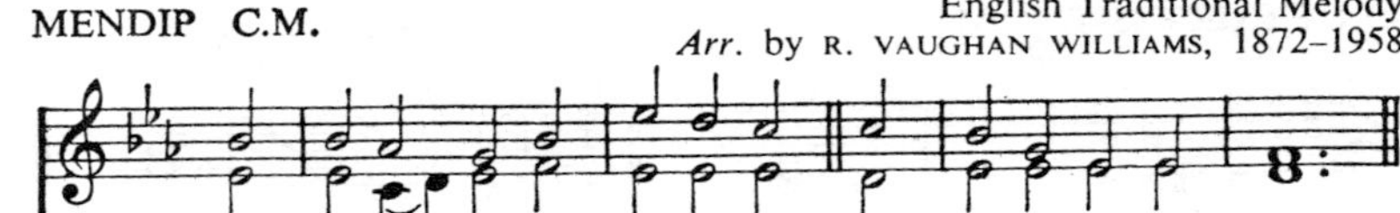

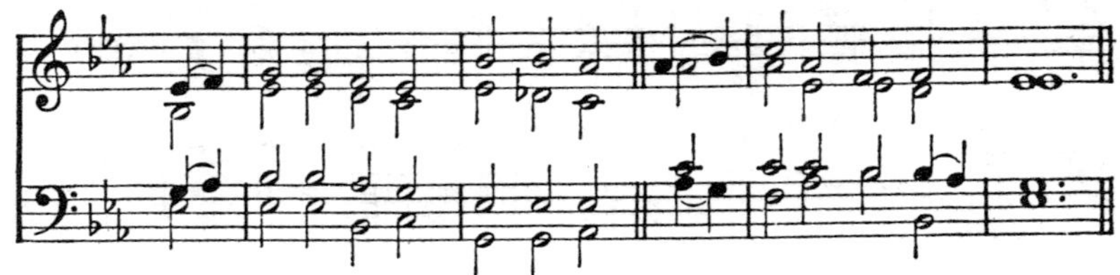

WE bless Thee for Thy peace, O God,
Deep as the unfathomed sea,
Which falls like sunshine on the road
Of those who trust in Thee.

2 We ask not, Father, for repose
Which comes from outward rest,
If we may have through all life's woes
Thy peace within our breast;

3 That peace which suffers and is strong,
Trusts where it cannot see,
Deems not the trial-way too long,
But leaves the end with Thee;

4 That peace which flows serene and deep,
A river in the soul,
Whose banks a living verdure keep,
God's sunshine o'er the whole.

5 O Father, give our hearts this peace,
Whate'er the outward be,
Till all life's discipline shall cease,
And we come home to Thee.

Author unknown

416

GREEN HILL C.M.

A. L. PEACE, 1844-1912

W HO fathoms the eternal thought?
Who talks of scheme and plan?
The Lord is God! He needeth not
The poor device of man.

2 Here in the maddening maze of things,
When tossed by storm and flood,
To one fixed ground my spirit clings;
I know that God is good!

3 I long for household voices gone,
For vanished smiles I long;
But God hath led my dear ones on,
And He can do no wrong.

4 I know not what the future hath
Of marvel or surprise,
Assured alone that life and death
His mercy underlies.

5 And if my heart and flesh are weak
To bear an untried pain,
The bruisèd reed He will not break,
But strengthen and sustain.

6 No offering of my own I have,
Nor works my faith to prove;
I can but give the gifts He gave,
And plead His love for love.

7 And so beside the silent sea
I wait the muffled oar;
No harm from Him can come to me
On ocean or on shore.

8 I know not where His islands lift
Their fronded palms in air;
I only know I cannot drift
Beyond His love and care.

John Greenleaf Whittier, 1807–92

HENSBURY   C.M.   R. BENNETT, 1788-1819 # 417

W HEN Israel, by divine command,
The pathless desert trod,
They found, through all that barren land,
A sure resource in God.

2 A cloudy pillar marked the road,
And screened them from the heat;
From the hard rock the water flowed,
And manna was their meat.

3 Like them we have a rest in view,
Secure from adverse powers;
Like them we pass a desert too,
But Israel's God is ours.

4 His word a light before us sheds,
By which our path we see;
His love, a banner o'er our heads,
From harm preserves us free.

5 Jesus, the Bread of Life, is given
To be our daily food;
And from the Rock that once was riven
We drink the streams of God.

John Newton, 1725–1807

See also
15 Come ye that love the Lord
496 Who is on the Lord's side?
589 For the might of Thine arm we bless Thee
688 Fierce was the wild billow
692 I dared not hope that Thou
694 I take Thy promise, Lord

MOZART 88.88.88

From Mozart's *Die Zauberflöte*, 1791

BEHOLD the servant of the Lord!
  I wait Thy guiding eye to feel,
To hear and keep Thy every word,
  To prove and do Thy perfect will,
Joyful from my own works to cease,
Glad to fulfil all righteousness.

2 Me, if Thy grace vouchsafe to use,
  Meanest of all Thy creatures, me:
The deed, the time, the manner
    choose,
  Let all my fruit be found of Thee;
Let all my works in Thee be wrought,
By Thee to full perfection brought.

3 My every weak, though good design,
  O'errule, or change, as seems Thee
    meet;
Jesus, let all my work be Thine!
  Thy work, O Lord, is all complete,
And pleasing in Thy Father's sight;
Thou only hast done all things right.

4 Here then to Thee Thy own I leave;
  Mould as Thou wilt Thy passive
    clay;
But let me all Thy stamp receive,
  But let me all Thy words obey,
Serve with a single heart and eye,
And to Thy glory live and die.

Charles Wesley, 1707–88

AUGUSTINE S.M.

PETER ABELARD, 1079-1142

B LEST are the pure in heart,
For they shall see our God,
The secret of the Lord is theirs,
Their soul is Christ's abode.

2   The Lord, who left the heavens
Our life and peace to bring,
To dwell in lowliness with men,
Their pattern and their King—

3   Still to the lowly soul
He doth Himself impart,
And for His dwelling and His throne
Chooseth the pure in heart.

4   Lord, we Thy presence seek:
May ours this blessing be;
Give us a pure and lowly heart,
A temple meet for Thee.

John Keble, vv. 1, 3, 1792–1866
William John Hall,
vv. 2, 4, 1793–1861

420

SLANE 10.11.11.12

Irish Traditional Melody

BE Thou my Vision, O Lord of my heart;
Naught be all else to me, save that Thou art—
Thou my best thought, in the day or the night,
Waking or sleeping, Thy presence my light.

2 Be Thou my Wisdom, be Thou my true Word;
I ever with Thee, and Thou with me, Lord;
Thou my great Father, and I Thy true son;
Thou in me dwelling, and I with Thee, one.

3 Be Thou my breastplate, my sword for the fight;
Be Thou my dignity, Thou my delight,
Thou my soul's shelter, and Thou my high tower;
Raise Thou me heavenward, O power of my power.

4 Riches I heed not, nor man's empty praise;
Thou mine inheritance, now and always:
Thou, and Thou only, be first in my heart,
High King of heaven, my treasure Thou art.

5 High King of heaven, Thou bright heaven's Sun,
Grant me its joys, after vict'ry is won;
Heart of my own heart, whatever befall,
Still be my Vision, O ruler of all.

Ancient Irish, tr. by Mary Elizabeth Byrne, 1880–1931
Versified by Eleanor Henrietta Hull, 1860–1935

VIGILATE   777.3

Melody by W. H. MONK, 1823-89

CHRISTIAN, seek not yet repose,
  Cast thy dreams of ease away;
Thou art in the midst of foes:
  Watch and pray.

2 Principalities and powers,
  Mustering their unseen array,
Wait for thy unguarded hours:
  Watch and pray.

3 Gird thy heavenly armour on,
  Wear it ever, night and day;
Ambushed lies the evil one:
  Watch and pray.

4 Hear the victors who o'ercame;
  Still they mark each warrior's way;
All with one sweet voice exclaim,
  Watch and pray.

5 Hear, above all, hear thy Lord,
  Him Thou lovest to obey;
Hide within thy heart His word:
  Watch and pray.

6 Watch, as if on that alone
  Hung the issue of the day;
Pray that help may be sent down:
  Watch and pray.

Charlotte Elliott, 1789–1871

422

BIRMINGHAM 10.10.10.10

From Rev. F. CUNNINGHAM'S
A Selection of Psalm Tunes, 1834

COME in, oh come! the door stands open now;
I knew Thy voice: Lord Jesus, it was Thou;
The sun has set long since; the storms begin;
'Tis time for Thee, my Saviour, oh come in!

2 Alas, ill-ordered shows the dreary room;
The household-stuff lies heaped amidst the gloom;
The table empty stands, the couch undressed;
Ah, what a welcome for the Eternal Guest!

3 Yet welcome, and to-day; this doleful scene
Is e'en itself my cause to hail Thee in;
This dark confusion e'en at once demands
Thine own bright presence, Lord, and ordering hands.

4 I seek no more to alter things, or mend,
Before the coming of so great a Friend;
All were at best unseemly; and 'twere ill
Beyond all else to keep Thee waiting still.

5 Come, not to find, but make this troubled heart
A dwelling worthy of Thee as Thou art;
To chase the gloom, the terror, and the sin:
Come, all Thyself, yea come Lord Jesus in!

Handley Carr Glyn Moule, 1841–1920

This hymn may also be sung to **Morecambe,** No. 600

REPTON 86.886   FIRST TUNE   C. H. H. PARRY, 1848-1918

DEAR Lord and Father of mankind,
  Forgive our foolish ways!
Re-clothe us in our rightful mind;
In purer lives Thy service find,
  In deeper reverence, praise.

2 In simple trust like theirs who heard,
  Beside the Syrian sea,
The gracious calling of the Lord,
Let us, like them, without a word
  Rise up and follow Thee.

3 Oh Sabbath rest by Galilee!
  Oh calm of hills above,
Where Jesus knelt to share with Thee
The silence of eternity,
  Interpreted by love.

4 With that deep hush subduing all
  Our words and works that drown
The tender whisper of Thy call,
As noiseless let Thy blessing fall
  As fell Thy manna down.

5 Drop Thy still dews of quietness,
  Till all our strivings cease;
Take from our souls the strain and
    stress:
And let our ordered lives confess
  The beauty of Thy peace.

6 Breathe through the heats of our
    desire
  Thy coolness and Thy balm;
Let sense be dumb—let flesh retire;
Speak through the earthquake, wind,
    and fire,
  O still small voice of calm!

John Greenleaf Whittier, 1807–92

423

REST 86.886

F. C. Maker, 1844-1927

Dear Lord and Father of mankind,
  Forgive our foolish ways!
Re-clothe us in our rightful mind;
In purer lives Thy service find,
  In deeper reverence, praise.

2 In simple trust like theirs who heard,
    Beside the Syrian sea,
The gracious calling of the Lord,
Let us, like them, without a word
    Rise up and follow Thee.

3 Oh Sabbath rest by Galilee!
    Oh calm of hills above,
Where Jesus knelt to share with Thee
The silence of eternity,
    Interpreted by love.

4 With that deep hush subduing all
    Our words and works that drown
The tender whisper of Thy call,
As noiseless let Thy blessing fall
    As fell Thy manna down.

5 Drop Thy still dews of quietness,
    Till all our strivings cease;
Take from our souls the strain and
    stress:
And let our ordered lives confess
    The beauty of Thy peace.

6 Breathe through the heats of our
    desire
    Thy coolness and Thy balm;
Let sense be dumb—let flesh retire;
Speak through the earthquake, wind,
    and fire,
    O still small voice of calm!
      John Greenleaf Whittier, 1807–92

424 SPOHR 86.86.86

From Spohr's *Calvary*, 1833

Father, I know that all my life
  Is portioned out for me;
The changes that are sure to come
I do not fear to see;
I ask Thee for a present mind,
Intent on pleasing Thee.

2 I ask Thee for a thoughtful love,
  Through constant watching wise
To meet the glad with joyful smiles,
  To wipe the weeping eyes;
A heart at leisure from itself,
  To soothe and sympathise.

3 I would not have the restless will
  That hurries to and fro,
Seeking for some great thing to do,
  Or secret thing to know;
I would be treated as a child,
  And guided where I go.

4 Wherever in the world I am,
  In whatsoe'er estate,
I have a fellowship with hearts
  To keep and cultivate;
A work of lowly love to do
  For Him on whom I wait.

5 I ask Thee for the daily strength,
  To none that ask denied,
A mind to blend with outward life,
  While keeping at Thy side;
Content to fill a little space,
  If Thou be glorified.

Anna Laetitia Waring, 1820–1910

MOUNT ZION   88.88.88

I. J. PLEYEL, 1757-1831   **425**

GIVE me the faith which can remove
  And sink the mountain to a
    plain;
Give me the child-like praying love,
  Which longs to build Thy house
    again;
Thy love, let it my heart o'erpower
And all my simple soul devour.

2 I would the precious time redeem,
  And longer live for this alone,
To spend, and to be spent, for them
  Who have not yet my Saviour
    known;
Fully on these my mission prove,
And only breathe, to breathe Thy
  love.

3 My talents, gifts, and graces, Lord,
  Into Thy blessèd hands receive;
And let me live to preach Thy word,
  And let me to Thy glory live;
My every sacred moment spend
In publishing the sinners' Friend.

4 Enlarge, inflame, and fill my heart
  With boundless charity divine:
So shall I all my strength exert,
  And love them with a zeal like
    Thine;
And lead them to Thy open side,
The sheep for whom their Shepherd
  died.

Charles Wesley, 1707–88

This hymn may also be sung to **Mozart,** No. 418

426

GOD BE IN MY HEAD Irregular

H. WALFORD DAVIES, 1869-1941

GOD be in my head,
  And in my understanding;
God be in mine eyes,
  And in my looking;
God be in my mouth,
  And in my speaking;

God be in my heart,
  And in my thinking;
God be at mine end,
  And at my departing. Amen.

Book of Hours, 1514

ELLERS 10.10.10.10

E. J. Hopkins, 1818-1901
Harmonized by A. S. Sullivan, 1842-1900

God made me for Himself, to serve Him here,
With love's pure service and in filial fear;
To show His praise, for Him to labour now;
Then see His glory where the angels bow.

2 All needful grace was mine through His dear Son,
Whose life and death my full salvation won;
The grace that would have strengthened me, and taught;
Grace that would crown me when my work was wrought.

3 And I, poor sinner, cast it all away;
Lived for the toil or pleasure of each day;
As if no Christ had shed His precious blood,
As if I owed no homage to my God.

4 O Holy Spirit, with Thy fire divine,
Melt into tears this thankless heart of mine;
Teach me to love what once I seemed to hate,
And live to God, before it be too late.

Henry Williams Baker, 1821–77

This hymn may also be sung to **Pax Dei**, No. 176

428

ST. BOTOLPH C.M.

GORDON SLATER, b. 1896

ENTHRONE thy God within thy heart,
  Thy being's inmost shrine;
He doth to thee the power impart
  To live the life divine.

2 Seek truth in Him with Christlike
    mind;
  With faith His will discern;
Walk on life's way with Him, and find
  Thy heart within thee burn.

3 With love that overflows thy soul
  Love Him who first loved thee;
Is not His love thy life, thy goal,
  Thy soul's eternity?

4 Serve Him in His sufficing strength:
  Heart, mind, and soul employ;
And He shall crown thy days at length
  With everlasting joy.

William Joseph Penn, 1875–1956

This hymn may also be sung to **Green Hill,** No. 158

429

OMBERSLEY L.M.

W. H. GLADSTONE, 1840-91

G OD of all power, and truth, and grace,
  Which shall from age to age endure,
Whose word, when heaven and earth shall pass,
  Remains and stands for ever sure;

2 That I Thy mercy may proclaim,
  That all mankind Thy truth may see,
Hallow Thy great and glorious name,
  And perfect holiness in me.

3 Purge me from every evil blot;
  My idols all be cast aside;
Cleanse me from every sinful thought,
  From all the filth of self and pride.

4 Give me a new, a perfect heart,
  From doubt, and fear, and sorrow free;
The mind which was in Christ impart,
  And let my spirit cleave to Thee.

5 Oh that I now, from sin released,
  Thy word may to the utmost prove,
Enter into the promised rest,
  The Canaan of Thy perfect love!

Charles Wesley, 1707–88

WARRINGTON L.M.   R. HARRISON, 1748-1810   430

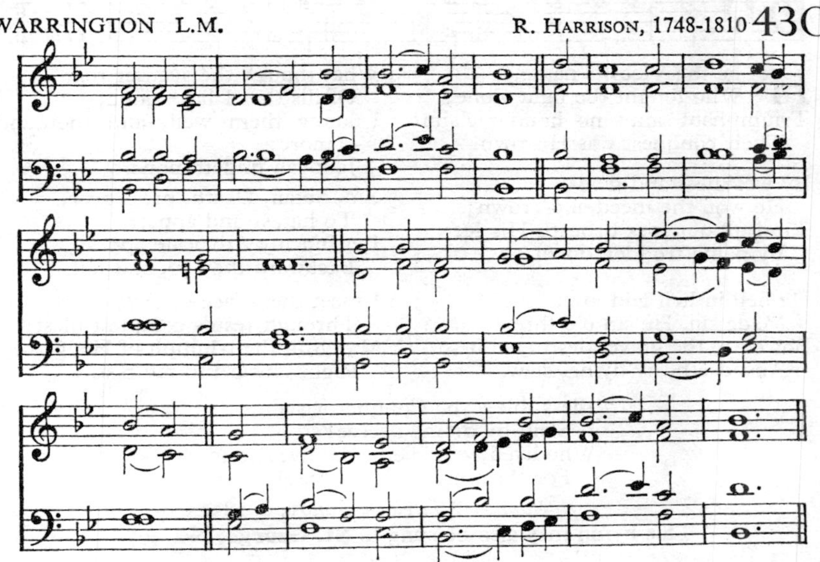

G REAT God, indulge my humble claim;
  Be Thou my hope, my joy, my rest:
The glories that compose Thy name
  Stand all engaged to make me blest.

2 Thou Great and Good, Thou Just and Wise,
  Thou art my Father and my God;
And I am Thine, by sacred ties,
  Thy son, Thy servant bought with blood.

3 With fainting heart and lifted hands,
  For Thee I long, to Thee I look,
As travellers in thirsty lands
  Pant for the cooling waterbrook.

4 With early feet I love to appear
  Among Thy saints, and seek Thy face;
Oft have I seen Thy glory there,
  And felt the power of sovereign grace.

5 Should I from Thee, my God, remove,
  Life could no lasting bliss afford;
My joy, the sense of pardoning love,
  My guard, the presence of my Lord.

6 I'll lift my hands, I'll raise my voice,
  While I have breath to pray or praise;
This work shall make my heart rejoice,
  And fill the circle of my days.

Isaac Watts, 1674-1748

431

CAMBRIDGE S.M.

R. Harrison, 1748-1810

His be the Victor's name,
  Who fought the fight alone;
Triumphant saints no honour claim:
  Their conquest was His own.

2 By weakness and defeat,
  He won the meed and crown;
Trod all our foes beneath His feet,
  By being trodden down.

3 He hell in hell laid low;
  Made sin, He sin o'erthrew;
Bowed to the grave, destroyed it so,
  And death, by dying, slew.

4 What though the accuser roar
  Of ills that I have done;
I know them well, and thousands more:
  Jehovah findeth none.

5 Sin, Satan, Death, press near,
  To harass and appal;
Let but my Advocate appear,
  Backward they go, and fall.

6 I meet them face to face,
  Through Jesu's conquest blest;
March in the triumph of His grace,
  Right onward to my rest.

7 Bless, bless the Conqueror slain,
  Slain by divine decree!
Who lived, who died, who lives again,
  For thee, my soul, for thee!

Samuel Whitelock Gandy, d. 1851

This hymn may also be sung to **St. George,** No. 497

432 ALSTONE L.M.

C. E. Willing, 1830-1904

How blest is life if lived for Thee,
  My loving Saviour and my
    Lord:
No pleasures that the world can give
  Such perfect gladness can afford.

2 To know I am Thy ransomed child,
  Bought by Thine own most precious
    blood,
And from Thy loving hand to take
  With grateful heart each gift of
    good;

3 All day to walk beneath Thy smile,
  Watching Thine eye to guide me
    still,
To rest at night beneath Thy care,
  Guarded by Thee from every ill;

4 To feel that though I journey on
  By stony paths and rugged ways,
Thy blessèd feet have gone before,
  And strength is given for weary
    days.

5 Such love shall ever make me glad,
  Strong in Thy strength to work or
    rest,
Until I see Thee face to face,
  And in Thy light am fully blest.
Prust's Supplementary Hymn Book, 1869
Author unknown

SAMUEL 66.66.88   A. S. SULLIVAN, 1842-1900 433

HUSHED was the evening hymn,
  The temple courts were dark
The lamp was burning dim
  Before the sacred ark:
When suddenly a voice divine
Rang through the silence of the shrine.

2 Oh give me Samuel's ear—
  The open ear, O Lord!
Alive and quick to hear
  Each whisper of Thy word:
Like him to answer at Thy call,
And to obey Thee first of all.

3 Oh give me Samuel's heart!
  A lowly heart, that waits
When in Thy house Thou art,
  Or watches at Thy gates
By day and night—a heart that still
Moves at the breathing of Thy will.

4 Oh give me Samuel's mind!
  A sweet, unmurmuring faith,
Obedient and resigned
  To Thee in life and death:
That I may read with childlike eyes,
Truths that are hidden from the wise.
James Drummond Burns, 1823–64

434

BULLINGER 85.83

First Tune

E. W. Bullinger, 1837-1913

Second Tune

STEPHANOS 85.83

H. W. Baker, 1821-77

I AM trusting Thee, Lord Jesus,
  Trusting only Thee!
Trusting Thee for full salvation,
  Great and free.

2 I am trusting Thee for pardon,
  At Thy feet I bow;
For Thy grace and tender mercy,
  Trusting now.

3 I am trusting Thee for cleansing,
  In the crimson flood;
Trusting Thee to make me holy,
  By Thy blood.

4 I am trusting Thee to guide me,
  Thou alone shalt lead;
Every day and hour supplying
  All my need.

5 I am trusting Thee for power;
  Thine can never fail!
Words which Thou Thyself shalt give
  me,
  Must prevail.

6 I am trusting Thee, Lord Jesus;
  Never let me fall;
I am trusting Thee for ever,
  And for all.

Frances Ridley Havergal, 1836–79

DOLOMITE CHANT 66.66   Austrian Melody arr. by J. T. Cooper, 1819-1879

I HUNGER and I thirst,
   Jesus, my manna be;
Ye living waters, burst
   Out of the rock for me.

2 Thou bruised and broken Bread,
   My life-long wants supply;
As living souls are fed,
   Oh feed me, or I die.

3 Thou true life-giving Vine,
   Let me Thy sweetness prove,
Renew my life with Thine,
   Refresh my soul with love.

4 Rough paths my feet have trod,
   Since first my course began,
Feed me, Thou Bread of God;
   Help me, Thou Son of Man.

5 For still the desert lies
   My thirsting soul before,
O living waters, rise
   Within me evermore.

John Samuel Bewley Monsell, 1811–75

436

WALDEN C.M.

J. E. Jones, 1866-1939

I would commune with Thee, my God,
  E'en to Thy seat I come;
I leave my joys, I leave my sins,
  And seek in Thee my home.

2 I stand upon the mount of God,
  With sunlight in my soul;
I hear the storms in vales beneath;
  I hear the thunders roll.

3 But I am calm with Thee, my God,
  Beneath these glorious skies:
And to the height on which I stand
  Nor storms nor clouds can rise.

4 Oh this is life, oh this is joy
  My God, to find Thee so;
Thy face to see, Thy voice to hear,
  And all Thy love to know.

George Burden Bubier, 1823–69

BISHOPTHORPE C.M.

Attributed to J. CLARK, *c.* 1670-1707

IMMORTAL Love, for ever full,
  For ever flowing free,
For ever shared, for ever whole,
  A never-ebbing sea!

2 Our outward lips confess the name
  All other names above;
Love only knoweth whence it came,
  And comprehendeth love.

3 We may not climb the heavenly steeps
  To bring the Lord Christ down:
In vain we search the lowest deeps,
  For Him no depths can drown.

4 But warm, sweet, tender, even yet
  A present help is He;
And faith has still its Olivet,
  And love its Galilee.

5 The healing of His seamless dress
  Is by our beds of pain;
We touch Him in life's throng and
    press,
  And we are whole again.

6 Through Him the first fond prayers
    are said
  Our lips of childhood frame,
The last low whispers of our dead
  Are burdened with His name.

7 O Lord and Master of us all!
  Whate'er our name or sign,
We own Thy sway, we hear Thy call,
  We test our lives by Thine.

8 We faintly hear, we dimly see,
  In differing phrase we pray;
But, dim or clear, we own in Thee
  The Light, the Truth, the Way!

John Greenleaf Whittier, 1807–92

438

CHURCH TRIUMPHANT L.M.　　　　　　　J. W. ELLIOTT, 1833-1915

JESUS, and shall it ever be,
A mortal man ashamed of Thee?
Ashamed of Thee, whom angels praise,
Whose glories shine through endless
　　days?

2 Ashamed of Jesus? – Sooner far
Let evening blush to own a star;
He shed the beams of light divine
O'er this benighted soul of mine.

3 Ashamed of Jesus?—Just as soon
Let midnight be ashamed of noon;
'Twas midnight with my soul till He,
Bright Morning Star, bade darkness
　　flee.

4 Ashamed of Jesus, that dear Friend
On whom my hopes of heaven depend?
No! when I blush, be this my shame,
That I no more confess His name.

5 Ashamed of Jesus?—Yes, I may,
When I've no guilt to wash away;
No tear to wipe, no good to crave,
No fears to quell, no soul to save.

6 Till then—nor is my boasting vain—
Till then I boast a Saviour slain.
And oh may this my glory be,
That Christ is not ashamed of me.

Joseph Grigg, 1722–68
and Benjamin Francis, 1734–99

This hymn may also be sung to Lledrod, No. 324

439 ST. ANDREW 87.87　　　　　　　E. H. THORNE, 1834-1916

JESUS calls us: o'er the tumult
Of our life's wild restless sea;
Day by day His sweet voice soundeth,
Saying, "Christian, follow Me."

2 As, of old, apostles heard it
By the Galilean lake,
Turned from home and toil and
　　kindred,
Leaving all for His dear sake.

3 Jesus calls us from the worship
  Of the vain world's golden store,
From each idol that would keep us,
  Saying, "Christian, love Me more."

4 In our joys and in our sorrows,
  Days of toil and hours of ease,
Still He calls, in cares and pleasures,
  "Christian, love Me more than these."

5 Jesus calls us: by Thy mercies,
  Saviour, may we hear Thy call,
Give our hearts to Thine obedience,
  Serve and love Thee best of all.

Cecil Frances Alexander, 1818–95

This hymn may also be sung to **St. Oswald,** 560, or **Drake's Broughton,** 557

TE LAUDANT OMNIA 77.77.77   J. F. SWIFT, 1847-1931 **440**

JESUS, Master, whose I am,
  Purchased Thine alone to be,
By Thy blood, O spotless Lamb,
  Shed so willingly for me,
Let my heart be all Thine own,
Let me live to Thee alone.

Open Thou mine eyes to see
All the work Thou hast for me.

2 Other lords have long held sway;
  Now, Thy name alone to bear,
Thy dear voice alone obey,
  Is my daily, hourly prayer:
Whom have I in heaven but Thee?
Nothing else my joy can be.

3 Jesus, Master, whom I serve,
  Though so feebly and so ill.
Strengthen hand and heart and nerve
  All Thy bidding to fulfil;

4 Jesus, Master, wilt Thou use
  One who owes Thee more than all?
As Thou wilt! I would not choose;
  Only let me hear Thy call.
Jesus, let me always be,
In Thy service, glad and free.

5 Jesus, Master! I am Thine;
  Keep me faithful, keep me near;
Let Thy presence in me shine
  All my homeward way to cheer.
Jesus! at Thy feet I fall,
Oh, be Thou my All-in-all.

Frances Ridley Havergal, 1836–79

This hymn may also be sung to **Wells,** No. 161

441

ST. CHRYSOSTOM 88.88.88

J. Barnby, 1838-96

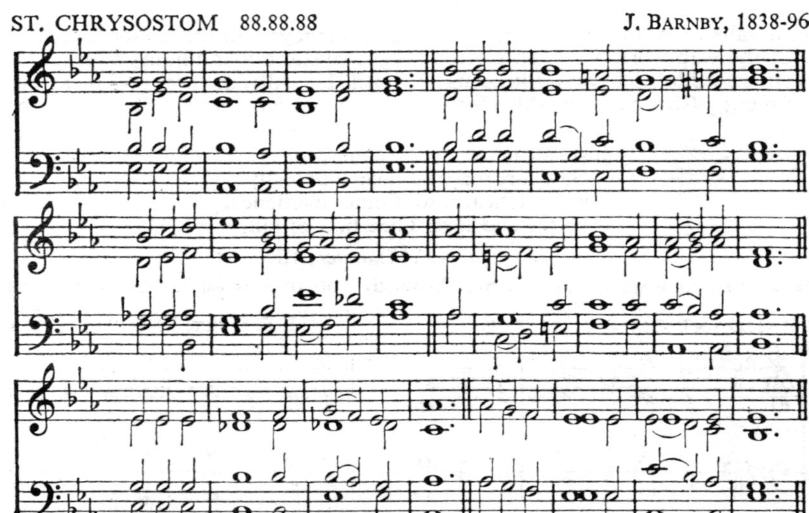

Jesus, my Lord, my God, my All,
  Hear me, blest Saviour, when I call;
Hear me, and from Thy dwelling-place
Pour down the riches of Thy grace;
  Jesus, my Lord, I Thee adore,
  Oh, make me love Thee more and more.

2 Jesus, too late I Thee have sought,
How can I love Thee as I ought?
And how extol Thy matchless fame,
The glorious beauty of Thy name?
  Jesus, my Lord, I Thee adore,
  Oh, make me love Thee more and more.

3 Jesus, what didst Thou find in me,
That Thou hast dealt so lovingly?
How great the joy that Thou hast brought
So far exceeding hope or thought!
  Jesus, my Lord, I Thee adore,
  Oh, make me love Thee more and more.

4 Jesus, of Thee shall be my song,
To Thee my heart and soul belong;
All that I have or am is Thine,
And Thou, blest Saviour, Thou art mine.
  Jesus, my Lord, I Thee adore,
  Oh, make me love Thee more and more.

Henry Collins, 1827–1919

442 WARWICK C.M.

S. Stanley, 1767-1822

JESUS, of Thee we ne'er would tire:
  The new and living food
Can satisfy our heart's desire;
  And life is in Thy blood.

2 If such the happy midnight song
    Our straitened spirits raise,
What boundless joys will cause, ere
    long,
    Eternal bursts of praise.

3 To look within and see no stain,
    Abroad no curse to trace;
To shed no tears, to feel no pain,
    But see Thee face to face.

4 To find each hope of glory gained,
    Fulfilled each precious word;
And fully all to have attained
    The image of our Lord.

5 For this we're pressing onward still,
    And in this hope would be
More subject to the Father's will,
    E'en now much more like Thee.

Mary Bowly Peters, 1813–56

This hymn may also be sung to **Evan**, No. 70

443

ST. OLAVE   66.66.66

J. BARNBY, 1838-96

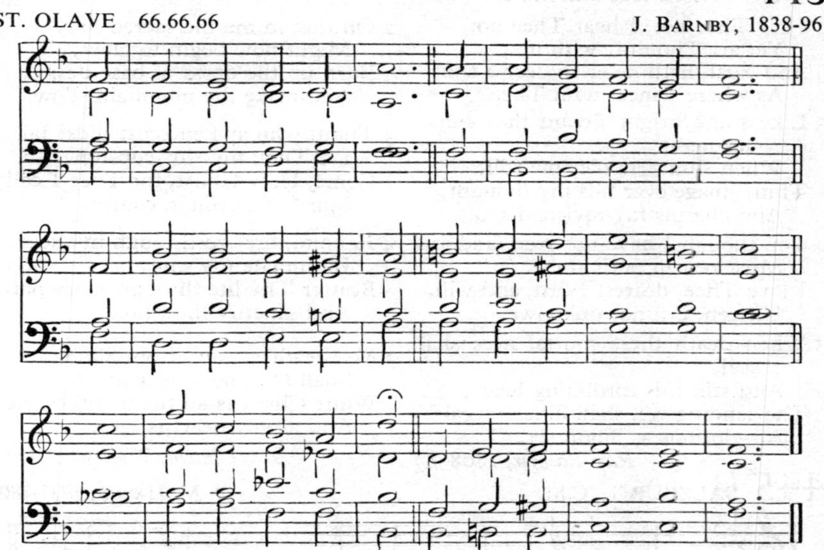

JESUS, the First and Last,
  On Thee my soul is cast:
Thou didst Thy work begin
By blotting out my sin;
Thou wilt the root remove,
And perfect me in love.

2 Yet when the work is done,
  The work is but begun:
Partaker of Thy grace,
I long to see Thy face;
The first I prove below,
The last I die to know.

Charles Wesley, 1707–88

MANOAH C.M.

G. A. Rossini, 1792-1868

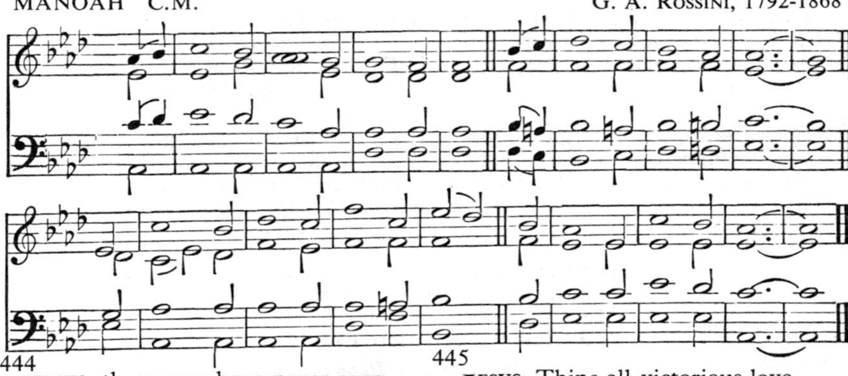

444

Jesus, these eyes have never seen
  That radiant form of Thine;
The veil of sense hangs dark between
  Thy blessèd face and mine.

2 I see Thee not, I hear Thee not,
  Yet art Thou oft with me;
And earth hath ne'er so dear a spot
  As where I meet with Thee.

3 Like some bright dream that comes
    unsought
  When slumbers o'er me roll,
Thine image ever fills my thought,
  And charms my ravished soul.

4 Yet, though I have not seen, and still
  Must rest in faith alone,
I love Thee, dearest Lord, and will,
  Unseen, but not unknown.

5 When death these mortal eyes shall
    seal,
  And still this throbbing heart,
The rending veil shall Thee reveal
  All-glorious as Thou art.
Ray Palmer, 1808–87

445

Jesus, Thine all-victorious love
  Shed in my soul abroad;
Then shall my heart no longer rove,
  Rooted and fixed in God.

2 Oh that in me the sacred fire
  Might now begin to glow;
Burn up the dross of base desire,
  And make the mountains flow.

3 Thou, who at Pentecost didst fall,
  Do Thou my sins consume;
Come, Holy Ghost, for Thee I call;
  Spirit of burning, come.

4 Refining fire, go through my heart,
  Illuminate my soul;
Scatter Thy life through every part,
  And sanctify the whole.

5 My steadfast soul, from falling free,
  Shall then no longer move,
While Christ is all the world to me,
  And all my heart is love.
Charles Wesley, 1707–88

445 SALZBURG C.M.

J. M. Haydn, 1737-1806

GIESSEN 88.88.88   GAUNTLETT's *Comprehensive Tune Book*, 1851

JESUS, Thy boundless love to me
  No thought can reach, no tongue
    declare:
Oh knit my thankful heart to Thee,
  And reign without a rival there.
Thine wholly, Thine alone, I'd live;
Myself to Thee entirely give.

2 Oh grant that nothing in my soul
  May dwell, but Thy pure love alone:
Oh may Thy love possess me whole,
  My joy, my treasure, and my crown:
Strange fires far from my soul remove,
May every act, word, thought, be love.

3 O Love, how cheering is Thy ray!
  All fear before Thy presence flies;
Care, anguish, sorrow melt away,
  Where'er Thy healing beams arise:
O Jesu, nothing may I see
Nothing desire or seek but Thee!

4 What in Thy love possess I not?
  My Star by night, my Sun by day;
My Spring of Life when parch'd with
    drought,
  My Wine to cheer, my Bread to
    stay,
My Strength, my Shield, my safe
    Abode,
My Robe before the throne of God!

5 In suffering be Thy love my peace;
  In weakness be Thy love my power;
And when the storms of life shall
    cease,
  Do Thou, in that important hour
In death, as life, be still my Guide,
My Saviour, who for me hast died!
    Paulus Gerhardt, 1607–76, tr. John Wesley, 1703–91

447

ST. CRISPIN L.M.
G. J. ELVEY, 1816-93

JESUS, Thy dying love I own,
A love unfathomed and unknown!
All other love can measured be,
But not Thy boundless love to me.

2 Oh, wonder to myself I am,
Thou loving, suffering, dying
Lamb,
That I can scan the mystery o'er,
And not be moved to love Thee more!

3 'Tis well, my Lord, that' twas Thy
love,
Not mine, that brought Thee from
above;
And well that 'twas Thy bitter grief,
Not mine, that gave my soul relief.

4 Oh, I am weary of my love,
That doth so little towards Thee move;
Yet do I constant, inly groan,
To know the depth of all Thine own.

5 Loved, and for ever on Thy throne,
Adored and loved, Thou timeless One!
Thou wilt through one eternal day,
The height and depth of love display.

6 Meanwhile, Thou precious, wondrous
Lamb,
Content at least with this I am,
To count my love too mean to own,
And know but Thine—Thy love alone.

Joseph Denham Smith, 1817-89

CAMBRIDGE 888.6   CHARLES FISHWICK

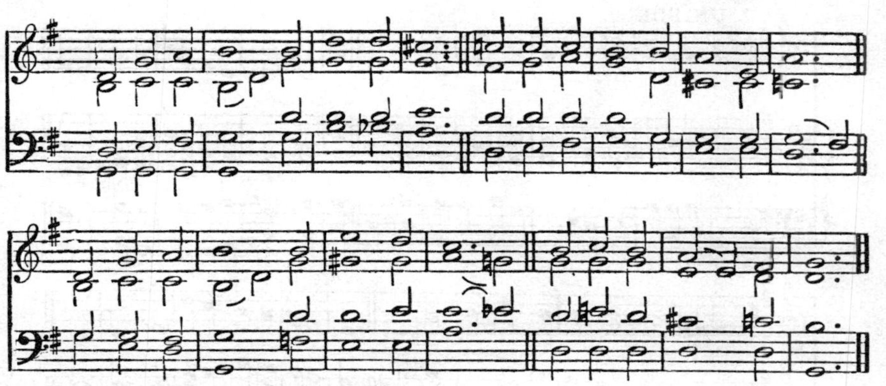

JUST as I am, Thine own to be,
  Friend of the young, who lovest
    me,
To consecrate myself to Thee,
  O Jesus Christ, I come

2 In the glad morning of my day,
My life to give, my vows to pay,
With no reserve, and no delay,
  With all my heart, I come.

3 I would live ever in the light,
I would work ever for the right,
I would serve Thee with all my might,
  Therefore to Thee I come.

4 Just as I am, young, strong, and free,
To be the best that I can be,
For truth, and righteousness, and
    Thee,
  Lord of my life, I come.

5 And for Thy sake to win renown,
And then to take the victor's crown,
And at Thy feet to lay it down,
  O Master, Lord, I come.

Marianne Farningham, 1834–1909

This hymn may also be sung to Trust, No. 322

449

WOODLANDS 10.10.10.10

W. GREATOREX, 1877-1949

"LIFT up your hearts!" We lift them, Lord, to Thee;
Here at Thy feet none other may we see;
"Lift up your hearts!" E'en so, with one accord,
We lift them up, we lift them to the Lord.

2 Above the level of the former years,
The mire of sin, the slough of guilty fears,
The mist of doubt, the blight of love's decay,
O Lord of Light, lift all our hearts to-day!

3 Above the swamps of subterfuge and shame,
The deeds, the thoughts that honour may not name,
The halting tongue that dares not tell the whole,
O Lord of Truth, lift every Christian soul!

4 Lift every gift that Thou Thyself hast given;
Low lies the best till lifted up to heaven:
Low lie the bounding heart, the teeming brain,
Till, sent from God, they mount to God again.

5 Then, as the trumpet-call, in after years,
"Lift up your hearts," rings pealing in our ears,
Still shall those hearts respond, with full accord:
"We lift them up, we lift them to the Lord!"

Henry Montagu Butler, 1833–1918

BERWYN 11.6.11.6 — CARADOG ROBERTS, 1879-1935

L IGHT of the world, for ever, ever
   shining,
  There is no change in Thee;
True light of life, all joy and health
  . enshrining,
  Thou canst not fade nor flee.

2 Thou hast arisen, but Thou declinest
   never;
  To-day shines as the past;
All that Thou wast Thou art, and
   shalt be ever,
  Brightness from first to last.

3 Night visits not Thy sky, nor storm,
   nor sadness;
  Day fills up all its blue,
Unfailing beauty and unfaltering
   gladness,
  And love for ever new.

4 Light of the world, undimming and
   unsetting,
  Oh shine each mist away!
Banish the fear, the falsehood, and the
   fretting;
  Be our unchanging day.

Horatius Bonar, 1803–89

451

SONG 1   10.10.10.10.10.10   Melody and Bass by ORLANDO GIBBONS, 1583-1625

LONG did I toil, and knew no earthly
    rest;
  Far did I rove, and found no certain
      home;
At last I sought them in His sheltering
      breast,
  Who opes His arms, and bids the
      weary come:
With Him I found a home, a rest
      divine;
And I since then am His, and He is
  mine.

2 The good I have is from His stores
      supplied;
  The ill is only what He deems the
      best;
With Him as Friend I'm rich, with
      nought beside,
  And poor without Him, though of
      all possest:
Changes may come—I take, or I
      resign,
Content while I am His, while He is
  mine.

3 Whate'er may change, in Him no
      change is seen;
  A glorious Sun, that wanes not, nor
      declines;
Above the clouds and storms He walks
      serene,
  And on His people's inward dark-
      ness shines:
All may depart—I fret not nor repine,
While I my Saviour's am, while He is
  mine.

4 While here, alas! I know but half His
      love,
  But half discern Him, and but half
      adore;
But when I meet Him in the realms
      above,
  I hope to love Him better, praise
      Him more,
And feel, and tell, amid the choir
      divine.
How fully I am His, and He is mine.
                    John Quarles, 1624–65
            Henry Francis Lyte, 1793–1847

STANLEY D.L.M.

A. H. MANN, 1850-1930

1. LORD! it is good for us to be
   High on the mountain here with Thee:
Here in an ampler, purer air,
Above the stir of toil and care
Of hearts oppressed with doubt and
   grief,
Believing in their unbelief,
Calling Thy servants all in vain
To ease them of their bitter pain.

2. Lord! it is good for us to be
With Thee, and with Thy faithful
   three:
Here, where the apostle's heart of
   rock
Is nerved against temptation's shock;
Here, where the son of thunder learns
The thought that breathes, the word
   that burns;
Here, where on eagles' wings we move
With him whose last, best word is
   love.

3. Lord! it is good for us to be
Entranced, enwrapped, alone with
   Thee,
Watching the glistening raiment glow
Whiter than Hermon's whitest snow,
The human lineaments which shine
Irradiant with a light divine,
Till we, too, change from grace to
   grace,
Gazing on that transfigured face.

4. Lord! it is good for us to be
Here on the holy mount with Thee,
When darkling in the depths of night,
When dazzled with excess of light,
We bow before the heavenly voice
Which bids bewildered souls rejoice:
Though love wax cold, and faith
   grow dim,
This is My Son: oh hear ye Him!

Arthur Penrhyn Stanley, 1815–81

453

ST. MATTHIAS 88.88.88

W. H. MONK, 1823-89

L ORD Jesus, Thou who only art
The endless source of purest joy,
Oh come and fill this longing heart,
Do Thou my every thought employ;
Teach me on Thee to fix my eye,
For Thou alone canst satisfy.

2 The joys of earth can never fill
The heart that once has known Thy love;
No portion would I seek until
I reign with Thee, my Lord, above,
When I shall gaze upon Thy face,
And know more fully all Thy grace.

3 Oh what is all that earth can give,
To one who shares in God's own joy?
Dead to the world, in Thee I live,
In Thee is bliss without alloy:
Well may I earthly joys resign—
All things are mine, since I am Thine!

4 Till Thou shalt come to take me home
Be this my one ambition, Lord,
Self, sin, the world, to overcome,
Fast clinging to Thy faithful Word.
More of Thyself each day to know,
And more into Thine image grow.

Author unknown

This hymn may also be sung to **Mozart, No. 418**

BLAENWERN 87.87.D

W. P. ROWLANDS, 1860-1937

L OVE Divine, all loves excelling,
  Joy of heaven, to earth come down;
Fix in us Thy humble dwelling,
  All Thy faithful mercies crown.
Jesus, Thou art all compassion;
  Pure, unbounded love Thou art;
Visit us with Thy salvation,
  Enter every longing heart.

2 Breathe, oh breathe Thy loving Spirit
  Into every troubled breast;
Let us all in Thee inherit,
  Let us find Thy promised rest;
Take away the love of sinning,
  Alpha and Omega be;
End of faith, as its beginning,
  Set our hearts at liberty.

3 Come, almighty to deliver,
  Let us all Thy grace receive;
Suddenly return, and never,
  Never more Thy temples leave.
Thee we would be always blessing,
  Serve Thee as Thy hosts above;
Pray, and praise Thee without ceasing,
  Glory in Thy perfect love.

4 Finish, then, Thy new creation;
  Pure and spotless may we be;
Let us see Thy great salvation,
  Perfectly restored in Thee;
Changed from glory into glory,
  Till in heaven we take our place;
Till we cast our crowns before Thee,
  Lost in wonder, love, and praise.

Charles Wesley, 1707–88

This hymn may also be sung to **Arwelfa**, No. 142

455

HOLLINGSIDE 77.77.D

J. B. Dykes, 1823-76

Loved with everlasting love,
  Led by grace that love to know;
Spirit, breathing from above,
  Thou hast taught me it is so!
Oh this full and perfect peace!
  Oh this transport all divine!
In a love which cannot cease
  I am His, and He is mine.

2 Heaven above is softer blue,
  Earth around is sweeter green!
Something lives in every hue
  Christless eyes have never seen:
Birds with gladder songs o'erflow,
  Flowers with deeper beauties shine,
Since I know, as now I know,
  I am His, and He is mine.

3 Things that once were wild alarms
  Cannot now disturb my rest;
Closed in everlasting arms,
  Pillowed on the loving breast.
Oh to lie for ever here,
  Doubt and care and self resign,
While He whispers in my ear—
  I am His, and He is mine!

4 His for ever, only His:
  Who the Lord and me shall part?
Ah, with what a rest of bliss
  Christ can fill the loving heart!
Heaven and earth may fade and flee,
  First-born light in gloom decline;
But, while God and I shall be,
  I am His, and He is mine.

George Wade Robinson, 1838-77

This hymn may also be sung to **Tichfield,** No. 545

LLANLLYFNI D.S.M.

John Jones (Talysarn), 1786-1857
Arr. by David Jenkins, 1848-1915

MAKE me a captive, Lord,
    And then I shall be free;
Force me to render up my sword,
And I shall conqueror be.
I sink in life's alarms
When by myself I stand;
Imprison me within Thine arms,
And strong shall be my hand.

2 My heart is weak and poor
    Until it master find;
It has no spring of action sure—
    It varies with the wind.
It cannot freely move,
    Till Thou hast wrought its chain;
Enslave it with Thy matchless love,
    And deathless it shall reign.

3 My power is faint and low
    Till I have learned to serve;
It wants the needed fire to glow,
    It wants the breeze to nerve;
It cannot drive the world,
    Until itself be driven;
Its flag can only be unfurled
    When Thou shalt breathe from
        heaven.

4 My will is not my own
    Till Thou hast made it Thine;
If it would reach a monarch's throne
    It must its crown resign;
It only stands unbent,
    Amid the clashing strife,
When on Thy bosom it has leant
    And found in Thee its life.

George Matheson, 1842–1906

This hymn may also be sung to **Leominster,** No. 518

457

ST. LEONARDS 87.85   A. C. Barham Gould, 1891-1953

May the mind of Christ my Saviour
Live in me from day to day,
By His love and power controlling
All I do and say.

2 May the Word of God dwell richly
In my heart from hour to hour,,
So that all may see I triumph
Only through His power.

3 May the peace of God my Father
Rule my life in everything,
That I may be calm to comfort
Sick and sorrowing.

4 May the love of Jesus fill me,
As the waters fill the sea;
Him exalting, self abasing,
This is victory.

5 May I run the race before me,
Strong and brave to face the foe,
Looking only unto Jesus
As I onward go.

6 May His beauty rest upon me
As I seek the lost to win,
And may they forget the channel,
Seeing only Him.

Katie Barclay Wilkinson, d. 1928

ADELBODEN C.M.D.

Swiss Melody

MY heart is resting, O my God;
 I will give thanks and sing;
My heart is at the secret source
 Of every precious thing.
Now the frail vessel Thou hast made,
 No hand but Thine shall fill;
For all the springs of earth have failed,
 And I am thirsting still.

2 I thirst for springs of heavenly life,
 And here all day they rise;
I seek the treasure of Thy love,
 And close at hand it lies:
And a new song is in my mouth,
 To long-loved music set:
Glory to Thee for all the grace
 I have not tasted yet!

3 I have a heritage of joy
 That yet I must not see:
The hand that bled to make it mine
 Is keeping it for me.
My heart is resting on His truth,
 Who hath made all things mine,
Who draws my captive will to Him,
 And makes it one with Thine.

4 My heart is resting, O my God,
 My heart is in Thy care;
I hear the voice of joy and praise
 Resounding everywhere.
"Thou art my portion," saith my soul,
 Ten thousand voices say!
The music of their glad Amen
 Will never die away.

Anna Laetitia Waring, 1820–1910

This hymn may also be sung to **Carol,** No. 103

459

REST C.M.

H. C. G. MOULE, 1841-1920

MY Saviour, Thou hast offered rest;
  Oh give it then to me;
The rest of ceasing from myself,
  To find my all in Thee.

2 This cruel self, oh how it strives
  And works within my breast,
To come between Thee and my soul,
  And keep me back from rest.

3 How many subtle forms it takes
  Of seeming verity,
As if it were not safe to rest
  And venture all on Thee.

4 O Lord, I seek a holy rest,
  A victory over sin;
I seek that Thou alone shouldst reign
  O'er all without, within.

5 In Thy strong hand I lay me down,
  So shall the work be done:
For who can work so wondrously
  As the Almighty One?

6 Work on then, Lord, till on my soul
  Eternal light shall break,
And, in Thy likeness perfected,
  I satisfied shall wake.

Eliza H. Hamilton, c. 1888

460 SUPREME SACRIFICE 10.10.10.10

C. HARRIS

NOT what I am, O Lord, but what
  Thou art!
That, that alone can be my soul's
  true rest;
Thy love, not mine, bids fear and
  doubt depart,
And stills the tempest of my tossing
  breast.

2 It is Thy perfect love that casts out fear;
  I know the voice that whispers "It is I;"
  And in Thy well-known words of heavenly cheer
  I find the joy that bids each sorrow fly.

3 Thy name is Love! I hear it from yon cross.
  Thy name is Love! I read it in yon tomb;
  All meaner love is perishable dross,
  But this shall light me through time's thickest gloom.

4 'Tis what I know of Thee, my Lord and God,
  That fills my soul with peace, my lips with song;
  Thou art my health, my joy, my staff and rod,
  Leaning on Thee, in weakness I am strong.

5 More of Thyself, oh show me, hour by hour,
  More of Thy glory, O my God and Lord:
  More of Thyself, in all Thy grace and power;
  More of Thy love and truth, Incarnate Word!

Horatius Bonar, 1808–89

This hymn may also be sung to **Bont Newydd,** No. 554, or **Dalkeith,** No. 699

461

EAGLEY C.M.

J. WALCH, 1837-1901

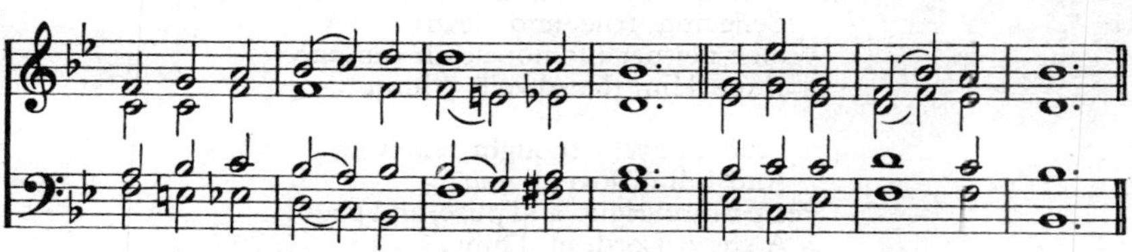

OH for a closer walk with God,
  A calm and heavenly frame,
A light to shine upon the road
That leads me to the Lamb.

2 Where is the blessedness I knew,
  When first I saw the Lord?
Where is the soul-refreshing view
Of Jesus and His Word?

3 What peaceful hours I once enjoyed,
  How sweet their memory still!
But they have left an aching void
The world can never fill.

4 The dearest idol I have known,
  Whate'er that idol be,
Help me to tear it from Thy throne,
And worship only Thee.

5 So shall my walk be close with God,
  Calm and serene my frame;
So purer light shall mark the road
That leads me to the Lamb.

William Cowper, 1731–1800

This hymn may also be sung to **Sawley,** No. 462

462

SAWLEY C.M.

J. WALCH, 1837-1901

OH for a heart to praise my God,
A heart from sin set free:
A heart that's sprinkled with the blood
So freely shed for me:

2 A heart resigned, submissive, meek,
My dear Redeemer's throne;
Where only Christ is heard to speak,
Where Jesus reigns alone:

3 A humble, lowly, contrite heart,
Believing, true, and clean;
Which neither life nor death can part
From Him that dwells within:

4 A heart in every thought renewed,
And full of love divine,
Perfect, and right, and pure, and good,
A copy, Lord, of Thine.

5 Thy nature, gracious Lord, impart,
Come quickly from above,
Write Thy new name upon my heart,
Thy new, best name of love.

Charles Wesley, 1707–88

This hymn may also be sung to **Eagley, No. 461**

463

CONTEMPLATION C.M.

F. A. G. OUSELEY, 1825-89

O JESUS Christ, grow Thou in me,
  And all things else recede:
My heart be daily nearer Thee
  From sin be daily freed.

2 Each day let Thy supporting might
  My weakness still embrace;
My darkness vanish in Thy light,
  Thy life my death efface.

3 In Thy bright beams which on me fall,
  Fade every evil thought;
That I am nothing, Thou art all,
  I would be daily taught.

4 More of Thy glory let me see,
  Thou Holy, Wise, and True!
I would Thy living image be,
  In joy and sorrow too.

5 Fill me with gladness from above,
  Hold me by strength divine!
Lord, let the glow of Thy great love
  Through my whole being shine.

6 Make this poor self grow less and less,
  Be Thou my life and aim;
Oh make me daily, through Thy grace,
  More meet to bear Thy name!

Johann Caspar Lavater, 1741–1801
tr. by Elizabeth Lee Smith, 1817–98

This hymn may also be sung to **Claremont**, No. 129

464

TAL-Y-LLYN 76.76.D

Welsh Hymn Melody

O Jesus, I have promised
  To serve Thee to the end;
Be Thou for ever near me,
  My Master and my Friend;
I shall not fear the battle
  If Thou art by my side,
Nor wander from the pathway,
  If Thou wilt be my guide.

2 Oh let me feel Thee near me:
  The world is ever near;
I see the sights that dazzle,
  The tempting sounds I hear;
My foes are ever near me,
  Around me and within;
But, Jesus, draw Thou nearer,
  And shield my soul from sin.

3 Oh let me hear Thee speaking
  In accents clear and still,
Above the storms of passion,
  The murmurs of self-will;
Oh speak to re-assure me,
  To hasten or control;
Oh speak, and make me listen,
  Thou Guardian of my soul.

4 O Jesus, Thou hast promised
  To all who follow Thee,
That where Thou art in glory
  There shall Thy servant be;
And, Jesus, I have promised
  To serve Thee to the end;
Oh give me grace to follow,
  My Master and my Friend.

5 Oh let me see Thy foot-marks,
  And in them plant mine own;
My hope to follow duly
  Is in Thy strength alone:
Oh guide me, call me, draw me,
  Uphold me to the end;
And then in heaven receive me,
  My Saviour and my Friend.

John Ernest Bode, 1816–74

This hymn may also be sung to **Day of Rest,** No. 663

MORNING LIGHT   76.76.D

G. J. WEBB, 1803-87

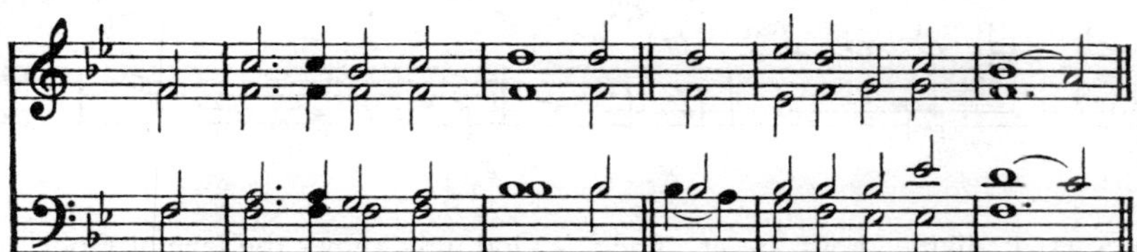

O Lamb of God, still keep me
  Close to Thy piercèd side;
'Tis only there in safety
  And peace I can abide.
What foes and snares surround me!
  What lusts and fears within!
The grace that sought and found me
  Alone can keep me clean.

2 'Tis only in Thee hiding
  I know myself secure;
Only in Thee abiding,
  The conflict can endure;
Thine arm the victory gaineth
  O'er every hateful foe;
Thy love my heart sustaineth
  In all its cares and woe.

3 Soon shall my eyes behold Thee,
  With rapture face to face;
One half hath not been told me
  Of all Thy power and grace.
Thy beauty, Lord, and glory,
  The wonders of Thy love,
Shall be the endless story
  Of all Thy saints above.

James George Deck, 1802-84

This hymn may also be sung to **Tal-y-Llyn,** No. 464

466

INNSBRUCK 886.D

HEINRICH ISAAK, *c.* 1460-1527

O LOVE divine, how sweet Thou art!
When shall I find my willing heart
  All taken up by Thee?
I thirst, I faint, I die to prove
The greatness of redeeming love,
  The love of Christ to me!

2 Stronger His love than death or hell;
Its riches are unsearchable;
  The first-born sons of light
Desire in vain its depths to see,
They cannot reach the mystery,
  The length, the breadth, the height.

3 God only knows the love of God;
Oh that it now were shed abroad
  In this poor stony heart!
For love I sigh, for love I pine;
This only portion, Lord, be mine,
  Be mine this better part!

4 Oh that I could for ever sit
With Mary at the Master's feet!
  Be this my happy choice:
My only care, delight, and bliss,
My joy, my heaven on earth, be this—
  To hear the Bridegroom's voice.

5 Oh that I could, with favoured John,
  Recline my weary head upon
    My dear Redeemer's breast!
From care, and sin, and sorrow free;
Give me, O Lord, to find in Thee
    My everlasting rest.

Charles Wesley, 1707–88

ST. MARGARET 88.886

A. L. PEACE, 1844-1912

O LOVE that wilt not let me go,
   I rest my weary soul in Thee:
I give Thee back the life I owe,
That in Thine ocean depths its flow
   May richer, fuller be.

2 O Light that followest all my way,
   I yield my flickering torch to Thee:
My heart restores its borrowed ray,
That in Thy sunshine's blaze its day
   May brighter, fairer be.

3 O Joy, that seekest me through pain,
   I cannot close my heart to Thee:
I trace the rainbow through the rain,
And feel the promise is not vain
   That morn shall tearless be.

4 O Cross, that liftest up my head,
   I dare not ask to fly from Thee:
I lay in dust life's glory dead,
And from the ground there blossoms
     red
   Life that shall endless be.

George Matheson, 1842–1906

GIESSEN   88.88.88   GAUNTLETT'S *Comprehensive Tune Book*, 1851

O LOVE, who formedst me to wear
    The image of Thy Godhead here;
Who soughtest me with tender care
    Through all my wanderings wild
    and drear:
O Love, I give myself to Thee,
Thine ever, only Thine to be.

2 O Love, who ere life's earliest dawn
    On me Thy choice hast gently laid;
O Love, who here as Man wast born,
    And wholly like to us wast made:
O Love, I give myself to Thee,
Thine ever, only Thine to be.

3 O Love, who once in time wast slain,
    Pierced through and through with
    bitter woe;
O Love, who wrestling thus didst gain
    That we eternal joy might know:
O Love, I give myself to Thee,
Thine ever, only Thine to be.

4 O Love, who once shalt bid me rise
    From out this dying life of ours;
O Love, who once above yon skies
    Shalt set me in the fadeless bowers:
O Love, I give myself to Thee,
Thine ever, only Thine to be.

Johann Scheffler, 1624–77
tr. Catherine Winkworth, 1827–78

This hymn may also be sung to **Stella**, No. 150

WILTON L.M.

S. STANLEY, 1767-1822

O THOU who camest from above
    The pure celestial fire to impart,
Kindle a flame of sacred love
    On the mean altar of my heart!

2 There let it for Thy glory burn
    With inextinguishable blaze;
And trembling to its source return,
    In humble prayer and fervent praise.

3 Jesus, confirm my heart's desire
    To work, and speak, and think for
        Thee;
Still let me guard the holy fire,
    And still stir up Thy gift in me.

4 Ready for all Thy perfect will,
    My acts of faith and love repeat,
Till death Thy endless mercies seal,
    And make the sacrifice complete.

Charles Wesley, 1707–88

This hymn may also be sung to **Hereford**, No. 275

470

MISSIONARY 76.76.D

L. MASON, 1792-1872

ON Thee my heart is resting!
  Ah, this is rest indeed!
What else, almighty Saviour,
  Can a poor sinner need?
Thy light is all my wisdom,
  Thy love is all my stay;
Our Father's home in glory
  Draws nearer every day.

2 My guilt is great, but greater
  The mercy Thou dost give,
Thyself, a spotless offering,
  Hast died that I should live.
With Thee, my soul unfettered,
  Has risen from the dust;
Thy blood is all my treasure,
  Thy word is all my trust.

3 Through me, Thou gentle Master,
  Thy purposes fulfil!
I yield myself for ever
  To Thy most holy will.
What though I be but weakness,
  My strength is not in me;
The poorest of Thy people
  Has all things, having Thee.

4 'Tis Thou hast made me happy,
  'Tis Thou hast set me free;
To whom shall I give glory
  For ever, but to Thee?
Of earthly love and blessing
  Should every stream run dry,
Thy grace shall still be with me,
  Thy grace, to live and die!

Theodore Monod, 1836–1921

This hymn may also be sung to **Penlan,** No. 358

LEAMINGTON 76.76.77.76   S. ARNOLD, 1740-1802

OPEN, Lord, my inward ear,
  And bid my heart rejoice;
Bid my quiet spirit hear
  Thy comfortable voice;
Never in the whirlwind found,
  Or where earthquakes rock the
    place,
Still and silent is the sound,
  The whisper of Thy grace.

2 From the world of sin and noise
    And hurry I withdraw;
For the small and inward voice
    I wait with humble awe;
Silent am I now and still,
    Dare not in Thy presence move;
To my waiting soul reveal
    The secret of Thy love.

3 Thou didst undertake for me,
    For me to death wast sold;
Wisdom in a mystery
    Of dying love unfold;

Teach the lesson of Thy Cross,
    Let me die with Thee to reign;
All things let me count but loss,
    So I may Thee regain.

4 Show me, as my soul can bear,
    The depth of inbred sin;
All the unbelief declare,
    The pride that lurks within;
Take me, whom Thyself hast bought,
    Bring into captivity
Every high aspiring thought
    That would not stoop to Thee.

5 Lord, my time is in Thy hand,
    My soul to Thee convert;
Thou canst make me understand,
    Though I am slow of heart;
Thine in whom I live and move,
    Thine the work, the praise is Thine;
Thou art wisdom, power, and love,
    And all Thou art is mine.

Charles Wesley, 1707–88

472

PATER MEUS 85.85.D

J. H. BURKE

P RECIOUS thought, my Father knoweth,
  In His love I rest:
For whate'er my Father doeth,
  Must be always best:
Well I know the heart that planneth
  Nought but good for me;
Joy and sorrow interwoven,
  Love in all I see.

2 Precious thought, my Father knoweth,
    Careth for His child;
  Bids me nestle closer to Him,
    When the storms beat wild;
  Though my earthly hopes are shattered,
    And the tear-drops fall,
  Yet He is Himself my solace,
    Yea, my "all in all."

3 Sweet to tell Him all He knoweth,
    Roll on Him the care;
  Cast upon Himself the burden
    That I cannot bear.
  Then without a care oppressing,
    Simply to lie still,
  Giving thanks to Him for all things,
    Since it is His will.

4 Oh to trust Him then more fully,
    Day by day to move,
  In the conscious, calm enjoyment
    Of the Father's love:
  Knowing that life's chequered pathway
    Leadeth to His rest,
  Satisfied the way He taketh
    Must be always best.

L. Woodbury

NORFOLK PARK 65.65.D

H. COWARD, 1849-1944

S^{AVIOUR}, blessèd Saviour,
  Listen whilst we sing,
Hearts and voices raising
  Praises to our King;
All we have to offer,
  All we hope to be,
Body, soul, and spirit,
  All we yield to Thee.

2 Nearer, ever nearer,
    Christ, we draw to Thee,
  Deep in adoration
    Bending low the knee:
  Thou, for our redemption,
    Cam'st on earth to die;
  Thou, that we might follow,
    Hast gone up on high.

3 Clearer still, and clearer,
    Dawns the light from heaven,
  In our sadness bringing
    News of sin forgiven;

Life has lost its shadows,
  Pure the light within;
Thou hast shed Thy radiance
  On a world of sin.

4 Onward, ever onward,
    Journeying o'er the road
  Worn by saints before us,
    Journeying on to God:
  Leaving all behind us,
    May we hasten on,
  Backward never looking
    Till the prize is won.

5 Higher then, and higher
    Bear the ransomed soul,
  Earthly toils forgotten,
    Saviour, to its goal;
  Where, in joys unthought of,
    Saints with angels sing,
  Never weary, raising
    Praises to their King.
        Godfrey Thring, 1823-1903

474

SAVIOUR, Thy dying love
    Thou gavest me,
Nor should I aught withhold,
    My Lord, from Thee:
In love my soul would bow,
My heart fulfil its vow,
Some offering bring Thee now,
    Something for Thee.

2 At the blest mercy-seat
    Pleading for me,
My feeble faith looks up,
    Jesus, to Thee;
Help me the cross to bear,
Thy wondrous love declare
Some song to raise, or prayer,
    Something for Thee.

3 Give me a faithful heart—
    Likeness to Thee—
That each departing day
    Henceforth may see
Some work of love begun,
Some deed of kindness done,
Some wanderer sought and won,
    Something for Thee.

4 All that I am and have—
    Thy gifts so free—
In joy and grief, through life,
    O Lord, for Thee;
And when Thy face I see,
My ransomed soul shall be,
Through all eternity,
    Something for Thee.

Sylvanus Dryden Phelps, 1816–95

DAY's *Psalter*, 1562

SEARCH me, O God! my actions try,
And let my life appear
As seen by Thine all-searching eye;
To mine my ways make clear.

2 Search all my sense, and know my heart,
Who only canst make known,
And let the deep, the hidden part
To me be fully shown.

3 Throw light into the darkened cells,
Where passion reigns within;
Quicken my conscience till it feels
The loathsomeness of sin.

4 Search all my thoughts, the secret springs,
The motives that control;
The chambers where polluted things
Hold empire o'er the soul.

5 Search, till Thy fiery glance has cast
Its holy light through all,
And I by grace am brought at last
Before Thy face to fall.

6 Thus prostrate I shall learn of Thee,
What now I feebly prove,
That God alone in Christ can be
Unutterable love!

Francis Bottome, 1823–94

This hymn may also be sung to **Nun danket all**, No. 63

476

AESCENDUNE   888.3 Trochaic

H. BLAIR, 1864-1932

SEEK ye first, not earthly pleasure,
Fading joy and failing treasure;
But the love that knows no measure
Seek ye first.

2 Seek ye first, not earth's aspirings,
Ceaseless longings, vain desirings;
But your precious soul's requirings
Seek ye first.

3 Seek ye first God's peace and bless-
ing—
Ye have all if this possessing;
Come, your need and sin confessing:
Seek Him first.

4 Seek Him first; then, when forgiven,
Pardoned, made an heir of heaven,
Let your life to Him be given:
Seek this first.

5 Seek this first: be pure and holy;
Like the Master, meek and lowly;
Yielded to His service wholly:
Seek this first.

6 Seek the coming of His kingdom;
Seek the souls around to win them;
Seek to Jesus Christ to bring them:
Seek this first.

7 Seek this first. His promise trying—
It is sure, all need supplying.
Heavenly things—on Him relying—
Seek ye first.

Georgiana Mary Taylor, 1871–1953

477

ABERAFON 77.77

J. H. ROBERTS, 1848-1924

TAKE my life, and let it be
Consecrated, Lord, to Thee:
Take my moments and my days,
Let them flow in ceaseless praise.

2 Take my hands, and let them move
At the impulse of Thy love:
Take my feet, and let them be
Swift and beautiful for Thee.

3 Take my voice, and let me sing
Always, only, for my King:
Take my lips, and let them be
Filled with messages from Thee.

4 Take my silver and my gold;
Not a mite would I withhold:
Take my intellect, and use
Every power as Thou shalt choose.

5 Take my will, and make it Thine;
It shall be no longer mine:
Take my heart: it is Thine own,
It shall be Thy royal throne.

6 Take my love: my Lord, I pour
At Thy feet its treasure-store:
Take myself, and I will be
Ever, only, all for Thee.

Frances Ridley Havergal, 1836–79

478

BRESLAU L.M.

Melody in *As Hymnodus Sacer*, Leipzig, 1625
Adapted and harmonized by F. MENDELSSOHN-BARTHOLDY, 1809-47

"TAKE up thy cross," the Saviour said,
"If thou wouldst My disciple be;
"Take up thy cross, with willing heart,
"And humbly follow after Me."

2 Take up thy cross; let not its weight
Fill thy weak soul with vain alarm;
His strength shall bear thy spirit up,
And brace thy heart, and nerve thine arm.

3 Take up thy cross, nor heed the shame,
    And let thy foolish pride be still;
Thy Lord refused not e'en to die
    Upon a cross, on Calvary's hill.

4 Take up thy cross, then, in His strength,
    And calmly every danger brave;
'Twill guide thee to a better home,
    And lead to victory o'er the grave.

5 Take up thy cross, and follow Christ,
    Nor think till death to lay it down;
For only he who bears the cross
    May hope to wear the glorious crown.

Charles William Everest, 1814–77

RUTHERFORD 76.76.76.75   C. URHAN, 1790-1845   479

THE sands of time are sinking,
    The dawn of heaven breaks;
The summer morn I've sighed for,
    The fair sweet morn, awakes:
Dark, dark hath been the midnight,
    But dayspring is at hand,
And glory, glory dwelleth
    In Immanuel's land.

2 Oh Christ! He is the fountain
    The deep, sweet well of love:
The streams on earth I've tasted,
    More deep I'll drink above;
There, to an ocean fulness,
    His mercy doth expand,
And glory, glory dwelleth
    In Immanuel's land.

3 Oh, I am my Belovèd's,
    And my Belovèd's mine.
He brings a poor vile sinner
    Into His "house of wine";
I stand upon His merit,
    I know no other stand,
Not e'en where glory dwelleth,
    In Immanuel's land.

4 With mercy and with judgment
    My web of time He wove,
And aye the dews of sorrow
    Were lustred with His love;
I'll bless the hand that guided,
    I'll bless the heart that planned,
When throned where glory dwelleth
    In Immanuel's land.

5 The Bride eyes not her garment,
    But her dear Bridegroom's face;
I will not gaze at glory,
    But on my King of grace;
Not at the crown He giveth,
    But on His piercèd hand:
The Lamb is all the glory
    Of Immanuel's land.

Anne Ross Cousin, 1824–1906

ARABIA 88.88.D

W. J. WHITE, *c.* 1820

THOU Shepherd of Israel, and mine,
   The joy and desire of my heart,
For closer communion I pine,
   I long to reside where Thou art:
The pasture I languish to find
   Where all, who their Shepherd obey,
Are fed, on Thy bosom reclined,
   And screened from the heat of the day.

2 Ah! show me that happiest place,
   The place of Thy people's abode,
Where saints in an ecstasy gaze,
   And hang on a crucified God;
Thy love for a sinner declare,
   Thy passion and death on the tree;
My spirit to Calvary bear,
   To suffer and triumph with Thee.

3 'Tis there, with the lambs of Thy flock,
   There only, I covet to rest,
To lie at the foot of the rock,
   Or rise to be hid in Thy breast;
'Tis there I would always abide,
   And never a moment depart,
Concealed in the cleft of Thy side,
   Eternally held in Thy heart.

Charles Wesley, 1707–88

See also
365   Oh happy day
488   O Master, let me walk with Thee
689   Hast thou seen Him
693   I lift my heart to Thee
696   I thirst, but not as once I did
707   One who is all unfit to count
710   Thou hidden love of God, whose height

SPOHR   86.86.86   From SPOHR's *Calvary*, 1833

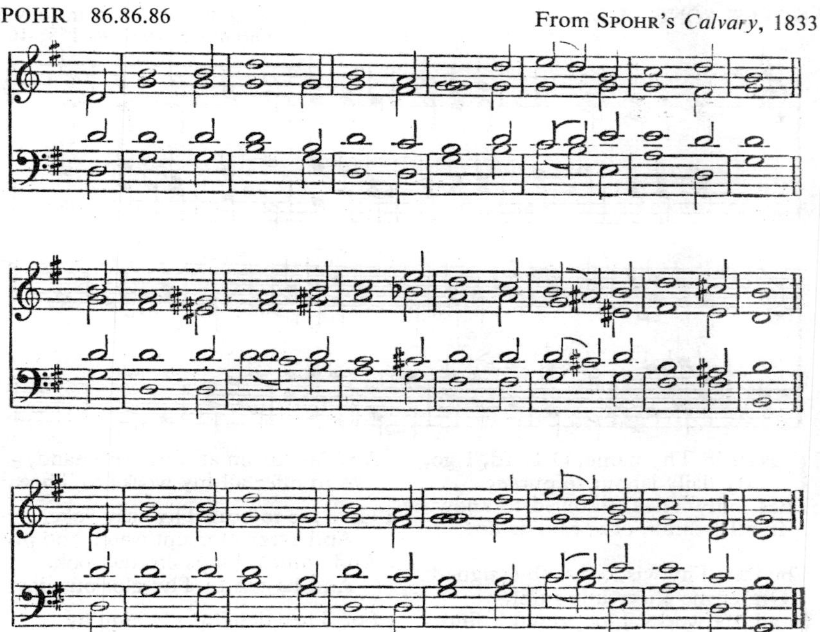

DISMISS me not Thy service, Lord,
　　But train me for Thy will;
For even I, in fields so broad,
　　Some duties may fulfil;
And I will ask for no reward,
　　Except to serve Thee still.

2 How many serve, how many more
　　May to the service come:
To tend the vines, the grapes to store
　　Thou dost appoint for some;
Thou hast Thy young men at the war,
　　Thy little ones at home.

3 All works are good, and each is best
　　As most it pleases Thee.
Each worker pleases when the rest
　　He serves in charity;
And neither man nor work unblest
　　Wilt Thou permit to be.

4 Our Master all the work hath done
　　He asks of us to-day;
Sharing His service, every one
　　Share too His Sonship may:
Lord, I would serve and be a son;
　　Dismiss me not, I pray.

Thomas Toke Lynch, 1818–71

482

ANGELS' SONG L.M.

Original version of melody by
ORLANDO GIBBONS, 1583-1625

FORTH in Thy name, O Lord, I go,
   My daily labour to pursue,
Thee, only Thee, resolved to know
In all I think, or speak, or do.

2 The task Thy wisdom hath assigned
   Oh let me cheerfully fulfil,
In all my works Thy presence find,
And prove Thy good and perfect will.

3 Thee may I set at my right hand,
   Whose eyes my inmost substance
      see,
And labour on at Thy command,
   And offer all my works to Thee.

4 Give me to bear Thy easy yoke,
   And every moment watch and pray,
And still to things eternal look,
   And hasten to Thy glorious day:

5 For Thee delightfully employ
   Whate'er Thy bounteous grace hath
      given,
And run my course with even joy,
   And closely walk with Thee to
      heaven.
         Charles Wesley, 1707–88

483

WHITBURN L.M.

H. BAKER, 1835-1910

GO, labour on; spend, and be
   spent,
   Thy joy to do the Father's will;
It is the way the Master went;
   Should not the servant tread it still?

2 Go labour on; 'tis not for nought;
   Thy earthly loss is heavenly gain;
Men heed thee, love thee, praise thee
   not,
   The Master praises, what are men?

3 Go, labour on while yet 'tis day;
  The world's dark night is hastening
    on:
  Speed, speed thy work, cast sloth
    away;
  It is not thus that souls are won

4 Men die in darkness at thy side,
  Without a hope to cheer the tomb;
  Take up the torch and wave it wide,
  The torch that lights time's thickest
    gloom.

5 Toil on, faint not, keep watch, and
    pray;
  Be wise the erring soul to win;
  Go forth into the world's highway,
  Compel the wanderer to come in.

6 Toil on, and in thy toil rejoice;
  For toil comes rest, for exile home;
  Soon shalt thou hear the Bridegroom's
    voice,
  The midnight peal, "Behold, I
    come!"
                    Horatius Bonar, 1808–89

This hymn may also be sung to **Glanllyfnwy,** No. 381

FULDA (WALTON) L.M.   GARDINER's *Sacred Melodies,* 1812 **484**

L   ORD, speak to me, that I may speak
      In living echoes of Thy tone;
  As Thou hast sought, so let me seek
  Thy erring children lost and lone.

2 Oh lead me, Lord, that I may lead
  The wandering and the wavering
    feet;
  Oh feed me, Lord, that I may feed
  Thy hungering ones with manna
    sweet.

3 Oh strengthen me, that while I stand
  Firm on the rock, and strong in
    Thee,
  I may stretch out a loving hand
  To wrestlers with the troubled sea!

4 Oh teach me, Lord, that I may teach
  The precious things Thou dost
    impart;
  And wing my words, that they may
    reach
  The hidden depths of many a heart.

5 Oh give Thine own sweet rest to me,
  That I may speak with soothing
    power
  A word in season, as from Thee,
  To weary ones in needful hour.

6 Oh fill me with Thy fulness, Lord,
  Until my very heart o'erflow
  In kindling thought and glowing
    word,
  Thy love to tell, Thy praise to
    show.

7 Oh use me, Lord, use even me
  Just as Thou wilt, and when, and
    where:
  Until Thy blessed face I see,
  Thy rest, Thy joy, Thy glory share.
              Frances Ridley Havergal, 1836–79
  This hymn may also be sung to **Llef,** No. 163

485

CHRISTCHURCH 66.66.88

C. STEGGALL, 1826-1905

MARCH on, my soul, with strength,
  March forward, void of fear;
He who hath led will lead,
  While year succeedeth year;
And as thou goest on thy way,
His hand shall hold thee day by day.

2 March on, my soul, with strength,
  In ease thou darest not dwell;
High duty calls thee forth;
  Then up, and quit thee well!
Take up thy cross, take up thy sword,
And fight the battles of thy Lord!

3 March on, my soul, with strength,
  With strength, but not thine own;
The conquest thou shalt gain,
  Through Christ thy Lord alone;
His grace shall nerve thy feeble arm,
His love preserve thee safe from harm.

4 March on, my soul, with strength,
  From strength to strength march on;
Warfare shall end at length,
  All foes be overthrown.
Then, O my soul, if faithful now,
The crown of life awaits thy brow.

William Wright, 1859-1924

486

CASTLE STREET (LUTHER'S CHANT)

H. C. ZEUNER, 1795-1857

MY gracious Lord, I own Thy right
  To every service I can pay,
And call it my supreme delight
  To hear Thy dictates and obey.

2 What is my being but for Thee,
  Its sure support, its noblest end;
Thy ever-smiling face to see,
  And serve the cause of such a Friend?

3 I would not breathe for worldly joy,
  Or to increase my earthly store;
Nor future days or powers employ
  To spread a sounding name the
  more.

4 'Tis to my Saviour I would live,
  To Him who for my ransom died;
Nor could untainted Eden give
  Such bliss as blossoms at His side.

5 His work my hoary age shall bless,
  When youthful vigour is no more;
And my last hour of life confess
  His love hath animating power.

Philip Doddridge, 1702–51

This hymn may also be sung to **Whitburn,** No. 156

STRENGTH AND STAY 11.10.11.10   J. B. DYKES, 1823-76 **487**

O LOVING Lord, who art for ever seeking
  Men of Thy mind, intent to do Thy will,
Strong in Thy strength, Thy power and grace bespeaking;
  Faithful to Thee, through good report and ill—

2 To Thee we come, and humbly make confession,
  Faithless so oft, in thought and word and deed,
Asking that we may have, in true possession,
  Thy free forgiveness in the hour of need.

3 In duties small, be Thou our inspiration,
  In large affairs endue us with Thy might;
Through faithful service cometh full salvation,
  So may we serve, Thy will our chief delight.

4 Not disobedient to the heavenly vision,
  Faithful in all things, seeking not reward,
Then, following Thee, may we fulfil our mission,
  True to ourselves, our brethren, and our Lord.

William Vaughan Jenkins, 1868–1920

This hymn may also be sung to **Charterhouse,** No. 629

488

PHILIPPINE L.M.

R. E. ROBERTS, 1878-1940

O MASTER, let me walk with Thee
In lowly paths of service free;
Tell me Thy secret; help me bear
The strain of toil, the fret of care.

2 Help me the slow of heart to move
By some clear winning word of love;
Teach me the wayward feet to stay,
And guide them in the homeward way.

3 Teach me Thy patience; still with
Thee
In closer, dearer company,
In work that keeps faith sweet and
strong,
In trust that triumphs over wrong.

4 In hope that sends a shining ray
Far down the future's broadening
way;
In peace that only Thou canst give,
With Thee, O Master, let me live.

Washington Gladden, 1836–1918

This hymn may also be sung to **Maryton**, No. 31

LANCASHIRE 76.76.D   H. SMART, 1813-1879

O MASTER! when Thou callest,
  No voice may say Thee nay,
For blest are they that follow
  Where Thou dost lead the way;
In freshest prime of morning,
  Or fullest glow of noon,
The note of heavenly warning
  Can never come too soon.

2 O Master! where Thou callest,
  No foot may shrink in fear,
For they who trust Thee wholly
  Shall find Thee ever near;
And quiet room and lonely,
  Or busy harvest field,
Where Thou, Lord, rulest only,
  Shall precious produce yield.

3 O Master! whom Thou callest,
  No heart may dare refuse;
'Tis honour, highest honour,
  When Thou dost deign to use
Our brightest and our fairest,
  Our dearest—all are Thine;
Thou who for each one carest,
  We hail Thy love's design.

4 They who go forth to serve Thee,
  We, too, who serve at home,
May watch and pray together
  Until Thy kingdom come;
In Thee for aye united,
  Our song of hope we raise,
Till that blest shore is sighted,
  Where all shall turn to praise!

Sarah Geraldina Stock, 1838–98

This hymn may also be sung to **Pearsall**, No. 406

490

BISHOPGARTH 77.87.D Iambic

A. S. SULLIVAN, 1842-1900

OMNIPOTENT Redeemer,
Our ransomed souls adore Thee;
Whate'er is done
Thy work we own,
And give Thee all the glory;
With thankfulness acknowledge
Our time of visitation;
Thine hand confess,
And gladly bless
The God of our salvation.

2 Thou hast employed Thy servants,
And blessed their weak endeavours,
And lo, in Thee
We myriads see
Of justified believers;
The church of pardoned sinners,
Exulting in their Saviour,
Sing all day long
The gospel song,
And triumph in Thy favour.

3 Thy wonders wrought already
Require our ceaseless praises;
But show Thy power,
And myriads more
Endue with heavenly graces.
But fill our earth with glory,
And, known by every nation,
God of all grace
Receive the praise
Of all Thy new creation.

Charles Wesley, 1707–88
This hymn may also be sung to **Goshen,** No. 223

SILCHESTER S.M.
C. H. A. MALAN, 1787-1864

491 REVIVE Thy work, O Lord!
   Thy mighty arm make bare:
Speak with the voice which wakes the dead,
   And make Thy people hear.

2 Revive Thy work, O Lord!
   Banish the sleep of death:
Quicken these smouldering embers now
   By Thine almighty breath.

3 Revive Thy work, O Lord!
   Exalt Thy precious name;
And, by the Holy Ghost, our love
   For Thee and Thine inflame.

4 Revive Thy work, O Lord!
   Give power unto Thy Word,
And may its pure and sacred truth
   In living faith be heard.

5 Revive Thy work, O Lord!
   Give Pentecostal showers;
The glory shall be all Thine own,
   The blessing, Lord, be ours!

Albert Midlane, 1825–1909

492 TEACH me, my God and King,
   In all things Thee to see;
And what I do in anything,
   To do it as for Thee.

2 A man that looks on glass,
   On it may stay his eye;
Or if he pleaseth, through it pass,
   And then the heaven espy.

3 All may of Thee partake:
   Nothing can be so mean,
Which with this tincture: For Thy sake,
   Will not grow bright and clean.

4 A servant with this clause
   Makes drudgery divine;
Who sweeps a room, as for Thy laws,
   Makes that and the action fine.

5 This is the famous stone
   That turneth all to gold:
For that which God doth touch and own,
   Cannot for less be told.

George Herbert, 1593–1632

SANDYS S.M. Traditional Carol from SANDYS' *Christmas Carols*, 1833 492

493

ELLACOMBE D.C.M.

Mainz Gesangbuch, c. 1833

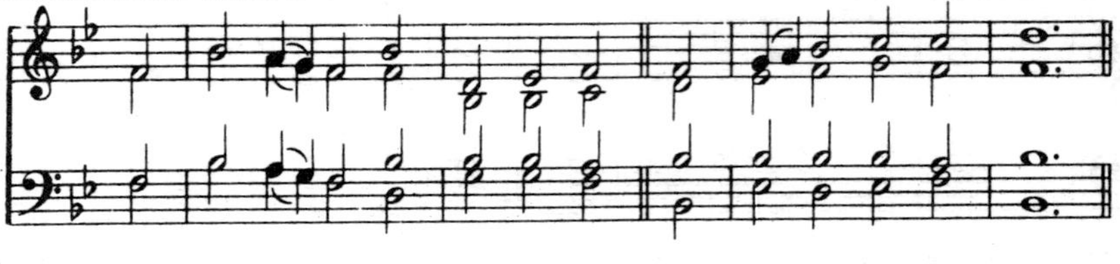

THE Son of God goes forth to war,
  A kingly crown to gain;
His blood-red banner streams afar!
  Who follows in His train?
Who best can drink his cup of woe,
  Triumphant over pain,
Who patient bears his cross below,
  He follows in His train.

2 The martyr first, whose eagle eye
  Could pierce beyond the grave;
Who saw his Master in the sky,
  And called on Him to save.
Like him, with pardon on his tongue,
  In midst of mortal pain,
He prayed for them that did the
    wrong:
  Who follows in his train?

3 A glorious band, the chosen few
  On whom the Spirit came,
Twelve valiant saints, their hope they
    knew,
  And mocked the cross and flame.
They met the tyrant's brandished
    steel,
  The lion's gory mane;
They bowed their necks, the death
    to feel:
  Who follows in their train?

4 A noble army, men and boys,
  The matron and the maid,
Around the Saviour's throne rejoice,
  In robes of light arrayed.
They climbed the steep ascent of
    heaven
  Through peril, toil, and pain;
O God, to us may grace be given
  To follow in their train.
      Reginald Heber, 1783–1826

494

RHODES S.M.   C. W. Jordan, 1840-1909

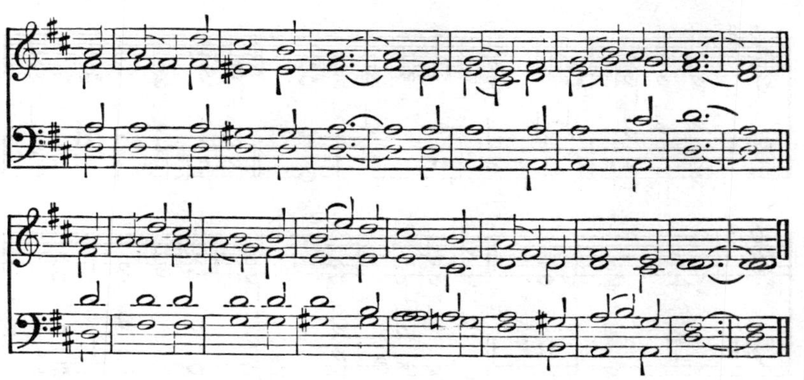

W^E give Thee but thine own,
   Whate'er the gift may be;
All that we have is Thine alone,
   A trust, O Lord, from Thee.

2   May we Thy bounties thus
     As stewards true receive,
  And gladly, as Thou blessest us,
     To Thee our first-fruits give.

3   For hearts are bruised and dead,
     And homes are bare and cold,
  And lambs, for whom the Shepherd
       bled,
     Are straying from the fold.

4   To comfort and to bless,
     To find a balm for woe,
  To tend the lone and fatherless,
     Is angels' work below.

5   The captive to release,
     To God the lost to bring,
  To teach the way of life and peace
     It is a Christ-like thing.

6   And we believe Thy word,
     Though dim our faith may be,—
  Whate'er for Thine we do, O Lord,
     We do it unto Thee.

William Walsham How, 1823–97

This hymn may also be sung to **Huddersfield,** No. 328

495

ST. CATHERINE 88.88.88   Melody by H. F. HEMY 1818-88

WE have not known Thee as we ought,
   Nor learned Thy wisdom, grace,
      and power:
The things of earth have filled our
      thought,
   And trifles of the passing hour:
Lord, give us light Thy truth to see,
And make us wise in knowing Thee.

2 We have not loved Thee as we ought,
   Nor cared that we are loved by
      Thee:
Thy presence we have coldly sought,
   And feebly longed Thy face to see:
Lord, give a pure and loving heart
To feel and know the love Thou art.

3 We have not served Thee as we ought;
   Alas! the duties left undone,
The work with little fervour wrought,
   The battles lost, or scarcely won!
Lord, give the zeal, and give the might,
For Thee to toil, for Thee to fight.

4 When shall we know Thee as we ought,
   When shall we love and serve aright?
When shall we, out of trial brought,
   Be perfect in the land of light?
Lord, may we day by day prepare
To see Thy face, and serve Thee there.

Thomas Benson Pollock, 1836–96

This hymn may also be sung to **Credo**, No. 117

496

W HO is on the Lord's side?
   Who will serve the King?
Who will be His helpers,
   Other lives to bring?
Who will leave the world's side?
Who will face the foe?
Who is on the Lord's side?
Who for Him will go?
   By Thy call of mercy
     By Thy grace divine,
   We are on the Lord's side;
     Saviour, we are Thine.

2 Not for weight of glory,
   Not for crown and palm,
Enter we the army,
   Raise the warrior-psalm;
But for love that claimeth
   Lives for whom He died:
He whom Jesus nameth
   Must be on His side.
   By Thy love constraining,
     By Thy grace divine,
   We are on the Lord's side;
     Saviour, we are Thine.

3 Jesus, Thou hast bought us,
   Not with gold or gem,
But with Thine own life-blood,
   For Thy diadem.
With Thy blessing filling
   All who come to Thee,
Thou hast made us willing,
   Thou hast made us free.
   By Thy grand redemption,
     By Thy grace divine,
   We are on the Lord's side;
     Saviour, we are Thine.

4 Fierce may be the conflict,
   Strong may be the foe,
But the King's own army
   None can overthrow.
Round His standard ranging,
   Victory is secure,
For His truth unchanging
   Makes the triumph sure.
   Master, Thou wilt keep us,
     By Thy grace divine,
   Always on the Lord's side,
     Saviour, always Thine!

Frances Ridley Havergal, 1836–79

496

RACHIE   65.65.D with refrain

CARADOG ROBERTS, 1879-1935

Who is on the Lord's side?
  Who will serve the King?
Who will be His helpers,
  Other lives to bring?
Who will leave the world's side?
  Who will face the foe?
Who is on the Lord's side?
  Who for Him will go?
    By Thy call of mercy
      By Thy grace divine,
  We are on the Lord's side;
    Saviour, we are Thine.

2 Not for weight of glory,
  Not for crown and palm,
Enter we the army,
  Raise the warrior-psalm;
But for love that claimeth
  Lives for whom He died:
He whom Jesus nameth
  Must be on His side.
    By Thy love constraining,
      By Thy grace divine,
  We are on the Lord's side;
    Saviour, we are Thine.

3 Jesus, Thou hast bought us,
   Not with gold or gem,
But with Thine own life-blood,
   For Thy diadem.
With Thy blessing filling
   All who come to Thee,
Thou hast made us willing,
   Thou hast made us free.
    By Thy grand redemption,
    By Thy grace divine,
    We are on the Lord's side;
    Saviour, we are Thine.

4 Fierce may be the conflict,
   Strong may be the foe,
But the King's own army
   None can overthrow.
Round His standard ranging,
   Victory is secure,
For His truth unchanging
   Makes the triumph sure.
    Master, Thou wilt keep us,
    By Thy grace divine,
    Always on the Lord's side,
    Saviour, always Thine!

Frances Ridley Havergal, 1836–79

ST. GEORGE S.M.   H. J. GAUNTLETT, 1805-76 **497**

Ye servants of the Lord,
   Each in his office wait,
Observant of His heavenly Word,
   And watchful at His gate.

2   Let all your lamps be bright,
     And trim the golden flame;
Gird up your loins as in His sight,
     For aweful is His name.

3   Watch! 'tis your Lord's command,
     And while we speak, He's near;
Mark the first signal of His hand,
     And ready all appear.

4   Oh happy servant he,
     In such a posture found!
He shall his Lord with rapture see,
     And be with honour crowned.

5   Christ shall the banquet spread,
     With His own royal hand,
And raise that faithful servant's head
     Amid the angelic band.

Philip Doddridge, 1702–51

ABBOT'S LEIGH 87.87.D   CYRIL V. TAYLOR, b.1907

YE that know the Lord is gracious,
   Ye for whom a corner-stone
Stands, of God elect and precious,
   Laid that ye may build thereon,
See that on that sure foundation
   Ye a living temple raise,
Towers that may tell forth salvation,
   Walls that may re-echo praise.

2 Living stones, by God appointed
   Each to his allotted place,
Kings and priests, by God anointed,
   Shall ye not declare His grace?
Ye, a royal generation,
   Tell the tidings of your birth,
Tidings of a new creation
   To an old and weary earth.

3 Tell the praise of Him who called you
   Out of darkness into light,
Broke the fetters that enthralled you,
   Gave you freedom, peace and sight:
Tell the tale of sins forgiven,
   Strength renewed and hope restored,
Till the earth, in tune with heaven,
   Praise and magnify the Lord!

Cyril Argentine Alington, 1872–1955

See also
405   Soldiers of Christ, arise
464   O Jesus, I have promised
518   Jesus, my strength, my hope
614   Lord of light, whose name outshineth
624   Sow in the morn thy seed
698   Jesus, my Lord, how rich Thy grace

FINGAL C.M.   J. S. ANDERSON, 1853-1945

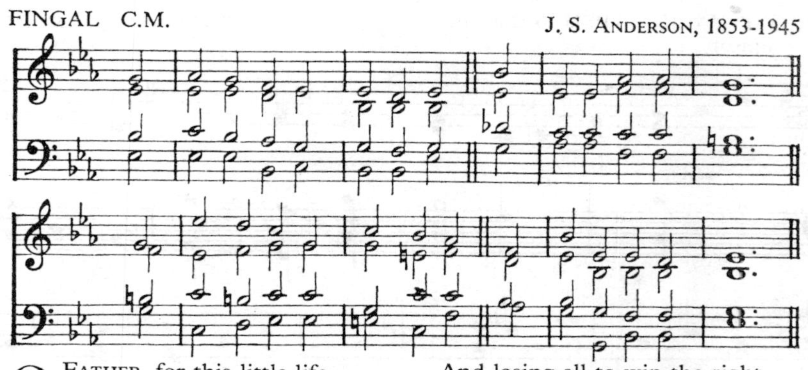

O FATHER, for this little life
    Entrusted from above,
Ere yet *he* face earth's sin and strife,
    We supplicate Thy love.

2 As Hannah to the Temple gate
    Her dearest treasure bore,
So, Lord, to Thee we dedicate
    This child for evermore.

3 Thy faithful soldier, may *he* fight
    With falsehood, sin, and shame,

And losing all to win the right
    Confess Thy holy name.

4 Thy faithful servant, may *he* learn
    To love and labour still,
And with a flaming spirit burn
    To know and do Thy will.

5 O Saviour, all *he* is is Thine,
    And all *he* yet may be:
Oh shelter *him* with love divine,
    And draw *him* near to Thee.
                    Gilbert White, 1859–1933

ST. BRIDE S.M.   SAMUEL HOWARD, 1710-82   500

O FATHER who didst give
    In Jesus Christ Thy Son
A Saviour for each child of earth,
    We bring our little one.

2 For Thou in tenderness
    Beyond all human care
Stooping to save the least, has said
    That such Thy kingdom share.

3 And we have known Thy grace,
    Creator, Healer, Friend;
Thy constant love enriches ours:
    We on Thy might depend.

4 So now in joyful trust
    Facing the years to be,
Our child, our daily life, ourselves
    We dedicate to Thee.

5 Oh may Thy wisdom lead;
    Our strength be Thine alone,
Until the faith we now confess
    This child shall make *his* own.

6 Here in this fellowship,
    Joined with our friends above,
In Christ's one church we yield *him*
        now
    To Thine unchanging love.
                Ralph Arnold Bethel, 1910–46

BROADWALK 11 10.11 10 Dactylic ROBERT ASHFIELD, b. 1911

unison

WHAT Thou has given us, Lord,
    here we bring Thee,
  Life that is dear to us, far beyond
    gold,
  Feet which must follow Thee, lips
    which must sing Thee,
  Hands which must toil for Thee ere
    they grow old.

2 What Thou hast given us, Lord, here
    we tender,
  Life of our own life, the child of
    our love;
  Take *him*, yet leave with us, till we
    shall render
  Count of the precious charge,
    kneeling above.

Charles Kingsley, 1819–75

This hymn may also be sung to **Epiphany Hymn**, No. 95

CWMGIEDD 76.76.D

Dan Protheroe, 1866-1934

AROUND Thy grave, Lord Jesus,
  In spirit here we stand;
With hearts all full of praises,
  To keep Thy blest command;
Our souls by faith rejoicing
  To trace Thy path of love,
Down through death's angry billows,
  Up to the throne above.

3 O Lord, Thou now art risen,
  Thy travail all is o'er!
For sin Thou once hast suffered;
  Thou liv'st to die no more;
Sin, death, and hell are vanquished
  By Thee, the Church's head;
And lo! we share Thy triumphs,
  Thou First-born from the dead.

2 Lord Jesus we remember
  The travail of Thy soul,
When in Thy love's deep pity,
  The waves o'er Thee did roll;
Baptized in death's dark waters,
  For us Thy blood was shed;
For us Thou, Lord of glory,
  Wast numbered with the dead.

4 Into Thy death baptizèd,
  We own with Thee we died;
With Thee, our Life, we're risen,
  And shall be glorified.
From sin, the world, and Satan,
  We're ransomed by Thy blood,
And here would walk as strangers,
  Alive with Thee to God.

James George Deck, 1802-84

This hymn may also be sung to **Aurelia,** No. 588

503

MELITA 88.88.88

J. B. DYKES, 1823-76

ETERNAL Father, whose great love
Encircles us where'er we rove,
By peak or plain, by sea or shore,
By crowded street or lonely moor,
Enfold within Thy sleepless care
Those who this day their faith
declare.

2 Eternal Saviour, whose rich grace
Did anguish, dark and drear, embrace;
Whose sweet compassions never fail,
Whose intercessions must prevail,
Uphold, we pray Thee, gracious
Lord,
Those who this day obey Thy word.

3 Eternal Spirit, whose still voice
Hath prompted every gracious choice;
Who taught our souls to loathe our sin,
And at the cross new life begin,
Preserve and lead for Jesus' sake,
Those who this day the world
forsake.

Frank William Boreham, 1871–1959

504

LLANGLOFFAN 76.76.D   Welsh Hymn Melody

L ord Jesus, in Thy footsteps
  We come to take our stand,
And pledge Thee loyal service
  In keeping Thy command.
As Thou in Jordan's river
  In faith and hope didst bow,
We would go through these waters
  To make our solemn vow.

2 We know we are unworthy;
  Our hearts are soiled within.
Lord, help us now to bury
  And here forsake our sin.
Lord, help us in the newness
  Of risen life with Thee
Henceforth by Thine enabling
  True witnesses to be.

3 As then at Thy baptizing
  Thy Father blessed Thy name,
And from the opened heaven
  The Spirit's favour came,
So, gracious Lord and Master,
  Do Thou Thy gift bestow,
That cleansed, inspired and guided,
  We in Thy likeness grow.

4 Upon Thy grace relying
  To meet temptation's hour,
We'd face life's tests with courage
  And conquer in Thy power.
Thy Kingdom's sway extending,
  Thy will our vital breath,
O Lord, may we Thy servants
  Prove faithful unto death.

Hugh Martin, 1890–1964

This hymn may also be sung to **Ewing**, No. 534

505

STEPHANOS. 85.83

H. W. BAKER, 1821-77

MASTER, we Thy footsteps follow,
We Thy word obey,
Hear us, Thy dear name confessing,
While we pray.

2 Now into Thy death baptizèd,
We ourselves would be
Dead to all the sin that made Thy
Calvary.

3 Rising with Thee, make us like Thee,
In Thy love and care,
In Thy zeal, and in Thy labour,
And Thy prayer.

4 Let the love that knows no failing
Cast out all our fears,
Let Thy pure and faithful spirit
Fill our years.

5 Till we hear the trumpets sounding
On the other side,
And for ever, in Thy heaven
We abide.

Frederick Arthur Jackson, 1867–1942

This hymn may also be sung to **Bullinger,** No. 434

See also
365 Oh happy day
464 O Jesus, I have promised
488 O Master, let me walk with Thee
693 I lift my heart to Thee

ST. FULBERT C.M.   H. J. GAUNTLETT, 1805-76

APPROACH, my soul, the mercy–seat,
Where Jesus answers prayer;
There humbly fall before His feet,
For none can perish there.

2 Thy promise is my only plea;
With this I venture nigh;
Thou callest burdened souls to Thee,
And such, O Lord, am I.

3 Bowed down beneath a load of sin,
By Satan sorely pressed,
By wars without, and fears within,
I come to Thee for rest.

4 Be Thou my shield and hiding-place,
That, sheltered near Thy side,
I may my fierce accuser face,
And tell him Thou hast died.

5 Oh, wondrous love! to bleed and die,
To bear the cross and shame,
That guilty sinners, such as I,
Might plead Thy gracious name!

John Newton, 1725–1807

This hymn may also be sung to **Bedford, No. 94**

507

LÜBECK 77.77

Freylinghausen's *Gesangbuch*, 1704

Come my soul, thy suit prepare,
    Jesus loves to answer prayer;
He himself has bid thee pray,
Therefore will not say thee nay.

2 Thou art coming to a King,
    Large petitions with thee bring;
For His grace and power are such,
None can ever ask too much.

3 With my burden I begin;
    Thou didst bear my load of sin,
Let Thy blood, for sinners spilt,
Set my conscience free from guilt.

4 Lord, I come to thee for rest,
    Take possession of my breast;
There Thy blood-bought right main-
        tain,
And without a rival reign.

5 While I am a pilgrim here,
    Let Thy love my spirit cheer;
As my Guardian, Guide and Friend;
Lead me to my journey's end.

John Newton, 1725–1807

This hymn may also be sung to **Nottingham**, No. 246

EVERTON   87.87.D

HENRY SMART, 1813-79

FAR beyond the storm and tempest,
  That untroubled calm above,
There the Son of God abideth,
  Resting in the Father's love.
Loved with all the love He claimeth,
  Who endured the cross and shame,
There, by God and man forsaken,
  Telling forth the Father's name.

2 Now in God's unmingled gladness,
  God's unmeasured, endless peace,
He abideth, and rejoiceth
  With a joy that cannot cease.
And amidst that joy and glory,
  In that peace no tongue can tell,
Far above the storm and tempest,
  There on high with Him we dwell.

3 Unto this His love has brought us,
  Nothing less than this He gives;
This the secret joy and power
  Of the heart wherein He lives.
Let us praise that love for ever,
  Fall in worship at His feet,
Lost in silent joy and wonder,
  Sinners made in Him complete.

Emma Frances Bevan, 1827–1909

This hymn may also be sung to **Bethany, No. 8**

509

PENITENTIA 10.10.10.10   E. DEARLE

FATHER, again in Jesu's Name we meet,
And bow in penitence beneath Thy feet:
Again to Thee our feeble voices raise,
To sue for mercy, and to sing Thy praise.

2 Lord, we would bless Thee for Thy ceaseless care,
And all Thy love from day to day declare:
Is not our life with hourly mercies crowned?
Does not Thine arm encircle us around?

3 Alas! unworthy of Thy boundless love,
Too oft with careless feet from Thee we rove:
But now encouraged by Thy voice we come,
Returning sinners to a Father's home.

4 Oh, by that name in whom all fulness dwells,
Oh, by that love which every love excels,
Oh, by that blood so freely shed for sin,
Open sweet mercy's gate and let us in!

Lucy Elizabeth Georgina Whitmore, 1792–1840

This hymn may also be sung to **Ellers**, No. 427

ST. JOHN 66.66.88

J. B. CALKIN, 1827-1905

FATHER, to seek Thy face
    Thy children now draw near;
Before the throne of grace
    With boldness we appear:
We plead His name, His precious
       blood,
Who made us kings and priests to
       God.

2   No more we shun the light,
       No more Thy presence fear;
    In robes of spotless white
       Before Thee we appear:
    Our great High Priest for us is there,
    And He presents our praise and prayer.

3   No power have we to praise
       Thy name, O God of love,
    Unless Thy Spirit raise
       Our thoughts and hearts above;
    His grace avails in all our need—
    May He our priestly worship lead.

4   Thy promises we plead,
       Thy true and faithful word—
    Grace for each time of need,
       Thou wilt to us afford:
    Thy promises in Christ are yea,
    In Him Amen! to endless day.
       James George Deck, 1802–84

511

MARYTON L.M

H. P. Smith, 1825-98

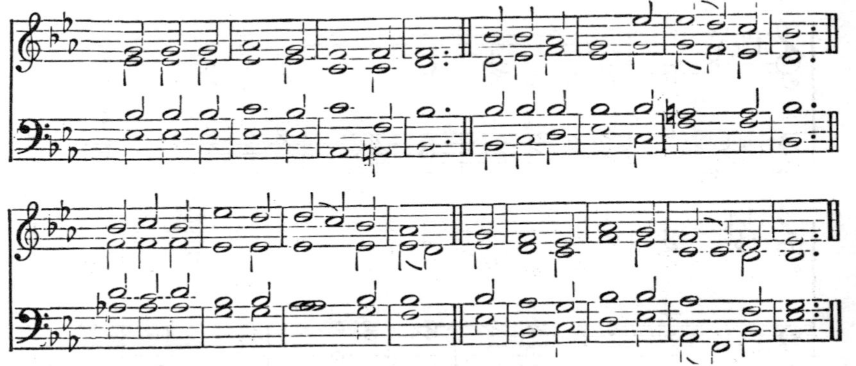

From every stormy wind that blows,
From every swelling tide of woes,
There is a calm, a safe retreat:
'Tis found beneath the mercy-seat.

2 There is a place where Jesus sheds
The oil of gladness on our heads,—
A place than all beside more sweet:
The blood-besprinkled mercy-seat.

3 There is a spot where spirits blend,
And friend holds fellowship with
friend;
Though sundered far, by faith they
meet
Around one common mercy-seat.

4 Ah, whither could we flee for aid,
When tempted, desolate, dismayed?
Or how the host of hell defeat,
Had suffering saints no mercy-seat?

5 There we on eagle-wings would soar,
Where time and sense are all no more;
There heavenly joys our spirits greet,
For glory crowns the mercy-seat.

Hugh Stowell, 1799–1865

512

PENMACHNO C.M.

T. Hopkin Evans, 1879-1940

Great Shepherd of Thy people,
hear;
Thy presence now display;
As Thou hast given a place for prayer,
So give us hearts to pray.

2 Within these walls let holy peace
And love and concord dwell;
Here give the troubled conscience ease,
The wounded spirit heal.

3 Show us some token of Thy love,
  Our fainting hope to raise;
And pour Thy blessings from above,
  That we may render praise.

4 The hearing ear, the seeing eye,
  The contrite heart bestow;

And shine upon us from on high,
  That we in grace may grow.

5 May we in faith receive Thy Word,
  In faith present our prayers,
And in the presence of our Lord
  Relinquish all our cares.

John Newton, 1725–1807

This hymn may also be sung to **Stracathro,** No. 88

TRYST 64.64.66.64

W. H. DOANE, 1832–1916 **513**

HERE from the world we turn,
  Jesus to seek;
Here may His loving voice
  Tenderly speak!
Jesus our dearest friend,
While at Thy feet we bend,
Oh let Thy smile descend!
  'Tis Thee we seek.

2 Come, holy Comforter,
  Presence divine,
Now in our longing hearts
  Graciously shine!

Oh for Thy mighty power!
Oh for a blessèd shower,
Filling this hallowed hour
  With joy divine!

3 Saviour, Thy work revive!
  Here may we see
Those who are dead in sin
  Quickened by Thee;
Come, to our hearts' delight,
Make every burden light,
Cheer Thou our waiting sight;
  We long for Thee.

Frances Jane van Alstyne, 1820–1915

This hymn may also be sung to **Glanhafren,** No. 407

514

BEVAN 85.85.D

G. F. KNOWLES, 1879-1970

IN the depths of His bright glory,
  Where the heavens rejoice,
I have seen Him, I have known Him,
  I have heard His voice.
Blessèd light, around me shining
  In the darkest day;
Precious words, as music sounding
  All along my way.

2 He has told me how He sought me,
  In the cloudy day,
On the waste and lonely mountains,
  Very far away.
I in wonder and in silence,
  Listen and adore,
Whilst the heart of God He tells me—
  Whilst my cup runs o'er.

3 Is it sweet to know He careth
  For my smallest need—
Know that He will ever tend me,
  Watch and guard and feed?
Yet exceedingly 'tis sweeter,
  Wondrous though it be,
His desire is ever toward me,
  He had need of me.

4 Words ineffable He speaketh,
  Words that none can tell—
Yet, O Lord, Thy wondrous secret
  Knows my heart full well.
Lost in silent love and wonder,
  There my soul abides,
Portion blest beyond all telling—
  Christ, and nought besides.

Emma Frances Bevan, 1827–1909

This hymn may also be sung to **Pater meus**, No. 472

BLAENCEFN   8.7.87.47   J. Thomas, 1839-1921

In Thy name, O Lord, assembling,
  We, Thy people, now draw near:
Teach us to rejoice with trembling,
  Speak and let Thy servants hear:
    Hear with meekness,
  Hear Thy word with godly fear.

2 While our days on earth are
    lengthened,
  May we give them, Lord, to Thee,
Cheered by hope, and daily
    strengthened,
  May we run, nor weary be;
    Till Thy glory,
  Without clouds, in heaven we see.

3 There in worship purer, sweeter,
  Thee Thy people shall adore,
Tasting of enjoyment greater
  Far than thought conceived before:
    Full enjoyment,
  Full, unmixed, and evermore.

Thomas Kelly, 1769–1855

This hymn may also be sung to **Regent Square,** No. 5

EVAN C.M.

W. H. HAVERGAL, 1793-1870

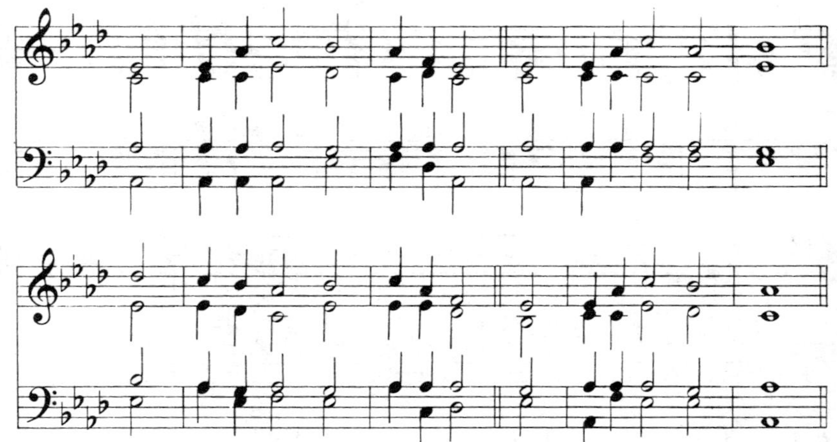

JESUS, do Thou my vision fill,
  My heart's affections claim:
Bid every troubled thought be still;
  My feeble faith sustain.

2 Oh let Thine all-transcendent love
  My highest powers employ;
Most wondrous theme! all themes
    above,
  Source of eternal joy.

3 My study and my boast be this,
  The love of Christ divine:
Oh deep, oh fathomless abyss!
  And mystery sublime.

4 My sins and griefs were made Thine
    own,
  Upon the awful tree,
That Thou might'st raise e'en to Thy
    Throne,
  A guilty worm like me.

5 'Tis here my soul finds sweetest rest,
  Beneath Thy sheltering cross;
And counts, while thus divinely blest,
  All other gain but loss.

6 And while a pilgrim in the land,
  I'm daily made to prove
The wonders which Thy gracious
    hand
  Hath wrought for me in love.

7 Adoringly I bow me down
  Before Thy Throne, O God;
And cast before Thy feet the crown,
  Made mine through Jesu's blood.

Charles Russell Hurditch, b. 1840

WAREHAM L.M. W. KNAPP, 1698-1768

JESUS, where'er Thy people meet,
There they behold Thy mercy-
seat:
Where'er they seek Thee Thou art
found,
And every place is hallowed ground.

2 For Thou, within no walls confined,
Inhabitest the humble mind;
Such ever bring Thee where they
come,
And going, take Thee to their home.

3 Dear Shepherd of Thy chosen few,
Thy former mercies here renew;
Here to our waiting hearts proclaim
The sweetness of Thy saving name.

4 Here may we prove the power of
prayer,
To strengthen faith and banish care,
To teach our faint desires to rise,
And bring all heaven before our eyes.

5 Lord! we are few, but Thou art near,
Nor short Thine arm, nor deaf Thine
ear;
Oh rend the heavens, come quickly
down,
And make a thousand hearts Thine
own!

William Cowper, 1731–1800

This hymn may also be sung to **Warrington**, No. 294

LEOMINSTER D.S.M.

G. W. Martin, 1828-1881

Jesus, my strength, my hope,
  On Thee I cast my care,
With humble confidence look up,
  And know Thou hear'st my prayer.
  Give me on Thee to wait,
  Till I can all things do,
On Thee, almighty to create,
  Almighty to renew.

2 I want a godly fear,
  A quick-discerning eye
That looks to Thee when sin is near,
  And sees the tempter fly:
  A spirit still prepared,
  And armed with jealous care,
For ever standing on its guard
  And watching unto prayer.

3 I want a true regard,
  A single, steady aim,
Unmoved by threatening or reward,
  To Thee and Thy great name;
  A jealous, just concern
  For Thine immortal praise;
A pure desire that all may learn
  And glorify Thy grace.

4 I rest upon Thy word;
  The promise is for me;
My succour and salvation, Lord,
  Shall surely come from Thee:
  But let me still abide,
  Nor from my hope remove,
Till Thou my patient spirit guide
  Into Thy perfect love.

Charles Wesley, 1707–88

ERNSTEIN 65.65

J. F. SWIFT, 1847-1931

JESUS, stand among us
In Thy risen power;
Let this time of worship
Be a hallowed hour.

2 Breathe Thy Holy Spirit
Into every heart;
Bid the fears and sorrows
From each soul depart.

3 Thus with quickened footsteps
We'll pursue our way;
Watching for the dawning
Of the eternal day.

William Pennefather, 1816–73

This hymn may also be sung to **North Coates,** No. 136

520

LORD, in this blest and hallowed hour
  Reveal Thy presence and Thy
    power;
Show to my faith Thy hands and side,
My Lord and God, the crucified.

2 Fain would I find a calm retreat
From vain distractions, near Thy feet;
And, borne above all earthly care,
Be joyful in Thy house of prayer.

3 Or let me through the opening skies
Catch one bright glimpse of paradise;
And realize, with raptured awe,
The vision dying Stephen saw.

4 But if unworthy of such joy,
Still shall Thy love my heart employ;
For of Thy favoured children's fare
'Twere bliss the very crumbs to share.

 5 Yet never can my soul be fed
With less than Thee, the Living Bread;
Thyself unto my soul impart,
And with Thy presence fill my heart.

Josiah Conder, 1789–1855

This hymn may also be sung to **Alstone,** No. 400

521

Lord Jesus Christ, we seek Thy face,
 Within the veil we bow the knee;
Oh let Thy glory fill the place,
 And bless us while we wait on Thee!

2 We thank Thee for the precious blood
 That purged our sins and brought
  us nigh,
All cleansed and sanctified, to God,
 Thy holy name to magnify.

3 Shut in with Thee, far, far above
 The restless world that wars below,
We seek to learn and prove Thy love,
 Thy wisdom and Thy grace to
  know.

4 The brow that once with thorns was
  bound,
 Thy hands, Thy side, we fain would
  see;
Draw near, Lord Jesus, glory-
  crowned,
 And bless us while we wait on Thee.

Alexander Stewart, 1843–1923

This hymn may also be sung to **Duke St.**, No. 365

522

LLOYD C.M.

C. Howard, 1856-1927

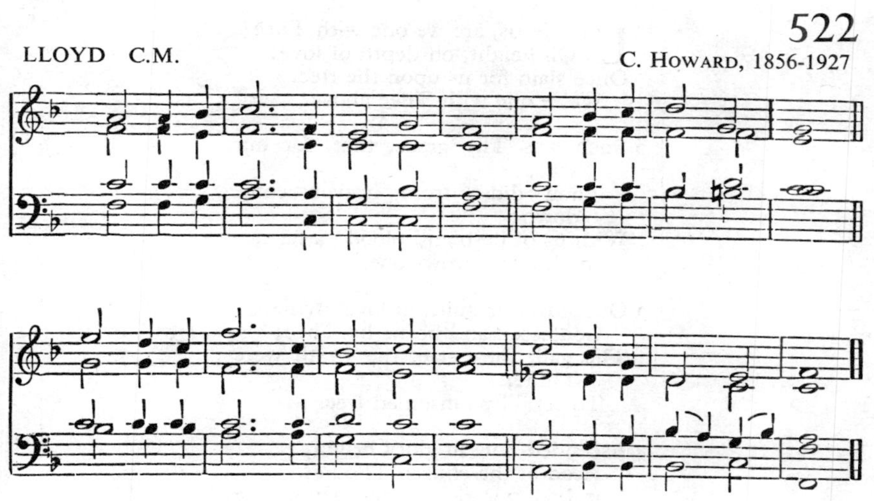

Lord Jesus Christ, our Saviour
 Thou,
 With joy we worship Thee,
We know Thou hast redeemèd us,
 By dying on the tree.

2 We know the love that brought Thee
  down,
 Down from that bliss on high;
To meet our ruined souls' deep need,
 On Calv'ry's cross to die.

3 Our Saviour and our Lord Thou art,
 Eternal is Thy love;
Eternal, too, our songs of praise,
 When with Thee, Lord, above.

4 E'en now we praise the grace divine,
 The love that shines in Thee:
The rich one Thou, for us made poor.
 By death to set us free.

5 We praise, we worship, we adore,
 As round Thyself we meet;
Thy beauty, Lord, our souls transports
 While bowing at Thy feet.

6 Our theme of praise art Thou alone,
 Thy cross, Thy work, Thy word:
Oh, who can fathom all Thy love,
 Thou living, blessèd Lord?

Thomas Eadie Purdom, c. 1852–1942

This hymn may also be sung to **Green Hill**, No. 158

523

HOLY TRINITY C.M.

J. Barnby, 1838-1896

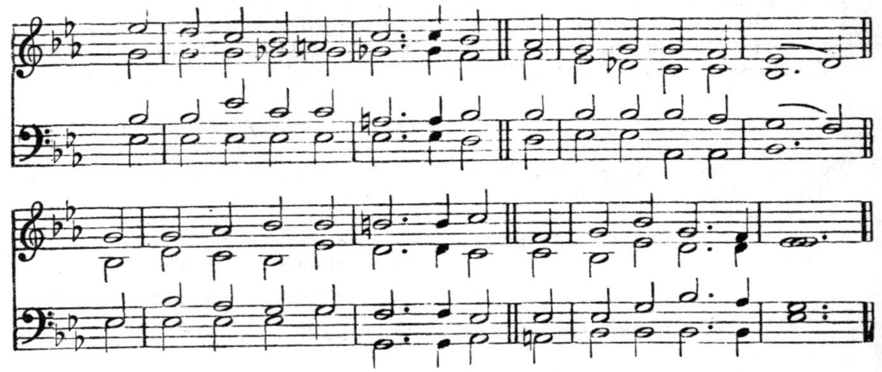

Lord Jesus, are we one with Thee?
  Oh height, oh depth of love!
Once slain for us upon the tree,
  We're one with Thee above.

2 Such was Thy grace, that, for our
    sake,
  Thou didst from heaven come
    down;
  With us of flesh and blood partake,
  In all our sorrows one.

3 Our sins, our guilt, in love divine
  Confessed and borne by Thee;
  The gall, the curse, the wrath were
    Thine,
  To set Thy ransomed free.

4 Ascended now in glory bright,
  Head of the church Thou art.
  Nor life, nor death, nor depth, nor
    height
  Thy saints and Thee can part.

5 Then teach us, Lord, to know and
    own
  This wondrous mystery,
  That Thou with us art truly one,
  And we are one with Thee.

6 Soon, soon shall come that glorious
    day,
  When, seated on Thy throne;
  Thou shalt to wondering worlds
    display,
  That Thou with us art one.

James George Deck, 1802-84

This hymn may also be sung to **Abridge,** No. 128

L ORD Jesus, gladly do our lips express
Our hearts' deep sense of all Thy worthiness;
Thou Risen One, the Holy and the True,
We give Thee now the praise so justly due.

2 Thou giv'st us, Lord, once more to taste down here,
The joy Thy presence brings, its warmth and cheer,
With great delight we 'neath Thy shadow rest
Thy fruit is sweet to those Thy love has blest.

3 Thou wast alone, till like the precious grain
In death Thou layest, but did'st rise again;
And in Thy risen life, a countless host
Are "all of one" with Thee, Thy joy and boast.

4 We bless Thee, Lord, Thou lov'st to take Thy place
Amongst Thine own, who taste Thy boundless grace;
'Tis here we learn Thee, as Thou'rt known above,
In heavenly glory—home of perfect love.

T. Willey

This hymn may also be sung to **Dalkeith**, No. 699

525

LLANBADARN 87.87.77

R. S. HUGHES, 1853-93

LORD of glory, we adore Thee!
  Christ of God, ascended high!
Heart and soul we bow before Thee,
  Glorious now beyond the sky;
    Thee we worship,
    Thee we praise—
Excellent in all Thy ways.

2 Mighty King, with glory crownèd,
  Rightful heir and Lord of all!
Once rejected, scorned, disownèd
  E'en by those Thou cam'st to call:
    Thee we honour,
    Thee adore—
Glorious now and evermore.

3 Lord of life! to death made subject;
  Blesser, yet a curse once made;
Of Thy Father's heart the object,
  Yet in depths of anguish laid:
    Thee we gaze on,
    Thee recall,
Bearing here our sorrows all.

4 Royal robes shall soon invest Thee,
  Royal splendours crown Thy brow;
Christ of God, our souls confess Thee
  King and sovereign even now!
    Thee we reverence,
    Thee obey,
Own Thee Lord and Christ alway.

Richard Holden, d. 1886

This hymn may also be sung to **Blaencefn,** No. 515

OLD 120TH 66.66.66   Melody from ESTE's *Book of Psalmes*, 1592

Not for our sins alone
  Thy mercy, Lord, we sue;
Let fall Thy pitying glance
  On our devotions too—
What we have done for Thee,
  And what we think to do.

2 The holiest hours we spend
  In prayer upon our knees,
The times when most we deem
  Our songs of praise will please,
Thou searcher of all hearts,
  Forgiveness pour on these.

3 And all the gifts we bring,
  And all the vows we make,
And all the acts of love
  We plan for Thy dear sake,
Into Thy pardoning thought,
  O God of mercy, take.

4 And most when we, Thy flock,
  Around Thy table bend,
And strange bewildering thoughts
  With those sweet moments blend,
By Him whose death we plead,
  O Lord, Thy help extend.

5 Bow down Thine ear and hear:
  Open Thine eyes and see:
Our very love is shame;
  And we must come to Thee,
To make it, of Thy grace,
  What Thou wouldst have it be.

Henry Twells, 1823–1900

527

ST. HUGH C.M.

E. J. Hopkins, 1818-1901

Lord, teach us how to pray aright
  With reverence and with fear;
Though dust and ashes in Thy sight,
  We may, we must draw near.

2 God of all grace, we come to Thee
  With broken contrite hearts;
Give, what Thine eye delights to see,
  Truth in the inward parts;

3 Give true humility; the sense
  Of godly sorrow give;
A strong desiring confidence
  To hear Thy voice and live;

4 Faith in the only sacrifice
  That can for sin atone;
To cast our hopes, to fix our eyes,
  On Christ, and Him alone;

5 Patience to watch, and wait, and weep,
  Though mercy long delay;
Courage, our fainting souls to keep,
  And trust Thee, though Thou slay;

6 Give these, and then Thy will be done;
  Thus, strengthened with all might,
We by Thy Spirit, through Thy Son,
  Shall pray, and pray aright.

James Montgomery, 1771–1854

This hymn may also be sung to **Dublin**, No. 188

529

Words at foot of next page.

ST. MICHAEL S.M.

Genevan Psalter, 1551

VENICE S.M.

W. AMPS, 1824-1910

O^H bless the Lord, my soul,
   His grace to thee proclaim,
And all that is within me join
   To bless His holy name.

2   Oh bless the Lord, my soul,
      His mercies bear in mind,
   Forget not all His benefits:
      The Lord to thee is kind.

3   He will not always chide;
      He will with patience wait;
   His wrath is ever slow to rise,
      And ready to abate.

4   He pardons all thy sins,
      Prolongs thy feeble breath,
   He healeth thine infirmities,
      And ransoms thee from death.

5   He clothes thee with His love,
      Upholds thee with His truth,
   And, like the eagle, He renews
      The vigour of thy youth.

6   Then bless His holy name,
      Whose grace hath made thee whole,
   Whose lovingkindness crowns thy
      days,
      Oh bless the Lord, my soul.

James Montgomery, 1771–1854

529

Tune at foot of previous page

O PATIENT, spotless One!
   Our hearts in meekness train
To bear Thy yoke and learn of Thee,
   That we may rest obtain.

2   Jesus, Thou art enough
      The mind and heart to fill:
   Thy life, to calm each anxious thought,
      Thy love, each fear dispel.

3   Oh fix our earnest gaze
      So wholly, Lord, on Thee,
   That, with Thy beauty occupied,
      We elsewhere none may see.

Christian Andreas Bernstein, d. 1699

This hymn may also be sung to Rhodes, No. 339

530

EDEN L.M.

T. B. MASON, 1801-61

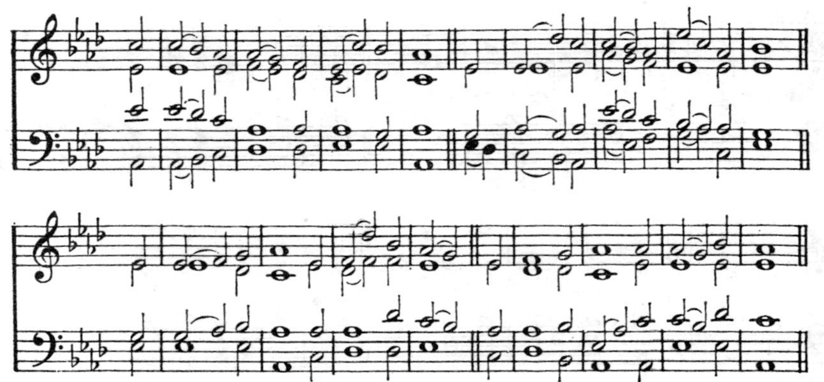

O COME Thou stricken Lamb of God,
Who shedd'st for us Thine own life-blood;
And teach us all Thy love: then pain
Were sweet, and life or death were gain.

2 O Lord, enlarge our scanty thought
To know the wonders Thou hast wrought;
Unloose our stammering tongues, to tell
Thy love immense, unsearchable.

3 What are our works but sin and death,
Till Thou Thy quickening Spirit breathe;
Thou giv'st the power Thy grace to move:
Oh wondrous grace! Oh boundless love!

4 How can it be, Thou heavenly King,
That Thou shouldst us to glory bring;
Make slaves the partners of Thy throne,
Decked with a never-fading crown?

5 First-born of many brethren, Thou!
To whom both heaven and earth must bow!
To Thee our hearts and hands we give;
Thine may we die, Thine may we live!

Nicolaus Ludwig von Zinzendorf, 1700–60
Johann Nitschmann, 1712–83
Anna Nitschmann, 1715–60
tr. John Wesley, 1703–91

This hymn may also be sung to **Bodmin,** No. 21

OH, the deep, deep love of Jesus!
  Vast, unmeasured, boundless, free;
Rolling as a mighty ocean
  In its fulness over me.
Underneath me, all around me,
  Is the current of Thy love;
Leading onward, leading homeward,
  To my glorious rest above.

2 Oh, the deep, deep love of Jesus!
  Spread His praise from shore to shore
How He loveth, ever loveth,
  Changeth never, nevermore;
How He watches o'er His loved ones,
  Died to call them all His own;
How for them He intercedeth,
  Watcheth o'er them from the throne.

3 Oh, the deep, deep love of Jesus!
  Love of every love the best:
'Tis an ocean vast of blessing,
  'Tis a haven sweet of rest.
Oh, the deep, deep love of Jesus!
  'Tis a heaven of heavens to me;
And it lifts me up to glory,
  For it lifts me up to Thee.

Samuel Trevor Francis, 1834–1925

This hymn may also be sung to Hyfrydol, No. 222

532

SAFFRON WALDEN 888.6

A. H. BROWN, 1830-1926

O SAVIOUR, I have nought to plead,
  In earth beneath, or heaven above,
But just my own exceeding need,
  And Thy exceeding love.

2 The need will soon be past and gone,
  Exceeding great, but quickly o'er:
The love unbought is all Thine own,
  And lasts for evermore.

Jane Fox Crewdson, 1809–63

533

SAWLEY C.M.

J. WALCH, 1837-1901

OH teach me more of Thy blest ways,
  Thou holy Lamb of God!
And fix and root me in Thy grace,
  As one redeemed by blood.

2 Oh tell me often of Thy love,
  Of all Thy grief and pain;
And let my heart with joy confess,
  That thence comes all my gain.

3 For this, oh may I freely count,
  Whate'er I have but loss;
The dearest objects of my love,
  Compared with Thee but dross.

4 Engrave this deeply on my heart
  With an eternal pen,
That I may, in some small degree,
  Return Thy love again.

James Hutton, 1715–95

EWING   76.76.D

ALEXANDER EWING, 1830-95

OUR Father, we would worship
  In Jesu's holy Name,
For He, whate'er our changes,
  For ever is the same;
Through Him Thy children's praises
  As incense sweet will be;
The songs Thy Spirit raises
  Can ne'er want melody.

2 The fire Thy love hath kindled
  Shall never be put out;
Thy Spirit keeps it burning,
  Though dimmed by sin and doubt;
Oh make it burn more brightly!
  By faith more freely shine!
That we may value rightly
  The grace that made us Thine.

Author unknown.

This hymn may also be sung to **Penlan**, No. 358

535

HOLY TRINITY C.M.

J. BARNBY, 1838-1896

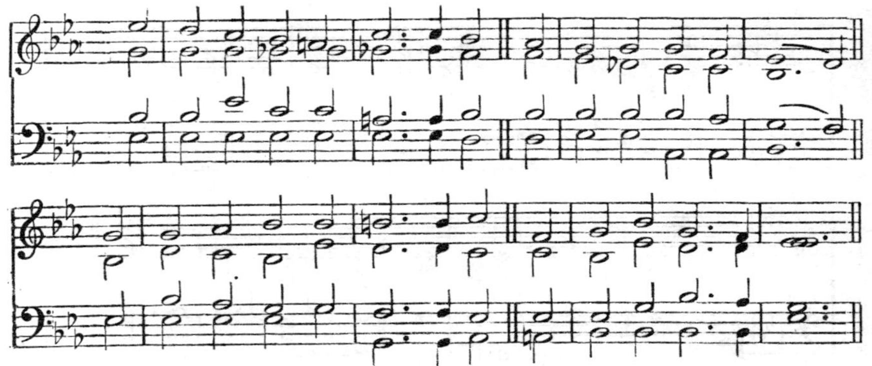

PRAYER is the soul's sincere desire,
  Uttered or unexpressed,
The motion of a hidden fire
  That trembles in the breast.

2 Prayer is the burden of a sigh,
  The falling of a tear,
The upward glancing of an eye
  When none but God is near.

3 Prayer is the simplest form of speech
  That infant lips can try;
Prayer, the sublimest strains that reach
  The Majesty on high.

4 Prayer is the contrite sinner's voice,
  Returning from his ways;
While angels in their songs rejoice,
  And cry, "Behold, he prays!"

5 Prayer is the Christian's vital breath,
  The Christian's native air,
His watchword at the gate of death;
  He enters heaven with prayer.

6 O Thou by whom we come to God,
  The Life, the Truth, the Way,
The path of prayer Thyself hast trod:
  Lord, teach us how to pray!

James Montgomery, 1771-1854

This hymn may also be sung to **Nox Praecessit,** No. 414

536   QUIETUDE 65.65

H. GREEN, 1871-1931

SPEAK, Lord, in the stillness,
  While I wait on Thee;
Hushed my heart to listen
  In expectancy.

2 Speak, O blessèd Master,
  In this quiet hour;
Let me see Thy face, Lord,
  Feel Thy touch of power.

3 For the words Thou speakest,
  They are life indeed;
Living Bread from heaven,
  Now my spirit feed!

4 Speak, Thy servant heareth!
  Be not silent, Lord;
Waits my soul upon Thee
  For the quickening word.

5 Fill me with the knowledge
  Of Thy glorious will;
All Thine own good pleasure
  In Thy child fulfil.

E. May Grimes, 1868–1927

LLANGLOFFAN 76.76.D   Welsh Hymn Melody 537

THE holiest we enter,
  In perfect peace with God;
He brings our thoughts to centre
  Round Jesus and His blood;
And while we mourn our dulness,
  In thought, and word, and deed,
We glory in the fullness
  That meets our utmost need.

2 Much incense is ascending
  Before our Father's throne;
His gracious ear is bending
  To hear our feeblest groan:

To all our prayers and praises
  Christ adds His sweet perfume;
And love the altar raises,
  These odours to consume.

3 O God, we come with singing,
  Because our great High Priest
Our names to Thee is bringing,
  Nor e'er forgets the least;
For us He wears the mitre,
  Where "Holiness" shines bright;
For us His robes are whiter
  Than heaven's unclouded light.

Mary Bowly Peters, 1813–56

This hymn may also be sung to **Aurelia,** No. 588

538

Thou life of my life, blessèd Saviour,
  Thy death was the death that was mine,
For me was Thy cross and Thine anguish,
  Thy love and Thy sorrow divine.
Thou hast suffer'd the cross and the judgment,
  That I might for ever go free—
A thousand, a thousand thanksgivings
  I bring, my Lord Jesus, to Thee!

2 For me hast Thou borne the reproaches,
  The mockery, hate, and disdain,
The blows and the spitting of sinners,
  The scourging, the shame, and the pain;
To save me from bondage and judgment,
  Thou gladly hast suffered for me—
A thousand, a thousand thanksgivings
  I bring, my Lord Jesus, to Thee!

SECOND TUNE

REDEMPTION 98.98.D

PETER BILHORN, 1865-1936

3 O Lord, from my heart do I thank
    Thee
    For all Thou hast borne in my
      room—
Thine agony, dying unsolaced,
    Alone in the darkness and gloom—
That I in the glory of heaven
    For ever and ever might be—
A thousand, a thousand thanksgivings
I bring, my Lord Jesus, to Thee!

Ernst Carl Homburg, 1605–81
tr. Emma Frances Bevan, 1827–1909

QUAM DILECTA 66.66 H. L. JENNER, 1820-98

WE love the place, O God,
  Wherein Thine honour dwells;
The joy of Thine abode
  All earthly joy excels.

2 It is the house of prayer,
    Wherein Thy servants meet;
  And Thou, O Lord, art there,
    Thy chosen flock to greet.

3 We love the word of life,
    The word that tells of peace,
  Of comfort in the strife
    And joys that never cease.

4 We love to sing below
    Of mercies freely given;
  But oh we long to know
    The triumph song of heaven!

5 Lord Jesus, give us grace,
    On earth to love Thee more,
  In heaven to see Thy face,
    And with Thy saints adore.

William Bullock, 1798–1874

CALON LÂN 87.87.D JOHN HUGHES (Glandŵr), 1872-1914

W HAT a Friend we have in Jesus,
  All our sins and griefs to bear;
What a privilege to carry
  Everything to God in prayer.
Oh what peace we often forfeit,
  Oh what needless pain we bear—
All because we do not carry
  Everything to God in prayer.

2 Have we trials and temptations?
  Is there trouble anywhere?
We should never be discouraged:
  Take it to the Lord in prayer.
Can we find a Friend so faithful,
  Who will all our sorrows share?
Jesus knows our every weakness—
  Take it to the Lord in prayer.

3 Are we weak and heavy-laden,
  Cumbered with a load of care?
Precious Saviour, still our refuge—
  Take it to the Lord in prayer.
Do thy friends despise, forsake thee?
  Take it to the Lord in prayer.
In His hands He'll take and shield
    thee,
  Thou wilt find a solace there.

John Medlicott Scriven, 1819–86
This hymn may also be sung to **Blaenwern,** No. 454

DATCHET 11.11.11.11   G. J. Elvey, 1816-93

WITH gladness we worship, rejoice as we sing,
Free hearts and free voices how blessèd to bring,
The old, thankful story shall scale Thine abode,
Thou King of all glory, most bountiful God.

2 Thy right would we give Thee—true homage Thy due,
And honour eternal, the universe through,
With all Thy creation, earth, heaven and sea,
In one acclamation we celebrate Thee.

3 Renewed by Thy Spirit, redeemed by Thy Son,
Thy children revere Thee for all Thou hast done.
O Father! returning to love and to light,
Thy children are yearning to praise Thee aright.

4 We join with the angels, and so there is given
From earth Hallelujah, in answer to heaven.
Amen! Be Thou glorious below and above,
Redeeming, victorious, and infinite Love!

George Rawson, 1807–89

This hymn may also be sung to **St. Denio,** No. 26

See also
269   Lord God the Holy Ghost
271   Spirit divine, attend our prayers
274   O breath of God, breathe on us now
288   Lord and Saviour, at Thy word
693   I lift my heart to Thee
700   My Lord, my Master, at Thy feet

MARTYRDOM C.M.

H. WILSON, 1766-1824
adapted by R. A. SMITH, 1780-1829

ACCORDING to Thy gracious word,
  In meek humility,
This will I do, my dying Lord,
  I will remember Thee.

2 Thy body broken for my sake,
  My bread from heaven shall be;
The cup of blessing I will take,
  And thus remember Thee.

3 Gethsemane can I forget,
  Or there Thy conflict see,
Thine agony and bloody sweat,
  And not remember Thee?

4 When to the cross I turn mine eyes,
  And rest on Calvary,
O Lamb of God, my sacrifice!
  I must remember Thee.

5 Remember Thee, and all Thy pains,
  And all Thy love to me;
Yea, while a breath, a pulse remains,
  Will I remember Thee.

6 And when these failing lips grow
      dumb,
  And mind and memory flee;
When thou shalt in Thy Kingdom
      come,
    Then, Lord, remember me.

James Montgomery, 1771–1854

543

SAXBY L.M.

T. R. MATTHEWS, 1826-1910

AMIDST us our Belovèd stands,
And bids us view His piercèd hands,
Points to His wounded feet and side—
Blest emblems of the Crucified.

2 What food luxurious loads the board
When at His table sits the Lord!
The wine how rich, the bread how sweet,
When Jesus deigns the guests to meet!

3 If now, with eyes defiled and dim,
We see the signs, but see not Him,
Oh may His love the scales displace,
And bid us see Him face to face!

4 Our former transports we recount,
When with Him in the holy mount;
These cause our souls to thirst anew
His marred but lovely face to view.

5 Thou glorious Bridegroom of our hearts,
Thy present smile a heaven imparts;
Oh lift the veil, if veil there be,
Let every saint Thy beauties see.

Charles Haddon Spurgeon, 1834–92

This hymn may also be sung to **Abends,** No. 297

544 MANCHESTER C.M.

R. WAINWRIGHT, 1748-82

AROUND Thy table, holy Lord,
In fellowship we meet;
Obedient to Thy gracious word,
This feast of love to eat.

2 Here every one that loves Thy name,
Our willing hearts embrace;
Our life, our hope, our joy the same,
The same Thy love and grace.

3 However poor, despised, or few,
   We know Thy changeless love
Is not one whit less warm and true,
   Now on the throne above.

4 Commune with each at this blest hour,
   And when we hence depart,
With deeds of love, or words of power,
   Engage each faithful heart.

Mary Bowly Peters, 1813–56

TICHFIELD   77.77.D   J. RICHARDSON, 1816-79 **545**

AT the Lamb's high feast we sing
   Praise to our victorious King,
Who hath washed us in the tide
Flowing from His piercèd side;
Praise we Him, whose love divine
Gave His outpoured blood for wine,
Gave His body for the feast,
Christ our Sacrifice and Priest.

2 Where the paschal blood was poured,
   Death's dark angel sheathed his
      sword;
Israel's hosts triumphant go
Through the wave that drowns the foe.
Praise we Christ, whose blood was
      shed,
Spotless victim, heavenly bread;
With sincerity and love
Eat we manna from above.

3 Mighty victim from the sky,
Hell's fierce powers beneath Thee lie;
Thou hast conquered in the fight,
Thou hast brought us life and light.
Now no more can death appal,
Now no more the grave enthral:
Thou hast opened Paradise,
And in Thee Thy saints shall rise.

4 Easter triumph, Easter joy,
Sin alone can this destroy;
From sin's power do Thou set free
Souls new-born, O Lord, in thee.
Hymns of glory and of praise,
Risen Lord, to Thee we raise:
Holy Father, praise to Thee,
With the Spirit, ever be.

Robert Campbell, 1814–68
Based on *Ad regias Agni dapes*

546

GLANLLYFNWY L.M.

E. Davies, b. 1870

At Thy command, our dearest Lord,
  Here we attend Thy dying feast;
Thy blood like wine adorns Thy board,
  And Thine own flesh feeds every guest.

2 Let the vain world pronounce it shame,
  And fling their scandals on His cause;
We come to boast our Saviour's name,
  And make our triumph in His cross.

3 With joy we tell the scoffing age,
  He that was dead has left His tomb;
He lives above their utmost rage,
  And we are waiting till He come.
                    Isaac Watts, 1674–1748

This hymn may also be sung to **Maryton,** No. 31

547

AUTHOR OF LIFE 66.66.88

J. Stainer, 1840-1901

AUTHOR of life divine,
    Who hast a table spread,
Furnished with mystic wine
    And everlasting bread,
Preserve the life Thyself hast given,
And feed and train us up for heaven.

2 Our needy souls sustain
        With fresh supplies of love,
    Till all Thy life we gain,
        And all Thy fullness prove,
    And, strengthened by Thy perfect grace
    Behold without a veil Thy face.

Charles Wesley, 1707–88

This hymn may also be sung to **Love unknown,** No. 122

548

BREAD OF HEAVEN 77.77.77   W. D. MACLAGAN, 1826-1910

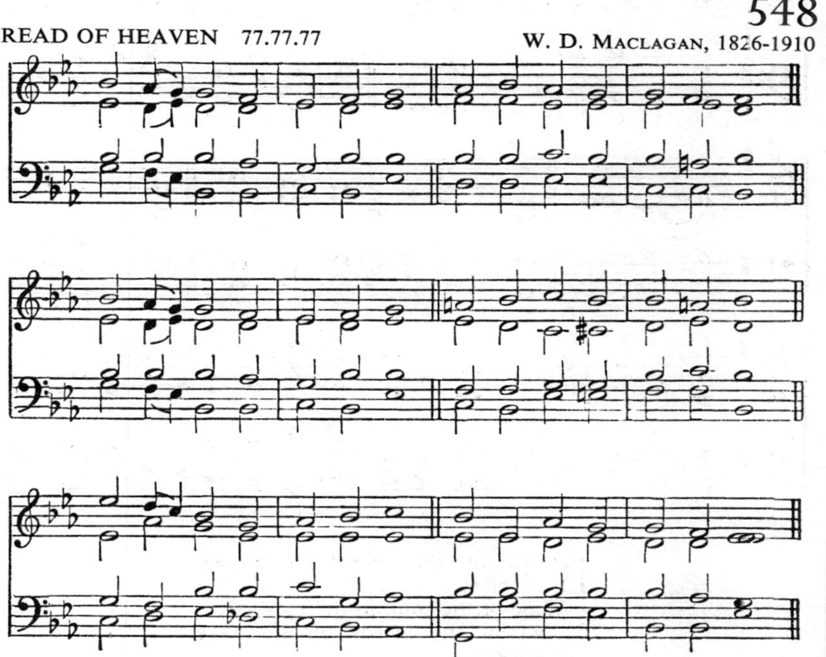

BREAD of heaven, on Thee I feed,
    For Thy flesh is meat indeed:
Ever may my soul be fed
With this true and living bread;
Day by day with strength supplied
Through the life of Him who died.

2 Vine of heaven, Thy blood supplies
This blest cup of sacrifice:
'Tis Thy wounds my healing give;
To Thy cross I look and live:
Thou my life, oh let me be
Rooted, grafted, built on Thee!

Josiah Conder, 1789–1855

RENDEZ À DIEU   98.98.D

Louis Bourgeois, 1510-61.
Psalm cxviii in *French Psalter*, 1542

BREAD of the world, in mercy
   broken;
Wine of the soul, in mercy shed;
By whom the words of life were
   spoken,
And in whose death our sins are
   dead:
Look on the heart by sorrow broken,
Look on the tears by sinners shed,
And be Thy feast to us the token
That by Thy grace our souls are fed.

Reginald Heber, 1783–1826

IN MEMORIAM 888.4

F. C. MAKER, 1844-1927

B^Y Christ redeemed, in Christ
restored,
We keep the memory adored,
And show the death of our dear Lord,
    Until He come.

2 His body, broken in our stead,
Is seen in this memorial bread,
And thus our feeble love is fed,
    Until He come.

3 His fearful drops of agony,
His life-blood, shed for us, we see—
This wine shall tell the mystery,
    Until He come.

4 And thus that dark betrayal-night
With His last advent we unite,
By one blest chain of loving rite,
    Until He come.

5 Until the trump of God be heard,
Until the ancient graves be stirred,
And, with His great commanding
    word,
The Lord shall come.

6 Oh blessed hope! with this elate,
Let not our hearts be desolate,
But strong in faith and patience, wait
    Until He come!

George Rawson, 1807–89

551

SONG 22   10.10.10.10

ORLANDO GIBBONS, 1583-1625

COME, risen Lord, and deign to be our guest;
  Nay, let us be Thy guests; the feast is Thine;
Thyself at Thine own board make manifest,
  In this memorial feast of bread and wine.

2 We meet, as in that upper room they met;
  Thou at the table, blessing, yet dost stand:
"This is my body": so Thou givest yet:
  Faith still receives the cup as from Thy hand.

3 One body we, one body who partake,
  One church united in communion blest;
One name we bear, one bread of life we break,
  With all Thy saints on earth and saints at rest.

4 One with each other, Lord, for one in Thee,
  Who art one Saviour and one living Head;
Then open Thou our eyes, that we may see;
  Be known to us in breaking of the bread.

George Wallace Briggs, 1875-1959

TROYTE'S CHANT 777.6

A. H. D. TROYTE, 1811-57
Arr. by F. A. J. Tonkin, b. 1926

For the bread and for the wine,
For the pledge that seals Him mine,
For the words of love divine,
    We give Thee thanks, O Lord.

2 Only bread and only wine,
Yet to faith the solemn sign
Of the heavenly and divine!
    We give Thee thanks, O Lord.

3 For the words that turn our eye
To the cross of Calvary,
Bidding us in faith draw nigh,
    We give Thee thanks, O Lord.

4 For the words that tell of home,
Pointing us beyond the tomb,
"Do ye this until I come,"
    We give Thee thanks, O Lord.

5 "Till He come" we take the bread,
Type of Him on whom we feed,
Him who liveth and was dead!
    We give Thee thanks, O Lord.

6 "Till He come" we take the cup;
As we at His table sup,
Eye and heart are lifted up!
    We give Thee thanks, O Lord.

7 For that coming here foreshown,
For that day to man unknown,
For the glory and the throne,
    We give Thee thanks, O Lord.

Horatius Bonar, 1808–89

553

CASTLE RISING   C.M.D.

F. A. J. HERVEY, 1846-1910

HERE, Lord, we come Thyself to meet,
  As to this feast we come;
Like Mary, resting at Thy feet,
  To learn of Thee alone:
Our hearts recall what Thou hast said,
  "This do," remembering Me;
So thus we take the wine, the bread,
  In memory of Thee.

2 From Thee, O Lord, the bread we take,
  From Thy pierced hand the wine;
At rest, accepted for Thy sake,
  Our meetness, Lord, is Thine!
We praise Thee for this quiet hour,
  Spent with Thyself alone,
We thank Thee for the Spirit's power,
  And His blest teachings own.

3 O Lord, we know that Thou art here;
    Enrich each memory!
  Thy faithful promise brings Thee
      near,
    And gathers us to Thee;
  Thy body broken, poured-out blood—
    Blest memories, ever dear!
  Thou Son of Man! Thou Lamb of
      God!
    Thy voice our hearts would hear!

Boethia Thompson

This hymn may also be sung to **St. Matthew**, No. 124

BONT-NEWYDD   10.10.10.10   John Roberts (Ieuan Gwyllt), 1822-77

Here, O my Lord, I see Thee face to face;
Here would I touch and handle things unseen;
Here grasp with firmer hand the eternal grace,
And all my weariness upon Thee lean.

2 Here would I feed upon the bread of God;
Here drink with Thee the royal wine of heaven;
Here would I lay aside each earthly load;
Here taste afresh the calm of sin forgiven.

3 Mine is the sin, but Thine the righteousness;
Mine is the guilt, but Thine the cleansing blood:
Here is my robe, my refuge, and my peace—
Thy blood, Thy righteousness, O Lord my God.

4 I have no help but Thine; nor do I need
Another arm save Thine to lean upon;
It is enough, my Lord, enough indeed;
My strength is in Thy might, Thy might alone.

5 Too soon we rise, the symbols disappear;
The feast, though not the love is past and gone;
The bread and wine remove, but Thou art here,
Nearer than ever, still my shield and sun.

6 Feast after feast thus comes and passes by;
Yet passing, points to the glad feast above;
Giving sweet foretaste of the festal joy,
The Lamb's great bridal feast of bliss and love.

Horatius Bonar, 1808–89

This hymn may also be sung to **St. Agnes,** No. 690

555

ST. HUGH C.M.

E. J. HOPKINS, 1818-1901

I AM not worthy, holy Lord,
  That Thou shouldst come to me;
Speak but the word; one gracious
    word
Can set the sinner free.

2 I am not worthy; cold and bare
  The lodging of my soul;
How canst Thou deign to enter there?
  Lord, speak, and make me whole.

3 I am not worthy; yet, my God,
  How can I say Thee nay—
Thee, who didst give Thy flesh and
    blood
My ransom price to pay?

4 Come, in this consecrated hour,
  Feed me with food divine;
And fill with all Thy love and power
  This worthless heart of mine.

Henry Williams Baker, 1821–77

556 BULLINGER 85.83

E. W. BULLINGER, 1837-1913

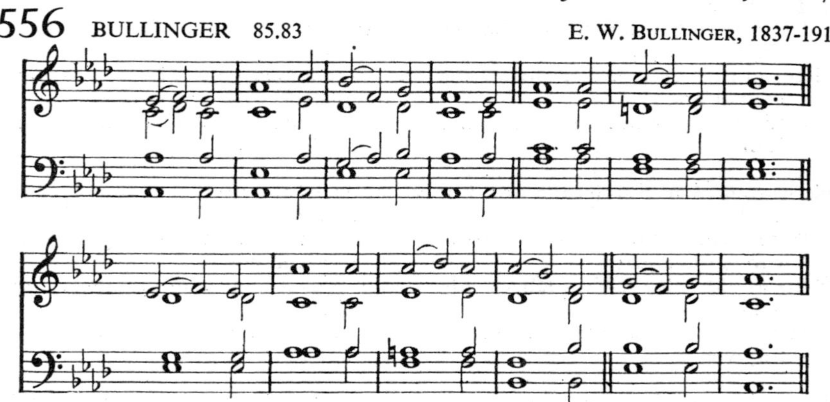

GATHERED, Lord, around Thy table,
  Now we seek Thy face;
Let us know Thy presence with us,
  Lord of grace!

2 Love divine first drew us to Thee,
  In our sin and need;
For our sin, in deep compassion,
  Thou did'st bleed.

3 Risen Lord, in glory seated,
  We are one with Thee;
Thou hast snapt the chains that
    bound us,
We are free.

4 Gratefully we Thee remember
  As we break the bread,
Symbol of Thy body broken
  In our stead.

5 Drink we too the cup of blessing
   Which Thy love has filled;
Through Thy blood we have re-
   demption,
   Fears are stilled.

6 Backward look we, drawn to Calvary,
   Musing while we sing;
Forward haste we to Thy coming,
   Lord and King!

Douglas Russell, 1842–1933

This hymn may also be sung to Cairnbrook, No. 144

557

DRAKE'S BROUGHTON 87.87   EDWARD ELGAR, 1857-1934

THEE we praise, High Priest and
   Victim,
   Of our hearts the Shepherd-king;
Living, dying, rising, saving;
   Now let alleluias ring.

2 Here, as priests around Thy table,
   We are met to worship Thee:
All Thy saints, on earth, in heaven,
   Humbly bend the adoring knee.

3 Here we see the mystery telling
   Of Thy wondrous love for men,
Here set forth in sacred symbol
   Love beyond our widest ken.

4 Lo! in adoration bending,
   We receive what Thou dost give;
Join the glad new song unending,
   Feed by faith on Thee, and live.

5 Praise to Thee, eternal Saviour,
   Praises from the earth ascend;
Praises from the saints in heaven,
   Alleluias without end!

William Robinson, b. 1888

558

DENNIS S.M.

J. G. Nägeli, 1773-1836

JESUS invites His saints
  To meet around His board;
Here pardoned rebels sit and hold
  Communion with their Lord.

2 Here we survey that love
  Which spoke in every breath,
Which crowned each action of His life,
  And triumphed in His death.

3 This feast of bread and wine
  Revives our fainting breath,
In union with our living Lord,
  And interest in His death.

4 Our heavenly Father calls
  Christ and His members one;
We the young children of His love,
  And He the first-born Son.

5 We are but several parts
  Of that same Living Bread;
Our body hath its several limbs,
  But Jesus is the Head.

6 Let all our powers be joined,
  His glorious name to raise;
Pleasure and love fill every mind,
  And every voice be praise.

Isaac Watts, 1674–1748

This hymn may also be sung to **St. Michael**, No. 529

CALON LÂN 87.87.D

JESUS, Lord, I know Thee present
  At Thy table freshly spread,
Seated at Thy priceless banquet,
  With Thy banner overhead.
Precious moments at Thy table,
  From all fear and doubt set free;
Here to rest, so sweetly able,
  Occupied alone with Thee.

2 Here rejoicing in Thy nearness,
  Gladly by Thy Spirit led;
Calmly in the blest remembrance
  Of Thy precious blood once shed.
Lord, I take each simple token
  In fond memory of Thee;
Muse upon Thy body broken,
  And Thy blood outpoured for me.

3 Oh what joy it is to see Thee,
  In these emblems gathered here!
In the bread and wine of blessing,
  Bread to strengthen, wine to cheer.
Lord, behold us met together,
  Members of our risen head,
Thus to take the cup of blessing,
  Thus to share the broken bread.

4 Lord, we know how true Thy promise,
  To be with us where we meet;
When in Thy loved name we gather
  To enjoy communion sweet.
Dearer still that looked-for promise
  To each waiting, yearning heart,
That we are to be with Thee, Lord,
  And for ever where Thou art.

Boethia Thompson

This hymn may also be sung to **Arwelfa**, No. 142

560

ST. OSWALD 87.87

J. B. DYKES, 1823-76

JESUS, Lord, we come together
  In the bonds of Thine own love;
Thou hast drawn our footsteps hither,
  Its deep meaning now to prove.

2 Closed the door, we leave behind us
  Toil and conflict, foes and strife;
And within, Thy love doth bind us
  In one fellowship of life.

3 Here together we recall thee,
  In Thy presence break the bread;
Never more can grief befall Thee,
  Thou art risen from the dead.

4 But Thy love remains, that entered
  Into death to make us Thine;
In that death all love was centred—
  Thankful now we drink the wine.

5 Thou dost make us taste the blessing,
  Soon to fill a world of bliss;
And we bless Thy name confessing
  Thine own love our portion is.

6 Sweet it is to sit before Thee,
  Sweet to hear Thy blessèd voice.
Sweet to worship and adore Thee,
  While our hearts in Thee rejoice.

Thomas H. Reynolds, 1830–1930

This hymn may also be sung to **All for Jesus,** No. 140

561

FIRST TUNE

REDHEAD No. 47 777.6

R. REDHEAD, 1820-1901

REMEMBRANCE 777.6   SECOND TUNE   Composer unknown

JESUS, we remember Thee!
Thy deep woe and agony,
All Thy suffering on the tree
Jesus, we adore Thee!

2 Calvary, oh Calvary!
Mercy's vast unfathomed sea,
Love, eternal love to me.

3 Darkness hung around Thy head,
When for sin Thy blood was shed,
Victim in the sinner's stead.

4 Jesus, hail, Thou now art risen!
Thou hast all our sins forgiven,
Haste we to our home in heaven.

5 Blessed Jesus, risen Head,
Feed us with the living bread:
Yea, our famished souls are fed.

6 From that piercèd hand of Thine
We would take this cup of wine;
Grace and mercy, how divine!

7 Soon, with joyful, glad surprise,
We shall hear Thy word: Arise!
Mounting upward to the skies.
Glory, glory, glory!

Samuel Trevor Francis, 1834–1925

562

AUGUSTINE S.M.

PETER ABELARD, 1079-1142

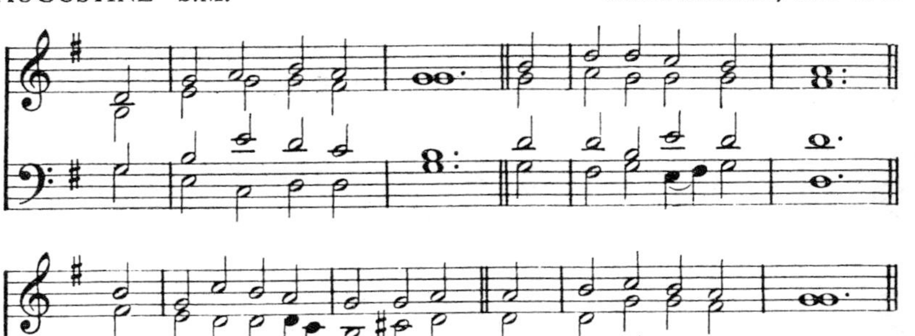

JESUS, we thus obey
  Thy last and kindest word;
Here, in Thine own appointed way,
  We come to meet Thee, Lord.

2 Our hearts we open wide,
  To make the Saviour room;
And lo! the Lamb, the Crucified,
  The sinner's Friend, is come.

3 Thus we remember Thee,
  And take this bread and wine
As Thine own dying legacy,
  And our redemption's sign.

4 Thy presence makes the feast;
  Now let our spirits feel
The glory not to be expressed,
  The joy unspeakable.

5 With high and heavenly bliss
  Thou dost our spirits cheer;
Thy house of banqueting is this,
  And Thou hast brought us here.

6 Now let our souls be fed
  With manna from above,
And over us Thy banner spread
  Of everlasting love.

Charles Wesley, 1707–88

563

FIRST TUNE

ST. JOHN'S, HOXTON 66.66

E. H. G. SARGENT, 1887-1973

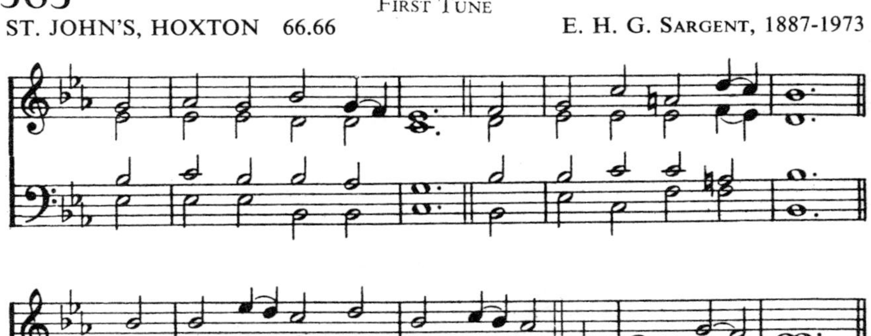

CORROUR BOTHY 66.84

SECOND TUNE

T. C. MICKLEM, b. 1925

LORD Jesus, in Thy name
  We round Thy table now
Remember thus Thy death of shame,
  Thy thorn-crowned brow.

2 Master, from Thy blest hand
  This broken bread we take,
Responsive to Thine own command
  For Thy name's sake.

3 We in this wine would see
  The measure of Thy love,
That love which bids us joy in Thee,
  Enthroned above.

4 Here would we rest, O Lord,
  Here banish doubt and fear,
Here feast on Thee, Thou Living
    Word,
  And know Thee near.

5 Keep us Thine own, we pray,
  Our Saviour, so may we
In thought, in word, in deed, alway
  Remember Thee.

Author unknown

564

ROCKINGHAM L.M.

E. MILLER, 1731-1807

LORD, we would ne'er forget Thy love,
Who hast redeemed us by Thy blood,
And now, as our High Priest above,
Dost intercede for us with God.

2 Lord, we would ne'er forget the pain,
The sweat of blood, the accursèd tree,
The wrath Thy soul did once sustain,
From sin and death to set us free.

3 We would remember we are one
With every saint that loves Thy name;
To Thee united on the throne—
Our life, our hope, our Lord, the same.

4 Here, in the broken bread and wine
We hear Thee say, "Remember me!
"I gave my life to ransom thine;
"I bore the wrath to set thee free."

5 Lord, we are Thine; we praise Thy love—
One with Thy saints, all one in Thee;
We would, until we meet above,
In all our ways, remember Thee.

James George Deck, 1802–84

This hymn may also be sung to **Castle Street,** No. 216

DIX 77.77.77

Adapted from a chorale by C. KOCHER, 1786-1872

MEETING in the Saviour's name,
  Breaking bread by His com-
mand,
To the world we thus proclaim
  On what ground we hope to stand,
When the Lord shall come with clouds,
Joined by heaven's exulting crowds.

2 From the cross our hope we draw,
  'Tis the sinner's blest resource;
Jesus magnified the law;
  Jesus bore its awful curse:
What a joyful truth is this!
Oh how full of hope it is!

3 Jesus died and then arose;
  Yes, He rose, He lives, He reigns!
Jesus vanquished all His foes,
  Jesus led them all in chains:
His the triumph and the crown,
His the glory and renown.

4 Sing we then of Him who died,
  Sing of Him who rose again;
By His blood we're justified,
  And with Him we hope to reign:
Yes, we wait to see our Lord,
And to share His bright reward.

Thomas Kelly, 1769–1855

This hymn may also be sung to **Heathlands**, No. 609

566

CROMER L.M.

J. A. LLOYD, 1815-74

MY God, and is Thy table spread?
And does Thy cup with love o'erflow?
Thither be all Thy children led,
And let them all its sweetness know.

2 Hail, sacred feast, which Jesus makes,
Rich banquet of His flesh and blood!
Thrice happy he who here partakes
That sacred stream, that heavenly food!

3 Why are its emblems all in vain
Before unwilling hearts displayed?
Was not for you the victim slain?
Are you forbid the children's bread?

4 Oh let Thy table honoured be,
And furnished well with joyful guests;
And may each soul salvation see,
That here its sacred pledges tastes.

5 Let us approach with hearts prepared,
With glowing hearts let all attend;
Nor when we leave our Father's board
The pleasure or the profit end.

6 Revive Thy fainting people, Lord,
And bid our drooping graces live;
That holy energy afford
A Saviour's love alone can give.

Philip Doddridge, 1702-51

This hymn may also be sung to **Warrington**, No. 294

VENI SPIRITUS S.M.

J. STAINER, 1840-1901

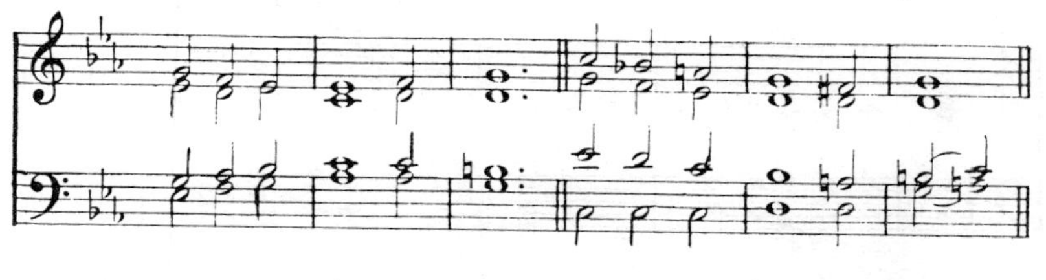

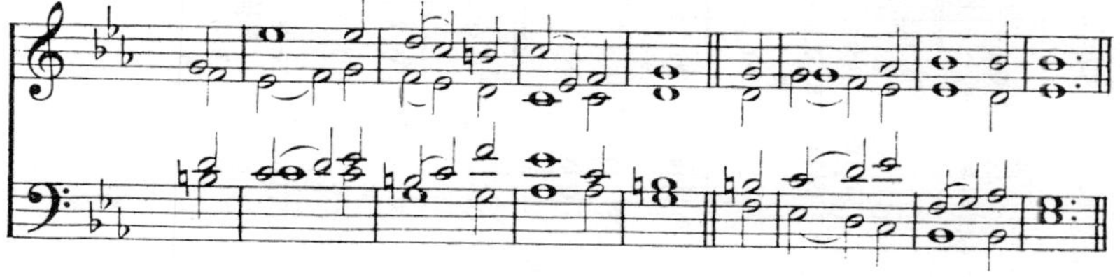

No gospel like this feast,
    Spread for us, Lord, by
Thee;
No prophet nor evangelist
    Preach the glad news so free.

2   All our redemption cost,
    All our redemption won;
All it has won for us, the lost,
    All it cost Thee, the Son.

3   Thine was the bitter price,
    Ours is the free gift given;
Thine was the blood of sacrifice,
    Ours is the wine of heaven.

4   For Thee the burning thirst,
    The shame, the mortal strife,
The broken heart, the piercèd side:
    To us, the bread of life.

5   Here we would rest midway,
    As on a sacred height;
That darkest and that brightest day
    Meeting before our sight.

6 From that dark depth of woes
    Thy love for us has trod,
We soar to heights of blest repose
    Thy love prepares with God.

7   Till, from self's chains released,
    One sight alone we see,
Still at the cross, as at this feast,
    Behold Thee, only Thee!

Elisabeth Rundle Charles, 1828–96

This hymn may also be sung to **Silchester**, No. 491

568

PASSION CHORALE 76.76.D

Melody by H. L. HASSLER, 1564-1612
Harmonised by J. S. BACH, 1685-1750

O BREAD to pilgrims given,
  O food that angels eat,
O manna sent from heaven,
  For heaven-born natures meet!
Give us, for Thee long pining,
  To eat till richly filled;
Till, earth's delights resigning,
  Our every wish is stilled.

2 O water, life-bestowing,
  Forth from the Saviour's heart
A fountain purely flowing,
  A fount of love Thou art:
Oh let us, freely tasting,
  Our burning thirst assuage;
Thy sweetness, never wasting,
  Avails from age to age.

3 Jesus, this feast receiving,
  We Thee unseen adore;
Thy faithful word believing,
  We take, and doubt no more:
Give us, Thou true and loving,
  On earth to live in Thee;
Then, death the veil removing,
  Thy glorious face to see.

Ray Palmer, 1808–87
from Thomas Aquinas, c. 1227–74

UNDE ET MEMORES 10.10.10.10.10.10   W. H. MONK, 1823-89

O HOLY Father, who in tender love
Didst give Thine only Son for us to die,
The while He pleads at Thy right hand above,
We in one Spirit now with faith draw nigh,
And, as we eat this bread and drink this wine,
Plead His once-offered sacrifice divine.

2 We are not worthy to be called Thy sons,
Nor gather up the fragments of Thy feast;
Yet look on us, Thy sorrowing contrite ones,
On us in Him, our Advocate and Priest,
Whose robe is fringed with mercy's golden bells,
Whose breastplate fathomless compassion tells.

3 Oh hear us, for Thou always hearest Him;
Behold us sprinkled with His precious blood;
And from between the shadowing Cherubim
Shine forth, and grant us in this heavenly food
Foretastes of coming glory, and meanwhile
A Father's blessing and a Father's smile.

4 Nor only, Father, in Thy presence here
Low at Thy footstool for ourselves we pray,
But for the loved ones to our hearts most near
At home or toiling in far lands away:
Oh guard them, guide them, comfort and befriend,
And keep them Thine unfaltering to the end.

5 And, Father, ere we leave Thy mercy-throne,
Bound by these sacred pledges, yet most free,
We give our hearts, and not our hearts alone,
But all we are and all we have to Thee;
Glad free-will offerings all our pilgrim days
Hereafter an eternity of praise.

Edward Henry Bickersteth, 1825–1906

This hymn may also be sung to **Song 1**, No. 451

570

SANDON 10.4.10.4.10.10

C. H. PURDAY, 1799-1885

OH teach us, Lord, Thy searchless
love to know,
Thou who hast died.
Before our feeble faith, Lord Jesus,
show
Thy hands and side;
That our glad hearts, responsive unto
Thine,
May wake with all the power of love
divine.

2 Thy death has brought to light the
Father's heart,
And ours has won;
And now we contemplate Thee as
Thou art,
God's glorious Son!
And know that we are loved with that
great love,
That rests on Thee in those bright
courts above.

3 Thy flesh is meat, Thy blood, blest
Saviour, shed,
Is drink indeed;
On Thee, the true, the heavenly,
living Bread,
Our souls would feed,
And live with Thee in life's eternal
home,
Where sin, nor want, nor woe, nor
death can come.

James Boyd

This hymn may also be sung to **Barton,** No. 391

PEN-YR-YRFA   76.76.D

Welsh melody, arr. W. JAMES, 1877-1964

ON that same night, Lord Jesus,
    When all around combined
To cast its darkest shadow
    Across Thy holy mind,
We hear Thy voice, blest Saviour,
    "This do, remember me;"
With grateful hearts responding,
    We now remember Thee.

2 We think of all the darkness
    Which round Thy spirit pressed,
Of all the waves and billows
    Which rolled across Thy breast;
'Tis there Thy grace unbounded
    And perfect love we see;
With joy and sorrow mingling,
    We do remember Thee.

3 We know Thee now as risen,
    The firstborn from the dead;
We see Thee now ascended,
    The church's glorious Head.
In Thee by grace accepted,
    The heart and mind set free
To think of all Thy sorrow,
    And thus remember Thee.

4 Till Thou shalt come in glory,
    And call us hence away,
To rest in all the brightness
    Of that unclouded day,
We show Thy death, Lord Jesus,
    And here would seek to be
More to Thy death conformèd,
    Whilst we remember Thee.

George West Fraser, 1840–96

This hymn may also be sung to **Bentley,** No. 292

572

ST. JOHN BAPTIST 65.65

O. M. FEILDEN, 1837-1924

ON this day of sharing
  Gladly do we come
To the Lord's own table,
  Gathering as one.

2 See the table laden
  With the bread and wine,
Sign of Christ's own presence,
  Pledge of love divine!

3 Food and drink, symbolic
  Of His life on earth:
Peace, good will to all men,
  Promised from His birth.

4 In the bread that's broken
  In the wine that's poured,
Be the name of Jesus
  Evermore adored!

5 Many urgent problems
  Face the human race—
War and vice and hunger:
  God seems out of place.

6 Yet our Saviour sends us
  To this world of sin,
Calling men to Jesus:
  "Let Christ enter in!"

7 Then, depart to serve Him;
  Worship Him as God;
Follow as He leads us
  In the way He trod.

David Kenneth Bentley, b. 1948
Doreen Margaret Jeal, b. 1940
Marsha Coburn Kahale, b. 1947
Robert Kyba, b. 1949

This hymn may also be sung to **Quietude**, No. 536

573 LOVE DIVINE 87.87.D

J. ZUNDEL, 1815-82

O THOU tender, gracious Shepherd,
   Shedding for us Thy life's
blood,
Unto shame and death delivered,
   All to bring us nigh to God!
Now our willing hearts adore Thee;
   Now we taste Thy dying love;
While by faith we come before Thee,
   Faith which lifts our souls above.

2 As our surety we behold Thee,
   Ransoming our souls from death;
As the willing victim view Thee,
   Yielding up to God Thy breath.

In this broken bread we own Thee,
   Bruised for us and put to shame;
And this cup, O Lord, we thank Thee,
   Speaks our pardon through Thy
name.

3 Blessèd supper of thanksgiving,
   Feast of more than angels' food!
Bread of life, and cup of blessing,
   This is fellowship with God.
Poor the praise we now are bringing;
   But when, Lord, we see Thy face,
Better songs of triumph singing,
   We shall own Thy matchless grace.

Amelia St. John Niblock Wellesley

DEEP HARMONY L.M.

HANDEL PARKER, 1857-1929   **574**

OURS is a rich and royal feast
   Provided by the King of heaven:
How privileged are they, and blest,
   To whom the bread of life is given!

2 In sacred fellowship we meet,
   To celebrate our Saviour's death;
His blood we drink, His flesh we eat,
   His people feed on Him by faith.

3 We worship Him who bore the cross;
   We glory in His death alone:
The world itself appears but loss
   To those by whom His name is
known.

4 The blood He shed supplied a stream
   That washed our crimson guilt
away;
How precious then the Lord should
   seem,
   Whose death we celebrate to-day.

5 On earth His dying love shall be
   Our spring of hope, our theme of
joy;
And when in heaven our Lord we see,
   His praise shall all our powers
employ.

Thomas Kelly, 1769–1855

This hymn may also be sung to **Arizona,** No. 162

575

BELMONT C.M.

GARDINER'S *Sacred Melodies*, 1812

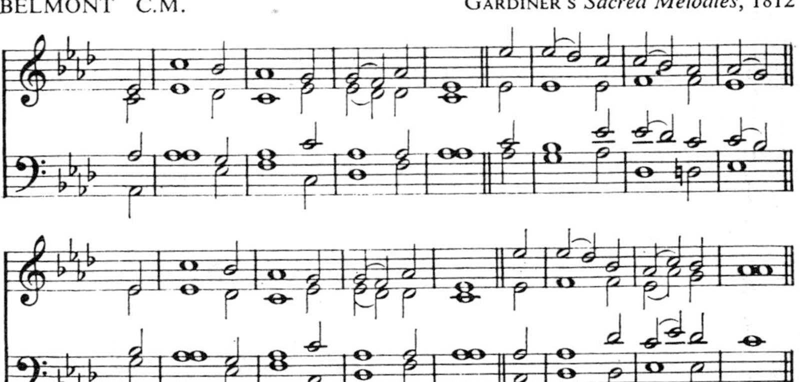

SHEPHERD of souls, refresh and bless
  Thy chosen pilgrim-flock,
With manna from the wilderness,
  With water from the rock.

2 Hungry and thirsty, faint and weak
  (As Thou when here below),
Our souls the joys celestial seek
  That from Thy sorrows flow.

3 We would not live by bread alone,
  But by Thy word of grace,
In strength of which we travel on
  To our abiding place.

4 Be known to us in breaking bread,
  But do not then depart;
Saviour, abide with us, and spread
  Thy table in our heart.

5 There sup with us in love divine:
  Thy body and Thy blood,
That living bread, that heavenly wine,
  Be our immortal food.

James Montgomery, 1771–1854

This hymn may also be sung to **Evan,** No. 70

576

CULBACH 77.77

SCHEFFLER'S *Heilige Seelenlust*, 1657

Spread the table of the Lord,
Break the bread and pour the wine;
Gathered at the sacred board,
We would taste the feast divine.

2 Saints and martyrs of the faith
To the cross have turned their eyes,
Sharing, in their life and death,
That eternal sacrifice.

3 Humbly now our place we claim
In that glorious company,
Proud confessors of the name,
Breaking bread, O Christ, with Thee.

4 By the memory of Thy love,
To the glory of the Lord,
Here we raise Thy cross above,
Gird us with Thy Spirit's sword.

5 Guided by Thy mighty hand,
All Thy mind we would fulfil,
Loyal to Thy least command,
Serving Thee with steadfast will.

George Osborn Gregory, 1881–1972

577

DOWNING S.M.

J. A. LLOYD, 1815-74

Sweet feast of love divine!
'Tis grace that makes us free
To feed upon this bread and wine,
In memory, Lord, of Thee.

2 Here every welcome guest
Waits, Lord, from Thee to learn
The secrets of Thy Father's breast,
And all Thy grace discern.

3 Here conscience ends its strife,
And faith delights to prove
The sweetness of the bread of life—
The fullness of Thy love.

4 That blood that flowed for sin,
In symbol here we see,
And feel the blessèd pledge within,
That we are loved of Thee.

5 Oh if this glimpse of love
Is so divinely sweet,
What will it be, O Lord, above,
Thy gladdening smile to meet!

6 To see Thee face to face,
Thy perfect likeness wear,
And all Thy ways of wondrous grace,
Through endless years declare!

Edward Denny, 1796–1889

This hymn may also be sung to **Rhodes,** No. 339

578

RHYS 11.10.11.10

W. J. Evans, 1866-1947

Sweet feast of love, in Jesu's name now meeting,
We share the banquet which His hand provides;
Earth's highest festive joy is vain and fleeting,
The joy of our pure feast of love abides.

2 The thoughts of God, through ages past unfolding,
Knit all His saints in hope and spirit one;
Yea, one with us, who now rejoice, beholding
Those thoughts of peace secured in Christ the Son.

3 His life of love, His death of unknown sorrow,
Have brought us joys that make the lips to sing;
These cheer the night of weeping; and, to-morrow—
Who shall describe the joys that morn shall bring?

4 Lord Jesus, then our longing hearts shall greet Thee,
Our bread and wine, the wilderness along,—
And oh to drink the new wine, drink it with Thee,
And with the Bridegroom sing the bridal song!

5 Filled with this hope, may we, with chaste affection,
Our feast of love, our walk of faith, now keep;
Thy fellowship and truth be our protection
From sloth and folly, 'midst a world asleep.

6 And, till Thy day, may we around be showing
Thy death, Lord Jesus, as life's only spring;
And, in the harvest field the seed be sowing,
Whence Thou wilt fruit to life eternal bring.

John Withy, 1809–92

This hymn may also be sung to **Strength and Stay,** No. 487

SURSUM CORDA   10.10.10.10   ALFRED M. SMITH, b. 1879

UNISON

THE bread and wine are spread upon
  the board,
The guests are here, invited by the
  Lord;
Why come they thus, why tarry for a
  space?
But for Thy presence, O Thou King
  of grace.

2 Hush, O our hearts, as in the sacred
  name
We bow in worship and the promise
  claim—
Where two or three are gathered there
  am I,
Unseen, yet present to faith's opened
  eye.

3 Here in our midst art Thou, O risen
  Lord;
Worthy, O Lamb once slain, to be
  adored;
Here in our midst to lead Thy people's
  praise,
And incense sweet unto the Father
  raise.

4 We do remember Thee, as Thou hast
  said,
And think upon Thee as we break
  the bread,
Recall Thy dying love, Thy cross and
  shame,
Drinking the cup of blessing in Thy
  name.

George Goodman, 1866–1944

This hymn may also be sung to **Toulon**, No. 630

BEVERLEY   87.887.77.77   W. H. MONK, 1823-1889

THOU art coming, O my Saviour!
  Thou art coming, O my King!
In Thy beauty all-resplendent,
In Thy glory all-transcendent;
  Well may we rejoice and sing!
Coming! in the opening east,
  Herald brightness slowly swells;
Coming! O my glorious Priest,
  Hear we not Thy golden bells?

2 Thou art coming, Thou art coming!
  We shall meet Thee on Thy way,
We shall see Thee, we shall know
    Thee,
We shall bless Thee, we shall show
    Thee
  All our hearts could never say!
What an anthem that will be,
  Ringing out our love to Thee,
Pouring out our rapture sweet
  At Thine own all-glorious feet!

3 Thou art coming! At Thy table
  We are witnesses for this,
While remembering hearts Thou
    meetest,
In communion clearest, sweetest,

Earnest of our coming bliss.
Showing not Thy death alone,
  And Thy love exceeding great,
But Thy coming and Thy throne,
  All for which we long and wait.

4 Thou art coming! We are waiting
  With a hope that cannot fail;
Asking not the day or hour,
Resting on Thy word of power
  Anchored safe within the veil.
Time appointed may be long,
  But the vision must be sure:
Certainty shall make us strong,
  Joyful patience can endure!

5 Oh, the joy to see Thee reigning,
  Thee, my own belovèd Lord!
Every tongue Thy name confessing,
Worship, honour, glory, blessing,
  Brought to Thee with glad accord!
Thee, my Master and my Friend,
  Vindicated and enthroned!
Unto earth's remotest end
  Glorified, adored, and owned!

Frances Ridley Havergal, 1836–79

581

WELLS 77.77.77

D. S. Bortnianski, 1752-1825

Till He come!—oh let the words
Linger on the trembling chords;
Let the "little while" between
In their golden light be seen;
Let us think, how heaven and home
Lie beyond that "Till He come!"

2 When the weary ones we love
Enter on their rest above,
Seems the earth so poor and vast,
Even heaven overcast?
Hush! be every murmur dumb,
It is only "till He come!"

3 Clouds and darkness round us press;
Would we have one sorrow less?
All the sharpness of the cross,
All that tells the world is loss,
Death, and darkness, and the tomb,
Only whisper, "Till He come!"

4 See, the feast of love is spread
Drink the wine and eat the bread;
Sweet memorials, till the Lord
Call us round His heavenly board,
Some from earth, from glory some,
Severed only "till He come!"

Edward Henry Bickersteth, 1825–1906

HOLY FAITH 88.88.88   G. C. MARTIN, 1844-1916

VICTIM divine, Thy grace we claim,
  While thus Thy precious death
    we show:
Once offered up, a spotless Lamb,
  In Thy great temple here below,
Thou didst for all mankind atone,
And standest now before the throne.

2 Thou standest in the holy place,
  As now for guilty sinners slain:
The blood of sprinkling speaks, 'and
    prays,
  All prevalent for helpless man;
Thy blood is still our ransom found,
And speaks salvation all around.

3 We need not now go up to heaven,
  To bring the long-sought Saviour
    down;
  Thou art to all already given,
    Thou dost e'en now Thy banquet
      crown:
  To every faithful soul appear,
  And show Thy real presence here.

Charles Wesley, 1707–88

This hymn may also be sung to **Pater omnium,** No. 111

DENNIS   S.M.

J. G. NÄGELI, 1773-1836

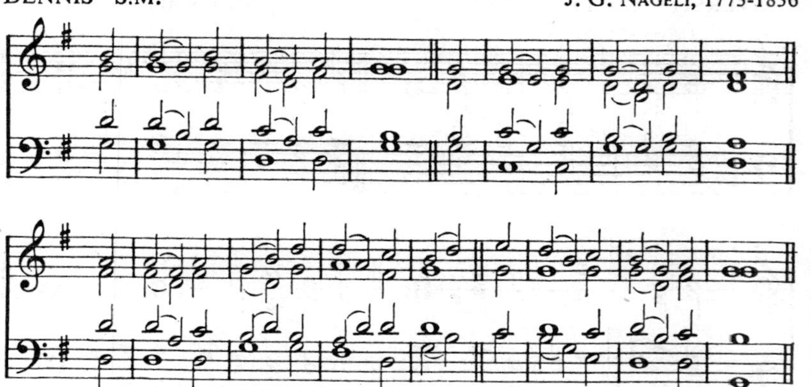

WITH Jesus in our midst,
    We gather round the board;
Though many, we are one in Christ,
    One body in the Lord.

2   Our sins were laid on Him
        When bruised on Calvary;
    With Christ we died and rose again,
        And sit with Him on high.

3   Faith eats the bread of life,
        And drinks the living wine;
    Thus we, in love together knit,
        On Jesu's breast recline.

4   Soon shall the night be gone,
        And we with Jesus reign;
    The marriage supper of the Lamb
        Shall banish all our pain.

Robert Cleaver Chapman, 1803–1902

UNIVERSITY COLLEGE 77.77   H. J. GAUNTLETT, 1805-76

CHRIST, from whom all blessings flow,
Perfecting the saints below,
Hear us, who Thy nature share,
Who Thy mystic body are.

2 Join us, in one spirit join,
Let us still receive of Thine;
Still for more on Thee we call,
Thou, who fillest all in all.

3 Move, and actuate, and guide:
Divers gifts to each divide;
Placed according to Thy will,
Let us all our work fulfil.

4 Sweetly may we all agree,
Touched with holy sympathy:
Kindly for each other care,
Every member feel its share.

5 Love, like death, hath all destroyed,
Rendered all distinctions void;
Names and sects and parties fall:
Thou, O Christ, art all in all.

Charles Wesley, 1707–88

This hymn may also be sung to **Ephraim**, No. 173

585 SAMUEL 66.66.88   A. S. SULLIVAN, 1842-1900

CHRIST is our corner-stone,
On Him alone we build;
With His true saints alone
The courts of heaven are filled;
On His great love
Our hopes we place
Of present grace
And joys above.

2 Oh then with hymns of praise
　These hallowed courts shall ring;
Our voices we will raise
　The Three in One to sing;
　　And thus proclaim
　　In joyful song,
　　Both loud and long,
　That glorious name.

3 Here may we gain from heaven
　The grace which we implore;
And may that grace, once given,
　Be with us evermore;
　　Until that day
　　When all the blest
　　To endless rest
　Are called away.

John Chandler, 1827–76

This hymn may also be sung to **Christchurch**, No. 265

586

NEANDER 87.87.87　　　From Chorale *Unser Herrscher* by J. Neander, 1650-80

COME, ye faithful, raise the anthem,
　Cleave the skies with shouts of praise;
Sing to Him who found the ransom,
　Ancient of eternal days,
God of God, the Word incarnate,
Whom the heaven of heaven obeys.

2 Ere He raised the lofty mountains,
　Formed the seas, or built the sky,
Love eternal, free, and boundless,
　Moved the Lord of life to die,
Foreordained the Prince of princes
For the throne of Calvary.

3 There, for us and our redemption,
　See Him all His life-blood pour!
There He wins our full salvation,
　Dies that we may die no more;
Then, arising, lives for ever,
Reigning where He was before.

4 Yet this earth He still remembers,
　Still by Him the flock are fed:
Yea, He gives them food immortal,
　Gives Himself, the Living Bread;
Leads them where the precious
　fountain
From the smitten Rock is shed.

5 Trust Him then, ye fainting pilgrims;
　Who shall pluck you from His hand?
Pledged He stands for your salvation,
　Pledged to give the promised land,
Where among the ransomed nations,
Ye around His throne shall stand.

Job Hupton, 1762–1849; John Mason Neale, 1818–66, and others

587

ALL SOULS 10.10.10.10

JOHN YOAKLEY, 1860-1932

COME ye yourselves apart and rest awhile,
Weary, I know it, of the press and throng,
Wipe from your brow the sweat and dust of toil,
And in My quiet strength again be strong.

2 Come ye aside from all the world holds dear,
For converse which the world has never known,
Alone with Me and with My Father here,
With Me and with My Father not alone.

3 Come, tell Me all that ye have said and done,
Your victories and failures, hopes and fears,
I know how hardly souls are wooed and won;
My choicest wreaths are always wet with tears.

4 Come ye and rest: the journey is too great,
And ye will faint beside the way and sink:
The bread of life is here for you to eat,
And here for you the wine of love to drink.

5 Then, fresh from converse with your Lord, return
And work till daylight softens into even:
The brief hours are not lost in which ye learn
More of your Master and His rest in heaven.

Edward Henry Bickersteth, 1825-1906

This hymn may also be sung to **Song 22, No. 551**

AURELIA 76.76.D S. S. WESLEY, 1810-76

D ISCIPLES, friends of Jesus,
The followers of the Lamb,
Now in His name assemble,
And there, saith He, "I AM"—
There, by the promised Spirit,
Unseen, but loved and known
By those His blood has pardoned,
And purchased for His own.

2 To His blest word obedient,
Loved with the Father's love,
By faith we claim the promise
That lifts our hearts above;
And through the Holy Spirit,
Abundantly bestowed,
We reach our heavenly dwelling,
The place of God's abode.

3 What wondrous, sweet communion!
What fellowship divine!
When, on our raptured vision,
Those inner glories shine.
As through the veil we enter,
Led by the Spirit's hand,
Within the holy places,
Where now by grace we stand.

4 Then, through the sacred silence,
The Spirit's voice is heard.
He leads the song of worship,
As every heart is stirred.
Thus cry we "Abba, Father"—
Thus Jesus "Lord" we call,
And join our hallelujahs
To crown Him Lord of all.

John G. Wheeler

This hymn may also be sung to **Ewing**, No. 534

VAUDOIS   Irregular   From the Hymn of the Vaudois Mountaineers

For the might of Thine arm we bless Thee, our God, our fathers' God;
Thou hast kept Thy pilgrim people by the strength of Thy staff and rod;
Thou hast called us to the journey which faithless feet ne'er trod;
For the might of Thine arm we bless Thee, our God, our fathers' God.

2 For the love of Christ constraining, that bound their hearts as one;
For the faith in truth and freedom in which their work was done;
For the peace of God's evangel wherewith their feet were shod;
For the might of Thine arm we bless Thee, our God, our fathers' God.

3 We are watchers of a beacon whose light must never die;
We are guardians of an altar that shows Thee ever nigh;
We are children of Thy freemen who sleep beneath the sod;
For the might of Thine arm we bless Thee, our God, our fathers' God.

4 May the shadow of Thy presence around our camp be spread;
Baptize us with the courage Thou gavest to our dead;
Oh keep us in the pathway their saintly feet have trod;
For the might of Thine arm we bless Thee, our God, our fathers' God.

Charles Silvester Horne, 1865-1914

ABBOT'S LEIGH 87.87.D — CYRIL V. TAYLOR, b. 1907

GLORIOUS things of thee are spoken,
  Zion, city of our God!
He, whose word cannot be broken,
  Formed thee for His own abode.
On the Rock of Ages founded,
  What can shake thy sure repose?
With salvation's walls surrounded,
  Thou mayst smile at all thy foes.

2 See the streams of living waters,
  Springing from eternal love,
Well supply thy sons and daughters,
  And all fear of want remove.
Who can faint while such a river
  Ever flows, their thirst to assuage?—
Grace which, like the Lord the Giver,
  Never fails from age to age.

3 Round each habitation hovering,
  See the cloud and fire appear!
For a glory and a covering,
  Showing that the Lord is near:
Blest inhabitants of Zion,
  Cleansed by the Redeemer's blood;
Jesus, whom their souls rely on,
  Makes them kings and priests to God.

4 Saviour, if of Zion's city
  I through grace a member am,
Let the world deride or pity,
  I will glory in Thy name:
Fading is the worldling's pleasure,
  All his boasted pomp and show:
Solid joys and lasting treasure,
  None but Zion's children know.

This hymn may also be sung to **Lux Eoi,** No. 33   *John Newton, 1725–1807*

591

FULDA (WALTON) L.M.

GARDINER'S *Sacred Melodies*, 1812

COMMAND Thy blessing from above,
  O God, on all assembled here:
Behold us with a Father's love,
  While we look up with filial fear.

2 Command Thy blessing, Jesus, Lord,
  May we Thy true disciples be;
Speak to each heart the mighty word,
  Say to the weakest, "Follow Me."

3 Command Thy blessing in this hour,
  Spirit of truth, and fill the place
With wounding and with healing
  power,
With quickening and confirming
  grace.

4 O Thou, our Maker, Saviour, Guide,
  One true eternal God confessed,
May nought in life or death divide
  The saints in Thy communion blest.

5 With Thee and these for ever found,
  May all the souls who here unite,
With harps and songs Thy throne
  surround,
Rest in Thy love, and reign in light.

James Montgomery, 1771–1854

592

RANDOLPH 98.89

R. VAUGHAN WILLIAMS, 1872-1958

Gᴏᴅ be with you till we meet again:
By His counsels guide, uphold you,
With His sheep securely fold you:
God be with you till we meet again.

2 God be with you till we meet again:
'Neath His wings securely hide you,
Daily manna still provide you:
God be with you till we meet again.

3 God be with you till we meet again:
When life's perils thick confound you
Put His arms unfailing round you:
God be with you till we meet again.

4 God be with you till we meet again:
Keep love's banner floating o'er you
Smite death's threatening wave before you:
God be with you till we meet again.

Jeremiah Eames Rankin, 1828–1904

593

SILCHESTER S.M.   C. H. A. Mᴀʟᴀɴ, 1787-1864

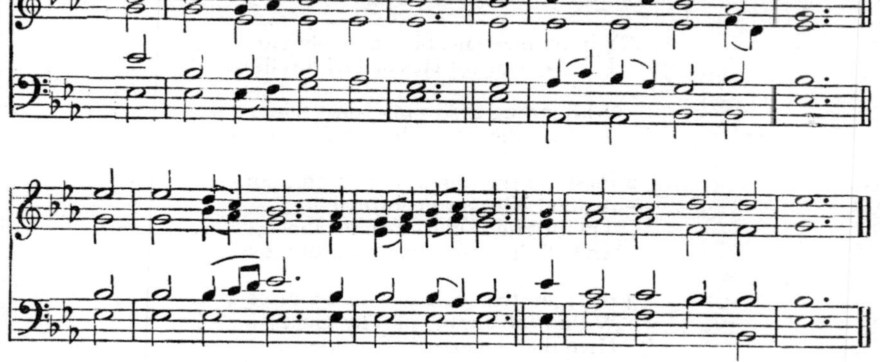

Jᴇꜱᴜꜱ, we look to Thee,
Thy promised presence claim;
Thou in the midst of us shalt be,
Assembled in Thy name.

2 Thy name salvation is,
Which now we come to prove;
Thy name is life, and health, and peace,
And everlasting love.

3 We meet, the grace to take,
Which Thou hast freely given;
We meet on earth for Thy dear sake,
As we shall meet in heaven.

4 Present we know Thou art;
But, oh Thyself reveal!
Now, Lord, let each expectant heart
The mighty comfort feel.

5 Oh may Thy quickening voice
The blight of sin remove;
And bid our inmost souls rejoice
In hope of perfect love!

Charles Wesley, 1707–88

This hymn may also be sung to **Carlisle,** No. 49

594

NICOMACHUS L.M.

A. H. MANN, 1850-1930

How pleasant, how divinely fair,
O Lord of Hosts, Thy dwellings are!
With strong desire my spirit faints
To meet the assemblies of Thy saints.

2 Blest are the saints that sit on high,
Around Thy throne of majesty;
Thy brightest glories shine above,
And all their work is praise and love.

3 Blest are the souls that find a place
Within the temple of Thy grace;
Here they behold Thy gentler rays,
And seek Thy face, and learn Thy praise.

4 Blest are the men whose hearts are set
To find the way to Zion's gate;
God is their strength, and through the road
They lean upon their helper God.

5 Cheerful they walk with growing strength,
Till all shall meet in heaven 'at length;
Till all before Thy face appear,
And join in nobler worship there.

Isaac Watts, 1674–1748

KIRKLAND   65.65.D

DAVID EVANS, 1874-1948

JESUS, Lord, Redeemer,
    Once for sinners slain,
Crucified in weakness,
    Raised in power to reign,
Dwelling with the Father,
    Endless in Thy days,
Unto Thee be glory,
    Honour, blessing, praise.

2 Faithful ones communing
    Towards the close of day,
Desolate and weary
    Met Thee in the way;
So, when sun is setting,
    Come to us and show
All the truth, and in us
    Make our hearts to glow.

3 In the upper chamber,
    Where the ten, in fear,
Gathered, sad and troubled,
    There Thou didst appear;
So, O Lord, this evening,
    Bid our sorrows cease:
Breathing on us, Saviour,
    Say, "I give you peace."

Patrick Miller Kirkland, 1857-1943

This hymn may also be sung to **Evelyns**, No. 98

596

WAVENEY (REDHEAD No. 66) C.M.   R. REDHEAD, 1820-1901

LIGHT up this house with glory, Lord;
  Enter, and claim Thine own;
Receive the homage of our souls,
  Erect Thy temple-throne.

2 We ask no bright shekinah-cloud
    To glorify the place;
  Give, Lord, the substance of that
      sign—
  A plenitude of grace.

3 Thou risen Lord, who cam'st to bless
    Gently as comes the dew,
  Here entering breathe on all around,
    "My peace be unto you."

4 No rushing mighty wind we ask,
    No tongues of flame desire;
  Grant us the Spirit's quickening light,
    His purifying fire.

5 Light up this house with glory, Lord—
    The glory of that love
  Which saves and forms a church
      below,
  And makes a heaven above.

John Harris, 1802–56

This hymn may also be sung to **Bedford,** No. 94

597

HOLLY L.M.   GEORGE HEWS, 1806-1873

L ORD Jesus, in Thy name alone
   Assembling, we Thy promise
      plead;
Thy presence in our midst be known,
   Our prayer and praise Thy Spirit
      lead.

2 Emmanuel, God with us, Thou art,
   This is Thy dear, Thy chosen
      name;
Its fragrance fills the loving heart,
   To-day, for evermore, the same.

3 Thou art the Light, our feet to guide,
   Our Sun, to cheer the desert way;

The Rock, beneath whose shade we
      hide,
   Whose waters flow and never stay.

4 Blest in Thy fellowship divine,
   The heart has found a perfect rest;
In joy or tears, we still recline
   For safety on Thy sheltering breast.

5 Here let our hearts for ever dwell,
   Live on Thy fullness, Lord, and be
Thy living witnesses, to tell
   The glories that are found in Thee.

John Withy, 1809–92

BISHOPTHORPE C.M. Attributed to J. CLARK, *c.* 1670-1707 **598**

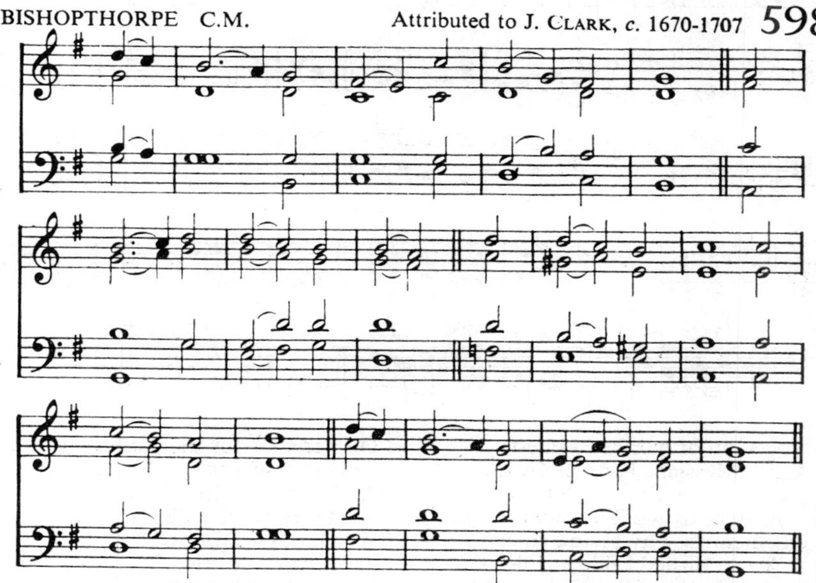

L ORD Jesus, Thy disciples see,
   The promised blessing give;
Met in Thy name, we look to Thee,
   Expecting to receive.

2 Thee we expect, our faithful Lord,
   Who in Thy name are joined;
We wait, according to Thy word,
   Thee in the midst to find.

3 With us Thou art assembled here;
   But oh Thyself reveal!
Son of the living God, appear!
   Let us Thy presence feel.

4 Whom now we seek, oh may we meet!
   Jesus the crucified,
Show us Thy wounded hands and
      feet,
   Thou who for us hast died.

5 Cause us the record to receive,
   Speak, and the tokens show—
"Oh be not faithless, but believe
"In Me, who died for you!"

Charles Wesley, 1707–88

599

LADYWELL D.C.M.

W. H. FERGUSON, 1874-1950

O GOD of glorious Majesty,
  Messiah, King of Grace,
Unveil to us Thy loveliness,
  And let us see Thy face!
Obedient to Thy loving voice
  We've turned aside awhile,
To rest beside Thy guiding feet,
  And bask beneath Thy smile.

2 Oh nerve us for the conflict, Lord,
    That thickens day by day,
  And in the midst of alien foes
    Thy banner to display.
  We've but a little while to fight,
    To work, to wait for Thee;
  Help us to labour in Thy cause
    With mighty energy.

3 Help us upon our watch to stand,
    And never quail for fear,
  Till in the glowing eastern sky
    The Morning Star appear.
  Then with Thy waiting saints above,
    Thine advent, Lord, we'll hail,
  And over death, and sin, and woe,
    With joy we shall prevail.

William Pennefather, 1816–73

This hymn may also be sung to **Ellacombe,** No. 85

600

MORECAMBE   10.10.10.10

F. C. ATKINSON, 1841-1948

O GOD our Father, who dost make us one
Heart bound to heart, in love of Thy dear Son,
Now as we part and go our several ways,
Touch every lip, may every voice be praise—

2 Praise for the fellowship that here we find,
The fellowship of heart and soul and mind,
Praise for the bonds of love and brotherhood,
Bonds wrought by Thee, who makest all things good.

3 Lord, make us strong, for Thou alone dost know
How oft we turn our faces from the foe;
How oft, when claimed by dark temptation's hour,
We lose our hold on Thee, and of Thy power.

4 Go with us, Lord, from hence; we only ask
That Thou be sharer in our daily task;
So, side by side with Thee, shall each one know
The blessedness of heaven begun below.

William Vaughan Jenkins, 1868–1920

This hymn may also be sung to **Farley Castle**, No. 694

601

ST. OSWALD 87.87

J. B. DYKES, 1823-76

OH how blest the hour, Lord Jesus,
When we can to Thee draw near,
Promises so sweet and precious
From Thy gracious lips to hear.

2 Be with us this day to bless us,
That we may not hear in vain;
With the saving truths impress us,
Which the words of life contain.

3 Open Thou our minds, and lead us
Safely on our heavenward way;
With the lamp of truth precede us,
That we may not go astray.

4 Make us gentle, meek, and humble,
And yet bold in doing right:
Scatter darkness, lest we stumble;
Men walk safely in the light.

5 Lord, endue Thy word from heaven
With such light, and love, and power,
That in us its silent leaven
May work on from hour to hour.

6 Give us grace to bear our witness
To the truths we have embraced;
And let others both their sweetness
And their quickening virtue taste.

Karl Johann Philipp Spitta, 1801–59
tr. Richard Massie, 1800–87

603

ST. FULBERT C.M.   *Words at foot of next page*   H. J. GAUNTLETT, 1805-76

602

ABRIDGE C.M.   I. Smith, *c.* 1725–*c.* 1800

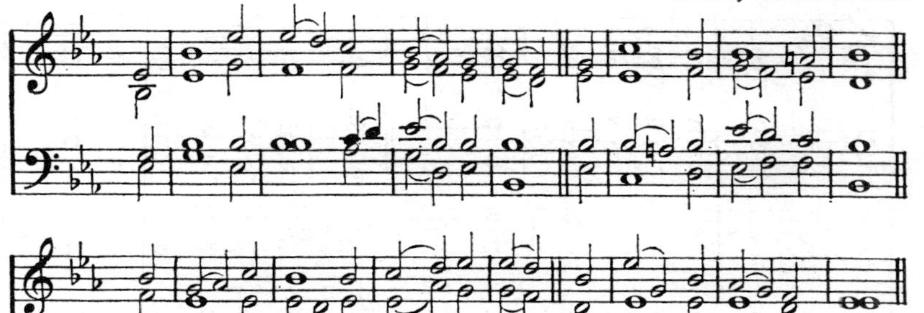

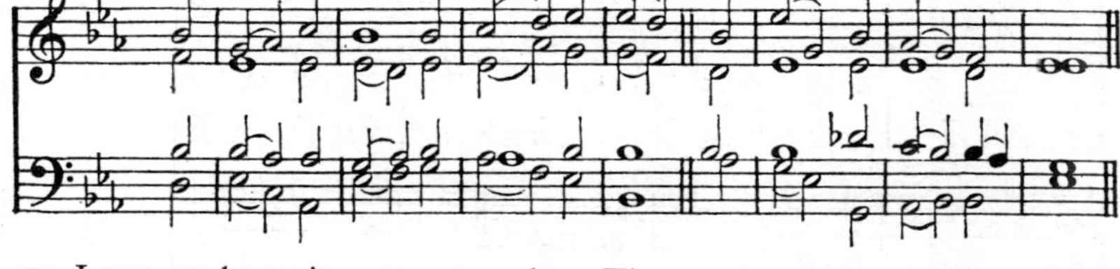

O Lord, we know it matters nought
　How sweet the sound may be,
No hearts but of the Spirit taught
　Make melody to Thee.

2 Then teach Thy gathered saints, O
　　Lord,
　To worship in Thy fear,
And dread, lest any idle word
　Should reach Thy holy ear.

3 Thy blood hath made poor sinners
　　meet,
　As saints in light, to come
And worship at the mercy-seat,
　Before the Father's throne.

4 Thy precious name is all we show,
　Our only passport, Lord!
And now our Father's love we know,
　Though we are self-abhorred.

5 Oh largely give—'tis all Thine own—
　The Spirit's goodly fruit;
Praise, issuing forth in life, alone
　Our living Lord can suit.

6 Henceforth let each belovèd child,
　With quickened step, proceed
To walk, with garments undefiled,
　Where'er Thy Spirit lead.

Mary Bowly Peters, 1813–56

603

Tune at foot of previous page

Talk with us, Lord, Thyself reveal,
　While here o'er earth we rove;
Speak to our hearts, and let us feel
　The kindling of Thy love.

2 With Thee conversing, we forget
　All time, and toil, and care;
Labour is rest, and pain is sweet,
　If Thou, my God, art here.

3 Here then, my God, vouchsafe to stay,
　And bid my heart rejoice;
My bounding heart shall own Thy
　　sway,
　And echo to Thy voice.

4 Thou callest me to seek Thy face;
　'Tis all I wish to seek;
To attend the whispers of Thy grace,
　And hear Thee inly speak.

5 Let this my every hour employ,
　Till I Thy glory see:
Enter into my Master's joy,
　And find my heaven in Thee.

Charles Wesley, 1707–88

604

AURELIA 76.76.D

S. S. WESLEY, 1810-76

THE church's one foundation
  Is Jesus Christ her Lord;
She is His new creation
  By water and the word:
From heaven He came and sought her
  To be His holy bride;
With His own blood He bought her,
  And for her life He died.

2 Elect from every nation,
  Yet one o'er all the earth;
Her charter of salvation—
  One Lord, one faith, one birth:
One holy name she blesses,
  Partakes one holy food;
And to one hope she presses,
  With every grace endued.

3 Though with a scornful wonder
  Men see her sore opprest,
By schisms rent asunder,
  By heresies distrest:
Yet saints their watch are keeping,
  Their cry goes up, "How long?"
And soon the night of weeping
  Shall be the morn of song.

4 'Mid toil and tribulation,
  And tumults of her war,
She waits the consummation
  Of peace for evermore;
Till with the vision glorious
  Her longing eyes are blest,
And the great church victorious
  Shall be the church at rest.

5 Yet she on earth hath union
  With God the Three in One,
And mystic sweet communion
  With those whose rest is won.
Oh happy ones and holy!
  Lord, give us grace, that we
Like them, the meek and lowly,
  On high may dwell with Thee.

Samuel John Stone, 1839–1900

This hymn may also be sung to
Bentley, No. 292

See also
351 Happy are they, they that love God
352 How firm a foundation
380 Children of the heavenly King
410 Thine for ever, God of love
432 How blest is life if lived for Thee
590 Glorious things of Thee are spoken

BISHOPGARTH 87.87.D Iambic   A. S. Sullivan, 1842-1900

"For My sake and the Gospel's, go
    "And tell redemption's story;"
His heralds answer, "Be it so,
    "And Thine, Lord, all the glory!"
They preach His birth, His life, His cross,
    The love of His atonement,
For whom they count the world but loss,
    His Easter, His enthronement.

2 Hark, hark, the trump of jubilee
    Proclaims to every nation,
From pole to pole, by land and sea,
    Glad tidings of salvation.
As nearer draws the day of doom,
    While still the battle rages,
The heavenly Day-spring, through the gloom,
    Breaks on the night of ages.

3 Still on and on the anthems spread
    Of hallelujah voices,
In concert with the holy dead,
    The warrior church rejoices:
Their snow-white robes are washed in blood,
    Their golden harps are ringing;
Earth and the paradise of God
    One triumph-song are singing.

4 He comes, whose Advent trumpet drowns
    The last of time's evangels—
Emmanuel crowned with many crowns,
    The Lord of saints and angels:
O Life, Light, Love, the great I AM,
    Triune, who changest never;
The throne of God and of the Lamb
    Is Thine, and Thine for ever!

Edward Henry Bickersteth, 1825-1906

606

BENSON Irregular

M. D. KINGHAM, 1866-1927

GOD is working His purpose out as year succeeds to year.
God is working His purpose out, and the time is drawing near;
Nearer and nearer draws the time, the time that shall surely be,
When the earth shall be filled with the glory of God as the waters cover the sea.

2 From utmost east to utmost west where'er man's foot hath trod,
By the mouth of many messengers goes forth the voice of God:
"Give ear to Me, ye continents, ye isles, give ear to Me,
That the earth may be filled with the glory of God as the waters cover the sea."

3 March we forth in the strength of
  God with the banner of Christ
  unfurled,
That the light of the glorious gospel of
  truth may shine throughout the
  world:
Fight we the fight with sorrow and sin,
  to set their captives free,
That the earth may be filled with the
  glory of God as the waters cover the
  sea.

4 All we can do is nothing worth unless
  God blesses the deed;
Vainly we hope for the harvest-tide
  till God gives life to the seed;
Yet nearer and nearer draws the time,
  the time that shall surely be.
When the earth shall be filled with the
  glory of God as the waters cover the
  sea.

Arthur Campbell Ainger, 1841–1919

MEAD HOUSE   87.87.D   Cyril V. Taylor, b.1907 **607**

God hath spoken—by His prophets,
  Spoken His unchanging word,
Each from age to age proclaiming
  God the One, the righteous Lord!
'Mid the world's despair and turmoil
  One firm anchor holdeth fast,
God is King, His throne eternal,
  God the first and God the last.

2 God hath spoken—by Christ Jesus,
  Christ, the everlasting Son,
Brightness of the Father's glory,
  With the Father ever one;
Spoken by the Word Incarnate,
  God of God ere time began,
Light of Light, to earth descending,
  Man, revealing God to man.

3 God yet speaketh—by his Spirit
  Speaketh to the hearts of men,
In the age-long word declaring
  God's own message, now as then;
Through the rise and fall of nations
  One sure faith yet standeth fast,
God abides, His word unchanging,
  God the first and God the last.

George Wallace Briggs, 1875–1959
This hymn may also be sung to Lux Eoi, No. 33

608

BIRLING L.M.

From an early 19th cent. MS.
Adapted by GEOFFREY SHAW, 1879-1943

B_E Thou exalted, holy Lord,
  Obeyed and honoured and
adored:
Let all the earth acknowledge Thee,
And heaven declare Thy majesty.

2 Look mercifully, O most High,
  On all who yet in darkness lie,
Who live in fear and fruitless strife,
Athirst for truth and peace and life.

3 How dare we rest, who bear Thy name
  Amidst ungodliness and shame,
Till men, ensnared in slavery,
Shall claim Thy glorious liberty?

4 Plant Thou Thy church in every place,
  Send forth ambassadors of grace;
And where Thy name is yet unkown,
Declare Thy word and claim Thine
  own.

5 Until the ransomed, in that day
  When sighs and sorrows flee away,
Sing praise, with all the heavenly
  host,
To Father, Son and Holy Ghost.

Edmund Robert Morgan, b. 1888

This hymn may also be sung to **Bodmin**, No. 21

609

HEATHLANDS 77.77.77

H. SMART, 1813-79

G OD of mercy, God of grace,
Show the brightness of Thy
face;
Shine upon us, Saviour, shine,
Fill Thy church with light divine;
And Thy saving health extend
Unto earth's remotest end.

2 Let the peoples praise Thee, Lord;
Be by all that live adored;
Let the nations shout and sing
Glory to their Saviour King;
At Thy feet their tribute pay,
And Thy holy will obey.

3 Let the peoples praise Thee, Lord;
Earth shall then her fruits afford;
God to man His blessing give,
Man to God devoted live;
All below, and all above,
One in joy, and light, and love.

Henry Francis Lyte, 1793–1847

610

MOEL LYS 75.75.77

S. G. STOCK, 1838-96

L ET the song go round the earth:
Jesus Christ is Lord,
Sound His praises, tell His worth,
Be His name adored;
Every clime and every tongue
Join the grand, the glorious song.

2 Let the song go round the earth,
From the eastern sea,
Where the daylight has its birth,
Glad, and bright, and free;
China's millions join the strains,
Waft them on to India's plains.

3 Let the song go round the earth,
Lands where Islam's sway
Darkly broods o'er home and hearth,
Cast their bonds away;
Let His praise from Afric's shore
Rise and swell her wide lands o'er.

4 Let the song go round the earth,
Where the summer smiles,
Let the notes of holy mirth
Break from distant isles;
Inland forests, dark and dim,
Snow-bound coasts give back the
hymn.

5 Let the song go round the earth:
Jesus Christ is King,
With the story of His worth,
Let the whole world ring,
Him creation all adore
Evermore and evermore.

Sarah Geraldina Stock, 1838–98

6II

LONDONDERRY   11.10.11.10.11.10.11.12

Irish Melody
Harmonized by JOHN HUGHES 1896-1968

I CANNOT tell why He, whom angels worship,
Should set His love upon the sons of men,
Or why, as Shepherd, He should seek the wanderers,
To bring them back, they know not how or when.
But this I know, that He was born of Mary,
When Bethlehem's manger was His only home,
And that He lived at Nazareth and laboured,
And so the Saviour, Saviour of the world, is come.

2 I cannot tell how silently He suffered,
As with His peace He graced this place of tears,
Or how His heart upon the cross was broken,
The crown of pain to three and thirty years.
But this I know, He heals the broken-hearted,
And stays our sin, and calms our lurking fear,
And lifts the burden from the heavy laden,
For yet the Saviour, Saviour of the world, is here.

3 I cannot tell how He will win the nations,
How He will claim His earthly heritage,
How satisfy the needs and aspirations
Of East and West, of sinner and of sage.
But this I know, all flesh shall see His glory,
And He shall reap the harvest He has sown,
And some glad day His sun shall shine in splendour
When He the Saviour, Saviour of the world, is known.

4 I cannot tell how all the lands shall worship,
When, at His bidding, every storm is stilled,
Or who can say how great the jubilation
When all the hearts of men with love are filled.
But this I know, the skies will thrill with rapture,
And myriad, myriad human voices sing,
And earth to heaven, and heaven to earth, will answer:
At last the Saviour, Saviour of the world, is King!

William Young Fullerton, 1857–1932

EVERTON 87.87.D   HENRY SMART, 1813-79

LORD, her watch Thy church is keeping;
 When shall earth Thy rule obey?
When shall end the night of weeping?
 When shall break the promised day?
See the whitening harvest languish,
 Waiting still the labourers' toil;
Was it vain, Thy Son's deep anguish?
 Shall the strong retain the spoil?

2 Tidings, sent to every creature,
 Millions yet have never heard;
Can they hear without a preacher?
 Lord Almighty, give the word:
Give the word; in every nation
 Let the gospel trumpet sound,
Witnessing a world's salvation
 To the earth's remotest bound.

3 Then the end: Thy church completed,
 All Thy chosen gathered in,
With their King in glory seated,
 Satan bound, and banished sin;
Gone for ever parting, weeping,
 Hunger, sorrow, death, and pain:
Lo! her watch Thy church is keeping;
 Come, Lord Jesus, come to reign!

Henry Downton, 1818–85

CORINTH 87.87.D

S. Webbe (the Elder), 1740-1816

L ORD, Thy ransomed church is waking
  Out of slumber far and near,
Knowing that the morn is breaking
  When the bridegroom shall appear;
Waking up to claim the treasure
  With Thy precious life-blood bought,
And to trust in fuller measure
  All Thy wondrous death hath wrought.

2 Praise to Thee for this glad shower,
    Precious drops of latter rain;
  Praise, that by Thy Spirit's power
    Thou hast quickened us again;
  That Thy gospel's priceless treasure
    Now is borne from land to land,
  And that all the Father's plesaure
    Prospers in Thy piercèd hand.

3 Praise to Thee for saved ones yearning
    O'er the lost and wandering throng;
  Praise for voices daily learning
    To upraise the glad new song;
  Praise to Thee for sick ones hasting
    Now to touch Thy garment's hem;
  Praise for souls believing, tasting
    All Thy love has won for them.

4 Set on fire our heart's devotion
    With the love of Thy dear name;
  Till o'er every land and ocean
    Lips and lives Thy cross proclaim:
  Fix our eyes on Thy returning,
    Keeping watch till Thou shalt come,
  Loins well girt, lamps brightly burning;
    Then, Lord, take Thy servants home.

Sarah Geraldina Stock, 1838–98

This hymn may also be sung to **Everton**, No. 612

614

AUSTRIA 87.87.D

F. J. HAYDN, 1732-1809

LORD of light, whose name outshineth
  All the stars and suns of space,
Deign to make us Thy co-workers
  In the kingdom of Thy grace;
Use us to fulfil Thy purpose
  In the gift of Christ Thy Son:
    Father, as in highest heaven,
    So on earth Thy will be done.

2 By the toil of lonely workers
    In some far outlying field;
  By the courage where the radiance
    Of the cross is still revealed;
  By the victories of meekness,
    Through reproach and suffering
      won:

3 Grant that knowledge, still increasing,
    At Thy feet may lowly kneel;
  With Thy grace our triumphs hallow,
    With Thy charity our zeal;
  Lift the nations from the shadows
    To the gladness of the sun:

4 By the prayers of faithful watchmen,
    Never silent day or night;
  By the cross of Jesus bringing
    Peace to men, and healing light;
  By the love that passeth knowledge,
    Making all Thy children one:
      Father, as in highest heaven,
      So on earth Thy will be done.

Howell Elvet Lewis, 1860–1953

This hymn may also be sung to **Everton**, No. 612

ST. HELENS   85.83

R. P. STEWART, 1825-1894

HE expecteth, He expecteth!
  Down the stream of time,
Still the words come softly ringing
  Like a chime.

2 Oft-times faint, now waxing louder
  As the hour draws near,
When the King, in all His glory,
  Shall appear.

3 He is waiting with long patience
  For His crowning day,
For that kingdom which shall never
  Pass away.

4 And till every tribe and nation
  Bow before His throne,
He expecteth loyal service
  From His own.

5 He expecteth—but He heareth
  Still the bitter cry
From earth's millions, "Come and help us,
  "For we die."

6 He expecteth—doth He see us
  Busy here and there,
Heedless of those pleading accents
  Of despair?

7 Shall we, dare we, disappoint Him?
  Brethren, let us rise!
He who died for us is watching
  From the skies—

8 Watching till His royal banner
  Floateth far and wide,
Till He seeth of His travail—
  Satisfied!

Alice Jane Janvrin, 1846–1908

616

BEDFORD C.M.

W. WEALE, 1690-1727

LIFT up your heads, ye gates of brass,
   Ye bars of iron, yield,
And let the King of glory pass,
   The cross is in the field.

2 A holy war His servants wage,
   Mysteriously at strife,
The powers of heaven and hell engage
   For more than death or life.

3 Ye armies of the living God,
   Ye warriors of His host,
Where hallowed footstep never trod
   Take your appointed post.

4 Though few and small and weak your
     bands,
   Strong in your Captain's strength,
Go to the conquest of all lands;
   All must be His at length.

5 Then fear not, faint not, halt not now,
   Quit you like men, be strong:
To Christ shall all the nations bow,
   And sing the triumph song:

6 Uplifted are the gates of brass,
   The bars of iron yield;
Behold the King of glory pass:
   The cross has won the field.

James Montgomery, 1771–1854

This hymn may also be sung to **St. Stephen**, No. 67

ST. GEORGE S.M.   H. J. GAUNTLETT, 1805-76

L ORD of the harvest, hear
   Thy needy servants' cry;
Answer our faith's effectual prayer,
   And all our wants supply.

2   On Thee we humbly wait;
     Our wants are in Thy view:
The harvest truly, Lord, is great;
     The labourers are few.

3   Convert, and send forth more
     Into Thy church abroad;
And let them speak Thy word of
     power,
     As workers with their God.

4   Give the pure gospel word,
     The word of saving grace;
Thee let them preach, the common
     Lord,
     Redeemer of our race.

5   Oh let them spread Thy name,
     Their mission fully prove,
Thy universal grace proclaim,
     Thy all-redeeming love!

           Charles Wesley, 1707–88

THE CHURCH OF GOD:

PEARSALL 76.76.D

R. L. DE PEARSALL, 1795-1856

LORD of the living harvest
  That whitens o'er the plain,
Where angels soon shall gather
  Their sheaves of golden grain;
Accept these hands to labour,
  These hearts to trust and love,
And deign with them to hasten
  Thy kingdom from above.

2 As labourers in Thy vineyard,
  Still faithful may we be,
Content to bear the burden
  Of weary days for Thee;
We ask no other wages,
  When Thou shalt call us home,
But to have shared the travail
  Which makes Thy kingdom come.

3 Come down, Thou Holy Spirit,
  And fill our souls with light,
Clothe us in spotless raiment,
  In vesture clean and white;
Within Thy sacred temple
  Be with us, where we stand,
And sanctify Thy people,
  Throughout this happy land.

4 Be with us, God the Father!
  Be with us, God the Son!
And God the Holy Spirit!
  O blessèd Three in One!
Make us a royal priesthood,
  Thee rightly to adore,
And fill us with Thy fullness,
  Both now and evermore.

John Samuel Bewley Monsell, 1811–75

WESTMINSTER ABBEY   87.87.87

The Psalmist, 1842
Adapted from HENRY PURCELL, 1659-95

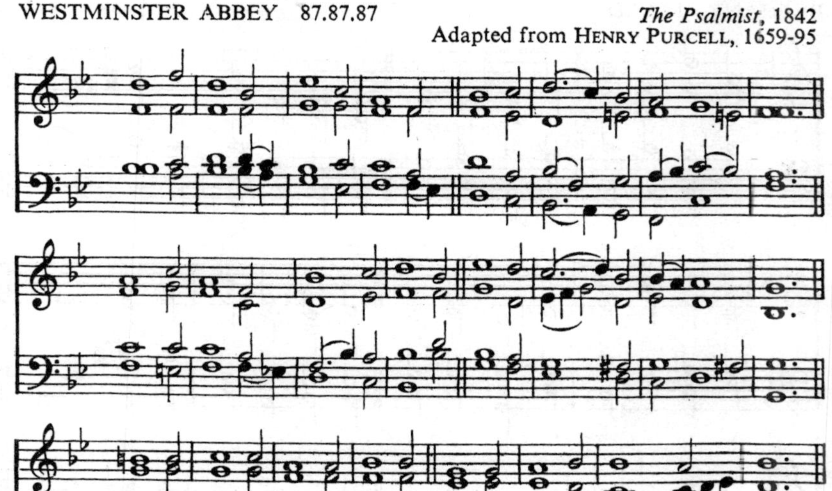

LORD, Thy servants forth are going,
  Each has heard the Master's call,
Seeds of life eternal sowing
  In His name who died for all;
    Oh sustain them
Till the shades of evening fall.

2 Then, where desert sands are glowing
  Neath the noontide's sultry heat,
Living streams shall soon be flowing
  Mid the meadow fair and sweet;
    And a harvest
Shall their raptured vision greet.

3 Lo! Thy hand is now bestowing
  Gifts abundant, rich and free;
Love, her wondrous debt still owing,
  Brings Thy gifts again to Thee
    That Thy kingdom
May extend from sea to sea.

4 Like the south wind gently blowing
  Comes Thy Spirit's breath of balm;
List! the sound is louder growing!
  Look! the Lord makes bare His arm!
    Hallelujah!
Wakes the universal psalm.

William Edward Winks, 1842–1926

This hymn may also be sung to **Blaencefn,** No. 244

620

BETHANY 87.87.D

H. Smart, 1813-79

Saviour, quicken many nations,
  Fruitful let Thy sorrows be;
By Thy pains and consolations
  Draw the Gentiles unto Thee:
Of Thy cross the wondrous story
  Be to all the nations told;
Let them see Thee in Thy glory
  And Thy mercy manifold.

2 Far and wide, though all unknowing,
  Pants for Thee each mortal breast;
Human tears for Thee are flowing,
  Human hearts in Thee would rest:
Thirsting, as for dews of even,
  As the new-mown grass for rain,
Thee they seek as God of heaven,
  Thee as Man for sinners slain.

3 Saviour, lo! the isles are waiting,
    Stretched the hand and strained the
    sight,
  For Thy Spirit, new creating,
    Love's pure flame, and wisdom's
    light;
  Give the word, and of the preacher
    Speed the foot, and touch the
    tongue,
  Till on earth by every creature
    Glory to the Lamb be sung.

Arthur Cleveland Coxe, 1818–96

ST. GEORGE'S, WINDSOR 77.77.D

G. J. ELVEY, 1816-93

SEE how great a flame aspires,
  Kindled by a spark of grace!
Jesu's love the nations fires,
  Sets the kingdoms on a blaze.
To bring fire on earth He came;
  Kindled in some hearts it is:
Oh that all might catch the flame,
  All partake the glorious bliss!

2 When He first the work begun,
  Small and feeble was His day:
Now the word doth swiftly run,
  Now it wins its widening way;
More and more it spreads and grows
  Ever mighty to prevail;
Sin's strongholds it now o'erthrows,
  Shakes the trembling gates of hell.

3 Sons of God, your Saviour praise!
  He the door hath opened wide;
He hath given the word of grace,
  Jesu's word is glorified;
Jesus, mighty to redeem,
  He alone the work hath wrought;
Worthy is the work of Him,
  Him who spake a world from
    nought.

4 Saw ye not the cloud arise,
  Little as a human hand?
Now it spreads along the skies,
  Hangs o'er all the thirsty land:
Lo! the promise of a shower
  Drops already from above;
But the Lord will shortly pour
  All the Spirit of His love!

Charles Wesley, 1707-88

622

O SPIRIT of the living God
   In all Thy plenitude of grace,
Where'er the foot of man hath trod,
Descend on our apostate race.

2 Give tongues of fire and hearts of love,
   To preach the reconciling word;
Give power and unction from above,
   Whene'er the joyful sound is heard.

3 Be darkness, at Thy coming, light;
   Confusion, order in Thy path;
Souls without strength inspire with
      might;
   Bid mercy triumph over wrath.

4 O Spirit of the Lord, prepare
   All the round earth her God to meet;
Breathe Thou abroad like morning air,
   Till hearts of stone begin to beat.

5 Baptize the nations; far and nigh
   The triumphs of the cross record;
The name of Jesus glorify,
   Till every kindred call Him Lord.

6 God from eternity hath willed
   All flesh shall His salvation see:
So be the Father's love fulfilled,
   The Saviour's sufferings crowned
      through Thee.

James Montgomery, 1771–1854

623 ARIZONA L.M.

R. H. EARNSHAW, 1856-1929

S^{END} forth the gospel! Let it run
  Southward and northward, east and west;
Tell all the earth Christ died and lives,
  Who giveth pardon, life, and rest.

2 Send forth Thy gospel, mighty Lord!
  Out of this chaos bring to birth
Thine own creation's promised hope;
  The better days of heaven on earth.

3 Send forth Thy gospel, gracious Lord!
  Thine was the blood for sinners shed;
Thy voice still pleads in human hearts;
  To Thee Thine other sheep be led.

4 Send forth Thy gospel, holy Lord!
  Kindle in us love's sacred flame;
Love giving all, and grudging naught
  For Jesu's sake, in Jesu's name.

5 Send forth the gospel! Tell it out!
  Go, brothers, at the Master's call;
Prepare His way, who comes to reign,
  The King of kings, and Lord of all.

Henry Elliott Fox, 1841–1926
This hymn may also be sung to **Church Triumphant,** No. 438

ARFRYN S.M.   W. J. EVANS, 1866-1947 **624**

S^{OW} in the morn thy seed,
  At eve hold not thy hand;
To doubt and fear give thou no heed,
  Broadcast it o'er the land.

2 Beside all waters sow,
  The highway furrows stock;
Drop it where thorns and thistles grow,
  Scatter it on the rock.

3 The good, the fruitful ground,
  Expect not here nor there;
O'er hill and dale by plots 'tis found,
  Go forth then everywhere.

4 Thou know'st not which may thrive,
  The late or early sown;
Grace keeps the precious germ alive,
  When and wherever strown.

5 And duly shall appear
  In verdure, beauty, strength,
The tender blade, the stalk, the ear,
  And the full corn at length.

6 Thou canst not toil in vain;
  Cold, heat, and moist, and dry,
Shall quicken and mature the grain,
  For garners in the sky.

7 And then the glorious end!—
  The Lord Himself shall come,
And thousand thousand saints attend,
  And heaven cry "Harvest Home!"

James Montgomery, 1771–1854
This hymn may also be sung to **St. George,** No. 497

625

TRIUMPH 87.87.87

H. J. GAUNTLETT, 1805-76

SPEED Thy servants, Saviour, speed them:
  Thou art Lord of winds and waves;
They were bound, but Thou hast freed them:
  Now they go to free the slaves:
    Be Thou with them,
  'Tis Thine arm alone that saves.

2 Friends and home and all forsaking,
  Lord, they go at Thy command;
As their stay Thy promise taking,
  While they traverse sea and land;
    Oh be with them!
  Lead them safely by the hand.

3 When no fruit appears to cheer them,
  And they seem to toil in vain—
Then in mercy, Lord, draw near them,
  Then their sinking hopes sustain!
    Thus supported,
  Let their zeal revive again.

4 In the midst of opposition,
  Let them trust, O Lord, in Thee;
When success attends their mission,
  Let Thy servants humble be:
    Never leave them
  Till Thy face in heaven they see:

5 There to reap in joy for ever,
  Fruit that grows from seed here sown:
There to be with Him, who never
  Ceases to preserve His own,
    And with triumph
  Sing a Saviour's grace alone.

Thomas Kelly, 1769–1855

This hymn may also be sung to **Bryn Calfaria**, No. 138

MELLING 77.77

SPREAD, oh spread, thou mighty
   word,
Spread the kingdom of the Lord,
Wheresoe'er His breath has given
Life to beings meant for heaven.

2 Tell them how the Father's will
Made the world, and keeps it still,
How He sent His Son to save
All who help and comfort crave.

3 Tell of our Redeemer's love,
Who for ever doth remove
By His holy sacrifice
All the guilt that on us lies.

4 Tell them of the Spirit given
Now to guide us up to heaven,
Strong and holy, just and true,
Working both to will and do.

5 Up! the ripening fields ye see,
Mighty shall the harvest be;
But the reapers still are few,
Great the work they have to do.

6 Lord of harvest, let there be
Joy and strength to work for Thee,
Till the nations, far and near,
See Thy light and learn Thy fear.

Jonathan Friedrich Bahnmaier,
1774-1841
tr. Catherine Winkworth, 1827-78

627

BIRLING L.M.

From an early 19th cent. MS.
Adapted by GEOFFREY SHAW, 1879-1943

WE have a gospel to proclaim,
  Good news for men in all the
earth;
The gospel of a Saviour's name:
  We sing His glory, tell His worth.

2 Tell of His birth at Bethlehem
  Not in a royal house or hall,
But in a stable dark and dim,
  The Word made flesh, a light for all.

3 Tell of His death at Calvary,
  Hated by those He came to save,
In lonely suffering on the cross;
  For all He loved His life He gave.

4 Tell of that glorious Easter morn:
  Empty the tomb, for He was free.
He broke the power of death and hell
  That we might share His victory.

5 Tell of His reign at God's right hand,
  By all creation glorified,
He sends His Spirit on His Church
  To live for Him, the Lamb who
died.

6 Now we rejoice to name Him King:
  Jesus is Lord of all the earth.
This gospel-message we proclaim:
  We sing his glory, tell His worth.

Edward John Burns, b. 1938

This hymn may also be sung to **Fulda**, No. 484

The World-wide Mission

LIMPSFIELD 73.73.77.73

Josiah Booth, 1852-1930

We have heard the joyful sound:
     Jesus saves!
Tell the message all around:
     Jesus saves!
Bear the news to every land,
     Climb the steeps and cross the
          waves;
Onward!—'tis our Lord's command:
     Jesus saves!

2 Waft it on the rolling tide:
     Jesus saves!
Say to sinners far and wide,
     Jesus saves!
Sing, ye islands of the sea;
     Echo back, ye ocean caves;
Earth shall keep her jubilee:
     Jesus saves!

3 Sing above the toil and strife,
     Jesus saves!
By His death and endless life
     Jesus saves!
Sing it softly through the gloom,
     When the heart for mercy craves;
Sing in triumph o'er the tomb,
     Jesus saves!

4 Give the winds a mighty voice:
     Jesus saves!
Let the nations now rejoice,
     Jesus saves!
Shout salvation full and free
     To every strand that ocean laves;
This our song of victory,
     Jesus saves!

Priscilla Jane Owens, 1829–1907

CHARTERHOUSE   11.10.11.10   DAVID EVANS, 1874-1948

"WE rest on Thee," our shield
    and our defender!
We go not forth alone against the
    foe;
Strong in Thy strength, safe in Thy
    keeping tender,
   "We rest on Thee, and in Thy
    name we go."

2 Yea, "in Thy name," O Captain of
    salvation!
In Thy dear name, all other names
    above;
Jesus our righteousness, our sure
    foundation,
   Our Prince of glory and our King
    of love.

3 "We go" in faith, our own great
    weakness feeling,
And needing more each day Thy
    grace to know:
Yet from our hearts a song of triumph
    pealing;
   "We rest on Thee, and in Thy name
    we go."

4 "We rest on Thee," our shield and
    our defender!
Thine is the battle, Thine shall be
    the praise
When passing through the gates of
    pearly splendour,
   Victors—we rest with Thee,
    through endless days.

Edith Gilling Cherry, d. 1897

This hymn may also be sung to **Strength and Stay**, No. 487

TOULON 10.10.10.10   *Genevan Psalter*, 1551

AND is it so? I shall be like Thy Son!
Is this the grace which He for me has won?
Father of glory, thought beyond all thought,
In glory, to His own blest likeness brought;

2 Oh, Jesus, Lord, who loved me like to Thee?
Fruit of Thy work, with Thee, too, there to see
Thy glory, Lord, while endless ages roll,
Myself the prize and travail of Thy soul.

3 Yet it must be, Thy love had not its rest
Were Thy redeemed not with Thee fully blest;
That love that gives not as the world, but shares
All it possesses with its loved co-heirs.

4 Nor I alone, Thy loved ones all, complete
In glory round Thee there with joy shall meet,
All like Thee, for Thy glory like Thee, Lord,
Object supreme of all, by all adored.

John Nelson Darby, 1800–82

This hymn may also be sung to **Farley Castle**, No. 694

631
THE CHURCH OF GOD:
SINE NOMINE   10.10.10.4
R. Vaughan Williams, 1872-1958
Unison, vv. 1,2,3,7,8.
small notes vv.2,8.
Harmony, vv. 4,5,6.

FOR all the saints, who from their labours rest,
Who Thee by faith before the world confessed,
Thy name, O Jesus, be for ever blessed.
　　Alleluia!

2 Thou wast their Rock, their Fortress, and their Might:
Thou, Lord, their Captain in the well-fought fight;
Thou, in the darkness drear, their one true Light.
　　Alleluia!

3 Oh may Thy soldiers, faithful, true, and bold,
Fight as the saints who nobly fought of old,
And win, with them, the victor's crown of gold.
　　Alleluia!

4 Oh blest communion, fellowship divine!
We feebly struggle; they in glory shine;
Yet all are one in Thee, for all are Thine.
　　Alleluia!

5 And when the strife is fierce, the warfare long,
Steals on the ear the distant triumph-song,
And hearts are brave again, and arms are strong.
　　Alleluia!

6 The golden evening brightens in the west;
Soon, soon, to faithful warriors cometh rest;
Sweet is the calm of Paradise the blest.
　　Alleluia!

7 But lo! there breaks a yet more glorious day;
The saints triumphant rise in bright array;
The King of Glory passes on His way.
　　Alleluia!

8 From earth's wide bounds, from ocean's farthest coast,
Through gates of pearl streams in the countless host,
Singing to Father, Son, and Holy Ghost—
　　Alleluia!

William Walsham How, 1823–97

This hymn may also be sung to **St. Philip (Pro Omnibus Sanctis)**, No. 20

632

NEARER HOME D.S.M.

I. B. WOODBURY, 1819-58
Arr. by A. S. SULLIVAN, 1842-1900

"For ever with the Lord!"
  Amen, so let it be;
Life from the dead is in that word,
  'Tis immortality.
  Here in the body pent,
  Absent from Him I roam,
Yet nightly pitch my moving tent
  A day's march nearer home.

2 My Father's house on high,
  Home of my soul, how near
At times to faith's foreseeing eye
  Thy golden gates appear!
  Ah! then my spirit faints
  To reach the land I love,
The bright inheritance of saints,
  Jerusalem above.

3 Though clouds may intervene,
  Rough seas and stormy skies,
Yet, by no mortal vision seen,
  Thy glory fills mine eyes.
  There shall the clouds depart,
  The winds and waters cease;
And sweetly shall my gladdened
    heart
  Enjoy eternal peace.

4 So when my latest breath
  Shall rend the veil in twain,
By death I shall escape from death
  And life eternal gain.
  That resurrection-word,
  That shout of victory;
Once more, "For ever with the Lord!"
  Amen, so let it be!

James Montgomery, 1771-1854

This hymn may also be sung to **St. Ishmael**, No. 378

ES IST KEIN TAG   888.4   Melody from MEYER's *Seelenfreud*, 1692

For those we love within the veil
  Who once were comrades of our way,
We thank Thee, Lord; for they have won
  To cloudless day.

2 And life for them is life indeed,
  The splendid goal of earth's strait race,
And where no shadows intervene,
  They see Thy face.

3 Not as we knew them any more,
  Toil-worn and sad with burdened care,—
Erect, clear-eyed, upon their brows
  Thy name they bear.

4 Free from the fret of mortal years,
  And knowing now Thy perfect will,
With quickened sense and heightened joy
  They serve Thee still.

5 Oh fuller, sweeter is that life,
  And larger, ampler is the air:
Eye cannot see nor heart conceive
  The glory there;

6 Nor know to what high purpose Thou
  Dost yet employ their ripened powers,
Nor how at Thy behest they touch
  This life of ours.

7 There are no tears within their eyes;
  With love they keep perpetual tryst,
And praise and work and rest are one
  With Thee, O Christ.

William Charter Piggott, 1872–1943

634

ST. CHRYSOSTOM 88.88.88

J. BARNBY, 1838-96

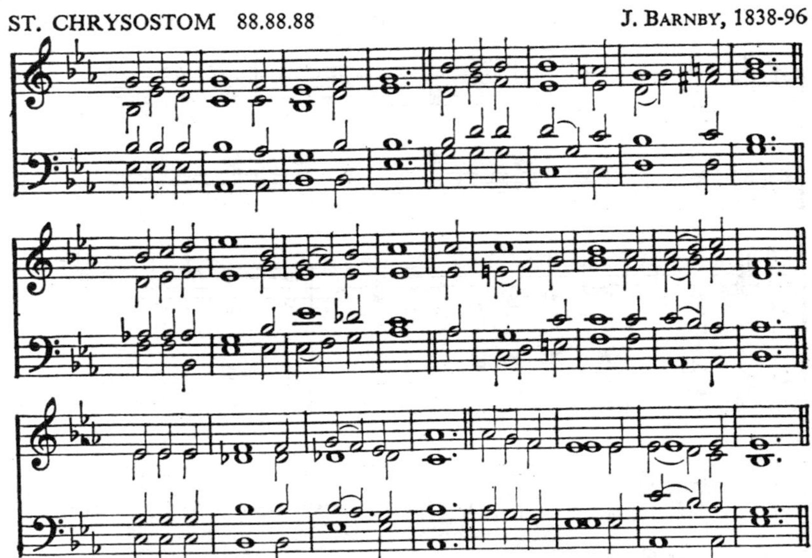

G OD of the living, in whose eyes
Unveiled Thy whole creation lies,
All souls are Thine—we must not say
That those are dead who pass away
From this our world of flesh set free;
We know them living unto Thee.

2 Released from earthly toil and strife
With Thee is hidden still their life;
Thine are their thoughts, their works,
their powers,
All Thine, and yet most truly ours;
For well we know, where'er they be,
Our dead are living unto Thee.

3 Thy word is true, Thy will is just;
To Thee we leave them, Lord, in trust;
And bless Thee for the love which gave
Thy Son to fill a human grave,
That none might fear that world to see
Where all are living unto Thee.

4 O giver unto man of breath,
O holder of the keys of death,
O quickener of the life within,
Save us from death, the death of sin;
That body, soul, and spirit be
For ever living unto Thee!

John Ellerton, 1826–93

635 ALL FOR JESUS 87.87

J. STAINER, 1840-1901

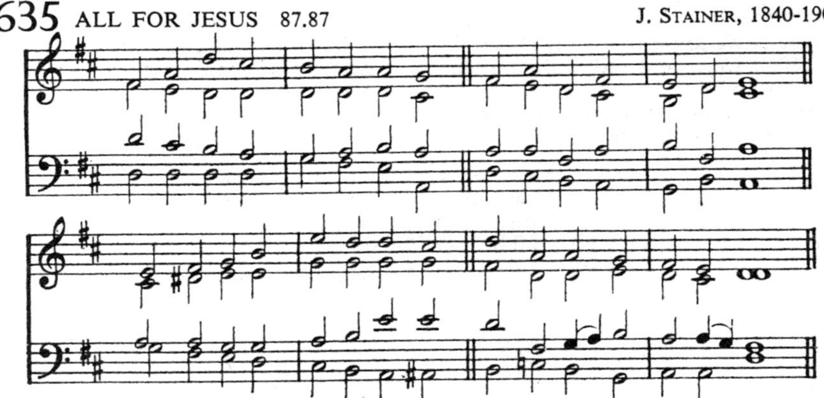

HARK, ten thousand voices crying,
  "Lamb of God" with one accord;
Thousand, thousand saints replying,
  Wake at once the echoing chord.

2 "Praise the Lamb" the chorus waking,
  All in heaven together throng,
Loud and far, each tongue partaking,
  Rolls around the endless song.

3 Grateful incense this, ascending
  Ever to the Father's throne;
Every knee to Jesus bending,
  All the mind in heaven is one.

4 All the Father's counsels claiming
  Equal honours to the Son;
All the Son's effulgence beaming,
  Makes the Father's glory known.

5 By the Spirit all pervading,
  Hosts unnumbered round the Lamb,
Crowned with light and joy unfading,
  Hail Him as the great "I AM."

6 Joyful now the new creation
  Rests in undisturbed repose,
Blest in Jesu's full salvation,
  Sorrow now, nor thraldom knows.

7 Hark! still louder swells their singing,
  As the notes are heard again;
Through creation's vault is ringing
  Joy's response, "Amen! Amen!"

John Nelson Darby, 1800–1882

BEATITUDO C.M.   J. B. DYKES, 1823-76 **636**

HOW bright those glorious spirits shine!
  Whence all their bright array?
How came they to the blissful seats
  Of everlasting day?

2 Lo! these are they from sufferings great,
  Who came to realms of light,
And in the blood of Christ have washed
  Their robes, which shine so bright.

3 Now, with triumphal palms they stand
  Before the throne on high;
And serve the Lord they love, amidst
  The glories of the sky.

4 Hunger and thirst are felt no more,
  Nor sun with scorching ray;
God is their sun, whose cheering beams
  Diffuse eternal day.

5 The Lamb, who dwells amidst the throne,
  Shall o'er them still preside,
Feed them with nourishment divine,
  And all their footsteps guide.

6 'Midst pastures green He'll lead His flock,
  Where living streams appear;
And God Himself from every eye
  Shall wipe away each tear.

*Isaac Watts, 1674–1748
and William Cameron, 1751–1811*

637

THERE'S A LIGHT UPON THE MOUNTAINS 15.15.15.15

M. L. WOSTENHOLM, b. 1887

1 I AM waiting for the dawning
    Of the bright and blessed day,
When the darksome night of sorrow
    Shall have vanished far away;
When for ever with the Saviour,
    Far beyond this vale of tears,
I shall swell the song of worship,
    Through the everlasting years.

2 I am looking at the brightness
    (See, it shineth from afar!)
Of the clear and joyous beaming
    Of the bright and morning Star;
Through the dark grey mist of morning
    Do I see its glorious light;
Then away with every shadow
    Of this sad and weary night.

3 I am waiting for the coming
    Of the Lord who died for me:
Oh His words have thrilled my spirit,
    "I will come again for thee!"
I can almost hear His foot-fall
    On the threshold of the door,
And my heart, my heart, is longing
    To be with Him evermore.

Samuel Trevor Francis, 1834–1925

638

ORLINGTON C.M.

J. CAMPBELL, 1807-1860

JERUSALEM, my happy home,
  Name ever dear to me!
When shall my labours have an end,
  In joy, and peace, and thee?

2 When shall these eyes thy heaven-
    built walls,
  And pearly gates behold?
Thy bulwarks with salvation strong,
  And streets of shining gold?

3 There happier bowers than Eden's
    bloom,
  Nor sin nor sorrow know:
Blest seats, through dark and stormy
    scenes
  I onward press to you.

4 Why should I shrink at pain and woe,
  Or feel, at death, dismay?
I've Canaan's goodly land in view,
  And realms of endless day.

5 Apostles, martyrs, prophets, there
  Around my Saviour stand;
And all I love in Christ below
  Will join the glorious band.

6 Do Thou, O Lord, my soul prepare
  For that bright home of love;
That I may see Thee and adore
  With all Thy saints above.

F.B.P. 15th cent.
Joseph Bromehead, 1748–1826

This hymn may also be sung to **Stracathro,** No. 88

639

EWING 76.76.D

ALEXANDER EWING, 1830-95

JERUSALEM, the golden,
  With milk and honey blest,
Beneath thy contemplation
  Sink heart and voice oppressed.
I know not, oh I know not,
  What height of joy is there,
What radiancy of glory,
  What light beyond compare.

2 They stand, those halls of Zion,
  All jubilant with song,
And bright with many an angel,
  And all the martyr throng:
The Prince is ever in them,
  The daylight is serene;
The pastures of the blessèd
  Are decked in glorious sheen.

3 With jasper glow thy bulwarks,
  Thy streets with emeralds blaze;
The sardius and the topaz,
  Unite in thee their rays:
Thine ageless walls are bonded
  With amethyst unpriced;
The saints build up its fabric,
  The Corner-Stone is Christ.

4 The cross is all thy splendour,
  The Crucified thy praise;
His laud and benediction
  Thy ransomed people raise:
Upon the Rock of Ages
  They raise thy holy tower;
Thine is the victor's laurel,
  And thine the golden dower.

Part 2

1 Jerusalem, the glorious,
  O paradise of joy!
Where tears are ever banished,
  And smiles have no alloy.
There grief is turned to pleasure,
  Such pleasure as below
No human voice can utter,
  No human heart can know.

2 And now we fight the battle,
  But then shall wear the crown
Of full and everlasting
  And passionless renown;
There He, whom now we trust in
  Shall then be seen and known;
And they, that know and see Him,
  Shall have Him for their own.

3 There is the throne of David,
  And there, from care released,
The shout of them that triumph,
  The song of those that feast;
And they who, with their Leader,
  Have conquered in the fight,
For ever and for ever
  Are clad in robes of white.

4 The light hath there no evening,
  The health hath there no sore,
The life hath there no ending,
  But lasteth evermore!
Exult, O dust and ashes,
  The Lord shall be thy part!
His only, His for ever,
  Thou shalt be, and thou art.

Bernard of Morlaix (Cluny), 12th cent.; tr. John Mason Neale, 1818–66

WESTMINSTER ABBEY   87.87.87   *The Psalmist, 1842*   640
Adapted from HENRY PURCELL, 1659-95

L IGHT's abode, celestial Salem,
  Vision whence true peace doth
    spring,
Brighter than the heart can fancy,
  Mansion of the highest King;
Oh how glorious are the praises
  Which of thee the prophets sing!

2 There for ever and for ever
  Alleluia is out-poured;
For unending, for unbroken
  Is the feast-day of the Lord;
All is pure and all is holy
  That within thy walls is stored.

3 There no cloud nor passing vapour
  Dims the brightness of the air;
Endless noon-day, glorious noon-day
  From the Sun of suns is there;
There no night brings rest from labour
  For unknown are toil and care.

4 Oh how glorious and resplendent,
  Fragile body, shalt thou be,
When endued with so much beauty,
  Full of health, and strong and free,
Full of vigour, full of pleasure
  That shall last eternally!

5 Now with gladness, now with courage,
  Bear the burden on thee laid,
That hereafter these thy labours
  May with endless gifts be paid;
And in everlasting glory
  Thou with brightness be arrayed.

Ascribed to Thomas a Kempis, 1380–1471; tr. John Mason Neale, 1818–66
This hymn may also be sung to **Regent Square**, No. 5

641

ST. ALPHEGE 76.76

H. J. GAUNTLETT, 1805-76

MY soul, there is a country
　Afar beyond the stars,
Where stands a wingèd sentry
　All skilful in the wars.

2 There, above noise and danger,
　Sweet peace sits, crowned with
　　smiles,
And One born in a manger
　Commands the beauteous files.

3 He is thy gracious friend,
　And—O my soul, awake!
Did in pure love descend,
　To die here for thy sake.

4 If thou canst get but thither,
　There grows the flower of peace,
The rose that cannot wither,
　Thy fortress, and thy ease.

5 Leave then thy foolish ranges;
　For none can thee secure,
But One, who never changes,
　Thy God, thy Life, thy Cure. *Henry Vaughan, 1621–95*

642 NEARER HOME D.S.M.

I. B. WOODBURY, 1819-58
Arr. by A. S. SULLIVAN, 1842-1900

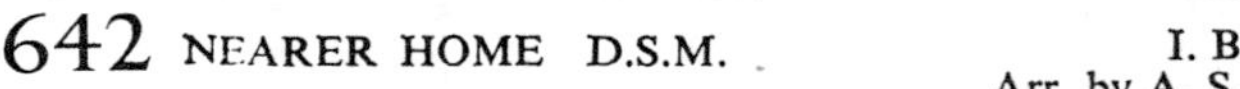

R EST of the saints above,
   Jerusalem of God!
Who, in thy palaces of love,
   Thy golden streets have trod,
Who shall to me the joy
   Of ransomed saints declare,
Tell of that constant sweet employ
   My spirit longs to share?

2   The Lamb is there, my soul!
   There, God Himself doth rest
In love divine diffused through all
   With Him supremely blest.

God and the Lamb! 'Tis well
   I know that source divine
Of joy and love, no tongue can tell,
   Yet know that all is mine.

3   There in effulgence bright,
   Saviour and Guide, with Thee
I'll walk, and in Thy heavenly light
   Whiter my robe shall be.
God and the Lamb shall there
   The light and temple be;
And radiant hosts for ever share
   The unveiled mystery.

John Nelson Darby, 1800–82

This hymn may also be sung to Falcon St, No. 664

CAMBRIDGE S.M.   R. HARRISON, 1748-1810   643

S ERVANT of God, well done!
   Rest from thy loved employ;
The battle fought, the victory won,
   Enter thy Master's joy.

2   The pains of death are past;
   Labour and sorrow cease;
And, life's long warfare closed at last,
   Thy soul is found in peace.

3   Rest from thy labour, rest,
   Soul of the just, set free;
Blest be thy memory, and blest
   Thy bright example be.

4   Now, toil and conflict o'er,
   Go, take with saints thy place;
But go, as each has gone before,
   A sinner saved by grace.

5   Soldier of Christ, well done!
   Praise be thy new employ;
And, while eternal ages run,
   Rest in thy Saviour's joy.

James Montgomery, 1771–1854

This hymn may also be sung to Huddersfield, No. 328

644

ALFORD 76.86.D

J. B. Dykes, 1823-76

Ten thousand times ten thousand,
In sparkling raiment bright,
The armies of the ransomed saints
Throng up the steeps of light;
'Tis finished, all is finished,
Their fight with death and sin;
Fling open wide the golden gates,
And let the victors in.

2 What rush of hallelujahs
Fills all the earth and sky;
What ringing of a thousand harps
Bespeaks the triumph nigh!
Oh day for which creation
And all its tribes were made!
Oh joy, for all its former woes
A thousandfold repaid!

3 Oh then what raptured greetings
On Canaan's happy shore,
What knitting severed friendships up,
Where partings are no more!
Then eyes with joy shall sparkle
That brimmed with tears of late;
Orphans no longer fatherless,
Nor widows desolate.

4 Bring near Thy great salvation,
Thou Lamb for sinners slain;
Fill up the roll of Thine elect,
Then take Thy power and reign;
Appear, Desire of nations,
Thine exiles long for home;
Show in the heaven Thy promised
sign:
Thou Prince and Saviour, come.

Henry Alford, 1810–71

WINCHESTER NEW L.M.

From a chorale in the
Musikalisches Handbuch, Hamburg, 1690
Arr. by W. H. Havergal, 1793-1870

THE countless multitude on high,
　　Who tune their songs to Jesu's
　　　　name,
All merit of their own deny,
　　And Jesu's worth alone proclaim.

2 Firm on the ground of sovereign grace,
　　They stand before Jehovah's throne;
The only song in that blest place
　　Is "Thou art worthy, Thou alone!"

3 Salvation's glory all be paid
　　To Him who sits upon the throne,
And to the Lamb whose blood was
　　　　shed;
　　"Thou, Thou art worthy, Thou
　　　　alone."

4 For Thou wast slain, and in Thy blood
　　These robes were washed so spotless
　　　　pure;
Thou mad'st us kings and priests to
　　　　God,
　　For ever let Thy praise endure.

5 Let us with joy adopt the strain
　　We hope to sing for ever there:
"Worthy's the Lamb for sinners slain,
　　Worthy alone the crown to wear!"

6 Without one thought that's good to
　　　　plead,
　　Oh what could shield us from
　　　　despair
But this: though we are vile indeed,
　　The Lord our Righteousness is
　　　　there.

Archibald Rutherford

This hymn may also be sung to **Mainzer**, No. 338

646

CLAUDIUS   D.C.M.

Adapted from a song by G. W. Fink, 1783-1846

THERE is a fold where none can
    stray,
  And pastures ever green,
Where sultry sun, or stormy day,
  Or night are never seen.
Far up the everlasting hills,
  In God's own light it lies;
His smile its vast dimension fills
  With joy that never dies.

2 There is a Shepherd living there,
    The First-born from the dead,
  Who tends with sweet unwearied care
    The flock for which He bled.
  There the deep streams of joy that
      flow,
    Proceed from God's right hand;
  He made them, and He bids them go
    To feed that happy land.

3 There congregate the sons of light,
    Fair as the morning sky,
  And taste of infinite delight
    Beneath their Saviour's eye;
  Where'er He turns, they willing turn,
    In unity they move;
  Their seraph spirits nobly burn
    In harmony of love.

4 There in the power of heavenly sight
    They gaze upon the throne,
  And scan perfection's utmost height,
    And know as they are known.
  Their joy bursts forth in strains of
      love,
    In one harmonious song,
  And all the azure heights above,
    The echoes roll along.

5 Oh may our faith take up that sound,
    Though toiling here below!
  'Midst trials may our joys abound,
    And songs amidst our woe;
  Until we reach that happy shore,
    And join to swell their strain,
  And from our God go out no more,
    And never weep again.

John East

This hymn may also be sung to **Castle Rising**, No. 553

MENDIP C.M.

English Traditional Melody
Arr. by R. VAUGHAN WILLIAMS, 1872–1958

THERE is a land of pure delight,
  Where saints immortal reign;
Infinite day excludes the night,
  And pleasures banish pain.

2 There everlasting spring abides,
  And never-withering flowers;
Death, like a narrow sea divides
  That heavenly land from ours.

3 Sweet fields, beyond the swelling
    flood,
  Stand dressed in living green;
So to the Jews old Canaan stood,
  While Jordan rolled between.

4 But timorous mortals start and shrink
  To cross this narrow sea;
And linger shivering on the brink,
  And fear to launch away.

5 Oh could we make our doubts remove,
  Those gloomy doubts that rise,
And see the Canaan that we love
  With unbeclouded eyes:

6 Could we but climb where Moses
    stood,
  And view the landscape o'er,
Not Jordan's stream, nor death's cold
    flood
  Should fright us from the shore!

Isaac Watts, 1674–1748

See also
177 The strife is o'er, the battle done
193 Crown Him with many crowns
194 Earth rejoice, our Lord is King!
206 Thy kingdom come, O God
359 Jesus, Thy blood and righteousness
479 The sands of time are sinking
713 When the day of toil is done

FIRST TUNE

CHRIST WHOSE GLORY 7777.77   MALCOLM WILLIAMSON, b. 1931

UNISON

SECOND TUNE

HEATHLANDS 77.77.77   H. SMART, 1813-79

CHRIST, whose glory fills the skies,
    Christ, the true, the only Light,
Sun of righteousness, arise,
    Triumph o'er the shades of night;
Day-spring from on high, be near;
Day-star, in my heart appear.

2 Dark and cheerless is the morn
   Unaccompanied by Thee:
Joyless is the day's return,
   Till Thy mercy's beams I see,
Till Thou inward light impart,
Glad my eyes, and warm my heart.

3 Visit then this soul of mine,
   Pierce the gloom of sin and grief;
Fill me, Radiancy divine,
   Scatter all my unbelief;
More and more Thyself display,
Shining to the perfect day.

Charles Wesley, 1707–88

649

MELCOMBE L.M.

S. Webbe (the Elder), 1740-1816

New every morning is the love
  Our wakening and uprising
    prove;
Through sleep and darkness safely
    brought,
Restored to life, and power, and
    thought.

2 New mercies, each returning day,
Hover around us while we pray;
New perils past, new sins forgiven,
New thoughts of God, new hopes of
    heaven.

3 If, on our daily course, our mind
Be set to hallow all we find,
New treasures still of countless price
God will provide for sacrifice.

4 Old friends, old scenes will lovelier be,
As more of heaven in each we see;
Some softening gleam of love and
    prayer
Shall dawn on every cross and care.

5 The trivial round, the common task,
Will furnish all we ought to ask:
Room to deny ourselves; a road
To bring us daily nearer God.

6 Only, O Lord, in Thy dear love
Fit us for perfect rest above,
And help us, this and every day,
To live more nearly as we pray.

John Keble, 1792–1866

LAUDES DOMINI 666.D   J. BARNBY, 1838-96

WHEN morning gilds the skies,
  My heart awaking cries,
    May Jesus Christ be praised!
Alike at work and prayer
To Jesus I repair:
    May Jesus Christ be praised!

2 To Thee, my God above,
  I cry with glowing love,
    May Jesus Christ be praised:
The fairest graces spring
In hearts that ever sing,
    May Jesus Christ be praised!

3 Does sadness fill my mind?
  A solace here I find,
    May Jesus Christ be praised!
Or fades my earthly bliss?
My comfort still is this,
    May Jesus Christ be praised!

4 When evil thoughts molest,
  With this I shield my breast,
    May Jesus Christ be praised!
The powers of darkness fear,
When this sweet chant they hear,
    May Jesus Christ be praised!

5 When sleep her balm denies,
  My silent spirit sighs,
    May Jesus Christ be praised!
The night becomes as day,
When from the heart we say,
    May Jesus Christ be praised!

6 Be this, while life is mine,
  My canticle divine,
    May Jesus Christ be praised!
Be this the eternal song
Through all the ages long,
    May Jesus Christ be praised!

Author unknown; tr. Edward Caswall,
1814–78

EVENTIDE 10.10.10.10   W. H. MONK, 1823-89

A BIDE with me—fast falls the eventide;
The darkness deepens; Lord, with me abide:
When other helpers fail, and comforts flee,
Help of the helpless, oh abide with me!

2 Swift to its close ebbs out life's little day;
Earth's joys grow dim, its glories pass away;
Change and decay in all around I see:
O Thou who changest not, abide with me!

3 Not a brief glance I beg, a passing word,
But as Thou dwell'dst with Thy disciples, Lord;
Familiar, condescending, patient, free,
Come not to sojourn, but abide with me.

4 I need Thy presence every passing hour;
What but Thy grace can foil the tempter's power?
Who like Thyself my guide and stay can be?
Through cloud and sunshine, oh abide with me!

5 I fear no foe, with Thee at hand to bless;
Ills have no weight, and tears no bitterness;
Where is death's sting? where, grave, thy victory?
I triumph still, if Thou abide with me.

6 Be Thou Thyself before my closing eyes,
Shine through the gloom, and point me to the skies:
Heaven's morning breaks, and earth's vain shadows flee;
In life, in death, O Lord, abide with me!

Henry Francis Lyte, 1793–1847

ANGELUS L.M.

Melody by GEORG JOSEPH
in SCHEFFLER's *Heilige Seelenlust*, 1657

A^T even when the sun was set,
   The sick, O Lord, around Thee lay;
Oh, in what divers pains they met!
Oh, with what joy they went away!

2 Once more 'tis eventide, and we,
   Oppressed with various ills, draw near;
What if Thy form we cannot see!
   We know and feel that Thou art here.

3 O Saviour Christ! our woes dispel;
   For some are sick, and some are sad,
And some have never loved Thee well,
And some have lost the love they had.

4 And some have found the world is vain,
   Yet from the world they break not free;
And some have friends who give them pain,
   Yet have not sought a friend in Thee.

5 And none, O Lord, have perfect rest,
   For none are wholly free from sin;
And they who fain would serve Thee best
   Are conscious most of wrong within.

6 O Saviour Christ! Thou too art Man;
   Thou hast been troubled, tempted, tried;
Thy kind but searching glance can scan
   The very wounds that shame would hide.

7 Thy touch has still its ancient power;
   No word from Thee can fruitless fall;
Hear, in this solemn evening hour,
And in Thy mercy heal us all.

Henry Twells, 1823–1900

This hymn may also be sung to **Abends,** No. 297

EVENING HYMN 887.D   W. Jackson, 1815-66

Father, in high heaven dwelling,
  May our evening song be telling
Of Thy mercy large and free:
Through the day Thy love hath fed us,
Through the day Thy care hath led us,
  With divinest charity.

2 This day's sins, oh pardon, Saviour,
  Evil thoughts, perverse behaviour,
    Envy, pride, and vanity:
  From the world, the flesh, deliver,
  Save us now, and save us ever,
    O Thou Lamb of Calvary!

3 From enticements of the devil,
  From the might of spirits evil,
    Be our shield and panoply:
  Let Thy power this night defend us,
  And a heavenly peace attend us,
    And angelic company.

4 Whilst the night-dews are distilling,
  Holy Ghost, each heart be filling
    With Thine own serenity:
  Softly let the eyes be closing,
  Loving souls on Thee reposing,
    Ever blessèd Trinity!
                    George Rawson, 1807–89

SEBASTE Irregular   J. Stainer, 1840-1901

HAIL, gladdening Light, of His
pure glory poured,
Who is the immortal Father, heavenly-
blest,
Holiest of holies, Jesus Christ our
Lord!

2 Now we are come to the sun's hour of
rest;
The lights of evening round us shine;
We hymn the Father, Son and Holy
Spirit Divine.

3 Worthiest art Thou at all times to be
sung
With undefilèd tongue,
Son of our God, giver of life, alone;
Therefore in all the worlds Thy
glories, Lord, they own.

Greek, 3rd cent.
tr. John Keble, 1792–1866

655

TALLIS' CANON L.M.

T. TALLIS, *c.* 1510-85

GLORY to Thee, my God, this night,
For all the blessings of the light;
Keep me, oh keep me, King of kings,
Beneath Thine own almighty wings.

2 Forgive me, Lord, for Thy dear Son,
The ills that I this day have done;
That with the world, myself, and Thee,
I, ere I sleep, at peace may be.

3 Teach me to live, that I may dread
The grave as little as my bed;
Teach me to die, that so I may
Rise glorious at the aweful day.

4 Oh may my soul on Thee repose,
And may sweet sleep mine eyelids close;
Sleep that shall me more vigorous make
To serve my God when I awake.

5 If in the night I sleepless lie,
My soul with heavenly thoughts supply;
Let no ill dreams disturb my rest,
Nor powers of darkness me molest.

6 Praise God, from whom all blessings flow,
Praise Him, all creatures here below,
Praise Him above, ye heavenly host,
Praise Father, Son and Holy Ghost.

Thomas Ken, 1637–1710

COMPANION 88.88.88   R. S. Newman, 1850-1927

<table>
<tr><td valign="top">

L ORD Jesus, in the days of old
    Two walked with Thee in
      waning light;
And love's blind instinct made them
    bold
    To crave Thy presence through the
      night,
As night descends, we too would pray:
Oh leave us not at close of day!

2 Did not their hearts within them
    burn?
    And though their Lord they failed
      to know,
Did not their spirits inly yearn?
    They could not let the Stranger go.
Much more must we who know Thee
    pray:
Oh leave us not at close of day!

</td><td valign="top">

3 Day is far spent, and night is nigh;
    Stay with us, Saviour, through the
      night;
Talk with us, touch us tenderly,
    Lead us to peace, to rest, to light;
Dispel our darkness with Thy face,
Radiant with resurrection grace.

4 Nor this night only, blessèd Lord,
    We, every day and every hour,
Would walk with Thee Emmaus-
    ward
    To hear Thy voice of love and
      power;
And every night would by Thy side
Look, listen, and be satisfied.

James Ashcroft Noble, 1844–96

</td></tr>
</table>

This hymn may also be sung to **Pater omnium**, No. 111

ELLERS 10.10.10.10

E. J. HOPKINS, 1818-1901
Harmonized by A. S. SULLIVAN, 1842-1900

SAVIOUR, again to Thy dear name we raise
With one accord our parting hymn of praise;
We rise to bless Thee ere our worship cease;
And now departing, wait Thy word of peace.

2 Grant us Thy peace upon our homeward way;
With Thee began, with Thee shall end the day;
Guard Thou the lips from sin, the hearts from shame,
That in this house have called upon Thy name.

3 Grant us Thy peace, Lord, through the coming night;
Turn Thou for us its darkness into light;
From harm and danger keep Thy children free,
For dark and light are both alike to Thee.

4 Grant us Thy peace throughout our earthly life,
Our balm in sorrow, and our stay in strife;
Then, when Thy voice shall bid our conflict cease,
Call us, O Lord, to Thine eternal peace.

John Ellerton, 1826–93

N̄ow God be with us, for the night
 is closing,
The light and darkness are of His
 disposing,
And neath His shadow here to rest
 we yield us,
 For He will shield us.

2 Let evil thoughts and spirits flee
 before us;
The morning cometh; do Thou,
 Lord, watch o'er us
In soul and body, and from harm
 defend us;
 Thine angels send us.

3 As Thy belovèd, soothe the sick and
 weeping;
And bid the sufferer lose his griefs in
 sleeping;
Widows and orphans, we to Thee
 commend them,
 Do Thou befriend them.

4 We have no refuge, none on earth to
 aid us,
Save Thee, O Father, who Thine
 own hast made us;
But Thy dear presence will not leave
 us lonely
 Who seek Thee only.

5 Let our last thoughts be Thine when
 sleep o'ertakes us;
Our earliest thoughts be Thine when
 morning wakes us;
All day serve Thee, in all that we are
 doing,
 Thy praise pursuing.

Petrus Herbert, d. 1571
tr. Catherine Winkworth, 1827–78

QUAM DILECTA 66.66   H. L. JENNER, 1820-98

ONCE more ·before we part,
   We bless the Saviour's name;
Let every tongue and heart
   Join to extol the Lamb.

2 We on Thy holy Word
   Would feed, and live, and grow;
Go on to know Thee, Lord,
   And practise what we know.

3 Lord, in Thy grace we came,
   Thy blessing still impart;
We met in Thine own name,
   And in Thy name ,we part.

Joseph Hart, 1712–68
and Robert Stephen Hawker, 1804–75

HURSLEY   L.M.

Katholisches Gesangbuch, c. 1774

Sun of my soul, Thou Saviour dear,
It is not night if Thou be near:
Oh may no earth-born cloud arise
To hide Thee from Thy servant's
eyes!

2 When the soft dews of kindly sleep
My wearied eyelids gently steep,
Be my last thought, how sweet to rest
For ever on my Saviour's breast!

·3 Abide with me from morn till eve,
For without Thee I cannot live;
Abide with me when night is nigh,
For without Thee I dare not die.

4 Watch by the sick, enrich the poor
With blessings from Thy boundless
store;
Be every mourner's sleep to-night,
Like infant's slumbers, pure and light.

5 Come near and bless us when we
wake,
Ere through the world our way we
take,
Till in the ocean of Thy love
We lose ourselves in heaven above.

John Keble, 1792–1866

This hymn may also be sung to **Abends**, No. 297

661

ST. ANATOLIUS 76.76.88   A. H. BROWN, 1830-1926

THE day is past and over;
　All thanks, O Lord, to Thee;
I pray Thee now that sinless
　The hours of dark may be:
Lord Jesus, keep me in Thy sight,
And guard me through the coming
　　night.

2　The joys of day are over;
　I lift my heart to Thee,
And ask Thee that offenceless
　The hours of dark may be:
Lord Jesus, keep me in Thy sight,
And guard me through the coming
　　night.

3　The toils of day are over;
　I raise the hymn to Thee,
And ask that free from peril
　The hours of dark may be:
Lord Jesus, keep me in Thy sight,
And guard me through the coming
　　night.

4　Be Thou my soul's preserver,
　For Thou alone dost know
How many are the perils
　Through which I have to go:
O Lord and Saviour, hear my call,
And guard and keep me through them
　　all.

Greek, 6th cent.
tr. John Mason Neale, 1818–66

ST. CLEMENT   98.98   C. C. SCHOLEFIELD, 1839-1904

THE day Thou gavest, Lord, is
 ended,
The darkness falls at Thy behest;
To Thee our morning hymns
 ascended,
Thy praise shall sanctify our rest.

2 We thank Thee that Thy church
 unsleeping,
While earth rolls onward into light,
Through all the world her watch is
 keeping,
And rests not now by day or night.

3 As o'er each continent and island
The dawn leads on another day,
The voice of prayer is never silent,
Nor dies the strain of praise away.

4 The sun that bids us rest is waking
 Our brethren 'neath the western
 sky,
And hour by hour fresh lips are
 making
 Thy wondrous doings heard on
 high.

5 So be it, Lord; Thy throne shall never,
 Like earth's proud empires, pass
 away;
Thy kingdom stands, and grows for
 ever,
 Till all Thy creatures own Thy
 sway.

John Ellerton, 1826–93

663

DAY OF REST 76.76.D

J. W. Elliott, 1833-1915

O DAY of rest and gladness,
  O day of joy and light,
O balm of care and sadness,
  Most beautiful, most bright;
On thee the high and lowly,
  Before the eternal throne,
Sing "Holy, Holy, Holy,"
  To the great Three in One.

2 On thee, at the creation,
  The light first had its birth;
On thee, for our salvation,
  Christ rose from depths of earth;
On thee our Lord victorious
  The Spirit sent from heaven;
And thus on thee most glorious
  A triple light was given.

3 Thou art a cooling fountain
  In life's dry, dreary sand,
From thee, like Pisgah's mountain,
  We view our promised land;
New graces ever gaining
  From this our day of rest,
We reach the rest remaining
  To spirits of the blest.

Christopher Wordsworth, 1807–85

This hymn may also be sung to Munich, No. 80

FALCON STREET S.M.   I. SMITH, *c.* 1725–*c.* 1800

THIS is the day of light:
Let there be light to-day;
O Day-spring, rise upon our night,
And chase its gloom away.

2   This is the day of rest:
Our failing strength renew;
On weary brain and troubled breast
Shed Thou Thy freshening dew.

3   This is the day of peace:
Thy peace our spirits fill;
Bid Thou the blasts of discord cease,
The waves of strife be still.

4   This is the day of prayer:
Let earth to heaven draw near;
Lift up our hearts to seek Thee there,
Come down to meet us here.

5   This is the first of days:
Send forth Thy quickening breath,
And wake dead souls to love and
praise,
O Vanquisher of death!

John Ellerton, 1826–93

This hymn may also be sung to **Huddersfield**, No. 328

BROMSGROVE　C.M. extended

Later form of melody from
Psalmodia Evangelica, 1789

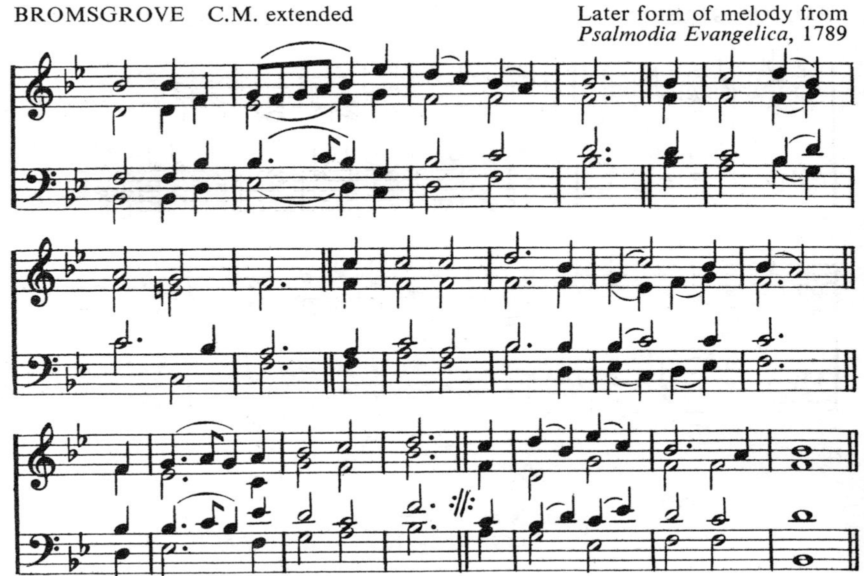

THIS is the day the Lord hath made,
　He calls the hours His own;
Let heaven rejoice, let earth be glad,
　And praise surround the throne.

2 To-day He rose and left the dead,
　And Satan's empire fell;
To-day the saints His triumphs spread,
　And all His wonders tell.

3 Hosanna to the anointed King,
　To David's holy Son!
Make haste to help us, Lord, and bring
　Salvation from Thy throne.

4 Blest be the Lord, who comes to men
　With messages of grace;
Who comes, in God His Father's name,
　To save our sinful race.

5 Hosanna in the highest strains
　The church on earth can raise;
The highest heavens in which He reigns
　Shall give Him nobler praise.

Isaac Watts, 1674–1748

This hymn may also be sung to **Richmond**, No. 18

LEOMINSTER D.S.M.

G. W. MARTIN, 1828-1881

O CHRIST, Thou Son of God,
  Thou glorious Lord of all,
Thou Living One who once wast
    slain,
  Before Thy face we fall!
  To Thee, O Lord, we look,
  To Thee ourselves we yield;
Be Thou throughout our earthly
    course
  Our refuge and our shield!

2 Though all around may change,
  No change Thou e'er shalt know;
The same art Thou upon the throne
  As Thou wast here below;
  The same to-day Thou art
  As yesterday Thou wast,
The same e'en to eternal days
  As in the wondrous past.

3 Lord Jesus, take our hearts,
  From self-love set them free;
Help us, however dark our path,
  To stay our souls on Thee:
  Though evil waxes worse,
  And many hearts grow cold,
Help us to cleave unto Thy name,
  Thy faithful Word to hold.

4 Help us to look beyond
  The dark and gloomy night,
To wait for that blest hour when Thou
  Wilt come in glory bright;
  When we Thy voice shall hear,
  Thy glorious face shall see,
And, like Thee, in Thy presence
    stand,
  And ever worship Thee.

William Henry Bennet, 1843–1920

See also
78 O God our help
399 O God of Bethel
464 O Jesus I have promised
477 Take my life and let it be
585 March on, my soul, with strength
694 I take Thy promise, Lord

667

ST. GEORGE'S, WINDSOR 77.77.D

G. J. ELVEY, 1816-93

COME, ye thankful people, come,
Raise the song of harvest-home!
All is safely gathered in,
Ere the winter storms begin;
God our Maker doth provide
For our wants to be supplied;
Come to God's own temple, come,
Raise the song of harvest-home!

2 All the world is God's own field,
Fruit unto His praise to yield;
Wheat and tares together sown,
Unto joy or sorrow grown;
First the blade, and then the ear,
Then the full corn shall appear;
Lord of harvest, grant that we
Wholesome grain and pure may be.

3 For the Lord our God shall come,
And shall take His harvest home;
From His field shall in that day
All offences purge away;
Give His angels charge at last
In the fire the tares to cast;
But the fruitful ears to store
In His garner evermore.

4 Even so, Lord, quickly come
To Thy final harvest-home.
Gather Thou Thy people in,
Free from sorrow, free from sin,
There for ever purified,
In Thy presence to abide:
Come, with all Thine angels, come,
Raise the glorious harvest-home!

Henry Alford, 1810–71

CONSTANCE 87.87.D Iambic

A. S. SULLIVAN, 1842-1900

To Thee, O Lord, our hearts we raise
  In hymns of adoration,
To Thee bring sacrifice of praise
  With shouts of exultation;
Bright robes of gold the fields adorn,
  The hills with joy are ringing,
The valleys stand so thick with corn
  That even they are singing.

2 And now, on this our festal day,
  Thy bounteous hand confessing,
Before Thee thankfully we lay
  The first-fruits of Thy blessing.
By Thee the souls of men are fed
  With gifts of grace supernal;
Thou who dost give us earthly bread,
  Give us the bread eternal.

3 We bear the burden of the day,
  And often toil seems dreary;
But labour ends with sunset ray,
  And rest comes for the weary:
May we, the angel-reaping o'er,
  Stand at the last accepted.
Christ's golden sheaves for evermore
  To garners bright elected.

4 Oh blessèd is that land of God
  Where saints abide for ever,
Where golden fields spread far and broad,
  Where flows the crystal river.
The strains of all its holy throng
  With ours to-day are blending;
Thrice blessèd is that harvest song
  Which never hath an ending.

William Chatterton Dix, 1837-98.

This hymn may also be sung to **Bishopgarth**, No. 490

WIR PFLÜGEN 76.76.D with refrain   J. A. P. Schulz, 1747-1800

We plough the fields, and scatter
  The good seed on the land;
But it is fed and watered
  By God's almighty hand:
He sends the snow in winter,
  The warmth to swell the grain;
The breezes, and the sunshine,
  And soft refreshing rain.

All good gifts around us
  Are sent from heaven above:
Then thank the Lord, oh thank the
  Lord,
For all His love!

2 He only is the Maker
    Of all things near and far:
  He paints the wayside flower,
    He lights the evening star;
  The winds and waves obey Him,
    By Him the birds are fed;
  Much more to us, His children,
    He gives our daily bread.

3 We thank Thee, then, O Father,
    For all things bright and good:
  The seed-time and the harvest,
    Our life, our health, our food.
  Accept the gifts we offer
    For all Thy love imparts:
  And—what Thou most desirest—
    Our humble, thankful hearts.

Matthias Claudius, 1740-1815
tr. Jane Montgomery Campbell, 1817-78

DOWNING S.M.　　　　　　　　　　　　J. A. LLOYD, 1815-74

How welcome was the call,
　And sweet the festal lay,
When Jesus deigned in Cana's hall
　To bless the marriage-day.

2　And happy was the bride,
　　And glad the bridegroom's heart;
For He who tarried at their side
　　Bade grief and ill depart.

3　His gracious power divine
　　The water-vessels knew;
And plenteous was the mystic wine
　　The wondering servants drew.

4　O Lord of life and love,
　　Come Thou again to-day,
And bring a blessing from above
　　That ne'er shall pass away.

5　Before Thy gracious throne
　　This mercy we implore:
As Thou dost knit them, Lord, in one,
　　So bless them evermore.

Henry Williams Baker, 1821–77

This hymn may also be sung to **St. George**, No. 497

671

MISSIONARY 76.76.D

L. MASON, 1792-1872

O FATHER, all-creating,
   Whose wisdom, love, and power
First bound two lives together
   In Eden's primal hour.
To-day to these Thy children
   Thine earliest gifts renew:
A home by Thee made happy,
   A love by Thee kept true.

2 O Saviour, guest most bounteous
   Of old in Galilee,
Vouchsafe to-day Thy presence
   With those who call on Thee;
Their store of earthly gladness
   Transform to heavenly wine,
And teach them in the tasting
   To know the gift is Thine.

3 O Spirit of the Father,
   Breathe on them from above,
So mighty in Thy pureness,
   So tender in Thy love,
That, guarded by Thy presence,
   From sin and strife kept free,
Their lives may own Thy guidance,
   Their hearts be ruled by Thee.

4 Except Thou build it, Father,
   The house is built in vain;
Except Thou, Saviour, bless it,
   The joy will turn to pain:
But nought can break the union
   Of hearts in Thee made one;
And love Thy Spirit hallows
   Is endless love begun.

John Ellerton, 1826–93

This hymn may also be sung to **Day of Rest,** No. 663

SAFFRON WALDEN 888.6

A. H. Brown, 1830-1926

O God of Love, to Thee we bow,
  And pray for these before Thee now,
That, closely knit in holy vow,
  They may in Thee be one.

2 When days are filled with pure delight,
  When paths are plain and skies are bright,
  Walking by faith and not by sight,
  May they in Thee be one.

3 When stormy winds fulfil Thy will,
  And all their good seems turned to ill,
  Then, trusting Thee completely, still
  May they in Thee be one.

4 Whate'er in life shall be their share
  Of quickening joy or burdening care,
  In power to do and grace to bear,
  May they in Thee be one.

5 Eternal Love, with them abide;
  In Thee for ever may they hide,
  For even death cannot divide
  Those whom Thou makest one.

William Vaughan Jenkins, 1868–1920

673

WELWYN 11.10.11.10

A. Scott-Gatty, 1847-1918

Oh happy home, where Thou art loved the dearest,
Thou loving Friend, and Saviour of our race;
And where among the guests there never cometh
One who can hold such high and honoured place.

2 Oh happy home, where two in heart united
In holy faith and blessèd hope are one,
Whom death a little while alone divideth,
And cannot end the union here begun!

3 Oh happy home, whose little ones are given
Early to Thee, in humble faith and prayer,
To Thee, their Friend, who from the heights of heaven
Guides them, and guards with more than mother's care.

4 Oh happy home, where each one serves Thee, lowly,
Whatever his appointed work may be,
Till every common task seems great and holy,
When it is done, O Lord, as unto Thee.

5 Until at last, when earth's day's work is ended,
All meet Thee in the blessed home above,
From whence Thou camest, where Thou hast ascended,
Thy everlasting home of peace and love!

Karl Johann Philipp Spitta, 1801–59; tr. Sarah Findlater, 1823–1907

This hymn may also be sung to Strength and Stay, No. 487

O PERFECT LOVE 11.10.11.10

J. BARNBY, 1838-96

O PERFECT Love, all human thought transcending,
Lowly we kneel in prayer before Thy throne,
That theirs may be the love which knows no ending
Whom Thou for evermore dost join in one.

2 O perfect Life, be Thou their full assurance
Of tender charity and steadfast faith,
Of patient hope, and quiet brave endurance,
With childlike trust that fears nor pain nor death.

3 Grant them the joy which brightens earthly sorrow;
Grant them the peace which calms all earthly strife,
And to life's day the glorious unknown morrow
That dawns upon eternal love and life.

Dorothy Frances (Blomfield) Gurney, 1853-1932

675

MELITA 88.88.88

ETERNAL Father, strong to save,
Whose arm has bound the restless wave,
Who bidd'st the mighty ocean deep
Its own appointed limits keep,
We pray, O Lord of Galilee,
For those who journey on the sea.

2 O Lord, who art Thyself the Way,
The Truth, the Life, to Thee we pray;
On mountain road and highway wide,
Where sweeps the traffic's roaring tide.
Beneath the shadow of Thy hand,
Guard those who travel on the land.

3 O Lord of sea, and earth, and sky,
Beyond the paths where eagles fly,
O'er empty sea and coloured land,
Do Thou control the pilot's hand.
They cannot soar beyond Thy care—
Keep those who travel in the air.

Edward Musgrave Blaiklock, b. 1903
William Whiting, 1825–78
(1st *four lines*)

ST. AËLRED 888.3 J. B. DYKES, 1823-76

F IERCE raged the tempest o'er the
deep;
Watch did Thine anxious servants
keep,
But Thou wast wrapped in guileless
sleep,
Calm and still.

2 "Save, Lord, we perish," was their
cry,
"Oh, save us in our agony!"
Thy word above the storm rose high,
"Peace, be still."

3 The wild winds hushed; the angry
deep
Sank, like a little child, to sleep;
The sullen billows ceased to leap,
At Thy will.

4 So, when our life is clouded o'er,
And storm-winds drift us from the
shore
Say, lest we sink to rise no more,
"Peace, be still."

Godfrey Thring, 1823–1903

See also
56 When all Thy mercies, O my God
205 There's a light upon the mountains
206 Thy kingdom come, O God
589 For the might of Thine arm

LASST UNS ERFREUEN (EASTER ALLELUIA)   L.M. with Alleluias

Geistliche Kirchengesang, Cologne, 1623
Arr. by R. VAUGHAN WILLIAMS, 1872–1958

FROM all that dwell below the skies,
  Let the Creator's praise arise;
Let the Redeemer's name be sung,
Through every land, by every tongue.

2 Eternal are Thy mercies, Lord!
Eternal truth attends Thy word;
Thy praise shall sound from shore to shore,
Till suns shall rise and set no more.

Isaac Watts, 1674–1748

CELESTE   88.88   *Lancashire Sunday School Songs*, 1857

How good is the God we adore,
  Our faithful unchangeable Friend!
His love is as great as His power,
  And knows neither measure nor end!

2 'Tis Jesus the First and the Last,
  Whose Spirit shall guide us safe home
We'll praise Him for all that is past,
  And trust Him for all that's to come.

Joseph Hart, 1712–68

679

SICILIAN MARINERS   87.87   W. TATTERSALL'S *Psalmody*, 1794

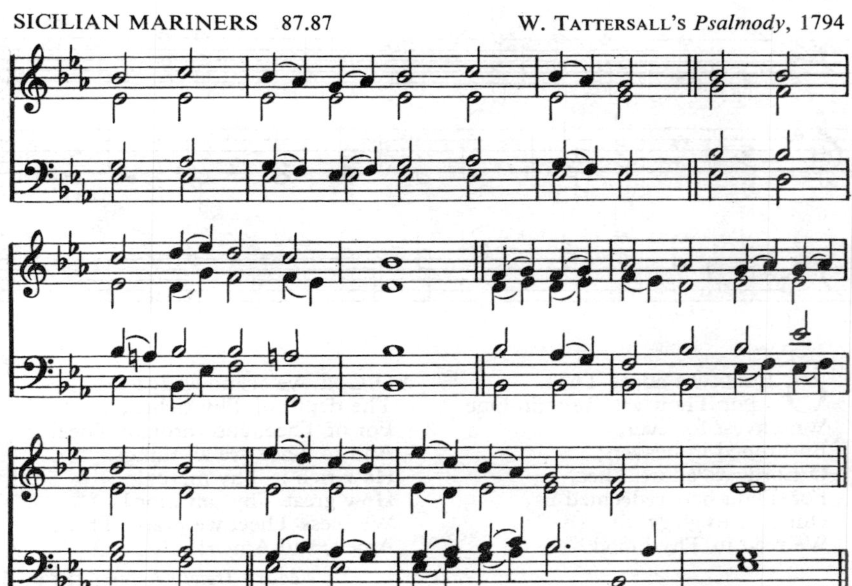

May the grace of Christ our Saviour,
  And the Father's boundless love,
With the Holy Spirit's favour,
  Rest upon us from above!

2 Thus may we abide in union,
  With each other and the Lord,
And possess in sweet communion
  Joys which earth can ne'er afford.

John Newton, 1725–1807

PENLEE Irregular

F. A. J. TONKIN, b. 1926

O LORD, we adore Thee,
    For Thou art the slain One
Who livest for ever,
Enthronèd in heaven;
O Lord, we adore Thee,
For Thou hast redeemed us;
Our title to glory
We read in Thy blood.

2 O God, we acknowledge
The depth of Thy riches;
For of Thee, and through Thee,
And to Thee are all things.
How rich is Thy mercy!
How great Thy salvation!
We bless Thee, we praise Thee:
Amen, and Amen!

Mary Bowly Peters, 1813–56

OLD 100TH   L.M. Melody from *Genevan Psalter*, 1551

DESCANT JOHN HUGHES, 1896-1968

PRAISE God, from whom all bless-
ings flow,
Praise Him all creatures here below;
Praise Him above, ye heavenly host,
Praise Father, Son, and Holy Ghost.

Thomas Ken, 1637–1710

This hymn may also be sung to Lasst uns erfreuen, No. 677

DIVA SERVATRIX (BAYEUX) 11.11.11.5   French Church Melody

UNISON

AH, holy Jesu, how hast Thou offended,
That man to judge Thee hath in hate pretended?
By foes derided, by Thine own rejected,
    O most afflicted.

2 Who was the guilty? Who brought this upon Thee?
Alas, my treason, Jesu, hath undone Thee;
'Twas I, Lord Jesu, I it was denied Thee:
    I crucified Thee.

3 Lo, the good Shepherd for the sheep is offered;
The slave hath sinnèd, and the Son hath suffered;
For man's atonement, while he nothing heedeth,
    God intercedeth.

4 For me, kind Jesu, was Thy incarnation,
Thy mortal sorrow, and Thy life's oblation;
Thy death of anguish and Thy bitter passion,
    For my salvation.

5 Therefore, kind Jesu, since I cannot pay Thee,
I do adore Thee, and will ever pray Thee,
Think on Thy pity and Thy love unswerving,
    Not my deserving.

Johann Heermann, 1585–1647
tr. Robert Seymour Bridges, 1844–1930.

This hymn may also be sung to **Integer Vitae,** No. 394

HEREFORD L.M.   S. S. WESLEY, 1810-76

B^E still, my heart, these anxious cares
To thee are burdens, thorns and snares;
They cast dishonour on the Lord,
And contradict His gracious word.

2 Brought safely by His hand thus far,
Why wilt thou now give place to fear?
How canst thou want if He provide,
Or lose thy way with such a guide?

3 When first before His mercy-seat
Thou didst to Him thine all commit;
He gave thee warrant from that hour
To trust His wisdom, love and power.

4 Did ever trouble yet befall,
And He refuse to hear thy call?
And has He not His promise passed,
That thou shalt overcome at last?

5 He who has helped me hitherto
Will help me all my journey through,
And give me daily cause to raise
New hymns of glory to His praise.

6 Though rough and thorny be the road,
It leads thee home apace to God:
Then count thy present trials small,
For heaven will make amends for all.

John Newton, 1725–1807

This hymn may also be sung to **Festus**, No. 17

684

MELCOMBE L.M.

S. Webbe (the Elder), 1740-1816

B EHOLD the eternal king and priest
Brings forth for me the bread
and wine;
Himself the master of the feast,
His flesh and blood the food divine!

2 Jesus, I come, for Thou dost call,
I eat and drink at Thy command;
Low at Thy feet I humbly fall,
Oh touch me with Thy piercèd
hand.

3 Wash throughly clean this heart of
mine,
That it may beat for Thee alone;
Oh let it lose its life in Thine,
And have no will except Thine own!

4 In weariness be Thou my rest,
In loneliness be Thou my friend,
In sorrow hold me to Thy breast,
And keep me, Jesus, to the end.

Anon., Congregational Church Hymnal, 1887

685 RIVAULX L.M.

J. B. Dykes, 1823-76

D EAR Master, in whose life I see
All that I would, but fail to be,
Let Thy clear light for ever shine,
To shame and guide this life of mine.

2 Though what I dream and what I do
In my weak days are always two,
Help me, oppressed by things undone,
O Thou, whose deeds and dreams
were one!

John Hunter, 1848-1917

This hymn may also be sung to **Maryton,** No. 31

MOZART 88.88.88

From Mozart's *Die Zauberflöte*. 1791

Come, Holy Ghost, all-quickening fire,
  Come, and in me delight to rest;
Drawn by the lure of strong desire,
  Oh come and consecrate my breast;
The temple of my soul prepare,
And fix Thy sacred presence there.

2 Eager for Thee I ask and pant;
    So strong, the principle divine
  Carries me out, with sweet constraint,
    Till all my hallowed soul is Thine;
  Plunged in the Godhead's deepest sea,
  And lost in Thine immensity.

3 My peace, my life, my comfort Thou,
    My treasure and my all Thou art;
  True witness of my sonship, now
    Engraving pardon on my heart,
  Seal of my sins in Christ forgiven,
  Earnest of love, and pledge of heaven.

4 Come then, my God, mark out Thine heir,
    Of heaven a larger earnest give;
  With clearer light Thy witness bear,
    More sensibly within me live;
  Let all my powers Thine entrance feel,
  And deeper stamp Thyself the seal.

Charles Wesley, 1707–88

687

RATISBON 77.77.77

WERNER'S *Choralbuch*, 1815

_FATHER, Son, and Holy Ghost,
   One in Three, and Three in One,
As by the celestial host,
   Let Thy will on earth be done;
Praise by all to Thee be given,
Glorious Lord of earth and heaven.

2 Vilest of the sinful race,
   Lo! I answer to Thy call;
Meanest vessel of Thy grace,
   Grace divinely free for all,
Lo! I come to do Thy will,
All Thy counsel to fulfil.

3 If so poor a worm as I
   May to Thy great glory live,
All my actions sanctify,
   All my words and thoughts receive;
Claim me for Thy service, claim
All I have and all I am.

4 Take my soul and body's powers;
   Take my memory, mind, and will,
All my goods, and all my hours,
   All I know, and all I feel,
All I think, or speak, or do;
Take my heart, but make it new.

5 Now, O God, Thine own I am,
   Now I give Thee back Thine own;
Freedom, friends, and health, and
      fame
   Consecrate to Thee alone:
Thine I live, thrice happy I;
Happier still if Thine I die.

6 Father, Son, and Holy Ghost,
   One in Three, and Three in One,
As by the celestial host,
   Let Thy will on earth be done;
Praise by all to Thee be given,
Glorious Lord of earth and heaven.

Charles Wesley, 1707–88

This hymn may also be sung to **Wells**, No. 161

QUEDLINBURG 10.10.10.10 Dactylic

From a chorale by
J. C. KITTEL, 1732-1809

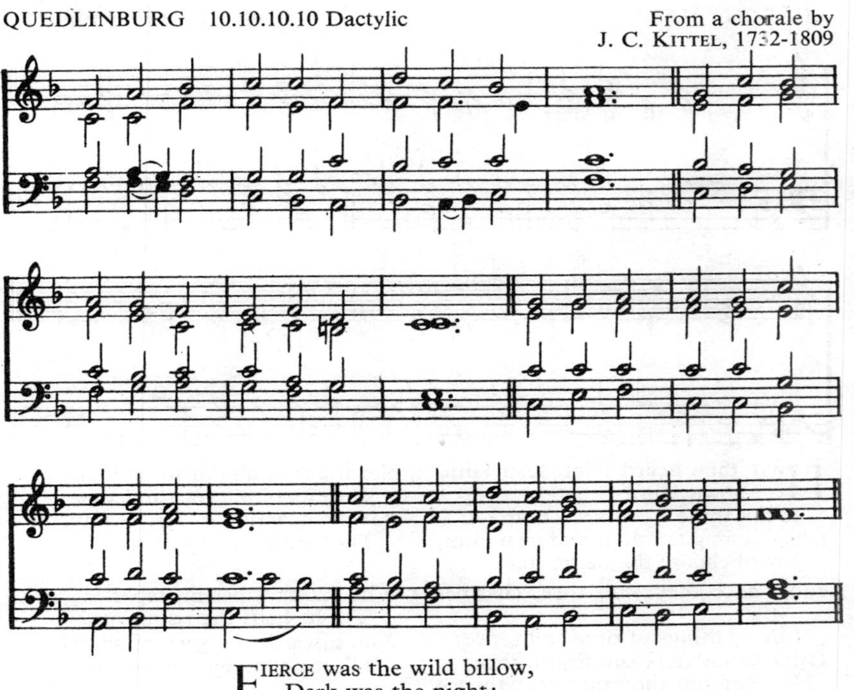

FIERCE was the wild billow,
  Dark was the night;
Oars laboured heavily,
  Foam glimmered white;
Trembled the mariners,
  Peril was nigh:
Then said the God of God,
  "Peace! It is I."

2 Ridge of the mountain-wave,
  Lower thy crest!
Wail of the hurricane,
  Be thou at rest!
Sorrow can never be,
  Darkness must fly,
Where saith the Light of Light,
  "Peace! It is I."

3 Jesus, deliverer,
  Nigh to us be;
Soothe thou my voyaging
  Over life's sea:
Thou, when the storm of death
  Roars, sweeping by,
Whisper, O Truth of Truth,
  "Peace! It is I."

Anatolius, tr. John Mason Neale, 1818–66

This hymn may also be sung to Moment by moment, No. 212

SHARON 87.87   William Boyce, 1710-79

Hast thou heard Him, seen Him, known Him?
  Is not thine a captured heart?
Chief among ten thousand own Him,
  Joyful choose the better part.

2 Idols once they won thee, charmed thee,
  Lovely things of time and sense:
Gilded thus does sin disarm thee,
  Honeyed lest thou turn thee thence.

3 What has stript the seeming beauty
  From the idols of the earth?
Not a sense of right or duty,
  But the sight of peerless worth.

4 Not the crushing of those idols,
  With its bitter void and smart;
But the beaming of His beauty,
  The unveiling of His heart.

5 Who extinguishes his taper
  Till he hails the rising sun?
Who discards the garb of winter
  Till the summer has begun?

6 'Tis the look that melted Peter,
  'Tis the face that Stephen saw,
'Tis the heart that wept with Mary,
  Can alone from idols draw:

7 Draw and win and fill completely,
  Till the cup o'erflow the brim;
What have we to do with idols
  Who have companied with Him?

Ora Rowan

690 ST. AGNES   10.10.10.10   Melody by J. Langran, 1835-1909

H E lovèd me, and gave Himself for
me;
Amazing love, amazing sacrifice:
I'll take my harp down from the
willow tree,
And bid its notes in praise of Jesus
rise.

2 He lovèd me, and gave Himself for
me;
And surely I myself to Him will give;
None, Jesus, will I ever love like Thee,
And to Thy glory only will I live.

3 Oh when I stand 'mid yonder shining
throng,
And on fair Canaan's coast my Saviour
see,
I'll add this chorus to their swelling
song,
"He lovèd me, and gave Himself for
me."

Fergus Ferguson, 1824–97

.This hymn may also be sung to **Song 22,** No. 551

691

CHILDHOOD   88.86   *University of Wales, 1923*

H IS are the thousand sparkling rills
That from a thousand fountains
burst,
And fill with music all the hills;
And yet he saith, "I thirst".

2 All fiery pangs on battle-fields,
On fever beds where sick men toss,
Are in that human cry He yields
To anguish on the Cross.

3 But more than pains that racked Him
then
Was the deep longing thirst divine
That thirsted for the souls of men:
Dear Lord! and one was mine.

4 O Love most patient, give me grace;
Make all my soul athirst for thee:
That parched dry lip, that fading face,
That thirst, were all for me.

Cecil Frances Alexander, 1818–95

SONG 1　10.10.10.10.10.10　　Melody and Bass by ORLANDO GIBBONS, 1583-1625

I DARED not hope that Thou wouldst deign to come
And make this lowly heart of mine Thy home,
That Thou wouldst deign, O King of kings, to be
E'en for one hour a sojourner in me:
Yet art Thou always here to help and bless,
And lift the load of my great sinfulness.

2 I dared not ever hope for such a Guide
To walk with me my faltering steps beside,
To help me when I fall, and, when I stray,
Constrain me gently to the better way:
Yet art Thou always at my side to be
A Counsellor and Comforter to me.

3 I do not always go where Thou dost lead,
I do not always Thy soft whispers heed;
I follow other lights, and, in my sin,
I vex with many a slight my Friend within:
Yet dost Thou not, though grieved, from me depart.
But guardest still Thy place within my heart.

Edwin Hatch, 1835–89

PRIVATE DEVOTION

693

BODLONDEB 64.64.10.10

DAVID EVANS, 1874-1948

SURSUM CORDA 64.64.10.10

GEORGE LOMAS, 1834-84

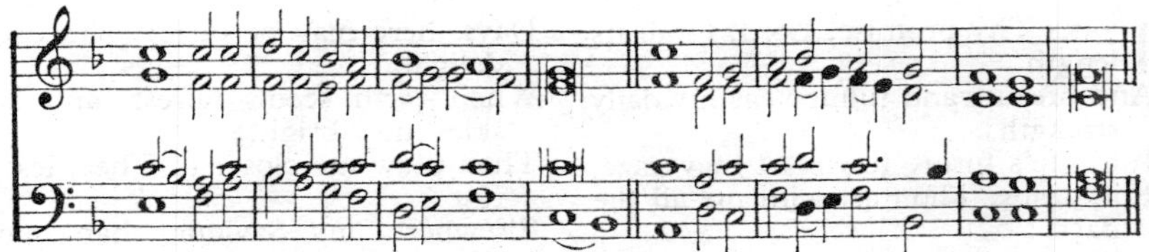

I LIFT my heart to Thee,
    Saviour Divine!
For Thou art all to me,
    And I am Thine.
Is there on earth a closer bond than
    this,
That "my Belovèd's mine, and I am
    His"?

2 Thine am I by all ties;
    But chiefly Thine,
That through Thy sacrifice
    Thou, Lord, art mine.
By Thine own cords of love, so
    sweetly wound
Around me, I to Thee am closely
    bound.

3 How can I, Lord, withhold
    Life's brightest hour
From Thee; or gathered gold
    Or any power?
Why should I keep one precious thing
    from Thee,
When Thou has given Thine own dear
    self for me?

4 I pray Thee, Saviour, keep
    Me in Thy love,
Until death's holy sleep
    Shall me remove
To that fair realm where, sin and
    sorrow o'er,
Thou and Thine own are one for
    evermore.

Charles Edward Mudie, 1818-90

694

FARLEY CASTLE 10.10.10.10   H. LAWES, 1596-1662

I TAKE Thy promise, Lord, in all its length,
And breadth and fullness, as my daily strength;
Into life's future fearless I may gaze,
For, Jesus, Thou art with me all the days.

2 Days may be coming fraught with loss and change,
New scenes surround my life and faces strange;
I thank Thee that no day can ever break,
Saviour, when Thou wilt leave me or forsake.

3 There may be days of darkness and distress,
When sin has power to tempt, and care to press—
Yet in the darkest day I will not fear,
For, 'mid the shadows, Thou wilt still be near.

4 Days there may be of joy, and deep delight,
When earth seems fairest, and her skies most bright;
Then draw me closer to Thee, lest I rest
Elsewhere, my Saviour, than upon Thy breast.

5 And all the other days that make my life,
Marked by no special joy or grief or strife,
Days filled with quiet duties, trivial care,
Burdens too small for other hearts to share;

6 Spend Thou these days with me, all shall be Thine—
So shall the darkest hour with glory shine.
Then when these earthly years have passed away,
Let me be with Thee in the perfect day.

Henry Legh Richmond Deck, 1858-1910

This hymn may also be sung to **Morecambe,** No. 600

ARTAVIA   10.10.10.6

E. J. HOPKINS, 1818-1901

I SOUGHT the Lord, and afterward I
  knew
He moved my soul to seek Him,
  seeking me;
It was not I that found, O Saviour
  true;
No, I was found of Thee.

2 Thou didst reach forth Thy hand and
    mine enfold;
I walked and sank not on the storm-
    vexed sea;
'Twas not so much that I on Thee
    took hold
As Thou, dear Lord, on me.

3 I find, I walk, I love, but oh the whole
Of love is but my answer, Lord, to
    Thee!
For Thou wert long beforehand with
    my soul;
Always Thou lovedst me.

Author unknown: 1880

696

HOLLY L.M.

GEORGE HEWS, 1806-1873

I THIRST, but not as once I did,
  The vain delights of earth to share:
Thy wounds, Emmanuel, all forbid
  That I should seek my pleasure there.

2 It was the sight of Thy dear cross
  First weaned my soul from earthly things,
And taught me to esteem as dross
  The mirth of fools and pomp of kings.

3 I want that grace that springs from Thee.
  That quickens all things where it flows,
And makes a wretched thorn like me
  Bloom as the myrtle or the rose.

4 Dear fountain of delight unknown!
  No longer sink below the brim;
But overflow, and pour me down
  A living and life-giving stream!

William Cowper, 1731-1800

698

Words at foot of next page

CHORUS ANGELORUM C.M.

ARTHUR SOMERVELL, 1863-1937

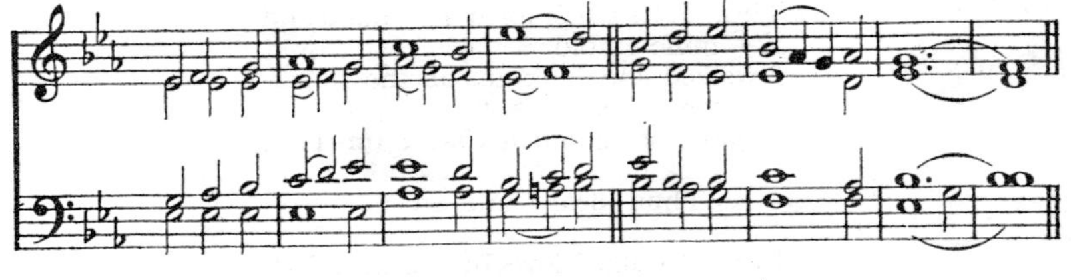

697

ST. ALPHEGE 76.76 H. J. GAUNTLETT, 1805-76

IN full and glad surrender,
  I give myself to Thee,
Thine utterly and only
  And evermore to be.

2 O Son of God, who lov'st me,
  I will be Thine alone;
And all I have and am, Lord,
  Shall henceforth be Thine own!

3 Reign over me, Lord Jesus;
  Oh, make my heart Thy throne:
It shall be Thine, dear Saviour,
  It shall be Thine alone.

4 Oh, come and reign, Lord Jesus;
  Rule over everything!
And keep me always loyal,
  And true to Thee, my King.

Frances Ridley Havergal, 1836–79

698

Tune at foot of previous page

JESUS, my Lord, how rich Thy grace,
  Thy bounties how complete!
How shall I count the matchless sum?
  How pay the mighty debt?

2 High on a throne of radiant light
  Dost Thou exalted shine;
What can my poverty bestow
  When all the worlds are Thine?

3 But Thou hast brethren here below,
  The partners of Thy grace,
And wilt confess their humble names
  Before Thy Father's face.

4 In them Thou may'st be clothed and
    fed,
  And visited and cheered,
And in their accents of distress
  My Saviour's voice is heard.

5 Thy face with reverence and with love
  I in Thy poor would see;
Oh let me rather beg my bread
  Than hold it back from Thee.

Philip Doddridge, 1702–51

699

DALKEITH 11.10.11.10

Thomas Hewlett, 1845-1874

"Lord, when thy Kingdom comes,
      remember me!"
Thus spake the dying lips to dying
      ears:
Oh faith, which in that darkest hour
      could see
   The promised glory of the far-off
      years!

2 No kindly sign declares that glory now,
   No ray of hope lights up that awful
      hour;
A thorny crown surrounds the bleed-
      ing brow,
   The hands are stretched in weak-
      ness, not in power.

3 Hark! through the gloom the dying
      Saviour saith,
   "Thou too shalt rest in Paradise
      to-day:"
Oh words of love to answer words of
      faith!
   Oh words of hope for those who
      live to pray!

4 Lord, when with dying lips my prayer
      is said,
   Grant that in faith Thy kingdom
      I may see;
And, thinking on Thy cross and
      bleeding head,
   May breathe my parting words,
      "Remember me."

5 Remember me, but not my shame or
      sin:
   Thy cleansing blood hath washed
      them all away;
Thy precious death for me did pardon
      win;
   Thy blood redeemed me in that
      awful day.

6 Remember me; and, ere I pass away,
   Speak Thou the assuring word that
      sets us free,
And make Thy promise to my heart,
      "To-day
   "Thou too shalt rest in Paradise
      with me."

Jacques Bridaine, 1701–67 ; tr. Thomas Benson Pollock, 1836–96

This hymn may also be sung to **Toulon**, No. 579

WELWYN 11.10.11.10

A. SCOTT-GATTY, 1847-1918

MY Lord, my Master, at Thy feet adoring,
  I see Thee bowed beneath Thy load of woe;
For me, a sinner, is Thy life-blood pouring:
  For Thee, my Saviour, scarce my tears will flow.

2 Thine own disciple to the Jews has sold thee,
  With friendship's kiss and loyal word he came;
How oft of faithful love my lips have told thee,
  While Thou hast seen my falsehood and my shame!

3 With taunts and scoffs they mock what seems Thy weakness,
  With blows and outrage adding pain to pain;
Thou art unmoved and steadfast in Thy meekness:
  When I am wronged how quickly I complain!

4 My Lord, my Saviour, when I see Thee wearing
  Upon thy bleeding brow the crown of thorn,
Shall I for pleasure live, or shrink from bearing
  Whate'er my lot may be of pain or scorn?

5 O victim of Thy love! O pangs most healing!
    O saving death! O wounds that I adore!
  O shame most glorious! Christ, before Thee kneeling,
    I pray thee keep me Thine for evermore.

William Dalrymple Maclagan, 1826–1910

This hymn may also be sung to **Rhys**, No. 330

70I

BONT-NEWYDD 10.10.10.10   JOHN ROBERTS (IEUAN GWYLLT), 1822-77

1 Not worthy, Lord, to gather up the crumbs
  With trembling hand that from Thy table fall,
A weary heavy-laden sinner comes,
  To plead Thy promise and obey Thy call.

2 I am not worthy to be thought Thy child,
  Nor sit the last and lowest at Thy board;
Too long a wanderer, and too oft beguiled,
  I only ask one reconciling word.

3 One word from Thee, my Lord, one smile, one look,
  And I could face the cold rough world again;
And with that treasure in my heart could brook
  The wrath of devils and the scorn of men.

4 And is not mercy Thy prerogative:
  Free mercy—boundless, fathomless, divine?
Me, Lord, the chief of sinners, me forgive!
  And Thine the greater glory, only Thine.

5 I hear Thy voice: Thou bidd'st me come and rest.
  I come, I kneel, I clasp Thy piercèd feet;
Thou bidd'st me take my place—a welcome guest
  Among Thy saints, and of Thy banquet eat.

6 My praise can only breathe itself in prayer,
  My prayer can only lose itself in Thee:
Dwell Thou for ever in my heart, and there,
  Lord, let me sup with Thee: sup Thou with me.

Edward Henry Bickersteth, 1825–1906

This hymn may also be sung to **All Souls**, No. 390

EDEN 66.66

O. M. FEILDEN, 1857-1924

MY spirit longs for Thee
  Within my troubled breast,
Unworthy though I be
  Of so divine a guest.

2 Of so divine a guest
  Unworthy though I be,
Yet has my heart no rest
  Unless it come from Thee.

3 Unless it come from Thee,
  In vain I look around;
In all that I can see
  No rest is to be found.

4 No rest is to be found
  But in Thy blessèd love;
Oh let my wish be crowned,
  And send it from above!

John Byrom, 1692-1763

This hymn may also be sung to **Quam dilecta**, No. 539

703

ARNOLD C.M.

S. ARNOLD, 1740-1802

Now from the altar of my heart
  Let incense flames arise;
Assist me, Lord, to offer up
  My evening sacrifice.

2 Awake, my love; awake, my joy;
  Awake, my heart and tongue!
Sleep not: when mercies loudly call,
  Break forth into a song.

3 This day my God was sun and shield,
  My keeper and my guide;
His care was on my frailty shown,
  His mercies multiplied.

4 New time, new favour, and new joys
  Do a new song require;
Till I shall praise Thee as I would,
  Accept my heart's desire.

John Mason, c. 1645–1694

This hymn may also be sung to **University**, No. 66

705 KEDRON C.M.

Words at foot of next page Arr. by F. A. J. TONKIN, b. 1926

ST. CRISPIN L.M.

G. J. ELVEY, 1816-93

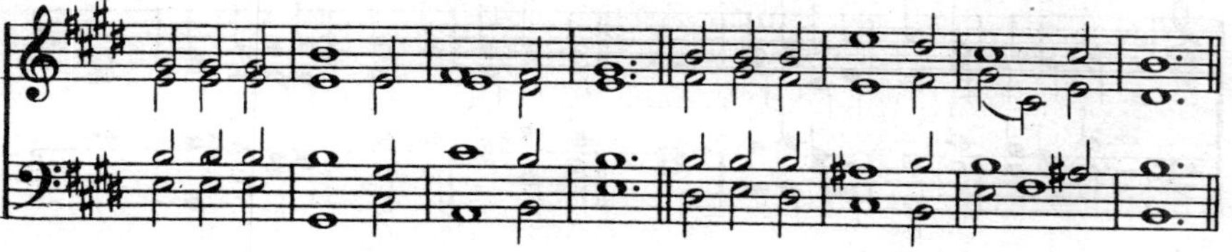

O Body bruisèd for my sake,
  And dying on the awful tree!
That I from death new life should take,
  And live engrafted into Thee.

2 O Living Bread! who once didst die,
  And lay Thee down in rocky tomb,
Within my heart for ever lie,
  And shed Thy brightness o'er its
    gloom.

3 O precious Blood! so freely shed,
  The pledge of pardon from above;
Speak to my heart, so cold and dead,
  And wake it into life and love.

4 Speak better things than Abel's
    blood—
  My ransom paid, my sins forgiven!
My soul restored to peace with God,
  My place prepared for me in
    heaven.

5 O sacred Food! O cleansing Stream!
  Fill all my soul with love divine;
O Thou, who didst my life redeem,
  Come to my heart, and make it
    Thine!

William Dalrymple Maclagan, 1826–1910

705

Tune at foot of previous page

O Dearest Lord, Thy sacred head
  With thorns was pierced for me;
Oh pour Thy blessing on my head
That I may think for Thee.

2 O dearest Lord, Thy sacred hands
  With nails were pierced for me;
Oh shed Thy blessing on my hands
That they may work for Thee.

3 O dearest Lord, Thy sacred feet
  With nails were pierced for me;
Oh pour Thy blessing on my feet
That they may follow Thee.

4 O dearest Lord, Thy sacred heart
  With spear was pierced for me;
Oh pour Thy spirit in my heart
That I may live for Thee.

Henry Ernest Hardy, 1869–1946

ST. AGNES   10.10.10.10   Melody by J. Langran, 1835-1909

SPIRIT of God, descend upon my heart;
  Wean it from earth; through all its pulses move;
Stoop to my weakness, mighty as Thou art,
  And make me love Thee as I ought to love.

2 I ask no dream, no prophet-ecstasies,
  No sudden rending of the veil of clay,
No angel-visitant, no opening skies;
  But take the dimness of my soul away.

3 Hast Thou not bid me love Thee, God and King—
  All, all Thine own, soul, heart, and strength, and mind?
I see Thy cross—there teach my heart to cling:
  Oh let me seek Thee, and oh let me find!

4 Teach me to feel that Thou art always nigh;
  Teach me the struggles of the soul to bear,
To check the rising doubt, the rebel sigh;
  Teach me the patience of unanswered prayer.

5 Teach me to love Thee as Thine angels love,
  One holy passion filling all my frame—
The baptism of the heaven-descended Dove,
  My heart an altar, and Thy love the flame.

George Croly, 1780–1860

This hymn may also be sung to **Song 22,** No. 551

708   ST. ETHELWALD S.M. *Words at foot of next page*   W. H. Monk, 1823-89

FINGAL C.M.

J. S. ANDERSON, 1853-1945

ONE who is all unfit to count
As scholar in Thy school,
Thou of Thy love hast named a
friend—
Oh kindness wonderful!

2 So weak am I, O gracious Lord,
So all unworthy Thee,
That e'en the dust upon Thy feet
Outweighs me utterly.

3 Thou dwellest in unshadowed light,
All sin and shame above—
That Thou shouldst bear our sin and
shame,
How can I tell such love?

4 Ah, did not He the heavenly throne
A little thing esteem,
And not unworthy for my sake
A mortal body deem?

5 When in His flesh they drove the
nails,
Did He not all endure?
What name is there to fit a life
So patient and so pure?

6 So, Love itself in human form,
For love of me He came;
I cannot look upon His face
For shame, for bitter shame.

7 If there is aught of worth in me,
It comes from Thee alone;
Then keep me safe, for so, O Lord,
Thou keepest but Thine own.

Narayan Vaman Tilak, 1862-1919.
tr. Nicol Macnicol, 1870-1952

708

Tune at foot of previous page

SAY not, my soul, "From whence
"Can God relieve my care?"
Remember that Omnipotence
Has servants everywhere.

2 God's help is always sure,
His method seldom guessed;
Delay will make our pleasure pure,
Surprise will give it zest.

3 His wisdom is sublime,
His heart profoundly kind;
God never is before His time,
And never is behind.

4 Hast thou assumed a load,
Which few will share with thee,—
And art thou carrying it for God,
And shall He fail to see?

5 Be comforted at heart,
Thou art not left alone;
Now, thou the Lord's companion art;
Soon, thou wilt share His throne.

Thomas Toke Lynch, 1818-71

709

BELMONT C.M.

GARDINER'S *Sacred Melodies*, 1812

THERE is a fountain filled with blood
    Drawn from Immanuel's veins;
And sinners plung'd beneath that
        flood,
    Lose all their guilty stains.

2 The dying thief rejoiced to see
    That fountain in his day;
And there may I, though vile as he,
    Wash all my sins away.

3 Dear dying Lamb, Thy precious blood
    Shall never lose its power,
Till all the ransomed church of God
    Be saved, to sin no more.

4 E'er since, by faith, I saw the stream
    Thy flowing wounds supply,
Redeeming love has been my theme,
    And shall be till I die.

5 Then in a nobler, sweeter song
    I'll sing Thy power to save,
When this poor lisping, stammering
        tongue
    Lies silent in the grave.

6 Lord, I believe Thou hast prepared—
    Unworthy though I be—
For me a blood-bought, free reward,
    A golden harp for me!

7 'Tis strung, and tuned for endless
        years,
    And form'd by power divine;
To sound in God the Father's ears
    No other name but Thine.

William Cowper, 1731–1800

MAGDALEN 88.88.88

John Stainer, 1840-1901

Thou hidden love of God, whose height,
  Whose depth unfathomed, no man knows,
I see from far Thy beauteous light,
  And inly sigh for Thy repose:
My heart is pained, nor can it be
At rest till it find rest in Thee.

2 'Tis mercy all, that Thou hast brought
  My mind to seek her peace in Thee:
Yet while I seek but find Thee not,
  No peace my wandering soul shall see:
Oh when shall all my wandering end,
And all my steps to Thee-ward tend?

3 Is there a thing beneath the sun
  That strives with Thee my heart to share?
Ah! tear it thence, and reign alone,
  The Lord of every motion there:
Then shall my heart from earth be free,
When it has found repose in Thee.

4 Each moment draw from earth away,
  My heart, that lowly waits Thy call;
Speak to my inmost soul and say,
  "I am thy Love—thy God—thy All!"
To feel Thy power, to hear Thy voice,
To know Thy love, be all my choice.

Gerhard Tersteegen, 1697–1769
tr. John Wesley, 1703–91

This hymn may also be sung to **Pater omnium**, No. 111

7II

OLD 120TH   66.66.66

Melody from ESTE's *Book of Psalmes*, 1592

THY life was given for me,
  Thy blood, O Lord, was shed
That I might ransomed be,
  And quickened from the dead:
Thy life was given for me;
What have I given for Thee?

2 Long years were spent for me
  In weariness and woe,
That through eternity
  Thy glory I might know:
Long years were spent for me;
Have I spent one for Thee?

3 Thy Father's home of light,
  Thy rainbow-circled throne,
Were left for earthly night,
  For wanderings sad and lone:
Yea, all was left for me;
Have I left aught for Thee?

4 Thou, Lord, hast borne for me
  More than my tongue can tell
Of bitterest agony,
  To rescue me from hell:
Thou sufferedst all for me;
What have I borne for Thee?

5 And Thou hast brought to me
  Down from Thy home above
Salvation full and free,
  Thy pardon and Thy love:
Great gifts Thou broughtest me;
What have I brought to Thee?

6 Oh let my life be given,
  My years for Thee be spent,
World-fetters all be riven,
  And joy with suffering blent.
Thou gav'st Thyself for me;
I give myself to Thee.

Frances Ridley Havergal, 1836–79

712

BUCKLAND 77.77

L. G. HAYNE, 1836-83

WHEN my love to Christ grows weak,
When for deeper faith I seek,
Then in thought I go to thee,
Garden of Gethsemane!

2 There I walk amid the shades,
While the lingering twilight fades;
See that suffering, friendless One,
Weeping, praying there alone.

3 When my love for man grows weak,
When for stronger faith I seek,
Hill of Calvary! I go
To thy scenes of fear and woe.

4 There behold His agony,
Suffered on the bitter tree:
See His anguish, see His faith,
Love triumphant still in death.

5 Then to life I turn again,
Learning all the worth of pain,
Learning all the might that lies
In a full self-sacrifice.

6 And I praise with firmer faith
Christ, who vanquished pain and death;
And to Christ enthroned above
Raise my song of selfless love.

John Reynell Wreford, 1800–81

713

FIRST TUNE

LLWYNCELYN 777.5

E. J. EVANS, 1877-1964

CHARITY 777.5

SECOND TUNE

J. STAINER, 1840-1901

WHEN the day of toil is done,
When the race of life is run,
Father, grant Thy wearied one
Rest for evermore.

2 When the strife of sin is stilled,
When the foe within is killed,
Be Thy gracious word fulfilled—
Peace for evermore.

3 When the darkness melts away
At the breaking of the day,
Bid us hail the cheering ray—
Light for evermore.

4 When the heart by sorrow tried
Feels at length its throbs subside,
Bring us, where all tears are dried,
Joy for evermore.

5 When for vanished days we yearn,
Days that never can return,
Teach us in Thy love to learn
Love for evermore.

6 When the breath of life is flown,
When the grave must claim its own,
Lord of Life, be ours Thy crown—
Life for evermore.

John Ellerton, 1826–93

BEULAH   C.M.

G. M. Garrett, 1834-97

WHEN, wounded sore, the stricken soul
Lies bleeding and unbound,
One only hand, a piercèd hand,
Can salve the sinner's wound.

2 When sorrow swells the laden breast,
And tears of anguish flow,
One only heart, a broken heart,
Can feel the sinner's woe.

3 When penitence has wept in vain
Over some foul dark spot,
One only stream, a stream of blood,
Can wash away the blot.

4 'Tis Jesus' blood that washes white,
His hand that brings relief,
His heart that's touched with all our joys,
And feeleth for our grief.

5 Lift up Thy piercèd hand, O Lord;
Unseal that cleansing tide;
We have no shelter from our sin,
But in Thy wounded side.

Cecil Frances Alexander, 1818–95

This hymn may also be sung to **St. Bernard**, No. 75

715

LLEF L.M.

WHEREWITH, O God, shall I draw near,
  And bow myself before Thy face?
How in Thy purer eyes appear?
  What shall I bring to gain Thy grace?

2 Whoe'er to Thee themselves approve
  Must take the path Thy Word hath showed,
Justice pursue, and mercy love,
  And humbly walk by faith with God.

3 But though my life henceforth be Thine,
  Present for past can ne'er atone;
Though I to Thee the whole resign,
  I only give Thee back Thine own.

4 What have I then wherein to trust?
  I nothing have, I nothing am;
Excluded is my every boast,
  My glory swallowed up in shame.

5 Guilty I stand before Thy face,
  On me I feel Thy wrath abide;
'Tis just the sentence should take place;
  'Tis just—but oh, Thy Son hath died!

6 Jesus, the Lamb of God, hath bled,
  He bore our sins upon the tree;
Beneath our curse He bowed His head;
  'Tis finished! He hath died for me!

7 See where before the throne He stands,
  And pours the all-prevailing prayer,
Points to His side, and lifts His hands,
  And shows that I am graven there.

8 He ever lives for me to pray;
  He prays that I with Him may reign:
"Amen" to what my Lord doth say!
  Jesus, Thou canst not pray in vain.

Charles Wesley, 1707–88

OLD 22ND. D.C.M.　　　　　*Anglo-Genevan Psalter, 1556*

<table>
<tr><td valign="top">

MY Lord, my Love, was crucified;
　He all the pains did bear:
But in the sweetness of His rest
　He makes His servants share.
How calmly rest Thy saints above
　Which in Thy bosom lie!
The Church below doth rest in hope
　Of that felicity.

</td><td valign="top">

2 Thou, Lord, who daily feed'st Thy
　　sheep,
　Mak'st them a weekly feast;
Thy flock meets in its several folds
　Upon this day of rest:
Welcome and dear unto my soul
　Are these glad feasts of love:
But what a sabbath shall I keep
　When I shall rest above!

</td></tr>
</table>

3 I bless Thy wise and wondrous love,
　Which binds us to be free;
Which makes us leave our earthly
　　snares,
　That we may come to Thee:
I come, I wait, I hear, I pray,
　Thy footsteps, Lord, I trace;
I sing to think this is the way
　Unto my Saviour's face.

John Mason, c. 1645-94

ACKNOWLEDGMENTS

The Publishers acknowledge with gratitude the kindness of many authors, composers, owners, or controllers of copyright, for permission to use the hymn-texts and tunes listed below. Where the second column is left blank permission has been granted direct by the author or composer. No effort in time or trouble has been spared to trace the owners or present holders of copyrights, or to ascertain if in fact such copyrights still exist. In a few instances these efforts have been unsuccessful, and if any rights still surviving have not been acknowledged, the Publishers ask that the omission be excused and express their willingness to make any necessary corrections in subsequent reprints.

HYMNS

Author or Translator	By Permission Of	Hymn No.
Alington, C. A.	Proprietors of *Hymns Ancient & Modern*	498
Alston, A. E.	E. C. Alston	4
Bennett, L. A.	R. Bennett	153
Bentley, D., Kahale, M., Jeal, D. and Kyba, R.		572
Bethel, R. A.	Mrs. R. A. Bethel	500
Blaiklock, E. M.		675
Boreham, F. W.		503
Bourne, G. H.	Oxford University Press	240
Bridges, R. S.	Oxford University Press, from the *Yattendon Hymnal*	336, 351, 682
Briggs, G. W.	Oxford University Press, from *Enlarged Songs of Praise*	551
Briggs, G. W.	The Hymn Society of America from *Ten New Bible Hymns*, © 1953	606
Burns, E. J.		627
Burroughs, E. A.	Society for Promoting Christian Knowledge	30
Burton, H.	Dr. M. M. Burton	206
Caird, G. B.		291
Chisholm, T. O.	Hope Publishing Co., Carol Stream, Ill., U.S.A.	350
Clarkson, E. M.	Inter-Varsity Christian Fellowship, U.S.A.	265
Dearmer, P.	Oxford University Press, from *The English Hymnal*	116, 384
Dudley-Smith, T.		52
Fox, H. E.	Church Missionary Society	623
Francis, S. T.	Pickering and Inglis, Ltd	23, 69, 532, 561, 637
Fullerton, W. Y.	Psalms and Hymns Trust	610
Goodman, G.	Executors of the late George Goodman	579
Greenaway, A. R.	Proprietors of *Hymns Ancient & Modern*	152, 330
Gregory, G. O.	B. W. Gregory	576
Grimes, E. M.	Africa Evangelical Fellowship	536
Gurney, D. F.	Oxford University Press	674
Hardy, H. E.	A. R. Mowbray and Co. Ltd	705
Head, B. P.	Rev. A. Hanbury Head	230
Holroyde, J.	Mrs. G. L. Cadell	272
Houghton, F.	Mrs. Houghton	114, 275
Hoyle, R. B.	Mrs. N. M. Mitchell	179
Hull, E. H.	Exors. of Miss E. H. Hull and Messrs. Chatto & Windus	420
Kirkland, P. M.	Misses M. & D. Kirkland	595
Lewis, Dr. Elvet	Caniedydd Committee, Union of Welsh Independents	301
Lowry, S. C.	Oxford University Press	211
Macnicol, N.	Trustees of the late Miss Helen M. Macnicol	707
Martin, H.		504
Morgan, E. R.	Church Society	608
Penn, W. J.	Miss E. J. Penn	428
Reed, M. C.	Evans Brothers Ltd	102
Robinson, W.	United Reformed Church	557
Rowley, F. H.	Marshall, Morgan and Scott	356
Russell, D.	Pickering and Inglis, Ltd	135, 556
Smith, L. J. E.	Miss M. E. Smith	20
Stewart, A.	Pickering and Inglis, Ltd	521
Wilkinson, K. B.	D. R. Gould	457
Wright, W.	National Council of Y.M.C.A.	485

MUSIC

Composer or Arranger	By Permission Of	Number
Allen, C. J.	G. Freeman Allen	318
Allen, H. P.	Exor. Lady Allen	293
Anderson, J. S.	Oxford University Press	499, 707
Ashfield, R. J.		501
Blair, H.	The Church Society	476
Brierley, M.	Josef Weinberger Ltd., Edward B. Marks Music Corpn. (U.S.A.); from *Thirty 20th Century Hymn Tunes*	225
Brown, A. H.	Oxford University Press	304, 531, 661, 672
Burroughs, E. A.	Society for Promoting Christian Knowledge	30
Button, E. H.	Novello & Co. Ltd.	496
Coward, H.	Roberton Publications	473
Davies, M. W.	Caniedydd Committee, Union of Welsh Independents	250
Davies, H. Walford	Oxford University Press	426
de Lloyd, David	Mrs. Lilian de Lloyd	112

ACKNOWLEDGMENTS

COMPOSER OR ARRANGER	BY PERMISSION OF	NUMBER
Duckworth, F. C.	Mrs. B. A. Duckworth	197
Elgar, E.	Search Press Ltd.	557
Evans, David	Oxford University Press	595, 629
Evans, Ernest	Mrs. Edith Evans	147
Evans, T. Hopkin	Exors. of T. Hopkin Evans	512
Evans, W. J.	Caniedydd Committee, Union of Welsh Independents	578, 624
Fink, G. W.	Royal School of Church Music	646
Finlay, K. G.		332
Ferguson, W. H.	Oxford University Press	225, 464
Francis, S. T.	Pickering & Inglis	23
Gabriel, C. H.	Alexander Copyrights Trust	202
Gould, A. C. Barham	D. R. Gould	457
Greatorex, Walter	Oxford University Press	52, 449
Green, Harold	Africa Evangelical Fellowship	536
Harkness, Robert	Alexander Copyrights Trust	386
Harris, W.	Mrs. A. P. Eggar	337
Harris, W. H.	Oxford University Press	413
Hartless, G.	Josef Weinberger Ltd., from *Thirty 20th Century Hymn Tunes*	6
Harwood, B.	Exors. of Dr. Basil Harwood	28
Holst, G.	Oxford University Press, from *The English Hymnal*	101
Howard, C.	George Taylor, Stainland, Halifax	127, 522
Hughes, John (Dolgllau)	Arwel Hughes	96, 142, 143
Hughes, John (Pontypridd)	Mrs. Dilys S. Webb	383
Hunt, J. E.	Miss E. K. Frank	279
Ireland, Dr. J.	Mrs. Norah Kirby	122
James, William	Miss Megan James	571
Jamouneau, A. J.	Methodist Conference	248
Jones, J. E.		133, 436
Kitson, C. H.	Year Book Press Ltd (Ascherberg, Hopwood & Crew, Ltd)	114
Lightwood, J. T.	Methodist Conference	391
Maker, F. C.	Psalms & Hymns Trust	62, 69, 134, 166, 423, 550
Maker, F. C.	Novello & Co. Ltd	496
Mann, A. H.	Dr. E. R. Goodliffe	452
	Novello & Co. Ltd	594
Marsh, C. H.	Alexander Copyrights Trust	232
Micklem, T. C.	United Reformed Church	563
Mudditt, B. H.		236, 282
Naylor, E. W.	Mr. Bernard Naylor	405
Northrop, A.	George Taylor, Stainland, Halifax	119
Palmer, F. M. Spencer	United Reformed Church	247
Palmer, G. H.	A. R. Mowbray & Co. Ltd., from *The Cowley Carol Book*	116
Parker, H.	Joshua Duckworth Ltd	574
Protheroe, D.	Mrs. M. Eryl Haydn Matthias	502
Richards, J. H.	Dan H. Morgan	48
Roberts, Caradoc	Caniedydd Committee, Union of Welsh Independents	450, 496
Rowlands, W. P.	G. A. Gabe	454
Runyan, W. M.	Hope Publishing Co., Carol Stream, Ill., U.S.A.	350
Rusbridge, A. E.	Mrs. A. E. Rusbridge	102, 109
Sargent, E. H. G.	Mrs. R. Prowse	563
Shaw, Geoffrey	Oxford University Press	110, 116, 608, 627
Shaw, Martin	Roberton Publications	412
	Oxford University Press, *The Oxford Book of Carols*	90
Sheldon, Robin	The Church Society	269
Slater, Gordon	Oxford University Press	428
Somervell, Arthur	Exors. Sir Arthur Somervell	44, 698
Stebbings, G. C.	Alexander Copyrights Trust	319, 349
Stewart, C. H.	Roberton Publications	272, 285
Swift, J. F.	George Taylor, Stainland, Halifax	10, 440
Swift, J. F.	Methodist Church Division of Education and Youth	519
Taylor, C. V.	Oxford University Press	498, 606
Thalben-Ball, G. H.	Oxford University Press, from the *B.B.C. Hymnbook*	323
Thiman, E. Harding	United Reformed Church	1
Thomas, D. Vaughan	Caniedydd Committee, Union of Welsh Independents	301
Tomblin, Norman		261
Tonkin, F. A. J.		47, 236, 262, 282, 311, 552, 680, 705
Vincent, C.	Exors. of Charles Vincent	115, 378
Williams, R. Vaughan	Oxford University Press	14, 105, 123, 141, 210, 320, 384, 592, 631, 677
Williams, W. J.	R. C. Williams	153
Williamson, M.	Josef Weinberger Ltd.; Edward B. Marks Music Corpn. (U.S.A.); from *12 New Hymn Tunes*	648
Wiseman, F. L.	Methodist Conference	299
Wostenholm, M. L.	Methodist Conference	205, 637

Permission for the use of copyright arrangements of traditional melodies has kindly been given as follows: Baptist Union of Wales, 324, 359, 504, 537.   Oxford University Press, 251, 442, 665. Union of Welsh Independents, 376

ALPHABETICAL INDEX OF TUNES

METRICAL INDEX

S.M.
Arfryn, 152, 624
Augustine, 419, 562
Bod Alwyn, 268
Cambridge, 431, 643
Carlisle, 49, 74
Cranbrook, 353
Dennis, 558, 583
Downing, 577, 670
Falcon Street, 664
Franconia, 76, 175
Gwengar, 252, 354
Holyrood, 269
Huddersfield, 328, 355
Rhodes, 339, 494
St. Bride, 131, 500
St. Ethelwald, 290, 708
St. George, 497, 617
St. Michael, 529
Sandys, 492
Silchester, 491, 593
Swabia, 397
Trentham, 234, 346
Veni Spiritus, 567
Venice, 528

D.S.M.
Ascension, 15
Cranbrook, 353
Diademata, 3, 281
Eden, 193
From strength to strength, 405
Leominster, 518, 666
Llanllyfni, 382, 456
Nearer home, 632, 642
St. Ishmael, 378
Studland, 30

C.M.
Abergele, 271
Abridge, 128, 602
Albano, 393
Allhallows, 260
Amazing grace, 64
Arnold, 703
Beatitudo, 198, 636
Bedford, 94, 616
Belmont, 575, 709
Beulah, 714
Binchester, 351
Bishopthorpe, 437, 598
Bromsgrove (extended), 665
Brother James' Air, 262
Byzantium, 257
Chorus angelorum, 44, 698
Claremont, 129
Contemplation, 463
Crediton, 61
Crimond, 409
Dalehurst, 253, 317
Diadem, 209
Dublin, 188
Dundee, 130, 160
Eagley, 229, 461
Evan, 70, 516
Fingal, 499, 707
Gerontius, 19
Godre'er coed, 56, 250
Glasgow, 83, 190
Green Hill, 158, 416
Harington, 187
Hensbury, 417
Holy Trinity, 523, 535
Horsley, 159
Irish, 35, 343
Jazer, 284
Jerusalem, 86
Kedron, 311, 705
Kilmarnock, 185
Lloyd, 127, 522
Lydia, 233
Lyngham, 250

Lynton, 248
Manchester, 204, 544
Manoah, 264, 444
Martyrdom, 314, 542
Mendip, 415, 647
Nativity, 215
Northrop, 119
Nox praecessit, 414
Nun danket all, 63, 363
Orlington, 225, 638
Penmachno, 512
Redhead No. 66 (Waveney), 596
Rest, 459
Richmond, 18
Rochester, 272, 285
St. Agnes, 235
St. Anne, 78
St. Bernard, 75, 93
St. Botolph, 428
St. Columba, 399
St. Flavian, 475
St. Fulbert, 506, 603
St. Hugh, 527, 555
St. Magnus, 117, 203
St. Peter, 230, 326
St. Saviour, 94, 254
St. Stephen, 67, 270
Salzburg, 445
Saron, 259
Sawley, 462, 533
Sennen Cove, 337
Southwell, 283, 398
Stracathro, 88
Stroudwater, 65
Tiverton, 286
University, 66, 357
Walden, 133, 436
Warwick, 251, 442
Waveney (Redhead No. 66), 596
Westminster, 34
Wetherby, 181
Wiltshire, 411
Winchester old, 119

D.C.M.
Adelboden, 458
Broyan, 126
Carol, 103
Castle Rising, 553
Claudius, 646
Ellacombe, 85, 493
Forest Green, 105, 123
Invocation, 402
Kingsfold, 320
Ladywell, 209, 599
Old 22nd, 716
Petersham, 295, 306
St. George's, Edinburgh (with Coda), 189, 207
St. Matthew, 124, 164

L.M.
Abends, 297, 315
Alstone, 400, 432
Angels' song, 482
Angelus, 652
Antwerp, 50, 360
Arizona, 162, 623
Birling, 608, 627
Bodmin, 21, 256
Boston, 521
Breslau, 478, 622
Calm, 274
Castle Street (Luther's chant), 216, 486
Church triumphant, 71, 438
Cromer, 566
Deep harmony, 574
Duke Street, 146, 365
Dunelm, 115

Eden, 154, 530
Eisenach, 58
Festus, 17, 182
Fulda, 484, 591
Galilee, 186, 273
Glanllyfnwy, 381, 546
Hembury Fort, 236
Hereford, 275, 683
Holly, 597, 696
Hursley, 660
Kent, 368
Lasst uns erfreuen (with alleluias), 14, 677
Lledrod, 324, 359
Llef, 163, 715
Luther's chant (Castle Street), 216, 486
Mainzer, 338, 341
Martham, 59
Maryton, 31, 511
Melcombe, 649, 684
Morning Hymn, 520
Niagara, 54
Nicomachus, 594
Old 100th, 11, 681
Ombersley, 403, 429
Philippine, 488
Rimington, 197
Rivaulx, 313, 685
Rockingham, 163, 564
St. Crispin, 447, 704
St. Drostane, 125
St. Polycarp, 81
Samson, 340, 379
Saxby, 543
Solothurn, 141
Tallis' Canon, 655
Torquay, 169
Truro, 197
Wareham, 517
Warrington, 294, 430
Whitburn, 156, 483
Wilton, 469
Winchester new, 16, 645

D.L.M.
Stanley, 452

447.447.44447
Infant Holy, 102

55.53.D
Bunessan, 96

55.55.65.65
Hanover, 40, 375
Houghton, 37, 342
Laudate dominum, 38

55.88.55
Spire, 388

55.11.D
Harwich, 132

64.64.664
Hiraeth, 327

64.64.6664
Glanhafren, 407
Something for Thee, 474
Tryst, 513

64.64.10.10
Sursum corda, 693

65.64
Christ arose (with refrain), 171

65.65
Ernstein, 519
Glenfinlas, 332
North Coates, 136
Quietude, 536
St. John Baptist, 572

87.87.47
Blaencefn, 244, 515
Bryn Aber, 301
Bryn Calfaria, 138
Crown Him, 200
Cwm Rhondda, 383
Helmsley, 199
Kingley Vale, 293

87.87.66.667
Ein' feste burg, 335

87.87.67
Groeswen, 336

87.87.77
Irby, 107
Llanbadarn, 525

87.87.87
Dismissal, 228, 392
Grafton, 138
Mannheim, 389
Neander, 191, 586
Praise, my soul, 41
Regent Square, 5, 137
Rhuddlan, 240, 371
Triumph, 625
Westminster Abbey, 619, 640

87.87.D Iambic
Bishopgarth, 490, 605
Constance, 226, 668

87.87.D Trochaic
Abbot's Leigh, 498, 590
Arwelfa, 142
Austria, 614
Banquet, 559
Bethany, 8, 620
Blaenwern, 454
Calon Lân, 540, 559
Corinth, 613
Ebenezer, 531
Everton, 508, 612
Hallelujah, 208
Hyfrydol, 222, 356
Love divine, 9, 573
Lux eoi, 33, 120
Mead House, 607
Morgenlied (with refrain), 166
Normandy, 217
Rex gloriae, 172
Sanctus, 13, 143

87.87.887
Mit freuden zart, 370

87.887.77.77
Beverley, 580

886.D
Ariel, 249
Innsbruck, 466
Manna, 291
Praise, 348

887.D
Evening hymn, 653

888
Victory (with alleluias), 177
Vulpius (with alleluias), 377

888.3
Aescendune, 476
St. Aëlred, 676

888.4
Almsgiving, 79
Es ist kein tag, 633
In memoriam, 550
Portland, 79

888.5
Kelly, 367

888.6
Cambridge, 448

Childhood, 691
Misericordia, 322
Saffron Walden. 532, 672
Trust, 322
Walford, 323

888.7
Ewhurst, 318

88.88
Celeste, 241, 678

88.886
St. Margaret, 467

88.88.88
Carey (Surrey), 243, 278
Colchester, 310
Companion, 296, 656
Credo, 118, 361
Giessen, 446, 468
Holy Faith, 582
Madrid, 364
Magdalen, 184, 710
Melita, 503, 675
Mount Zion, 298, 425
Mozart, 418, 686
Pater omnium, 111, 183
Rhyd-y-groes, 72

St. Catherine, 331, 495
St. Chrysostom, 441, 634
St. Matthias, 287, 453
Sagina, 308
Sovereignty, 72
Stella, 150, 263

888.D
Monmouth, 25
Nashville, 82

88.88.D Anapaestic
Arabia, 480
Trewen, 334

8.10.10.4
Ellasgarth, 247

98.98
Spiritus vitae, 280

98.89
Randolph (with refrain), 592

98.98
St. Clement, 662

98.98.98
Fragrance, 114

98.98.D
Crugybar, 538
Redemption, 538
Rendez à dieu, 549

10.4.66.66.10.4
Luckington, 28

10.4.10.4.10.10
Alberta, 413
Barton, 391
Sandon, 570

10.4.10.7.4.10
Wonderful love, 299

10.10
Song 46, 366

10.10.10.4
St. Philip, 20
Sine nomine, 211, 631

10.10.10.6
Artavia, 121, 695

10.10.10.10
All souls, 390, 587
Birmingham, 51, 422
Bodlondeb, 693
Bont-newydd, 554, 701

Dalkeith, 699
Ellers, 427, 657
Eventide, 651
Farley Castle, 694
Hurdle End, 282
Morecambe, 600
Pax Dei, 176, 524
Penitentia, 509
St. Agnes, 690, 706
Slane, 420
Song 22, 551
Supreme sacrifice, 460
Sursum corda, 579
Toulon, 630
Woodlands, 52, 449

10.10.10.10 Dactylic
Glory song, The, 202
Moment by moment, 212
Quedlinburg, 688
Trisagion, 212

10.10.10.10.10.10
Song 1, 451, 692
Unde et memores, 344, 569
Yorkshire, 97

10.11.11.11
Maccabaeus (with refrain), 179

11.6.11.6
Berwyn, 450

11.10.11.10
Broadwalk, 501
Charterhouse, 629
Epiphany hymn, 95
Faithfulness, 350
Hold Thou my hand, 385
Montreal, 139
O perfect Love, 46, 674
One day (with refrain), 232
Rhys, 330, 578
Strength and stay, 487
Was lebet, 232
Welwyn, 673, 700

11.10.11.10.11.10.11.12
Londonderry, 611

11.11.11.5
Christe sanctorum, 4
Diva Servatrix, 658, 682
Integer vitae, 394

11.11.11.11
Addoliad, 352
Cradle song, 91
Datchet, 541
Fortunatus, 180
Montgomery, 352
Richmond Hill, 112
St. Denio, 26
To God be the glory, 84

11.12.12.10
Nicaea, 6
Tersanctus, 6

12.10.12.10
Was lebet, 39

14.14.4.7.8
Lobe den herren, 45

15.15.15.15
There's a light, 205, 637

Irregular
Adeste fideles, 106
Benson, 606
Cranham, 101
God be in my head, 426
Margaret, 113
Penlee, 680
Puer nobis, 116
Sebaste, 654
Stille nacht, 109
Vaudois, 589

INDEX OF COMPOSERS, ARRANGERS AND SOURCES OF TUNES

INDEX OF AUTHORS AND TRANSLATORS

Index of First Lines and Tunes

*In addition to the tunes indicated, over 300 suggested alternatives
will be found on the relevant pages*

Index of First Lines

Index of First Lines

Index of First Lines

Index of First Lines